THE LANGUAGE AND STYLE OF THE GOSPEL OF MARK

SUPPLEMENTS TO
NOVUM TESTAMENTUM

VOLUME LXXI

THE LANGUAGE AND STYLE OF THE GOSPEL OF MARK

An Edition of C.H. Turner's "Notes on Marcan Usage" Together with Other Comparable Studies

BY

J.K. ELLIOTT

TUTA SUB AEGIDE PALLAS · 1683 ·

E.J. BRILL
LEIDEN · NEW YORK · KÖLN
1993

The paper in this book meets the guidelines for permanence and durability of the Committee on Production Guidelines for Book Longevity of the Council on Library Resources.

Chapter Twelve, Nigel Turner's *The Style of Mark* was originally published in J.H. Moulton, *A Grammar of New Testament Greek* IV (Edinburgh 1976). It is printed here with kind permission from T&T Clark Publishers.

Library of Congress Cataloging-in-Publication Data

93-35404
CIP

ISSN 0167-9732
ISBN 90 04 09767 8

PRINTED IN THE NETHERLANDS

PREFACE

The purpose of this book is primarily to reproduce the influential and important series of articles entitled "Notes on Marcan Usage" contributed by C.H. Turner to the *Journal of Theological Studies* between 1924-1928. References to these studies continue to be found in monographs, articles, grammars and commentaries. These "Notes" are reprinted here with only minor alterations.

No attempt has been made to bring the "Notes" up-to-date or to expand them, except in the form of a few additional notes I have appended to this section of the present book. The Introduction attempts to set Turner's work in its context and to provide a critical assessment of his achievements. In addition to the "Notes" which Turner published I have added one further "Note" (Note XI), Turner's typescript of which is in my possession. For readers wishing to pursue Turner's work on this Gospel it is to be noted that his commentary on Mark was published posthumously in 1931. He also published other articles on Mark: "*ὁ υἱός μου ὁ ἀγαπητός*" with special reference to Mark i 11; ix 7 in *JTS* xxvii (1926) pp. 113-29; "A Textual Commentary on Mark i" *JTS* xxviii (1927) pp. 145-58; "Western Readings in the Second Half of St. Mark's Gospel" *JTS* xxix (1927) pp. 1-16. The bulk of Turner's other publications are in the field of Latin Patristics: over eighty papers in that area are to be found in the *Journal of Theological Studies* from 1899-1931.

In addition to C.H. Turner's papers on Mark, I have also included a few studies by G.D. Kilpatrick who was a successor to Turner in the Dean Ireland chair at Oxford and who acknowledged on many occasions the influence on his own work of Turner's studies on Mark. Turner's prime motive in writing his "Notes" was to further study of the Synoptic Problem, but he was also alert to textual variation and the part Mark's usage could play in establishing the original text. Kilpatrick emphasised that aspect of Marcan usage in the notes he contributed to *The Bible Translator* and elsewhere. It is these which are included now. Some previously unpublished papers by Kilpatrick also appear here in print for the first time. I also include a couple of studies I have published in this area. To conclude this volume I reproduce the chapter in Nigel Turner's book on style that is concerned with Mark's grammar and usage: this book forms volume IV of J.H. Moulton, *A Grammar of New Testament*

Greek (Edinburgh, 1976). Nigel Turner's work in this volume shows the influence of his namesake's essays of some fifty year's previous.

Permission to reproduce articles published in *The Journal of Theological Studies*, *The Bible Translator*, in E.J.Epp and G.D.Fee (editors), *New Testament Textual Criticism*, in *Theologische Zeitschrift*, and in J.H.Moulton, *Grammar* IV has been granted by the original publishers, and I gratefully acknowledge their ready agreement. Financial assistance for the preparation of this book came from the British Academy and the University of Leeds: their help is gratefully acknowledged. The preparation of camera-ready copy was made by the staff of Nota Bene (UK) Ltd, whose expertise is apparent throughout: my thanks also go to them.

CONTENTS

Original Places of Publication xii
Introduction xiii

C.H. Turner

1. Marcan Usage: Notes, Critical and Exegetical on the Second Gospel
 Introductory Words 3
 I The Impersonal Plural 4
 II φέρειν in Mark 13
 III εἰς and ἐν in Mark 16
 IV Parenthetical Clauses in Mark 23
 V The Movements of Jesus and his Disciples and the Crowd . 36
 i) The Impersonal Plural followed by the Singular 39
 ii) The Singular followed by Mention of the Disciples (or the Twelve) 42
 iii) The Lord, the Disciples and the Multitude 45
 iv) "His Disciples", "The Disciples" 47
 v) "The Crowd" or "The Multitudes" 49
 vi) The Word "to follow" ἀκολουθεῖν 50
 VI The Use of Numbers in Mark 53
 VII Particles
 1. ὅτι Interrogative 63
 2. ὅτι Recitative (after λέγειν or similar Verbs) 68
 3. Asyndeta or Absence of Particles in Mark 74
 4 Particles Absent from Mark
 i) ναί 78
 ii) οὖν 79
 iii) ἰδού in Narrative 81
 VIII* "The Disciples" and "The Twelve" 82
 VIII* Auxiliary and Quasi-Auxiliary Verbs
 i) The past Tense of the Substantive Verb with Present Active, Present or Perfect Passive, Participle as Auxiliary 90

* Turner gave both these sections the same number. The first section VIII was originally planned as an appendix to section V.

ii) The Verb *ἄρχομαι* (*ἤρξατο, ἤρξαντο*) with Present Infinitive as Auxiliary for the Imperfect 93
iii) The Verb *δύναμαι* as Auxiliary 95
iv) The Verb *θέλω* as Auxiliary 97
v) The Verb *ἔχω* 99
Appendix.
εἰδέναι, γινώσκειν, ἐπιγινώσκειν substantially identical in Sense in Mark 102
IX Lexical Notes
1. *ἀποστερεῖν* 104
κεφαλιόω 105
προδοῦναι 105
πυγμῇ 107
2. *ἀλλά* 107
(*πρὸς*) *ἑαυτοὺς* 108
ἐκ, ἀπό 110
πάλιν 111
ὑπάγω and *πορεύεσθαι*
A. *ὑπάγω* 116
B. *πορεύεσθαι* and its Compounds 117
X Usage of Mark 120
1. Titles used in addressing Christ
i) Ῥαββεί (Ῥαββουνεί) 121
ii) Διδάσκαλε 121
iii) Κύριε 122
iv) Ἰησοῦ 122
2. Diminutives in Mark
i) *θυγάτριον* 123
ii) *ἰχθύδιον* 123
iii) *κοράσιον* 124
iv) *κυνάριον* 124
v) *σανδάλιον* 124
vi) *ψιχίον* 124
vii) *ὠτάριον* 125
παιδίον 125
3. The Verb at the End of the Sentence, after Noun or Personal Pronoun
a) With the Verb *ἅπτεσθαι* 126
b) Other Instances in Mark of the Verb placed last, after its Object, or the Noun after the Pronoun depending on it 127

4. *ἵνα* (Non-purposive Uses) 130
5. Absence of λέγων (λέγοντες) after Verbs introducing a Statement or a Question
i) *ἀγανακτεῖν* 133
ii) *ἀποκρίνεσθαι* 134
iii) *βοᾶν* 134
iv) *διαλογίζεσθαι* 134
v) *διαστέλλεσθαι* 134
vi) *ἐπερωτάω* (*ἐρωτάω*) 134
vii) *ἐπιτιμάω* 135
viii) *κατακρίνειν* 135
ix) *κηρύσσειν* 135
x) *κράζω* 135
xi) *λαλεῖν* 136
XI *ὁ* 'Ιησοῦς and 'Ιησους 137
Additional Notes (J.K.Elliott) 140

G.D.Kilpatrick

2. Mark i 45 and the Meaning of λόγος 151

3. Mark i 45 153

4. 'Επάνω Mark xiv .5. 155

5. Πορεύεσθαι and its Compounds
A. Compounds of Πορεύεσθαι 157
B. Πορευέσθαι and ἔρχεσθαι in Mark 157

6. Some Notes on Marcan Usage
i. *ὡς* 159
The Perfect 160
ii. λόγος 166
εὐθύς 168
πάλιν 168
οἶκος and *οἰκία* 169
ἐπιτιμᾶν 170
ἀκολουθεῖν 171
πολλά 172
Periphrastic *εἶναι* and Participle 173

7. Recitative λέγων 175

8. Verbs of Seeing 179

9. Particles
δέ 181
γάρ 182
ἀλλά 183
Causal ὅτι 183
ἤ 184
μέν 184
οὖν 184
Other Particles 184

J.K.Elliott
10. An Eclectic Textual Commentary on the Greek Text of Mark's Gospel 189
i 4 191
i 27 192
i 41 194
v 22 195
vi 3 196
vi 22 197
vi 41 197
ix 38 199
x 2 200
xi 24 201

11. The Text and Language of the Endings to Mark's Gospel 203

N.Turner
12. The Style of Mark
(1) Literary Sources in Mark 215
(2) Aramaic Influence on the Style of Mark 215
(3) Hebraic Influence on the Style of Mark 219
(4) Semitic Influence on the Style of Mark 224
(5) Mark's Mannered Style 231
(6) Latinisms in the Gospels 235

End Note (J.K.Elliott) 239

Indexes
Index of Marcan Verses 243
Index of Biblical and other Texts 249
Index of Themes 251
Index of Greek Words 254

ORIGINAL PLACES OF PUBLICATION

C.H.Turner
"Notes on Marcan Usage" *JTS* (I) xxv (1924) pp. 377-86; (II) xxvi (1924) pp. 12-14; (III) xxvi (1924) pp. 14-20; (IV) xxvi (1925) pp. 145-56; (V) xxvi (1925) pp. 225-40; (VI) xxvi (1925) pp. 337-46; (VII) xxvii (1926) pp. 58-62; xxviii (1926) pp. 9-22; (VIII) xxviii (1926) pp. 22-30, (1927) pp. 349-62; (IX) xxix (1928) pp. 275-89; (X) xxix (1928) pp. 346-61.

G.D.Kilpatrick
"Mark i 45 and the Meaning of λόγος" *JTS* xl (1939) pp. 389-40

"Mark i 45" *JTS* xlii (1941) pp. 67-8

"Ἐπάνω Mark xiv.4" *JTS* xlii (1941) pp. 181-2 cf. *JTS* xlv (1944) p.177

"Πορευέσθαι and its Compounds" *JTS* xlviii (1947) pp. 61-3.

"Some Notes on Marcan Usage" *Bible Translator* vii (1956) pp. 2-9, 51-6, 146.
[The above are reprinted in J.K.Elliott (ed.), *The Principles and Practice of New Testament Textual Criticism: Collected Essays of G.D. Kilpatrick* (Leuven, 1990) pp. 223-4, 261-79, 280-1, 282-3, 305-6. (=BETL 96).]

J.K.Elliott
"An Eclectic Textual Commentary on the Gospel Text of Mark's Gospel" in E.J.Epp and G.D.Fee (eds.) *New Testament Textual Criticism its Significance for Exegesis Essays in Honour of Bruce M.Metzger* (Oxford, 1981) pp. 47-60 reprinted as chapter 13 in J.K.Elliott, *Essays and Studies in New Testament Textual Criticism* (Cordoba, 1991) pp. 159-70 (=*Estudios de Filología Neotestamentaria* 3).

"The Text and Language of the Endings to Mark's Gospel" *Theologische Zeitschrift* 27 (1971) pp. 255-62.

Nigel Turner
"The Style of Mark" in J.H. Moulton, *A Grammar of New Testament Greek* IV (Edinburgh, 1976) pp. 11-30.

INTRODUCTION

C.H. Turner (1860-1930)

Cuthbert Hamilton Turner was born in London and went to Winchester as a scholar in 1872 and to New College, Oxford with a Winchester Scholarship in 1879. After graduating in Greats then in Theology he was elected to an open Fellowship at Magdalen[1]. In 1920 he became Dean Ireland's Professor of the Exegesis of Holy Scripture in the University of Oxford. The papers reproduced here were written during the time he was the holder of that chair; but in many ways the influence on his work can be traced to 1881 and Westcott and Hort's edition of the Greek New Testament.

It is striking that scholars who grew up almost in the shadow of Westcott and Hort (hereafter WH) in England were unconvinced by some of their conclusions and proceeded in some independence to advance beyond WH's position. This is especially noteworthy in F.C. Burkitt who already in 1896 contributed "Supplementary Notes" to the second edition of WH's Greek Testament. In his article on "Text and Versions" in the *Encyclopaedia Biblica* IV (1903) col. 4991f. he questions the pre-eminence given by WH to B over the Western text and discusses several passages where he thinks that the Western text may be right against B. We find discussions elsewhere in Burkitt's work, for example in *Evangelion Da-Mepharreshe* II (Cambridge, 1904) and in *The Gospel History and its Transmission* (Edinburgh,[3] 1911) pp. 40-58.

These items, instructive as they were, did not however amount to a systematic investigation. This came from C.H. Turner. Turner applied himself to the study of the text of various authors of the Ancient Church, in particular to Cyprian's *Testimonia* and to the Latin versions of the Shepherd of Hermas. His concern with Latin texts and manuscripts gave him a respect for Latin witnesses that had important consequences.

---

[1] A memoir and photograph of Turner preface the collection of papers published posthumously under the title *Catholic and Apostolic* (London and Oxford, 1931) edited by his friend H.W. Bate.

In his earlier work on the New Testament text he followed to a considerable extent the lines laid down by WH, but like Burkitt he occasionally suggested departures from their text, very often with encouragement from Western witnesses. These suggestions however remained haphazard.

This character holds true for much of his inaugural lecture on October 1920 (*The Study of the New Testament 1883 and 1920*) (Oxford, 1920, [3] 1926). In addition it contained a number of conjectures on which Turner was later tacitly to turn his back. It also contained the first hints of a different approach, a systematic study of the text of Mark to appear as a series of papers on "Marcan Usage" in *The Journal of Theological Studies* xxv-xxix (1924-1928). At the outset of this series he echoes Hort's statement, 'Knowledge of documents should precede final judgement upon readings' with his own principle 'Knowledge of an author's usage should precede final judgement'. This related "to readings", "to exegesis" and "to the mutual relations of the Synoptic Gospel". Turner's papers thus insisted on the importance of language as a criterion for text, for exegesis and the Synoptic Problem and applied this criterion to the style of Mark. In this way they are fundamental, but the emphasis throughout on the relevance of Mark's style for the Synoptic Problem inevitably restricted the choice of material included. Turner was of course arguing in favour of Marcan priority and the use of Mark by Matthew and Luke.

The impact of these articles can be seen in subsequent commentaries on Mark, for example, that of Vincent Taylor. In their own day the studies marked a great step forward. F.C. Burkitt in his departures from WH was moved by the consideration that it was unlikely that the Western text, especially when it was allied with the Old Syriac, was wrong all the time. Apart from attestation the only criterion that Burkitt mentioned was that of harmonisation. Language, invoked to the extent that Turner invoked it, was something new.

Now let us define Turner's contribution more precisely. First he did not have all the tools that we have. For example, the edition of the Greek New Testament on which he principally relied was Tischendorf's and he seems to have used von Soden little. (In our use of Turner's examples we shall need to remind ourselves that differences will sometimes be apparent when we compare the text he cites to that in e.g. Nestle-Aland, *Novum Testamentum Graece* 26th edition, but this we must do if we are to apply

Turner's work in our own day.) Turner was naturally at home with the major discoveries of New Testament manuscripts but he did not have access to all the materials available in S.C.E. Legg's *St. Mark* (Oxford, 1935) nor to the convenience of Jülicher-Aland's *Itala* II *Marcus-Evangelium* (Berlin 1938, ^{2}1970). The Chester Beatty Papyri came to light after his day. Unlike his colleagues who wrote on the Gospels, W.C. Allen and C.F. Burney, C.H. Turner was not a Semitic scholar. Consequently he was not alert to the traces of Semitic idiom in Mark to the same extent as W.C. Allen, but he had received a classical education and this showed itself in his extensive knowledge of Latin and Greek. A casual reference to A.E. Housman's introduction to volume 1 of his *Manilius* showed that Turner kept in touch with classical scholarship more than otherwise might be suspected. To this he added a great knowledge of Patristic Greek and Latin.

Another development was in palaeography. He was intimate with many Latin Christian manuscripts and had a fair working knowledge of Greek palaeography, but showed little acquaintance with the papyri. He accepted their contribution to the knowledge of the Greek of the period, but he did not enlarge it.

Great as his knowledge of ancient and Biblical Greek was, he showed little knowledge of its historical development or of its cultural stratification, nor does he show any sign of the stimulus of modern linguistic studies. In his discussion of particles (Notes VII) he does not try to set out Mark's usage in the light of the history of the particles between Attic and mediaeval Greek. If he had done so, he might have made other interesting discoveries in Mark.

His treatment of asyndeton shows no acquaintance with the Greek writers on style. Had he pondered their doctrine, he might well have reversed several of his decisions for asyndeton in Mark. He does not appear to have read any of the Greek writers on vocabulary or grammar and it is doubtful if his knowledge of them goes far beyond the indications furnished by dictionaries.

Yet when all is said and done, he had, quite apart from the Scriptures, a knowledge of ancient Christian Greek and Latin literature which few have paralleled. We may suspect that his article in *JTS* xxvii (1926) pp. 113-129 "*ὁ υἱός μου ὁ ἀγαπητός*" has not always had the impact that it should have done, partly because consultants have not always been able to feel the impact of its learning.

We may also remember that the papers on Marcan usage were pioneering work. Apart from Charles' commentary on Revelation, British scholarship does not seem to have known a comparable work where the systematic study of the language of an author has been used, not merely to compile an inventory of his language, but also to use this inventory as a tool for his exegesis, textual criticism and cultural exploration. Consequently when we have gladly recognised that Turner has made his point, it does not surprise us to discover that Turner has here and there left something to be done.

If we go through his studies of Marcan usage we can detect instances where we might depart from Turner's conclusions, but these departures often come about because we follow Turner's principles more rigorously or have more information. He himself had the same experience in the course of writing his papers. For example he changed his mind about the plural *ὄχλοι* at Mark x 1 (see his "Western Readings in the Second Half of St Mark's Gospel" *JTS* xxix (1927) pp. 4f.)

We may witness another development. When he set out on his exploration of Marcan usage Turner relied principally on the usage of his author as a criterion for determining his text. We may turn this into a maxim: When one reading in distinction from the rest accords with Marcan usage, that reading other things being equal is to be preferred. How then did the other readings come into being? Already in his first paper on Marcan usage Turner implied that harmonisation was responsible for some of the secondary variants.[2]

In the course of his papers he adds another: "Another *vera causa* of Alexandrian corruption of the text of Mark is the desire to remove the imperfections or non-literary elements of Mark's Greek".[3] Turner

---

[2] Of all the synopses available today, Greeven's revision of Huck's *Synopse* (Tübingen,[13] 1981) establishes the text by means of a rigorous application of the role of dissimilarity whenever harmonizing variants are encountered (see J.K. Elliott, "An Examination of the Text and Apparatus of Three Recent Greek Synopses" *NTS* 32 (1986) pp.557-82).

[3] "Western Readings in the Second Half of St.Mark's Gospel" *JTS* xxix (1927) p.15.

enlarges on this point elsewhere (cf. *JTS* xxvi (1924) p.20 (=Note III); xxix (1928) p.358(=Note X). Unfortunately he was deflected from considering the nature of this stylistical correction further by his attempts to find an explanation of these non-literary features in the influence of Latin idiom, an attempt which, apart from a few occasional expressions, seems unconvincing.

As can be seen from "Western Reading in the Second Half of St.Mark's Gospel", Turner's method knocked a big hole in the WH theory of the text. Over Mark as a whole he found a number of Western readings which mainly on grounds of language and style seemed to be right over against the Alexandrian alternatives.

Nonetheless Turner retained a considerable respect for WH's work and for the Alexandrian text.[4] For him the Alexandrian text was "a product of the highest kind of Alexandrian scholarship".[5] This gave him a clue to an explanation why this text sometimes fell short of success where Western witnesses preserved the original reading. The Alexandrian scholars with their critical standards sometimes improved on their authors. A considerable protection against this was a knowledge of the author's usage. Frequently this knowledge profited from the evidence provided by Western manuscripts in that they, from time to time, and not the Alexandrian witnesses provided the reading the Marcan usage seemed to require.

It is noteworthy that Turner found no place for Hort's Syrian (or majority) text or the *Textus Receptus* in this picture. Writing of πάλιν in Mark he states "The most definite result that emerges is the bad record of the *Textus Receptus*" (Note IX(2)) and this remark seems to represent his general view. Growing up at a time when WH had definitely supplanted the *Textus Receptus* it is understandable that he should take this view, but an examination of conflation not only in the Syrian text but also in the Alexandrian witnesses might have encouraged him to think again to the extent of allowing that sometimes the reading of the majority text might be right. We must therefore be cautious in accepting Turner's judgement about the worth of certain manuscripts or types of text. On the other hand his awareness of textual variation is an example to be followed and

---

4 "A Textual Commentary in Mark I" *JTS* xxviii (1927) pp.146f.

5 *ibid*. p.147.

occasionally he was prepared to argue for the originality of a reading which had only limited manuscript support if that reading conformed to Marcan usage (e.g.Note V (i) No.13)

He questioned WH's estimate of the Western text and to that extent modified their condemnation of it. To do this he employed criteria of author's usage, of harmonisation and stylistic correction, but his explorations remained largely a defence of the Western text of Mark. We should follow his criteria but extend them throughout the whole manuscript tradition.

In particular, Turner did not apply his criteria to readings from other than the Western-Alexandrian witnesses. As we have recognised, not merely did he accept WH's overthrow of the *Textus Receptus*, but he had no use for their Syrian text, though he developed the tools which enable us to reassess the Syrian text and the evidence of other witnesses which lie outside the Western-Alexandrian ambit. In rereading Turner's Notes we ought now check all his examples against a *full* critical apparatus. Turner created the tools which were needed in his attempt to deal with this problem, the Western text, without seeing the full consequences of this innovation.

Innovation it was. In trying to solve his problem he did not appeal to the mass of the evidence as Burgon and others have done, he did not appeal to genealogy nor to a couple of "best" manuscripts. Despite his respect for WH, for a decision he appealed not to such external considerations but to internal ones such as knowledge of an author's usage. If he left 't's to cross and 'i's to dot, this could only be done with his tools; he left us the means to complete his work.

Over the period 1920-1930 his methods steadily developed and refined themselves and we can detect certain tendencies. Conjecture is one example of this. In his inaugural lecture Turner made a number of textual conjectures but in the course of his studies in Marcan usage he turned his back on some of them and indulged less and less in new conjectures. He found that many of the problems he had been prone to solve by conjecture were better dealt with through a knowledge of the author's language.

If his principal contribution to New Testament studies lay in textual criticism, Turner also made other contributions to the methods of interpretation. He showed the value of a knowledge of the author's language for this kind of task. What he began with Mark we can only carry further both there and in the rest of the New Testament.

His great patristic knowledge enabled him to use the evidence of the Fathers both to illuminate the language of the New Testament and to provide interpretations of its difficulties. Many of them used a Greek which was so little different from that of the New Testament authors themselves. Turner shows himself well aware of this and can for example use the Apostolic Fathers as a continuation of the New Testament as far as the Greek language is concerned.

An extension of this is his knowledge of the Latin Christian authors and of the Latin Bible, especially of the New Testament. When the meaning of an expression in the Greek New Testament is in question, he is always happy to tell us how the Latin witnesses rendered it. The fact that he found illumination there should encourage us to continue in the same practice.

Turner knitted his study of Marcan usage with a general view of the Petrine origin and purpose of Mark. This view may seem to us today old-fashioned and limited. Many aspects of Mark which had been profitably explored by others are ignored in Turner's work, and of course the study of the gospels in general and Mark in particular has advanced greatly since 1930.

Nevertheless the methods Turner developed promised and still promise discoveries that can illuminate all parts of the New Testament to which they are applied. If Turner had to pay for his concentration by a narrowing of his achievement, we may feel that others have not always achieved what they might because they have not fully exploited his methods. His achievement should encourage us to persist in his methods as well as in those which others have developed.

C.H.Turner

CHAPTER ONE

MARCAN USAGE: NOTES, CRITICAL AND EXEGETICAL ON THE SECOND GOSPEL

Introductory Words

Dr Hort, in the great *Introduction* to his edition of the Greek Testament, lays down as fundamental the principle that 'Knowledge of documents should precede final judgement upon readings' (§ 38), using capitals in the text and italics in the table of contents to call special attention to the importance of the words. I want to enter a similar plea for what I conceive to be an even more important principle, namely that 'Knowledge of an author's usage should precede final judgement' alike as to readings, as to exegesis, and — in this case — as to the mutual relations of the Synoptic Gospels. The studies that follow are intended to be a contribution to the textual criticism and the exegesis of St Mark, and also to the better understanding of that department of the Synoptic problem which is concerned with the agreements of Matthew and Luke against Mark. So long as it is supposed that there is a residuum of agreements between Matthew and Luke against Mark in matter taken from Mark — apart, that is, from passages found also in Q — which cannot be explained without assuming literary contact either of Matthew and Luke with one another or of both with some other document than our extant Mark, so long will research into the Synoptic question be hampered and final solution delayed. We can only see things in their true proportions if we consider the evidence over a wide field, and note not only the agreements but the disagreements of the two later Synoptists in the handling of their common material. 'Use large maps' is a piece of advice that applies to other people besides politicians.

I propose therefore to treat in succession various characteristic Marcan usages, isolating each usage and examining it over the whole field of the Gospel. So and so only shall we be able to establish our inductions on a secure basis. And I cannot help thinking that the method proves itself to be unexpectedly fruitful in results.

I – The Impersonal Plural†[1].

By the impersonal plural is here meant the use of a plural verb with no subject expressed, and no subject implied other than the quite general one 'people'. This form of phrase, common in Aramaic as a substitute for the passive, is very characteristic of St Mark's narrative, and is generally altered in the other Synoptists either by the insertion of a definite subject or (and this especially in St Luke) by the substitution of the passive voice for the impersonal active. With the exception of two passages which present rather more difficulty than the rest and are therefore reserved for the end, the order of the Gospel is followed.

1. i 21, 22 *καὶ εὐθὺς τοῖς σάββασιν ἐδίδασκεν εἰς τὴν συναγωγὴν καὶ ἐξεπλήσσοντο ἐπὶ τῇ διδαχῇ αὐτοῦ, ἦν γὰρ διδάσκων αὐτοὺς ὡς ἐξουσίαν ἔχων.* There is no subject to *ἐξεπλήσσοντο*, though we can of course supply 'the congregation'; but I think what Mark meant was simply 'people were astonished'. Luke eases the construction by transferring *ἦν διδάσκων αὐτούς* from the second part of the sentence to the first, so that *αὐτούς* explains *ἐξεπλήσσοντο.* Matthew characteristically inserts *οἱ ὄχλοι*, 'the multitudes were astonished'.

2. i 29, 30 *καὶ εὐθὺς ἐκ τῆς συναγωγῆς ἐξελθόντες ἦλθον εἰς τὴν οἰκίαν Σίμωνος καὶ Ἀνδρέου μετὰ Ἰακώβου καὶ Ἰωάννου. ἡ δὲ πενθερὰ Σίμωνος κατέκειτο πυρέσσουσα καὶ εὐθὺς λέγουσιν αὐτῷ περὶ αὐτῆς.* St Mark means, I think, 'immediately He is told about her': he does not mean that 'Simon and Andrew with James and John' told Him, to the exclusion of the family in the house. Matthew, with his usual tendency to compress a story, omits the detail. Luke retains, only changing present to past tense and substituting a more definite word *ἠρώτησαν*, 'consulted Him', for Mark's recurring and colourless *λέγουσιν*.

3. i 32 *ὀψίας δὲ γενομένης ... ἔφερον πρὸς αὐτὸν πάντας τοὺς κακῶς ἔχοντας.* Matthew retains, with the past tense *προσήνεγκαν.* Luke inserts a nominative *πάντες ὅσοι εἶχον ἀσθενοῦντας νόσοις ποικίλαις.*

4. i 45 *ἔξω ἐπ' ἐρήμοις τόποις ἦν· καὶ ἤρχοντο πρὸς αὐτὸν πάντοθεν.* Matthew, omitting the whole verse, offers no parallel. Luke inserts *ὄχλοι πολλοί.*

5. ii 2, 3 *καὶ συνήχθησαν πολλοὶ ... καὶ ἐλάλει αὐτοῖς τὸν λόγον. καὶ ἔρχονται φέροντες πρὸς αὐτὸν παραλυτικόν.*

Obviously a new nominative must be supplied with *ἔρχονται* — 'there arrive people bringing a paralytic ...' So in terms Luke, *καὶ ἰδοὺ ἄνδρες*

---

[1] A dagger indicates an 'Additional Note' which is to be found at the end of this chapter.

φέροντες ...· Matthew is content with *καὶ ἰδοὺ προσέφερον*, but then, having omitted the previous verse of Mark, he has at least had no rival nominative in his preceding words.

6. ii 18 *καὶ ἦσαν οἱ μαθηταὶ Ἰωάννου καὶ οἱ Φαρισαῖοι νηστεύοντες. καὶ ἔρχονται καὶ λέγουσιν αὐτῷ· Διατί οἱ μαθηταὶ Ἰωάννου καὶ οἱ μαθηταὶ τῶν Φαρισαίων νηστεύουσιν, οἱ δὲ σοὶ μαθηταὶ οὐ νηστεύουσιν;*

A singularly instructive example. It does not seem to me doubtful that St Mark means, neither that John's disciples came to put the question, nor that the Pharisees came, but simply that the question was put. Some of the people of the place noticed that there was a remarkable difference of religious observance at the moment between two sections of 'disciples' and a third: and they apply to the head of the section which was in a minority for an explanation of its difference from the others. But neither Matthew nor Luke likes to leave the matter so. They interpret Mark, and both of them interpret him to mean that it was one of the two opposing sections which put the question: Matthew places it in the mouth of the disciples of John, inserting *οἱ μαθηταὶ Ἰωάννου*, Luke with *οἱ δὲ εἶπαν* treats the interlocutors as those of the preceding verses *οἱ Φαρισαῖοι καὶ οἱ γραμματεῖς αὐτῶν*.

7. iii 1, 2 *καὶ εἰσῆλθεν πάλιν εἰς συναγωγήν, καὶ ἦν ἐκεῖ ἄνθρωπος... καὶ παρετήρουν αὐτὸν εἰ τοῖς σάββασιν* ... Mark's *εἰς συναγωγήν* is I think almost exactly 'He went to church'. There is therefore no nominative to *παρετήρουν*, and the equivalent English is 'watch was kept on him to see if ...' Matthew having written *εἰς συναγωγὴν αὐτῶν* has an implied nominative ready for his verb *ἐπηρώτησαν*, Luke inserts *οἱ γραμματεῖς καὶ οἱ Φαρισαῖοι*.

8. iii 31, 32 *καὶ ἔρχεται ἡ μήτηρ αὐτοῦ καὶ οἱ ἀδελφοὶ αὐτοῦ καὶ ἔξω στήκοντες ἀπέστειλαν πρὸς αὐτὸν καλοῦντες αὐτόν· καὶ ἐκάθητο περὶ αὐτὸν ὄχλος, καὶ λέγουσιν αὐτῷ· Ἰδοὺ ἡ μήτηρ σου....* Clearly it is not the crowd who give the message. The porter or some one of that sort is charged to convey to Jesus the news that His mother wants to see Him: the inserted words *καὶ ἐκάθητο περὶ αὐτὸν ὄχλος* logically belong to *v.*34; but Peter visualizes the scene as he remembers it. Luke excellently represents the impersonal plural by the passive *ἀπηγγέλη*. Matthew's text, xii 47, offers a problem of some difficulty. It seems preposterous at first sight to suppose that words can be genuine which are absent from ℵ B L, the African Latin (*k*), the Old Syriac, and the Sahidic. But a sound instinct led Westcott and Hort to admit the words at least to their margin. For in the first place they are necessary to the sense: and in the second place experience of manuscripts establishes no rule on a more certain basis than that, where *homoioteleuton* will account for omission, the omitted words are probably genuine. It is therefore possible to say with some confidence that Mt. xii 47 is genuine, and that Matthew represented Mark's λέγουσιν by εἶπεν δέ τις. But even if they are not genuine, Matthew's τῷ λέγοντι in the next verse shews that he avoided the impersonal plural.

9. v 14 *καὶ οἱ βόσκοντες αὐτοὺς ἔφυγον καὶ ἀπήγγειλαν εἰς τὴν πόλιν καὶ εἰς τοὺς ἀγρούς. καὶ ἦλθον ἰδεῖν τί ἐστιν τὸ γεγονός.*

What St Mark of course means is that the inhabitants of the town and the villages came to see what had happened: Luke too thought that the words *εἰς τὴν πόλιν καὶ εἰς τοὺς ἀγρούς* sufficiently prepared for the change of subject, and retained Mark's language practically unaltered. Matthew on the other hand inserted *πᾶσα ἡ πόλις* as nominative.

10. v 35 *ἔτι αὐτοῦ λαλοῦντος ἔρχονται ἀπὸ τοῦ ἀρχισυναγώγου λέγοντες ὅτι Ἡ θυγάτηρ σου ἀπέθανεν.*

'Messengers come from the ruler of the synagogue's house with the news that ...' Matthew's form of this story is an extreme instance of his tendency to compression: three successive verses in Mark, v 35-37, are entirely unrepresented, so we can only say 'no parallel'. Luke's *ἔρχεταί τις ... λέγων* reminds us of Matthew's *εἶπέν τις* in no.**8**. Nothing is clearer throughout the series of these passages than the independence of Matthew and Luke in their treatment of the Marcan material. For the solitary coincidence between them see no.**12**.

11. vi 14 *καὶ ἤκουσεν ὁ βασιλεὺς Ἡρῴδης, φανερὸν γὰρ ἐγένετο τὸ ὄνομα αὐτοῦ, καὶ ἔλεγον ὅτι Ἰωάννης ὁ βαπτίζων ἐγήγερται ... ἄλλοι δὲ ἔλεγον ... ἄλλοι δὲ ἔλεγον ... ἀκούσας δὲ ὁ Ἡρῴδης ἔλεγεν ... .*

An interesting instance, because of the doubt as to the reading in the case of the first *ἔλεγον*. Most authorities give *ἔλεγεν*, 'Herod said'. The authorities which give the plural are few but good: B D, now reinforced by W, and some Old Latins. And the plural is absolutely certain, for it is guaranteed by the parallel in Mark viii 28 (*τίνα με λέγουσιν οἱ ἄνθρωποι εἶναι; οἱ δὲ εἶπαν αὐτῷ λέγοντες ὅτι Ἰωάννην τὸν βαπτιστήν, καὶ ἄλλοι Ἠλείαν, ἄλλοι δὲ ὅτι Εἷς τῶν προφητῶν*), and it is implied by the reproduction of the passage in Luke ix 7, *διὰ τὸ λέγεσθαι ὑπό τινων ὅτι Ἰωάννης ἠγέρθη* ... Matthew omits all reference to the divergent contemporary views about Jesus, and therefore offers, no real parallel. St Mark assuredly meant 'His reputation was now considerable, and different ideas were held about Him in different circles by His contemporaries: people were saying, Why, it's John the Baptizer *redivivus*, others No, it's Elijah, and others again A new prophet, just as there have been prophets from time to time before'.

12. vi 33 *καὶ εἶδον αὐτοὺς ὑπάγοντας καὶ ἔγνωσαν πολλοί· καὶ πεζῇ ἀπὸ πασῶν τῶν πόλεων συνέδραμον ἐκεῖ καὶ προῆλθον αὐτούς.*

Obviously [2] the many who recognized them were not the same necessarily as the people who ran on foot from all the cities. Rather the many who recognized the intention of Jesus and His disciples spread the news, and with many to circulate the report a large concourse of people from different directions could collect, all heading for the place of landing on the other side. I am not even sure that we should not put a comma after *ὑπάγοντας*, and translate 'And they were seen going, and many recognized them, and people ran on foot to the common meeting-point and anticipated their arrival'. All these details seemed to the later Evangelists superfluous, and they pruned them remorselessly. Both reduce Mark's four verbs to the single word — the only single word which would express the complete idea — *ἠκολούθησαν*: both supply *οἱ ὄχλοι* as again the only single noun which would cover those who saw, those who recognized, and those whose concourse was directed to the landing-place.

It should be noted that this is the solitary occasion on our list where Matthew and Luke make the *same* rectification of Mark's impersonal plural. But it has just been shewn what an obvious change it is: and Matthew inserts the same noun *ὄχλοι* on two other occasions in our list (**1** and **15**), Luke on one (**4**).

13. vi 42, 43 *καὶ ἔφαγον πάντες καὶ ἐχορτάσθησαν· καὶ ἦραν κλάσματα δώδεκα κοφίνων πληρώματα.*

It was not the 5,000 who ate and were filled who picked up the fragments. Luke correctly interprets Mark when he substitutes *ἤρθη* for *ἦραν*. So still more expressly the Fourth Evangelist — who in the story of this miracle follows in Mark's footsteps — *λέγει τοῖς μαθηταῖς αὐτοῦ Συναγάγετε τὰ περισσεύσαντα κλάσματα* (Jo. vi 12). Matthew alone retains Mark's phrase unaltered.

14. vi 53, 54 *καὶ διαπεράσαντες ἐπὶ τὴν γῆν ἦλθον εἰς Γεννησαρὲτ … καὶ ἐξελθόντων αὐτῶν ἐκ τοῦ πλοίου εὐθὺς ἐπιγνόντες αὐτὸν περιέδραμον* … . We have now arrived at the long lacuna in Luke's copying of Mark: for our three instances **14**, **15**, and **16** there are no parallels in the third Synoptist.

Mark meant that the people of the district where Jesus landed recognized Him: Matthew states that expressly, *ἐπιγνόντες αὐτὸν οἱ ἄνδρες τοῦ τόπου ἐκείνου.*

---

[2] I think it quite obvious: but I have to admit that Swete *in loc.* appears to take *πολλοί* as subject to all the three verbs.

15. vii 31, 32 *καὶ πάλιν ... ἦλθεν ... εἰς τὴν θάλασσαν τῆς Γαλιλαίας ... καὶ φέρουσιν αὐτῷ κωφὸν καὶ μογιλάλον.*

Matthew generalizes from Mark's single instance, inserting *ὄχλοι πολλοί* as the subject, *καὶ προσῆλθον αὐτῷ ὄχλοι πολλοί, ἔχοντες μεθ' ἑαυτῶν χωλοὺς τυφλοὺς κωφοὺς κυλλούς.*

16. viii 22 *καὶ ἔρχονται εἰς Βηθσαϊδάν. καὶ φέρουσιν αὐτῷ τυφλόν.*

Those who came to Bethsaida were our Lord and His disciples. Those who brought the blind man to Him were people of the place: our English equivalent would probably be 'and a blind man was brought to Him'. The whole passage is absent from Matthew (though it presumably contributed the *τυφλούς* to Matthew's generalization in xv 30, see just above under **15**) as well as from Luke.

17. x 1, 2 *καὶ συνπορεύονται πάλιν ὄχλοι πρὸς αὐτόν, καὶ ὡς εἰώθει πάλιν ἐδίδασκεν αὐτούς. καὶ ἐπηρώτων αὐτὸν εἰ ἔξεστιν ἀνδρὶ γυναῖκα ἀπολῦσαι.*

The passage is included here with a little hesitation: but I believe both that this is the true reading, and that *ἐπηρώτων αὐτόν* is the impersonal plural — not 'the multitudes asked Him' but 'the question was asked of Him'. It would not be reasonable to suppose that the question of divorce was the dominant one in the minds of the crowds: Peter simply remembered the question being raised at that time. There is no parallel in Luke: Matthew supplies *προσῆλθον αὐτῷ οἱ Φαρισαῖοι*, from which many authorities have borrowed *προσελθόντες οἱ Φ.* for the text of Mark.

18. x 13 *καὶ προσέφερον αὐτῷ παιδία ἵνα αὐτῶν ἅψηται.*

Luke retains the impersonal plural: Matthew substitutes the passive, *τότε προσενέχθησαν αὐτῷ παιδία.*

19. x 49 *καὶ εἶπεν Φωνήσατε αὐτόν. καὶ ἐφώνησαν τὸν τυφλόν.*

This passage is again included doubtfully, since it is possible to understand St Mark as meaning that our Lord addressed the command 'Call him' to definite persons who obeyed the command. I should rather understand the Evangelist to mean that our Lord ordered generally that Bartimaeus should be called, and that the order was carried out by somebody or other. In any case the detail was omitted by Matthew and only indicated by Luke.

20. xiii 9-11 *βλέπετε δὲ ὑμεῖς ἑαυτούς· παραδώσουσιν ὑμᾶς εἰς συνέδρια καὶ εἰς συναγωγὰς δαρήσεσθε ... καὶ ὅταν ἄγωσιν ὑμᾶς παραδιδόντες, μὴ προμεριμνᾶτε τί λαλήσητε.*

Both Matthew and Luke retain the impersonal plural here — it is the solitary instance in our series in which both do so, but then it is also the solitary instance in our series in which the idiom is employed in the record of our Lord's words [3] — but in an earlier place in Matthew (x 17, where the substance of the Marcan passage is much more closely reproduced than it is at xxiv 9) we have, instead of *βλέπετε ἑαυτούς*, *προσέχετε ἀπὸ τῶν ἀνθρώπων*, and in that way a subject is supplied.

21. xiv 12 *καὶ τῇ πρώτῃ ἡμέρᾳ τῶν ἀζύμων ὅτε τὸ πάσχα ἔθυον.*

Matthew, either because he thought the information superfluous or perhaps because he thought it absolutely misleading, omitted the clause *ὅτε τὸ πάσχα ἔθυον*. Luke transposed the impersonal active, as in **8**, **11**, **13**, into a passive, *ἐν ᾗ ἔδει θύεσθαι τὸ πάσχα*.

Of these twenty-one passages there are three for which there is no Matthaean parallel, **4**, **10**, **16**, and four for which there is no Lucan parallel, **14**, **15**, **16**, **17**. Again, the actual phrase in which the impersonal plural occurs is dropped on four occasions by Matthew, **2**, **11**, **19**, **21**, and on one by Luke, **19**. There remain fourteen passages in Matthew, sixteen in Luke, to consider.

The most common expedient in both Matthew and Luke is the insertion of a nominative as subject for the verb, which thus ceases to be impersonal. The expedient is adopted eight times by Matthew **1**, **6**, **8**, **9**, **12**, **14**, **15**, **17**, seven times by Luke, **3**, **4**, **5**, **6**, **7**, **10**, **12**. Each of them uses *τις* once, Matthew 8, Luke 10: for the rest they used plural nouns or nouns of multitude. Only once do they agree on the nominative inserted, 12, where *οἱ ὄχλοι* is common to both. Since the particular word *ὄχλος* was one of the most obvious nouns, if not the most obvious, to insert, the single coincidence is nothing unnatural.

Besides this, there was the possibility of using what we should feel in English the most idiomatic method of rendering St Mark's usage, and substituting a passive. Matthew does this once, **18**, Luke four times, **8**, **11**, **13**, **21**.

These two expedients reduce the series to five passages apiece in Matthew and Luke, where the impersonal plural is retained. The evidence shews conclusively that the idiom is a regular and common one in Mark's narrative, and that on two occasions on an average out of three it is in some way got rid of by the other Synoptists.

With these results before us, let us now consider the two reserved passages, Mark iii 21 (**22**), xiv 1 (**23**).

---

[3] Matthew and Luke shew a fair number of instances of the idiom in the record of Christ's teaching. What is remarkable is Mark's fondness for it, and their dislike of it, in narrative. No doubt they allowed themselves far greater latitude in recasting Mark's own story than in recasting the record of the *Λόγοι* of Christ.

22. iii 21 *καὶ ἀκούσαντες οἱ παρ' αὐτοῦ ἐξῆλθον κρατῆσαι· αὐτόν ἔλεγον γὰρ ὅτι Εξέστη.*

The impression ordinarily and naturally caused by these words is that our Lord's family left home to get hold of Him, because they thought He was out of His senses. But in the light of what we now know of Mark's fondness for the impersonal plural, an alternative rendering becomes at once possible, 'for it was reported that He was out of His senses'. And the possible rendering becomes I think probable, or more than probable, if we consider the weakness of the reason given, on the ordinary view, for the action of Christ's family. They said He was mad: on what grounds? On the rather inadequate ground that the crowd was so great that nobody had room to eat. But on the view now proposed, St Mark has rounded off his story of the Call of the Twelve by the summary statement that the call was followed by a resumption of the work at Capernaum. Then begins a new paragraph, verses 21-35, dealing with two alternative explanations offered by those who criticized the new teacher's work: *ἔλεγον ὅτι 'Εξέστη, ἔλεγον ὅτι Βεελζεβοὺλ ἔχει.* The former was a local criticism, which reached the ears of His family at Nazareth, and they left home to see what restraining influence they could exert over Him: the latter was the suggestion of emissaries from Jerusalem. This is dealt with first: it is the sin against the Holy Ghost, the refusal to recognize that good deeds must come from the good God. The story then returns to the former. It is over-subtle to regard the intercalation of verses 22-30 as intended to allow time for the journey from Nazareth to Capernaum. It is rather that the mention of the earlier and more naïve criticism of people at Capernaum suggests at once to the writer the other more evil-minded but more logical theory of people from Jerusalem, and being reminded of it he deals with it first. [4]

23. xiv 1 *ἦν δὲ τὸ πάσχα καὶ τὰ ἄζυμα μετὰ δύο ἡμέρας, καὶ ἐζήτουν οἱ ἀρχιερεῖς καὶ οἱ γραμματεῖς πῶς αὐτὸν ἐν δόλῳ κρατήσαντες ἀποκτείνωσιν ἔλεγον γὰρ Μὴ ἐν τῇ ἑορτῇ, μή ποτε ἔσται θόρυβος τοῦ λαοῦ.*

'Next day was the Passover: and the chief-priests were on the look out for some underhand way of arresting Him: for it had been urged that an (open) arrest at the feast might lead to a riot'. That is I think what St Mark means. The emphasis in the second clause is, as the position of the

---

[4] I think myself that by the *ἔλεγον* of verse 30, *ὅτι ἔλεγον Πνεῦμα ἀκάθαρτον ἔχει*, St Mark means again the impersonal plural 'because it was said', though it is of course possible that he is harking back to 'the scribes' of verse 22.

word indicates, on δόλῳ: and what reason would there be for any emphasis on δόλῳ, if the point were that they were going to make *no* arrest during the festival? But if the conditions were (1) that the chief-priests were determined to arrest Jesus before He left Jerusalem, (2) that some of the Sanhedrists, to whom they felt bound to defer in order to secure unanimity, made a timid *caveat* against any action which might involve the chance of a riot at the moment of arrest, then the need for δόλος explains itself. An arrest effected by δόλος would avoid the chance of a riot, whether it was effected during the festival or no. Hence the value to them of Judas, and of the information which enabled them to carry out their *coup* in the late evening and at a retired spot.

It has been suggested that the mysterious directions given by our Lord to disciples in xi 2 and xiv 13, where no names are named, were intended to prevent Judas from obtaining previous knowledge of our Lord's movements which he could convey to the Jewish authorities. However that may be, it seems clear that δόλος meant just the securing of a time and place for the arrest where popular support for Jesus would have no opportunity of asserting itself. It is difficult to suppose that it is intended to imply a contrast between an arrest on Thursday and an arrest on Friday. And the solitary change which Matthew makes in copying Mark is in this respect very instructive: for, understanding ἔλεγον to refer back to the chief priests, he alters ἔλεγον γάρ into ἔλεγον δέ. The chief priests, that is to say, determined to arrest Jesus, but determined at the same time that an arrest during the feast must be avoided. Later exegesis has, as in so many other passages, interpreted Mark by Matthew. But if Mark's account is taken as the primary one, ἔλεγον γάρ gives the reason for δόλος. On the ordinary view, St Mark ought to have written 'Next day being passover, the authorities determined to effect the arrest of Jesus before passover began: for they said, Not during the feast ... ' But that is not what St Mark says. He says, 'The feast being now imminent, the authorities determined to avoid a direct and open arrest, for the objection had been taken that such methods were too dangerous at such a time: they had to have recourse therefore to some secret *coup*'.

I add, by way of appendix, yet one more passage, where, if we may assume the use of the impersonal plural, the reading which is perhaps the more probable would receive its explanation and justification:

24. xv 10 (8-11) *καὶ ἀναβὰς ὁ ὄχλος ἤρξατο αἰτεῖσθαι καθὼς ἐποίει αὐτοῖς. ὁ δὲ Πειλᾶτος ἀπεκρίθη αὐτοῖς λέγων Θέλετε ἀπολύσω ὑμῖν τὸν βασιλέα τῶν Ἰουδαίων; ἐγίνωσκεν γὰρ ὅτι διὰ φθόνον παραδεδώκεισαν* *αὐτόν. οἱ δὲ ἀρχιερεῖς ἀνέσεισαν τὸν ὄχλον ἵνα μᾶλλον τὸν Βαραββᾶν ἀπολύσῃ αὐτοῖς.*

The above reading, *παραδεδώκεισαν αὐτόν* without *οἱ ἀρχιερεῖς* to follow, is that of B 1 *k* and the Sinai Syriac, and is supported by Matt. xxvii 18 *ᾔδει γὰρ ὅτι διὰ φθόνον παρέδωκαν αὐτόν*: and since it was certainly not the multitude who had handed Jesus over to the governor, we must take *παραδεδώκεισαν* as impersonal plural, and translate 'it was for envy's sake that Jesus had been brought before him'. The alternative reading supplies a nominative to *παραδεδώκεισαν*: but it would be awkward even for Mark to end one sentence with *οἱ ἀρχιερεῖς* and begin the next sentence with *οἱ δὲ ἀρχιερεῖς*, and I incline to think that the first *οἱ ἀρχιερεῖς* is just an early scribal insertion, or more probably gloss, intended to make the sense of *παραδεδώκεισαν* clear to the reader.

II – Φέρειν in St Mark

φέρειν is one of the words specially characteristic of the Second Gospel, and Sir John Hawkins rightly includes it in his list *Horae Synopticae*[2] p.13. If we make abstraction of the technical usage of *φέρειν* 'to bear fruit', the figures for the four Gospels are Mark 14, Matthew 4, Luke 4, John 8. Sir John Hawkins leaves the matter there: but examination of the passages concerned reveals the secret of the disproportionate occurrence of the word in Mark. The other three Evangelists, in fact, limit the meaning of *φέρειν*, speaking generally, to the sense of 'carry': Mark, on the other hand, uses it also, and more frequently, in the sense 'bring'. The difference is therefore a lexical one. It is well illustrated in the treatment of Mark **2** (ii 3) by Luke, and of Mark **7** (xi 2, 7) by both Matthew and Luke.

1. Mark i 32 *ἔφερον πρὸς αὐτὸν πάντας τοὺς κακῶς ἔχοντας.* Here *ἔφερον*, as in the parallel cases **2**, **4**, **5**, **6**, **7**, **9**, means certainly 'brought', not 'carried': and therefore Matthew substitutes *προσήνεγκαν* and Luke *ἤγαγον*.

2. ii 3 *καὶ ἔρχονται φέροντες πρὸς αὐτὸν παραλυτικὸν αἰρόμενον ὑπὸ τεσσάρων.* So far is Mark from implying the sense of 'carry' in *φέροντες* that he finds it necessary to add *αἰρόμενον* to convey the further idea: 'they bring to him a paralytic, carried by four men'. Matthew again substitutes *προσφέρειν*: Luke transfers *φέροντες* to take the place of *αἰρόμενον* 'men (come) carrying on a bed a man who was paralysed'.

3*a*. vi 27 *καὶ εὐθὺς ἀποστείλας ὁ βασιλεὺς σπεκουλάτορα ἐπέταξεν ἐνέγκαι τὴν κεφαλὴν αὐτοῦ.*

***b*.** 28 *καὶ ἤνεγκεν τὴν κεφαλὴν αὐτοῦ ἐπὶ πίνακι.*

Here the natural rendering in verse 27 would be 'bring', but in verse 28 we could no doubt say either 'he brought his head on a dish' or 'he bore his head on a dish'. The episode is absent from Luke: Matthew's abbreviated narrative dispenses with the *ἐνέγκαι* of verse 27, but retains the *ἤνεγκεν* of verse 28 in the passive form *ἠνέχθη* 'his head was borne on a dish.'

4. vii 32 *καὶ φέρουσιν αὐτῷ κωφὸν καὶ μογιλάλον.* Obviously they 'bring' the man, not 'carry' him. So Matthew (Luke again has no parallel) paraphrases with *προσῆλθον ... ἔχοντες μεθ' ἑαυτῶν*, once more refusing Mark's usage of *φέρειν*.

5. viii 22 *καὶ ἔρχονται εἰς* Βηθσαιδάν. *καὶ φέρουσιν αὐτῷ τυφλόν.* Neither Matthew nor Luke retains this episode: if they had retained it, we may presume that they would have done as they regularly do elsewhere and have avoided the *φέρειν*.

6*a*. ix 17 *διδάσκαλε, ἤνεγκα τὸν υἱόν μου πρὸς σέ.*
***b*.** 19 *φέρετε αὐτὸν πρός με.*
***c*.** 20 *καὶ ἤνεγκαν αὐτὸν πρὸς αὐτόν.*

Luke reduces the triple use of the word to a single occasion, and there substitutes *προσάγαγε*. Matthew inserts *προσήνεγκα* at one point, drops the *ἤνεγκα, ἤνεγκαν*, of verses 17 and 20, but retains the *φέρετε* of verse 19. Here (Matt. xvii 17) we have the solitary instance in which Mark's *φέρειν* = 'bring' retains its place in either of the other Synoptists. Probably the use was felt to be more tolerable in the imperative[1]: possibly it is eased by Matthew's addition of *ὧδε*. So Matt. xiv 18 of the loaves and fishes *φέρετέ μοι ὧδε αὐτούς*.

7*a*. xi 2 *εὑρήσετε πῶλον δεδεμένον ... λύσατε αὐτὸν καὶ φέρετε.*
***b*.** 7 *καὶ φέρουσιν τὸν πῶλον πρὸς τὸν Ἰησοῦν.*

Both Matthew and Luke substitute *ἀγάγετε* in *a*, *ἤγαγον* in *b*. Luke therewith makes his regular alteration: Matthew for once deserts *προσφέρω* for *ἄγω*, presumably because 'leading' is a natural word to employ of an animal.

8*a*. xii 15 *φέρετέ μοι δηνάριον ἵνα ἴδω.*
***b*.** 16 *οἱ δὲ ἤνεγκαν.*

Matthew *ἐπιδείξατέ μοι ... οἱ δὲ προσήνεγκαν*. Luke *δείξατε*, omitting the addition that a *δηνάριον* was then brought. Neither would talk of *φέρειν* in connexion with a coin: but Luke's normal substitution of *ἄγειν* was inappropriate here, and he had to find another word. That he and Matthew should have found the same substitute for *φέρετε* in *δείξατε* (*ἐπιδείξατε*) naturally challenges our attention. But coincidences will happen: they have no significance unless they bear an undue proportion to the total number of cases in which they could happen. And if the chances were — as presumably they were — that one or other of the group of Pharisees and Herodians had a *denarius* on his person, then 'show me one' was an even more natural phrase than 'bring me one'.

9. xv 22 (*ἀγγαρεύουσιν ... Σίμωνα ... ἵνα ἄρῃ τὸν σταυρὸν αὐτοῦ*) *καὶ φέρουσιν αὐτὸν ἐπὶ τὸν Γολγοθὰν τόπον ...* (*καὶ σταυροῦσιν αὐτόν*).

Mark uses *αἴρω*, as in ii 3, for 'carrying' the cross: Luke, as there, substitutes *φέρειν*. Mark's *φέρειν* for 'bring' him to Golgotha is of course rejected by both Matthew and Luke, who agree in simplifying the sentence into the form 'on their arrival (*ἐλθόντες, ὅτε ἀπῆλθον*) at Golgotha ... they crucified him'. Again a coincidence, but surely a very obvious one, once it is postulated that the word *φέρειν* had somehow to

---

[1] See for the imperative also Luke xv 23 (quoted in the next note), and Jo. xx 27 *φέρε τὸν δάκτυλον*.

be got rid of, and that the four verbs connected by *καί* in Mark xv 22-24 offered an irresistible temptation to revision.

In the result, out of fourteen instances of *φέρειν* in Mark, the word is never retained by Luke,[2] once only by Matthew; though Luke twice (v 18, xxiii 26) transfers it to the immediate context, displacing Mark's *αἴρειν* to make room for it. For *φέρειν* Luke's favourite alternative is *ἄγειν* (three times) or *προσάγειν* (once). Mark only once has *ἄγειν* in the ordinary transitive use: Matthew, save in the episode of the 'bringing' of the colt to Jesus, shares Mark's avoidance of *ἄγειν*, and replaces *φέρειν* by *προσφέρειν* (four times), a word which he employs nearly twice as often as the other three Evangelists put together.

---

[2] Yet compare Luke xv 23 *φέρετε τὸν μόσχον τὸν σιτευτόν* (again however in the imperative, as Matt. xiv 18, xvii 17, see above under *6b*), Acts v 16 *φέροντες ἀσθενεῖς*.

III – εἰς and ἐν in St Mark

On εἰς (εἰς and ἐν) in the New Testament see Winer-Moulton, *Grammar of New Testament Greek*[9] pp.514, 516-518, who give the older view that there is no, or next to no, real confusion between the two prepositions: on the other side J.H.Moulton, *Prolegomena to a Grammar of New Testament Greek* (1906) pp.62-63, and especially 234; Fr.Blass, *Grammatik des Neutestamentlichen Griechisch* (1896) § 39. 3 (4, 5) pp.119-121; L. Radermacher, *Neutestamentliche Grammatik: Das Griechisch des Neuen Testaments im Zusammenhang mit der Volkssprache* (1911) pp. 16, 10: and for εἰς in modern Greek A.Thumb, *Handbuch der neugriechischen Volkssprache* (1895) § 202, p.120

The following list of passages is intended to justify the conclusion that in Mark's usage εἰς is frequently used in the place of ἐν, ἐν perhaps occasionally where we should rather expect εἰς (see **2**, **10**): that the other two Synoptists, and Matthew more consistently than Luke, dislike the confusion of the two prepositions and generally alter Mark's phraseology: and that the volume of evidence for εἰς = ἐν as a favourite usage of Mark is sufficient to turn the scale where the witnesses happen to be divided, some giving an εἰς = ἐν reading and others either having ἐν in place of εἰς (**6**, **15**) or more often introducing into the text a verb of motion (**3**, **4**, **14**).

1. i 9 *ἐβαπτίσθη εἰς τὸν Ἰορδάνην*. It is quite impossible, in my judgement, to suppose that by this phrase Mark means anything at all different from i 5 *ἐβαπτίζοντο ἐν τῷ Ἰορδάνῃ*: the phrases were to him synonymous. Matthew retains *ἐβαπτίζοντο ἐν τῷ Ἰορδάνῃ* of the multitudes, and for the baptism of Jesus alters the construction to *παραγίνεται ... ἐπὶ τὸν Ἰορδάνην ... τοῦ βαπτισθῆναι*. Luke omits both *ἐν τῷ Ἰορδάνῃ* and *εἰς τὸν Ἰορδάνην*.

[**2.** i 16 *ἀμφιβάλλοντας ἐν τῇ θαλάσσῃ*. Matthew more correctly *βάλλοντας ἀμφίβληστρον εἰς τὴν θάλασσαν*: Luke has no parallel. Most MSS of Mark insert a noun (some *ἀμφίβληστρον* from Matthew, others, possibly rightly, *τὰ δίκτυα*) to give *ἀμφιβάλλοντας* an object: but the insertion only makes the use of *ἐν* odder still.]

3. i 21 *ἐδίδασκεν εἰς τὴν συναγωγήν*. So ℵ C L Δ 28 33 Ferrar group syr^{sin} Origen: *εἰσελθὼν εἰς τὴν συναγωγὴν ἐδίδασκεν* A B D W Θ latt. The latter group is in itself the stronger, and I cannot regard ℵ Origen as more than a single witness. But Westcott-Hort give the shorter reading a place in their margin, and the close parallels of **4** and **14** suggest that the scholar who produced the B text, whenever he found *εἰς* without any idea of motion expressed, systematically put matters right from a grammatical point of view by the insertion of the verb *ἔρχομαι* (*εἰσέρχομαι*). Still in view of the Latin evidence, and of the Greek support for the same reading, the decision is perhaps less easy than in any other instance of reading on our list. Neither of the other Synoptists has a parallel text here.

4, 5. i 39 *καὶ ἦν κηρύσσων εἰς τὰς συναγωγὰς αὐτῶν εἰς ὅλην τὴν Γαλιλαίαν*. So A C D W Δ latt. syr^{sin}: *ἦλθεν* ℵ B L Θ. With regard to the prepositions, Matthew changes *εἰς* both times into *ἐν*, *ἐν ὅλῃ τῇ Γαλιλαίᾳ διδάσκων ἐν ταῖς συναγωγαῖς αὐτῶν*: Luke retains *εἰς* on the first occasion, but by combining the two phrases into *εἰς τὰς συναγωγὰς τῆς Γαλιλαίας* [*Ἰουδαίας*] avoids the second. With regard to the verb, Matthew changes to *περιῆγεν* 'went about', Luke has *ἦν*. It is much more likely that Luke repeated *ἦν κηρύσσων εἰς* from Mark than that he altered *ἦλθεν εἰς* into *ἦν εἰς*. It is further much more likely that scribes or editors of Mark should have substituted *ἦλθεν εἰς* for *ἦν εἰς* than *vice versa*. I cannot doubt that ℵ B represent here an intentional correction of a non-literary usage of St Mark.

6. ii 1 *ἠκούσθη ὅτι εἰς οἶκόν ἐστιν*. So A C Δ and the margin of Westcott-Hort: *ἐν οἴκῳ ἐστίν* ℵ B D W Θ 33. Versions hardly count; but authority, it is clear, is preponderant for *ἐν οἴκῳ*: it is only the consideration that the temptation to alter *εἰς οἶκον* to *ἐν οἴκῳ* was infinitely greater than the converse which makes it likely that the inferior witnesses are right. There is no parallel in either Matthew or Luke.

7a. iv7 *ἔπεσεν εἰς τὰς ἀκάνθας*.

b. 18 *οἱ εἰς τὰς ἀκάνθας σπειρόμενοι*.

Both Matthew and Luke alter Mark on the first occasion, the former to *ἐπὶ τὰς ἀκάνθας*, the latter to *ἐν μέσῳ τῶν ἀκανθῶν*: both, on the other hand, retain Mark's *εἰς* on the second occasion. There is indeed some authority for *ἐπὶ τὰς ἀκάνθας* both times in Mark, C D 33 in verse 7, ℵ C Δ in verse 18: the former is doubtless borrowed from the parallel in Matthew. And the parallel in Jeremiah iv 3 must not be overlooked, *νεώσατε ἑαυτοῖς νεώματα, καὶ μὴ σπείρητε ἐπ' ἀκάνθαις*.

8. iv 8 *ἔπεσεν εἰς τὴν γῆν τὴν καλήν*.

cf. verse 20 *οἱ ἐπὶ τὴν γῆν τὴν καλὴν σπαρέντες*.

Here Matthew changes *εἰς* to *ἐπί* in verse 8,[1] thus giving *ἐπί* in both places. Luke, more tolerant than Matthew of the Marcan use of *εἰς*,

---

[1] *εἰς* tends to take the place of *ἐπί* (*πρός*) as well as of *ἐν* in Mark. i 10 *καταβαίνων εἰς αὐτόν* is changed by both Matthew and Luke to *ἐπί*: xiii 3 *καθημένου αὐτοῦ εἰς τὸ ὄρος τῶν ἐλαιῶν*, Matthew writes *ἐπὶ τοῦ ὄρους* (see no. **19** below): and the very odd *καθῆσθαι ἐν τῇ θαλάσσῃ* of iv 1, where Matthew omits *ἐν τῇ θαλάσσῃ* (Luke again gives no parallel), would at least be less odd if Mark had written *ἐπὶ τῆς θαλάσσης*. But *εἰς τὸ πέραν* (iv 35, v 1, 21, vi 45, viii 13) and *εἰς τὸν οὐρανόν* (vi 41, vii 34) are freely reproduced by Matthew and Luke, and have precedent in classical usage.

retains it[2] in Mark's verse 8, while he changes ἐπὶ τήν to ἐν τῇ in Mark's verse 20.

9. iv 8 *εις τριάκοντα καὶ εις ἑξήκοντα καὶ εις ἑκατόν* (with variant *εν*).

cf. verse 20 *εν τριάκοντα καὶ εν ἑξήκοντα καὶ εν ἑκατόν*.

By a curious freak of the Greek language *εις εν* can mean, according as breathing and accent differ, either the two correlated prepositions *εἰς ἐν*, or the masculine and neuter of the cardinal number one, *εἷς ἕν*. And since breathings and accents were not part of the usage of MSS at the time when our Gospels were written, we are thrown back on internal evidence to decide between possible interpretations. Matthew on each occasion substitutes *ὃ μὲν ... ὃ δὲ ... ὃ δέ*: he would therefore seem to have read *ἕν*, and certainly to have understood Mark to mean 'one ... another ... another'. Luke, with the dislike of an educated Greek for the Jewish use of symbolic numbers, omits the details on both occasions

εἷς in verse 8 would be ungrammatical after *ἄλλα*, and if we translate with Matthew 'one ... another ... another' we must read the neuter *ἕν* throughout, against the testimony of ℵ B C* L Δ. The Latins followed Matthew's interpretation, and rendered *unum*: and so among moderns Blass *op.cit.* § 46. 2 p. 142. But in view of the Semitic idiom, which uses the preposition 'in' to mean 'at the rate of', I suspect that Mark had in his mind here the preposition and not the numeral. Further, if the mass of evidence adduced in these notes convinces us that the evangelist used the two prepositions *ἐν* and *εἰς* almost interchangeably, it becomes simple enough to suppose that he had the same idiom in his mind whether he expressed it by *ἐν*, as certainly in verse 20, or by *εἰς*, as perhaps in verse 8. Nay, it becomes even possible that cod. B is right in interchanging the two in a single verse: in verse 8 if B's *εἰς τριάκοντα καὶ ἐν ἑξήκοντα καὶ ἐν ἑκατόν* is the true text, we can the better understand why ℵ should have *εἰς ... εἰς ... εἰς* and A D *ἐν ... ἐν ... ἐν*.

[**10**. iv 36 *παραλαμβάνουσιν αὐτὸν ὡς ἦν ἐν τῷ πλοίῳ*. As in [2] above, this is an instance not of *εἰς* where we expect *ἐν*, but of *ἐν* where we expect *εἰς*. Luke omits the detail: Matthew restores the more correct use, *ἐμβάντι αὐτῷ εἰς πλοῖον*.]

11. v 14 *ἀπήγγειλαν εἰς τὴν πόλιν καὶ εἰς τοὺς ἀγρούς*. An instance on the border-line, where *εἰς* might just be rendered 'announced it to the city', though it is hardly doubtful that the real meaning is 'in the city and in the country'. So, while Luke retains the Marcan phrase unaltered,

---

[2] If D here, Luke viii 8, has *ἐπί*, *a c d* 'super', the variant is probably due to a simple assimilation to Matthew.

Matthew, with his more rigid canon of exactness in respect of this preposition, inserts ἀπελθόντες before εἰς τὴν πόλιν ἀπήγγειλαν.

12. v 34 *ὕπαγε εἰς εἰρήνην*. Once more Matthew omits the phrase, and Luke, with the change of ὕπαγε into πορεύου, retains it. While μετ' εἰρήνης and ἐν εἰρήνῃ are common in the LXX, εἰς εἰρήνην is the characteristic use, following the Semitic idiom, with πορεύου and βάδιζε. Mark's phrase is therefore not destitute of precedent, though it is more likely that Luke consciously sheltered himself under this than that Mark did.

13. vi 8 *ἵνα μηδὲν αἴρωσιν εἰς ὁδὸν ... μὴ πήραν, μὴ εἰς τὴν ζώνην χαλκόν*. Here the usual conditions are reversed, and it is Luke who omits, Matthew who retains, εἰς τὴν ζώνην. It is of course just possible to say 'take no money for your purse', though the more natural phrase is undoubtedly 'in your purse'.

14. viii 26 *μηδε[νὶ] εἰς τὴν κώμην εἴπῃς*. There are no parallels from the other Synoptists: but the instance is a most significant one, and the case for the reading adopted above is in my judgement unanswerable. Westcott and Hort, *Introduction* § 140 cite this verse with good cause as a typical 'conflate' reading of the received text: it is demonstrable that behind the form μηδὲ εἰς τὴν κώμην εἰσέλθῃς μηδὲ εἴπῃς τινὶ ἐν τῇ κώμῃ lie two earlier readings, (1) μηδὲ εἰς τὴν κώμην εἰσέλθῃς, and (2) μηδὲ εἴπῃς τινὶ ἐν τῇ κώμῃ, which the Antiochene text has combined. Westcott-Hort treat the two briefer readings as rivals, and decide for the former, which is given by ℵ B L W 1 syr$^{sin.}$ But what if we repeat the process of analysis, and ask whether both (1) and (2) cannot be explained as developments of a reading that lay further back than either of them? If we bear in mind (α) the accumulation of evidence in favour of the Marcan use of εἰς for ἐν: (β) the tendency of codex B to get rid of this unclassical idiom, on the more startling occasions of its employment, by the introduction of ἔρχομαι or εἰσέρχομαι see 3, 4 above: (γ) the actual presence of the phrase μηδενὶ εἴπῃς εἰς τὴν κώμην as part of the reading in D, and of 'ne cui diceret in castellum' as the whole reading in the Old Latin MS *c*: (δ) the ease with which the other early readings can be explained if we postulate μηδε[νὶ] εἰς τὴν κώμην εἴπῃς as the original source of the different developments: then I do not think it too much to say that the problem has solved itself.[3]

---

[3] When I first published my Inaugural Lecture, *The Study of the New Testament: 1883 and 1920* (1920), I had not grasped the evidence for St Mark's usage of εἰς = ἐν, and thought that the original text must have run μηδὲ εἰς τὴν κώμην, without any verb: but my friend the Rev.H.N.Bate had already divined the true reading, as I have there recorded (p. 59 *ad fin*).

15. x 10 *καὶ εἰς τὴν οἰκίαν πάλιν οἱ μαθηταὶ περὶ τούτου ἐπηρώτων αὐτόν*. Luke is no longer parallel to Mark: Matthew drops the whole phrase. But the reading is that of ℵ B D L Δ Ψ, and it must not be assumed that because the Latins give the ablative they found *ἐν τῇ οἰκίᾳ* in their Greek exemplars. It cannot be too often repeated that a large element in our critical apparatus is vitiated because it is forgotten that the earliest translators translated by the sense and not by the letter, and followed the idiom of their own language. It is only the late pedantry of the Greek O.T. of Aquila, or the Harclean Syriac, or the English Revised Version of N.T., which so translates as to enable one to reconstruct the exact phraseology and order of their original.[4] So we are free to follow the reading of our best Greek MSS without reference on this occasion to the versions. The temptation to scribes to substitute *ἐν τῇ οἰκίᾳ* in so palpable a case of *εἰς* = *ἐν* was obvious: it is rather matter for wonder that the few MSS escaped it than that the many fell victims to it.

16. xi 8 *πολλοὶ τὰ ἱμάτια αὐτῶν ἔστρωσαν εἰς τὴν ὁδόν*. The verb 'to strew' might be conceived of as implying motion, 'strewed their garments on to the road': and if Mark never used *εἰς* for *ἐν*, some such explanation would be feasible. But in view of the evidence here accumulated, it is by far the simpler view that he meant 'on the road'. So certainly Matthew and Luke understood it, since both substitute *ἐν τῇ ὁδῷ*. This is the first occasion on which we find them agreeing on *ἐν* for *εἰς*; but see also below, no. **20**.

[**17**. xiii 3 *καθημένου αὐτοῦ εἰς τὸ ὄρος τῶν ἐλαιῶν*, 'as he was sitting on the Mount of Olives'. In English we can only render by 'on'. But that does not mean that the proper Greek word was necessarily *ἐν*: Matthew's *ἐπὶ τοῦ ὄρους* (Luke omits the whole detail) is doubtless more idiomatic. It remains, however, that it is a real example of the encroachments in vulgar use of *εἰς* upon other prepositions.]

18. xiii 9 *παραδώσουσιν ὑμᾶς εἰς συνέδρια καὶ εἰς συναγωγὰς δαρήσεσθε καὶ ἐπὶ ἡγεμόνων καὶ βασιλέων σταθήσεσθε*. How is the sentence to be punctuated? Luke, omitting *δαρήσεσθε* entirely, is able to construct a simple sentence with two pairs of parallel nouns, *παραδιδόντες εἰς τὰς συναγωγὰς καὶ φυλακάς, ἀπαγομένους ἐπὶ βασιλεῖς καὶ ἡγεμόνας*. Matthew (x 17) sacrificed the connexion of *συνέδρια* and *συναγωγάς*, constructing the former with the verb that precedes it and the latter with the verb that follows it, *παραδώσουσιν γὰρ*

[4] The Vulgate was saved from this pitfall of revision because Jerome was not only a good Greek scholar, but a great Latin stylist.

ὑμᾶς εἰς συνέδρια, καὶ ἐν ταῖς συναγωγαῖς αὐτῶν μαστιγώσουσιν ὑμᾶς, καὶ ἐπὶ ἡγεμόνας δὲ καὶ βασιλεῖς ἀχθήσεσθε. I cannot doubt that Matthew is so far right that εἰς συναγωγὰς δαρήσεσθε was intended by Mark to be taken together, and that therefore εἰς συναγωγάς means nothing more nor less than 'in synagogues'. But I am also inclined to believe that Luke interprets correctly when he joins συναγωγὰς καὶ φυλακάς — i.e. συνέδρια and συναγωγάς — in one construction: for it seems as odd to think that Mark meant to contrast the usage to be experienced in sanhedrins and in synagogues respectively, as that he should have contrasted governors and kings. If I am right, Mark's thought implies a comma after ὑμᾶς, and another after δαρήσεσθε: 'they shall give you in charge, in sanhedrins and synagogues shall you be beaten, and before governors and kings shall you be made to stand.' The absolute use of παραδιδόναι is found in i 14 μετὰ τὸ παραδοθῆναι τὸν Ἰωάννην, and in frequent references to Judas and the Betrayal of Christ. Anyhow a clear case is established of εἰς = ἐν: Mark, we may be quite sure, had no thought of 'the simplest rendering' "Ye shall be scourged into the synagogues"', even though it 'presents no archaeological difficulty' (Winer-Moulton[9] p. 518).

19. xiii 10 καὶ εἰς πάντα τὰ ἔθνη πρῶτον δεῖ κηρυχθῆναι τὸ εὐαγγέλιον. 'Preached to all nations' would be a possible rendering: but when Matthew xxiv 14 wrote κηρυχθήσεται ... ἐν ὅλῃ τῇ οἰκουμένῃ (Luke has no parallel), he must have taken Mark to be once more using εἰς for ἐν.

20. xiii 15, 16 ὁ ἐπὶ τοῦ δώματος μὴ καταβάτω [εἰς τὴν οἰκίαν] μηδὲ εἰσελθάτω τι ἆραι ἐκ τῆς οἰκίας αὐτοῦ, καὶ ὁ εἰς τὸν ἀγρὸν μὴ ἐπιστρεψάτω εἰς τὰ ὀπίσω ἆραι τὸ ἱμάτιον αὐτοῦ. Both the other Synoptists recognize the clear implication of ὁ εἰς τὸν ἀγρόν 'the man in the field'; Matthew writes ὁ ἐν τῷ ἀγρῷ, Luke οἱ ἐν ταῖς χώραις. For the second time (see **16** above) they agree in the very obvious substitution of ἐν for εἰς.

21. xiv 20 ὁ ἐμβαπτόμενος μετ' ἐμοῦ εἰς τὸ [ἓν] τρύβλιον. As in 16, it is possible to argue that ἐμβάπτεσθαι implies motion, so that 'dips into the dish' could stand. But Matthew at any rate (Luke omits the whole phrase) interpreted Mark's εἰς as equivalent to ἐν, ὁ ἐμβάψας μετ' ἐμοῦ τὴν χεῖρα ἐν τῷ τρυβλίῳ. I think it is not unlikely that the ἕν of B in Mark does not really mean 'the one dish' (there seems no trace in Marcan usage of τὸ ἕν = 'the same') but it is the descendant of a marginal gloss suggesting the substitution of ἐν for εἰς.

These instances, taken together — even after allowance is made for the two, **2** and **10**, where ἐν appears instead of εἰς, and another **17**, where εἰς has ousted ἐπί rather than ἐν — do seem to establish a definite tendency in Marcan usage for εἰς to encroach on ἐν. That encroachment is not peculiar to Mark, though among New Testament writings there is none where the encroachment is so marked as in his Gospel. The process which was commencing in the common speech of our Lord's time has ended in the complete supersession of ἐν in modern Greek. But it was still resented by scribes and scholars, or at any rate by some of them, in the first and second centuries A.D. If Matthew regularly, and Luke frequently, are found to desert Mark's use in this respect, it is reasonable to expect that the same tendency will have influenced scribes, and not least the more skilled among them. The evidence of undoubted cases like **1**, **15**, **18**, **20**, may fairly be used to turn the scale where the evidence is divided, and justifies the conclusion that the scribe of codex B or its ancestor, admirable as is his general fidelity, did not rise superior to the temptation of altering an incorrect idiom into accordance with the traditions of literary Greek.

IV – Parenthetical clauses in Mark. †

Ancient manuscripts were written without signs of punctuation or even of interrogation. In the hands of a master of the Greek language its highly developed structure and its numerous particles made punctuation to a large extent superfluous, and enabled any intelligent reader to punctuate for himself as he read. But St Mark was not a master of the Greek language and his fondness for brief co-ordinate clauses, not helped out by appropriate particles, often leaves us in doubt whether, for instance, we should read a clause interrogatively or not. Take a simple case, where both Matthew and Luke already felt the difficulty, and took care to insert words to shew which interpretation they adopted — and, in fact, one interpreted one way, and one the other: xvi 6 *μὴ ἐκθαμβεῖσθε* | *Ἰησοῦν ζητεῖτε τὸν Ναζαρηνὸν τὸν ἐσταυρωμένον* | *ἠγέρθη* | *οὐκ ἔστιν ὧδε.* Here the second clause can be punctuated either as a statement of fact (with Vulgate, A.V., R.V., and Westcott-Hort) 'Ye seek Jesus the Nazarene the Crucified', or as a question 'Are you seeking Jesus the Nazarene the Crucified?': and Matthew by prefixing the words *οἶδα γὰρ ὅτι* shews that he takes the former view, while Luke, writing *τί ζητεῖτε*, shews us as clearly that he takes the latter.[1]

The present note envisages a special group of cases where St Mark employs parenthetical clauses, and a modern writer or printer would place these within dashes or brackets. In some cases the parenthesis is so brief and so obvious that no real difficulty arises. If in vii 2 Mark writes *κοιναῖς χερσίν, τοῦτ' ἔστιν ἀνίπτοις, ἐσθίουσιν τοὺς ἄρτους*, 'they eat their bread with defiled, i.e. unwashed, hands', we understand of course that the Pharisees used the Aramaic equivalent of *κοινός* 'defiled' and that the Evangelist explains to his Gentile readers in what the defilement consisted. But in many more cases, as I think, Mark has made use of this expedient in a way which has misled scribes or commentators or both. The process of my argument would be more cogent and more logical if the clearer cases were cited first, and advance was then made from the more to the less certain. But convenience of reference appears to dictate the simpler course of taking the passages in the order of the Gospel.

1. Mark i 1-4 *Ἀρχὴ τοῦ εὐαγγελίου Ἰησοῦ Χριστοῦ υἱοῦ θεοῦ (καθὼς γέγραπται ἐν τῷ Ἡσαΐᾳ τῷ προφήτῃ Ἰδοὺ ... τὰς τρίβους αὐτοῦ) ἐγένετο Ἰωάννης ὁ βαπτίζων ἐν τῇ ἐρήμῳ κηρύσσων βάπτισμα μετανοίας εἰς ἄφεσιν ἁμαρτιῶν.*

---

[1] For a similar difficulty as to the second of three clauses see Mark i 24.

Here the text of Westcott-Hort (apart from the insertion of the words *υἱοῦ θεοῦ*, which do not concern the problem before us) is followed, but not their punctuation. Westcott-Hort place a full stop before *καθὼς γέγραπται*, and a comma after *αὐτοῦ*: Swete prints a full-stop in both places; Tischendorf a comma before *καθώς*, a full-stop after *αὐτοῦ*. Wellhausen wants to remove the whole of the quotation (verses 2 and 3) as not genuine, but retains the full-stop after verse 1. And, in general, modern exegetes are more or less agreed in segregating verse 1 as a sort of title,[2] though it is hard to see what real meaning *ἀρχή* has on this supposition.

But ancient exegetes had at least this advantage over modern, that they were accustomed to read unpunctuated Greek MSS, and therefore in problems of this sort especial weight attaches to their interpretation. We have only to remember how the true meaning of Mark vii 19 (no.10 below) was rescued by Field from Origen and Chrysostom (to whom Burgon added Gregory Thaumaturgus) where modern interpreters had been baffled, and we shall be prepared on the present problem to listen respectfully to Origen, Basil, and Victor of Antioch. The two latter are quoted by Swete: Basil *c. Eunomium* ii 15 *ὁ δὲ Μᾶρκος ἀρχὴν τοῦ εὐαγγελίου τὸ Ἰωάννου πεποίηκε κήρυγμα*, Victor *Ἰωάννην οὖν τελευταῖον τῶν προφητῶν ἀρχὴν εἶναι τοῦ εὐαγγελίου φησίν*. And Origen should, I believe, be cited on the same side: *in Io.* i 13 *ἡ ἀρχὴ τοῦ εὐαγγελίου ... ἤτοι πᾶσά ἐστιν ἡ παλαιὰ διαθήκη, τύπου αὐτῆς ὄντος Ἰωάννου, ἢ ... τὰ τέλη τῆς παλαιᾶς διὰ Ἰωάννου παριστάμενα*, and a few lines further on *ὅθεν θαυμάζειν μοι ἔπεισι πῶς δυσὶ θεοῖς προσάπτουσιν ἀμφοτέρας τὰς διαθήκας οἱ ἑτερόδοξοι, οὐκ ἔλαττον καὶ ἐκ τούτου τοῦ ῥητοῦ ἐλεγχόμενοι. πῶς γὰρ δύναται ἀρχὴ εἶναι τοῦ εὐαγγελίου (ὡς αὐτοὶ οἴονται ἑτέρου τυγχάνων θεοῦ) Ἰωάννης, ὁ τοῦ δημιουργοῦ ἄνθρωπος;* (Brooke i 17. 26, 18. 2). Place then verses 2 and 3 within brackets as a parenthesis, and construct *ἀρχὴ* with *ἐγένετο*. 'The beginning of the proclamation of good news about Jesus as Messiah and Son of God, was John the Baptizer's preaching in the wilderness of a baptism of repentance for remission of sins'.†

2. ii 10, 11 *ἵνα δὲ εἰδῆτε ὅτι ἐξουσίαν ἔχει ὁ υἱὸς τοῦ ἀνθρώπου ἀφιέναι ἁμαρτίας ἐπὶ τῆς γῆς (λέγει τῷ παραλυτικῷ) Σοὶ λέγω, ἔγειρε.*

---

[2] Lagrange *Évangile selon Saint Marc* ad loc. cites Zahn, Nestle, J.Weiss, on this side.

The parenthesis is so obvious that it is retained with practically no change by both Matthew and Luke. We could express it in English '(he turns to the paralytic)'.

3. ii 15, 16 *καὶ πολλοὶ τελῶναι καὶ ἁμαρτωλοὶ συνανέκειντο τῷ Ἰησοῦ καὶ τοῖς μαθηταῖς αὐτοῦ — ἦσαν γὰρ πολλοί, καὶ ἠκολούθουν αὐτῷ — καὶ οἱ γραμματεῖς τῶν Φαρισαίων ἰδόντες ὅτι ἐσθίει μετὰ τῶν ἁμαρτωλῶν καὶ τελωνῶν* ...

The words within dashes are, I am sure, to be taken as strictly parenthetical: if they were removed altogether the main emphasis would remain unaltered — 'Many "publicans and sinners" sat at table with Jesus and his disciples, and the Pharisee scribes seeing that Jesus was eating with them ... ', or, as in the logical order we might put it, 'And the Pharisee scribes, seeing that many "publicans and sinners" were at the dinner with Jesus and his disciples, and that he ate freely with them ... ' The parenthesis has nothing to do with the *τελῶναι καὶ ἁμαρτωλοί*. We have no reason to suppose that large numbers of revenue collectors deserted their employment to follow our Lord, nor is there anything in the rest of the Gospel to suggest it. What St Mark really does here is to lay stress on the mention, for the first time, of the word 'disciples'. Before this we have only heard from him of the call of Peter and Andrew, James and John, and perhaps of a growing company in the 'Simon and his friends' of i 36. Now in ii 15 he reminds us by the way that already a considerable body of followers had gathered round Jesus and accompanied him wherever he went: *μαθηταί* is the noun to be supplied with *ἦσαν γὰρ πολλοί*. Weiss and Loisy interpret correctly: Lagrange and Swete are on the other side. Wellhausen gives two alternative explanations, but misses the true one.

4. ii 22 *καὶ οὐδεὶς βάλλει οἶνον νέον εἰς ἀσκοὺς παλαιούς — εἰ δὲ μή, ῥήξει ὁ οἶνος τοὺς ἀσκούς, καὶ ὁ οἶνος ἀπόλλυται καὶ οἱ ἀσκοί — ἀλλὰ οἶνον νέον εἰς ἀσκοὺς καινούς*.

The arrangement above given (which is that adopted by Swete) is the only possible one if the last six words are genuine. They are omitted by D and many Old Latin MSS (not *e*, which borrows the full form of the verse from Matthew), but the agreement of Matthew and Luke in giving exactly these six words in common, while they provide different forms of *βάλλω* to complete the construction, is a strong argument for their genuineness in Mark. ℵ B, therefore, should be followed against the rest: and if *εἰ δὲ μή* ... *οἱ ἀσκοί* is printed as a parenthesis, there is no real difficulty about the construction. But Matthew and Luke, not recognizing or not liking the parenthesis, give the final clause a construction of its own with *βάλλει* (Matthew) or *βλητέον* (Luke).

5. ii 26*b* *καὶ τοὺς ἄρτους τῆς προθέσεως ἔφαγεν* (*οὓς οὐκ ἔξεστιν φαγεῖν εἰ μὴ τοὺς ἱερεῖς*) *καὶ ἔδωκεν καὶ τοῖς σὺν αὐτῷ οὖσιν.*

The case for parenthesis is less certain here, but I believe that the words 'which only the priests are allowed to eat' is an addition by Peter or Mark to make it clear to Gentile hearers or readers in what way the instance of David and his company afforded a parallel and justification for the action of Jesus and his disciples. It looks, at any rate, as if Luke felt that there was something wrong with the Marcan passage, for he transposes the words treated above as parenthetical to the end of the sentence. If they were not parenthetical, that was the natural thing to do.

Commentators have perhaps not sufficiently realized Mark's habit of introducing explanations for those unfamiliar with the details of Jewish customs, see vii 2; vii 3, 4; vii 26a; xiv 36: compare the note introduced by him in xiii 14.

6. iii 22-30.

It would be misleading to print so long a passage as parenthetical: yet we lose something if the direct connexion of verse 21 with verse 31 escapes our notice. It would seem as though the Evangelist, after he has begun to tell us of the charge about our Lord that he was out of his senses, diverged to put on record the much graver charge that he was possessed by Beelzebub, and then, having dealt with that, recurs to the story he was beginning to tell and goes on to finish it. A similar case is that of the two verses viii 14, 16, which are directly connected with one another, though there is only a single verse which intervenes. And possibly the same sort of consideration will help to unravel the complicated connexions of ix 33-50, where verses 37 and 42 are the necessary complement to one another.

7. vi 14, 15 *καὶ ἤκουσεν ὁ βασιλεὺς Ἡρῴδης* (*φανερὸν γὰρ ἐγένετο τὸ ὄνομα αὐτοῦ, καὶ ἔλεγον ὅτι Ἰωάννης ὁ βαπτίζων ἐγήγερται ἐκ νεκρῶν ... ἄλλοι δὲ ἔλεγον ὅτι Ἠλείας ἐστιν, ἄλλοι δὲ ἔλεγον ὅτι προφήτης ὡς εἷς τῶν προφητῶν*). *ἀκούσας δὲ ὁ Ἡρῴδης ἔλεγεν Ὃν ἐγὼ ἀπεκεφάλισα Ἰωάννην, οὗτος ἠγέρθη.*

Here *ἀκούσας ὁ Ἡρῴδης* is simply resumptive of *ἤκουσεν ὁ βασιλεὺς Ἡρῴδης*, 'Herod then, on hearing about Jesus, said'. The parenthetical arrangement assumes that *ἔλεγον* is the right reading in verse 14, not ἔλεγεν,[3] for the parenthesis gives the vivid popular interest in the personality of Jesus of Nazareth as the reason for his fame coming to Herod's ears.

The whole passage vi 17-29 is parenthetical in the sense that the story of the martyrdom of John the Baptist is inserted here out of its historical place. All that belongs to the period at which St Mark's narrative has arrived is just Herod's knowledge about Jesus. And perhaps it is one of the curious links that connect the Fourth Gospel with the Second, that we learn in John vi 15 (cf.Mark vi 31b, 33) that there was at this time a movement, such as might naturally attract 'King' Herod's attention, to make Jesus king.

8. vii 2 *ἰδόντες τινὰς τῶν μαθητῶν αὐτοῦ ὅτι κοιναῖς χερσὶν (τοῦτ' ἔστιν ἀνίπτοις) ἐσθίουσιν τοὺς ἄρτους ...*

κοινός in the sense of 'unclean' does not occur elsewhere in the Gospels: but it is used throughout the story of St Peter and Cornelius in Acts x-xi, being there combined with *ἀκάθαρτος*. The usage is technical and Jewish, and Mark explains to his Gentile readers that it means in this case 'unwashed'. Presumably St Peter in relating the story had employed the word and intended to represent by it the actual phraseology in Aramaic employed by the Pharisees. The interpretation being editorial would best be put within brackets: cf. nos. 5 (ii 26b), 9 (vii 3, 4), 11 (vii 26a), 16 (xiii 14) and probably 17 (xiv 36).

From 8 to 12 there are no parallels in Luke.

9. vii 3, 4 *οἱ γὰρ φαρισαῖοι ... ξεστῶν καὶ χαλκίων [καὶ κλινῶν]*.

The editors rightly print these verses within dashes: the Evangelist remembers that his readers would hardly understand the religious value set by the Pharisees on such an observance as washing the hands before meals, unless he correlated it with their general attitude to other similar purifications. Matthew discards the explanation: what was necessary for Gentile readers in Rome was unnecessary in Palestinian circles.

10. vii 18, 19 *καὶ λέγει αὐτοῖς* Οὕτως *καὶ ὑμεῖς ἀσύνετοί ἐστε; οὐ νοεῖτε ὅτι πᾶν τὸ ἔξωθεν ... ἐκπορεύεται; καθαρίζων πάντα τὰ βρώματα.*

A very interesting example, for it shews how the Greek fathers may be better guides to the intelligent reading of the Gospels than the best equipped modern critics. Origen, Gregory Thaumaturgus, and Chrysostom

---

[3] See Note I 11.

saw that *καθαρίζων* (the reading is quite certain, though later scribes attempted to make it more grammatical, as they thought, by changing it to the neuter) goes back to the beginning of the sentence, and means that Christ when he said this 'cleansed all meats': and we owe to Dr Field, *Otium Norvicense* iii (= *Notes on the Translation of the New Testament* p. 31) and to Dean Burgon, (*Last Twelve Verses of St Mark* p. 179 note u) the recovery of the true exegesis from the patristic comments. Wellhausen ad loc. still takes *καθαρίζων* with *τὸν ἀφεδρῶνα*! Loisy (*Les Évangiles Synoptiques* p. 965) is acquainted with the recovered interpretation, but thinks that if it is correct it can only be treated as a gloss, seeing that it 'interrupts the thread of the argument too unskilfully to be original'. But I do not think that any one who studies the series here enumerated of parentheses in the Second Gospel will accept the suggestion that unskilful interruption of the context is decisive against genuineness. If the parentheses were wholly normal and intelligible, the other Synoptists would not have got rid of them so consistently.

11. vii 25, 26a *ἀκούσασα γυνὴ περὶ αὐτοῦ, ἧς εἶχεν τὸ θυγάτριον αὐτῆς πνεῦμα ἀκάθαρτον, ἐλθοῦσα προσέπεσεν πρὸς τοὺς πόδας αὐτοῦ (ἡ δὲ γυνὴ ἦν Ἑλληνίς, Συροφοινίκισσα τῷ γένει) καὶ ἠρώτα αὐτὸν ...*

Mark reflects as he writes that the sequel of the story will be unintelligible if he does not explain that the woman was not a Jewess either by race or religion, but on the contrary a Syrophoenician in the one respect, a heathen in the other.[4] Matthew reduces the statement to the single word 'a Canaanite' — which by itself implied both things to those for whom he wrote — and put it at its logical place in the forefront of the story.

12. viii 14-17 *καὶ ἐπελάθοντο λαβεῖν ἄρτους, καὶ εἰ μὴ ἕνα ἄρτον οὐκ εἶχον μεθ' ἑαυτῶν ἐν τῷ πλοίῳ. (καὶ διεστέλλετο αὐτοῖς λέγων Ὁρᾶτε, βλέπετε ἀπὸ τῆς ζύμης τῶν Φαρισαίων καὶ τῆς ζύμης Ἡρῴδου). καὶ διελογίζοντο πρὸς ἀλλήλους ὅτι ἄρτους οὐκ ἔχουσιν. καὶ γνοὺς λέγει αὐτοῖς Τί διαλογίζεσθε ὅτι ἄρτους οὐκ ἔχετε; οὔπω νοεῖτε οὐδὲ συνίετε;*

If the bracketed words are omitted from the sequence of the argument, everything seems plain sailing: and whatever explanation we give of the

---

[4] I feel sure that St Mark means by *Ἑλληνίς* not 'Greek speaking' (as Swete) but 'heathen', and I think that Matthew so understood him when he substituted for *Ἑλληνὶς Συροφοινίκισσα τῷ γένει* the single word *Χαναναία*. If Mark had meant 'Greek by language, Phoenician by race', he must have added something like *τῇ γλώσσῃ*. The normal meaning of *Ἕλλην* in N.T. is 'pagan', and that is precisely the sense needed to lead up to the contrast between 'children' and 'dogs'.

words in question, it can hardly be doubtful that our Lord's meaning, as reported in this Gospel, is that his disciples shewed grievous want of perception in not recognizing, after the miracles of the multiplication of the loaves, that their Master had at command a power from God to provide, if need were, their necessary food. This straightforward sequence of thought is broken by one intrusive verse. It is not an interpolation: the substance of it is present in the Matthaean parallel, and *διαστέλλομαι* is a characteristically Marcan word, never found in the other Gospels apart from a single passage, and that a doubtful one, in Matthew (xvi 20); Marcan, too, is the combination 'Pharisees and Herod'. The parallels give us no help: Matthew follows Mark closely. Luke omits the whole passage. But Luke, though he omits the passage, does give in quite another context (xii 1) the single verse 'Beware for yourselves of the leaven of the Pharisees, which is hypocrisy'. He may of course have borrowed it from this passage: it is more likely that it was in Q. Anyhow it seems that the context of 'bread' must have reminded St Mark of the saying about the leaven of the Pharisees and Herod, and he inserted it here, though strictly speaking it was foreign to the context. In other words, it must be regarded as a parenthesis, an extreme example of Mark's naïve and non-logical construction of his narrative. A modern writer would have put it in a note at the foot of the page, and introduced it with the phrase 'compare ... ' The ancients, lacking such devices, were shut up within the alternatives of intercalation into the body of the text and omission. The modern editor of an ancient text, in which such intercalations occur, can only guide his readers by the typographical expedients of the dash and the bracket.

13. ix 36-42 (38-41) *καὶ λαβὼν παιδίον ἔστησεν αὐτὸ ἐν μέσῳ αὐτῶν, καὶ ἐναγκαλισάμενος αὐτὸ εἶπεν αὐτοῖς Ὃς ἂν ἕν τῶν τοιούτων παιδίων δέξηται ἐπὶ τῷ ὀνόματί μου, ἐμὲ δέχεται· καὶ ὃς ἂν ἐμὲ δέχηται, οὐκ ἐμὲ δέχεται ἀλλὰ τὸν ἀποστείλαντά με. (Ἔφη αὐτῷ ὁ Ἰωάννης Διδάσκαλε, εἴδαμέν τινα ... ὃς γὰρ οὐκ ἔστιν καθ' ἡμῶν, ὑπὲρ ἡμῶν ἐστίν. ὃς γὰρ ἂν ποτίσῃ ὑμᾶς ποτήριον ὕδατος ἐν ὀνόματι ὅτι Χριστοῦ ἐστέ, ἀμὴν λέγω ὑμῖν ὅτι οὐ μὴ ἀπολέσῃ τὸν μισθὸν αὐτοῦ.) καὶ ὃς ἂν σκανδαλίσῃ ἕνα τῶν μικρῶν τούτων τῶν πιστευόντων, καλόν ἐστιν αὐτῷ μᾶλλον εἰ περίκειται μύλος ὀνικὸς περὶ τὸν τράχηλον αὐτοῦ καὶ βέβληται εἰς τὴν θάλασσαν. καὶ ἐὰν σκανδαλίσῃ σε ἡ χείρ σου ...*

In the ninth chapter of his Gospel St Mark devotes a larger proportion than hitherto to the Sayings of Christ. There are indeed in the earlier chapters episodes introduced which led up to Sayings, and without the Sayings the episode would have no special point. Such would be, for instance, the plucking of the ears of corn, ii 23-28. But in the second half of the Gospel the training of the disciples gives more occasion to direct and systematic teaching, either not dependent upon special episodes at all, or at any rate more loosely connected with them than before. And the verses cited at the head of the paragraph exemplify this new feature of his story. It is hardly possible to suppose either that verses 35-50 are all continuous and belong to a single occasion, or that verses 35-37 record one conversation introduced by the episode of the child placed in the midst, 38-50 another conversation introduced by the remark of John. What we have is something more complex than that, and less easy to disentangle.

As in the last passage treated, no. 12, it seems likely that the Evangelist has interwoven with one another Sayings originally independent, though very probably belonging to the same cycle of teaching. And the method of combination seems to be on the same lines as before: a word or phrase brings to the writer's mind another Saying on a similar topic and he sets it down, returning later on to the original topic. The intervening words may once more be treated as an example of Mark's fondness for parenthesis.

If we read verses 37 and 42 consecutively, it is difficult not to think that they are connected with one another. 'Whosoever shall receive one of such children as this, receiveth me ... and whosoever shall offend one of these little ones that believe, it were better for him ... ' St Mark will have inserted the episode of John's remark and the Lord's answer, because it seemed to him to illustrate the same general idea: but having so inserted it, he returns to the topic from which he started and completes the saying which the parenthesis had interrupted.

Wellhausen too, points out the connexion of verses 37 and 42. But he brings an arbitrary element into his exegesis of the passage by making a contrast between verses 43 and following, which he regards as genuine words of Christ, and verses 42 and preceding which appear to him to imply the period of the Apostolic age and not the period of the Ministry. He follows D in verse 40, reading ὑμῶν for ἡμῶν, 'Whosoever is not against you is with you', and supposes that the Evangelist or his authority has in his mind attempts in the primitive community to dispense with the leadership of the Twelve. Even if he is right in the reading he adopts, there is an obvious objection to his interpretation which he has not attempted to meet. The Gospel according to Mark puts in the foreground the selection of the Twelve and their subsequent training, and not less the prominence of Peter as spokesman of the inner company of the disciples.

If there was in the early Church any tendency to minimize the one or the other, it certainly could not be proved from our Second Gospel. Except on the postulate that Jesus cannot have contemplated the continued existence of preaching in his name after his death, it is surely far simpler and more reasonable to suppose that the Saying or Sayings which inculcate the principle laid down in these verses came from no other lips than his.

14. xii 12*a* *καὶ ἐζήτουν αὐτὸν κρατῆσαι (καὶ ἐφοβήθησαν τὸν ὄχλον), ἔγνωσαν γὰρ ὅτι πρὸς αὐτοὺς τὴν παραβολὴν εἶπεν.*

Obviously the recognition on the part of the Jewish authorities that the Parable of the Vineyard and the Husbandmen had been directed against them, was the reason not for their fear of the multitude but for their desire to arrest Jesus. The words 'and they feared the multitude' interrupt the connexion, and it is from that point of view necessary to bracket them. The Evangelist ought logically to have put first the reason for the desire before mentioning the obstacle which interfered with its fulfilment.

The sense is clear enough, and Luke (xx 19) left Mark's order of the clauses unaltered. Matthew (xxi 46) felt a difficulty in the sentence as it stood, and substitutes a reason for their fearing the people in place of Mark's reason for their desire to arrest Jesus: 'they feared the multitudes because they [the multitudes] held him for a prophet.'

15. xiii 9-11 *παραδώσουσιν ὑμᾶς εἰς συνέδρια καὶ εἰς συναγωγὰς δαρήσεσθε, καὶ ἐπὶ ἡγεμόνων καὶ βασιλέων σταθήσεσθε, ἕνεκεν ἐμοῦ εἰς μαρτύριον αὐτοῖς — καὶ εἰς πάντα τὰ ἔθνη πρῶτον δεῖ κηρυχθῆναι τὸ εὐαγγέλιον — καὶ ὅταν ἄγωσιν ὑμᾶς παραδιδόντες, μὴ προμεριμνᾶτε τί λαλήσητε ...*

The connexion of verses 9 and 11 is obvious: it is broken by verse 10 which Luke in his parallel passage (xxi 13, 14) and Matthew in an earlier parallel (x 18, 19) entirely omit, while Matthew at this point (xxiv 9) transfers the verse to the end of the section (after Mark xiii 13) *καὶ κηρυχθήσεται τοῦτο τὸ εὐαγγέλιον τῆς βασιλείας ἐν ὅλῃ τῇ οἰκουμένῃ εἰς μαρτύριον πᾶσιν τοῖς ἔθνεσιν, καὶ τότε ἥξει τὸ τέλος.* This Matthaean paraphrase does probably supply the answer to the two questions which suggest themselves about the Marcan parenthesis. In the first place it is the words *εἰς μαρτύριον αὐτοῖς* which give the cue for the parenthetic reference to the preaching of the Gospel to all nations: in the second place *πρῶτον* is correctly interpreted by Matthew to mean 'before the end come'.

16. xiii 14 *ὅταν δὲ ἴδητε τὸ βδέλυγμα τῆς ἐρημώσεως ἑστηκότα ὅπου οὐ δεῖ (ὁ ἀναγινώσκων νοείτω), τότε οἱ ἐν τῇ Ἰουδαίᾳ ...*

An obvious and acknowledged parenthesis, copied by Matthew, omitted by Luke. Whether Matthew retained it because he understood what it meant, whether Luke omitted it because he saw that it was no longer necessary, I am not sure: but I am quite sure what Mark meant by it.

In the first place *ὁ ἀναγινώσκων* has nothing to do with the Reader, or with any reading of the Gospel in the Christian congregation. It would be an anachronism to suppose that the Evangelist contemplated the use of his Gospel in public worship: and it is a pure misunderstanding of the meaning of *ἀναγινώσκειν* to suppose that it excludes private reading. It was the custom of the ancients to read aloud to themselves: St Augustine relates it of St Ambrose as something unusual that he read to himself, as we do, without using his voice.[5] Mark simply means 'my readers'.

In the second place *νοεῖν*, as in Rev. xiii 18 *ὁ ἔχων νοῦν ψηφισάτω*, means 'to read between the lines', 'to penetrate below the surface'. Evangelist and Apocalyptist alike mean something that neither can afford to put down in black and white. In both cases there is veiled reference to the Roman power, and just as St Paul conceals allusion to empire and emperor by employing both masculine and neuter, *ὁ κατέχων* and *τὸ κατέχον*, in 2 Thess. ii 6, 7, so St Mark with a bold disregard of grammar writes *τὸ βδέλυγμα ἑστηκότα* because he wants to indicate that Daniel's 'abomination of desolation' has a human reference. Matthew, seeing in the capture of the Temple the fulfilment of the prediction, paraphrases 'standing in the holy place': Mark, writing with the prediction still unfulfilled — though it is possible that the Jewish war had already broken out — reproduces, we may well believe, the very phrase employed by Jesus, and adds to it parenthetically his own comment.

Wellhausen ad loc. goes preposterously wrong. 'The warning to the reader to take note', he says, 'fits only with the context of Matthew,

---

[5] Aug. *Confess.* vi 3 'Sed cum legebat, oculi ducebantur per paginas, et cor intellectum rimabatur, uox autem et lingua quiescebant. saepe cum adessemus (non enim uetabatur quisquam ingredi aut ei uenientem nuntiari mos erat), sic eum legentem vidimus tacite, et aliter numquam; sedentesque in diuturno silentio — quis enim tam intento esse oneri auderet? — discedebamus, et coniectabamus eum, paruo ipso tempore quod reparandae menti suae nanciscebatur, feriatum ab strepitu causarum alienarum nolle in aliud auocari et cauere fortasse ne, auditore suspenso et intento, si qua obscurius posuisset ille quem legeret etiam exponere necesse esset aut de aliquibus difficilioribus disceptare quaestionibus, atque huic operi temporibus impensis minus quam uellet uoluminum euolueret: quamquam et causa seruandae uocis, quae illi facillime obtundebatur, poterat esse iustior tacite legendi. quolibet tamen animo id ageret, bono utique ille uir agebat.'

where express reference is made to Daniel — the reader of Daniel, that is, is to note how his prophecy is fulfilled — and has therefore been inserted in Mark out of Matthew'. If critics would take a little more trouble to master the meaning of the words before them, counsel would less often be darkened, and textual problem and Synoptic problem would arrive more speedily and surely at solution. Wellhausen's work is full of acute exegesis: but this comment is perverse.

17. xiv 36 'Αββὰ (ὁ πατήρ).

So St Paul in Gal. iv 6, Rom. viii 15. The early Church as we know it was, as were all the Jews of the Dispersion from Alexandria round to Rome, Greek-speaking. But just as Greek survived in the Roman church and other Western churches for purposes of worship after it had ceased to be the language of ordinary speech — witness the *Agios agios agios* of Saturus's vision in the Acts of Perpetua — just as Latin has remained the liturgical language of south-western Europe, or Old Slavonic of Slav Churches, or Coptic of the Monophysite church of Egypt, so Aramaic phrases survived in the Greek-speaking churches founded by St Paul. The ἀββά of the Christians of Galatia and Rome, the μαρὰν ἀθά of the Christians of Corinth, are like the *Kyrie eleison* in the Latin liturgy of to-day.[6]

What then of ὁ πατήρ? It is the Greek equivalent inserted to explain the ἀββά for those of the congregation who were ignorant of Aramaic. I cannot think (with Sanday and Headlam on Rom. viii 15) that we are to suppose that our Lord used both words in his prayer — any more than he used Greek as well as Aramaic on the other occasions on which St Mark records the actual Aramaic (or Hebrew[7]) words employed by him. Ὁ πατήρ, then, is one more of St Mark's parentheses. But it differs from his other parentheses in being provided for him, so to say, ready made. It was in familiar use — possibly in connexion with the Lord's Prayer in the church of the Apostolic age. But St Mark's testimony is the last that

---

[6] I do not mean to assert that the *Kyrie* in the Mass goes back to the second or third century, though I am not convinced to the contrary. But there is at any rate some probability that the *Agios agios agios* of Mozarabic and Gallican books is a survival rather than a later introduction.

[7] In Mark xv 34 I believe the true text to be that of D *k* (with some support from other Old Latins and B) ἠλεὶ ἠλεὶ λαμὰ ζαφθάνει (עֲזַבְתָּנִי), that is to say, that the Evangelist reports our Lord's cry according to the Hebrew of the Psalm and not in Aramaic (שְׁבַקְתָּנִי): Matthew substituted the Aramaic, and the Matthaean reading, as so often elsewhere, has ousted the original reading in St Mark. On our Lord's knowledge of the Hebrew Scriptures see Dr Headlam's *Life and Teaching of Jesus the Christ* pp.107f.

we have for it. After the destruction of Jerusalem the Aramaic element in Greek-speaking Christianity disappeared. Matthew and Luke agree in substituting Πάτερ for the earlier Ἀββὰ ὁ πατήρ.

18. xvi 3, 4 *καὶ ἔλεγον πρὸς ἑαυτάς Τίς ἀποκυλίσει ἡμῖν τὸν λίθον ἐκ τῆς θύρας τοῦ μνημείου; (καὶ ἀναβλέψασαι θεωροῦσιν ὅτι ἀνακεκύλισται ὁ λίθος) ἦν γὰρ μέγας σφόδρα.*

I cannot doubt that St Mark's motive in the words 'for it was very great' was to account for the anxiety of the women to find help in the rolling away of the stone. If it had been a small one, they could have rolled it away unaided: as it is, they doubt their own capacity to do so without assistance. The parenthesis explains that after all their anxiety was unnecessary: the stone had been, not indeed rolled away, but shifted, 'rolled a little' (*κυλισθεὶς ἐπεχώρησε παρὰ μέρος*, *Ev. Petri*), sufficiently to permit of their entrance. The structure of the sentence closely resembles that of xii 12, no. 14 *supra*.

The detail is so unimportant that it can only have come from the artless narrative of one who was relating individual experience. Fortunately perhaps for us, the Evangelist was no more given to distinguishing the essential and the unessential features of a story than was his informant, and it re-appeared untrimmed in his record. Matthew, true to his methods of condensation, omits the whole episode of the two verses, though he has transferred to his account of the entombment, a few verses higher up, the detail that the stone was 'great': Luke simply states that the women found 'the stone' rolled away from the sepulchre, but he had said nothing of the closing of the tomb and no doubt simply means his readers to understand that the normal proceeding had been adopted, and the tomb closed with a slab which was now found 'rolled away'.

19. xvi 7 *εἴπατε τοῖς μαθηταῖς αὐτοῦ καὶ τῷ Πέτρῳ ὅτι Προάγει ὑμᾶς εἰς τὴν Γαλιλαίαν — ἐκεῖ αὐτὸν ὄψεσθε — καθὼς εἶπεν ὑμῖν.*

The natural exegesis of these words, if printed without punctuation or brackets, is that our Lord had told the disciples that they would see him in Galilee. But the Gospel contains no record of any such Saying. Matthew, therefore, by substituting the first person for the third, *εἶπον* for *εἶπεν*, changes the sense from a prediction of our Lord's to a statement by the angel, 'You will see him in Galilee: I tell you so categorically'.[8]

---

[8] Hort *ad loc.* proposes to restore *εἶπεν* in the text of Matthew. But I think Matthew was puzzled by Mark's statement as he understood it, and deliberately altered it: unless indeed he read *εἶπον* in his copy of Mark. In either case, *ἰδού* appears to me to exclude *εἶπεν*. It introduces a new speaker.

Luke retains the third person; but as his Gospel records appearances of the Risen Christ in Jerusalem and its neighbourhood only, he has to connect Galilee not with the appearances but with the prediction, 'He spake yet being in Galilee'. But St Mark had recorded one prediction by Jesus, uttered as recently as the Last Supper (xiv 28), *μετὰ τὸ ἐγερθῆναί με προάξω ὑμᾶς εἰς τὴν Γαλιλαίαν*, in language of which the angel's words seem an obvious echo, xvi 6, 7, *ἠγέρθη ... προάγει ὑμᾶς εἰς τὴν Γαλιλαίαν ... καθὼς εἶπεν ὑμῖν*. Apart from the three intrusive words, *ἐκεῖ αὐτὸν ὄψεσθε*, the correspondence is exact. Treat them as a parenthesis after the Marcan manner, place them between dashes, and all difficulty disappears.

V – The movements of Jesus and his disciples and the crowd.†

The present instalment of these Notes on Marcan Usage deals with what seems to me a singularly interesting feature of the Second Gospel in comparison and contrast with the other two Synoptic Gospels, namely the position and relative prominence which in the structure of the narrative attaches to the disciples or the Twelve. This prominence is not to all appearance the result of a conscious attempt on the evangelist's part to emphasize it or in any way to advertise it: you might read the Gospel superficially without noticing it: but when once attention is drawn to it, it is seen to be there, and the natural and obvious explanation is that we have before us the experience of a disciple and apostle who tells the story from the point of view of an eyewitness and companion, who puts himself in the same group as the Master, who distinguishes the group of companions from the crowd at large. Matthew and Luke are Christian historians who stand away from the events, and concentrate their narrative on the central figure: in contrast with it other contrasts lose something of their importance, and on occasion the disciples and the crowd almost melt — as they never do in Mark — into one.

The first and perhaps of all the most significant distinction between the three Synoptists in this sphere is the distinction between the use of the plural and the singular in the narrative of the movements of Jesus and his disciples. Twenty-one instances are enumerated in § 1 of these notes, in which the plural is used by Mark, denoting the coming and going of Jesus and his disciples — in fifteen of them the word is *ἔρχεσθαι* or one of its compounds — followed at once by the singular in reference to Jesus alone. Obviously it was simpler and saved space to construct the whole sentence in the singular, and this is what the other Synoptists, concentrating attention on the Master, tend to do: on five occasions both substitute the singular for the plural, and on three more occasions Luke does so, while Luke five times and Matthew three times omit the whole clause containing the plural verb. The net result is that the retention of Mark's plural is rare in Matthew, rarer still in Luke. And the scribes of Mark, whether affected by the presence of the singular in the Synoptic parallels, or influenced independently by the same motives as influenced Matthew and Luke, tend themselves too to get rid of the plural: and in one or two cases it is not unreasonable to allow 'Marcan usage' a decisive voice and to accept the plural on what is apparently the weaker body of witness.

Why then did our earliest Evangelist tell his story in the plural, not being himself one of the company who went about with Jesus, save because he is repeating the story of one to whom the plural came natural as being himself an actor in the events he relates? 'We went across, and as he left the boat there met him ... ' 'Next morning after we had left Bethany he was hungry ... ' 'We come again to Jerusalem: and as he was walking up and down the Temple ... ' The mixture of nominatives is less glaring between the first person and the third — 'we' and 'he', instead of 'they' and 'he': and that may perhaps be the reason why St Mark so rarely writes 'Jesus'. Peter would be content with 'He': there could be no question who was meant.[1]

In one passage in particular, i 29, 'they left the synagogue and came into the house of Simon and Andrew with James and John', the hypothesis that the third person plural of Mark represents a first person plural of Peter makes what as it stands is a curiously awkward phrase into a phrase which is quite easy and coherent. 'We left the synagogue and came into our house with our fellow-disciples James and John. My mother-in-law was in bed with fever, and he is told about her ... '[2] So too, i 16, 'He saw me and Andrew my brother'.

The usages of which details are given in the other sections of this paper are all intended to re-inforce the conclusion that Mark's story is told as from a disciple and companion, while Matthew and Luke are less directly interested in that particular point of view.

In § ii nine passages are enumerated where the sentence begins with a singular verb in reference to our Lord and goes on to mention the disciples: and more often than not this mention of the disciples falls out in one or both of the derivative accounts.

The passages collected in the following section (§ 3) differ only from these by the additional mention of the crowd. They witness to the more articulated conceptions of the Second Gospel: in later Gospels the lines become a little blurred and indistinct. Out of eleven passages there is practically none where something of the Marcan distinction of elements is not lost by both the other two evangelists.

This definite articulation, characteristic of Mark, is further brought out with regard to 'the crowd', ὄχλος, in § v. Alone among the three Synop-

[1] Mark very rarely writes ὁ Ἰησοῦς in narrative, not infrequently in the give and take of question and answer: though scribes have tried to insert it, e.g. xii 41. Matthew adds ὁ Ἰησοῦς not less than some forty times, especially at the beginning of a paragraph. Luke is even more sparing than Mark with ὁ Ἰησοῦς, and like Mark, but oftener, makes use of αὐτός, 'He himself', 'The Master', or better still a stressed 'He': it is almost equivalent to our use of the capital H.

[2] My colleague Mr Brightman points out to me that this suggestion was anticipated by Godet: see his *Biblical Studies: New Testament* ch.i § 2, p. 24.

tists he uses the word only in the singular — the one exception in x 1 refers to the gathering together of crowds from different quarters — because he or his informant visualizes as a single whole the body of people who came together to hear Jesus, and according to their numbers on each occasion describes them as 'a crowd' or 'a big crowd' or 'a considerable crowd' or 'a very big crowd'. Mark never uses the definite article in the nominative, *ὁ ὄχλος*, *πᾶς ὁ ὄχλος* (at any rate till the scene shifts to Jerusalem), except in relation to an indefinite 'crowd' mentioned just previously.[3] They are not a fixed quantity, so to say, not *ὁ ὄχλος* but *ὄχλος*, a necessary element in the picture but a variable and varying one. To the other evangelists, or at any rate to Matthew, they are a stereotyped but vague generality, 'the multitudes'.

A similar conclusion results from the study of the word *ἀκολουθεῖν* in § vi. In Mark this verb has ordinarily something still about it to suggest the literal sense: it is never used of the crowds — as it is in the other Synoptists — but only of the call to 'leave all and follow' Jesus. And more significant still are the changes which the two later Synoptists make by introducing *ἀκολουθεῖν* of the disciples 'following' Jesus, where Mark had spoken of Jesus and the disciples as a single group; see iv 36, ix 38.[4]

Finally, as to the terms used of the disciples themselves, St Mark's Gospel reveals its archaic and primitive character by its predominant use of the phrase 'his disciples' (§ iv below); whereas the other Gospels tend to introduce the absolute statement 'the disciples', a usage which doubtless goes back to a very early stage in the separate history of the Christian Society but does not go back to the time of the Ministry itself. And St Mark's Gospel is distinguished again from the other two by its fondness, especially in the later chapters, for the phrase *οἱ δώδεκα*, which comes to all appearance to be practically a synonym, during the last journey to Jerusalem and at Jerusalem, for 'the disciples'.[5]

---

[3] *ὁ ὄχλος* in iii 20 (but note *ὄχλος* ℵ* C with W-H margin) would refer to the *πλῆθος πολύ* of iii 8: in ix 25 (but again *ὄχλος* ℵ^{c} B D Δ) to the *ὄχλον πολύν* of ix 14: *πᾶς ὁ ὄχλος* (*ὄχλος* D*) ii 13 to the *πολλοί* of ii 2 and the *διὰ τὸν ὄχλον* of ii 4: *πᾶς ὁ ὄχλος* of iv 1 *b* to *ὄχλος πλεῖστος* earlier in the same verse, and in ix 15 to *ὄχλον πολύν* of ix 14. In xv 8 D a k give, for 'the crowd', 'the whole crowd'. In oblique cases the article is of course essential, and implies nothing as between *ὄχλος* and *ὁ ὄχλος*: e.g. in ii 4 *διὰ τὸν ὄχλον* was the only possible phrase, just like 'because of the crowd' in English. You could not say *δὶ ὄχλον*, 'because of a crowd'.

[4] Of the crowd Matt. iv 25, viii 1, xii 15, xiv 13, xix 2, xx 29; Lk. vii 9, ix 11: and of the disciples Matt. viii 23, Lk. ix 49, xxii 39.

[5] In Note *VIII* (pr.) below I examine the theory urged by Eduard Meyer in his important work *Ursprung und Anfänge des Christentums* that *οἱ μαθηταὶ (αὐτοῦ)* and *οἱ δώδεκα* indicate two separate sources employed by St Mark. As far as I can see at present, this

i. The impersonal plural, followed by the singular.†

1. i 21 *καὶ εἰσπορεύονται εἰς Καφαρναούμ. καὶ εὐθὺς τοῖς σάββασιν ἐδίδασκεν εἰς τὴν συναγωγήν.*

The plural is found in all authorities save *fam.* 1 Origen and a very few others (*om.* syr-sin). Matthew omits the notice entirely: Luke gives the singular; but as the call of the first disciples comes at a later point in his story, he was naturally bound to do so.

2. i 29, 30 *καὶ εὐθὺς ἐκ τῆς συναγωγῆς ἐξελθόντες ἦλθον εἰς τὴν οἰκίαν Σίμωνος ... καὶ εὐθὺς λέγουσιν αὐτῷ ...*

ἐξελθόντες ... ἦλθον ℵ A C L Δ Vulg. with W-H text: B D W Θ *fam.* 1, *fam.* 13 and the Old Latins and Armenian *ἐξελθὼν ... ἦλθεν*: syr-sin combines the two readings 'and he went forth ... and they came', and so *l* 'et protinus egrediens de synagoga uenerunt': *a* and the Sahidic are defective. Matthew and Luke both have the singular. It is so much more probable that the singular would have been substituted for the plural by scribes of Mark than *vice versa*, that, in spite of the strong authority for *ἐξελθὼν ...ἦλθεν*, I can feel little doubt that W-H are right in putting the plural in their text.[6]

3. v 1, 2 *καὶ ἦλθον εἰς τὸ πέραν ... καὶ ἐξελθόντος αὐτοῦ ἐκ τοῦ πλοίου εὐθὺς ὑπήντησεν αὐτῷ ...*

ἦλθεν C L W Δ etc. syr-sin. Matthew omits the first clause altogether: Luke has the plural with Mark. External authority and intrinsic probability combined are decisive for *ἦλθον*.

4. v 38 *καὶ ἔρχονται εἰς τὸν οἶκον τοῦ ἀρχισυναγώγου· καὶ θεωρεῖ θόρυβον ...*

ἔρχονται ℵ A B C D 1 33, the better half of Old Latin MSS (*b e i*) Vulg. and Sahidic: *ἔρχεται* L W Θ *a c ff* arm: def. syr-sin. Matthew and Luke both substitute the singular. There is no doubt about the reading in Mark: exactly the same instinct which actuated the other two Synoptists accounts for the reading of the minority.

5. vi 53, 54 *καὶ διαπεράσαντες ἐπὶ τὴν γῆν ἦλθον εἰς Γεννησαρὲτ καὶ προσωρμίσθησαν. καὶ ἐξελθόντων αὐτῶν ἐκ τοῦ πλοίου εὐθὺς ἐπιγνόντες αὐτὸν ...*

---

theory has no adequate basis at all.

[6] In Mk. ii 13 ℵ* gives ἐξῆλθον for ἐξῆλθεν: but though it may conceivably be right, the authority is too slight to justify the inclusion of the passage in this list.

Luke is now defective: Matthew retains the first plurals, *διαπεράσαντες ἦλθον*, but drops the other two as superfluous detail.[7]

6. viii 22 *καὶ ἔρχονται εἰς Βηθσαϊδάν. καὶ φέρουσιν αὐτῷ ...*

ἔρχονται ℵ^c B C D L W Δ Θ *fam.* 13 Latins Sahidic Armenian: *ἔρχεται* ℵ* A syr-sin etc. Again no doubt at all: but again we note the persistent inclination by some or other witnesses to substitute the singular. There are no Synoptic parallels.

7. ix 14, 15 *καὶ ἐλθόντες πρὸς τοὺς μαθητὰς εἶδον ὄχλον πολὺν ... καὶ εὐθὺς πᾶς ὁ ὄχλος ἰδόντες αὐτὸν ἐξεθάμβησαν.*

ἐλθόντες ... εἶδον ℵ B L W Δ k sah arm: *ἐλθὼν ... εἶδεν* A C D Θ and all Latins except *k*, etc.: syr-sin, as in no 2, gives a conflate reading 'when he came to his disciples, they saw by them a great multitude'. Both Matthew and Luke keep the plural of Mark, though Matthew, as on some other occasions, omits all mention of the multitude. There are only eight witnesses (or nine, if we count syr-sin) for the plural in Mark, but their quality makes up for their quantity. Note that *k* is the only MS of the Westerns (in the literal sense) in the group: it preserves on not a few occasions a purer text than D.

8. ix 30 *κἀκεῖθεν ἐξελθόντες παρεπορεύοντο διὰ τῆς Γαλιλαίας, καὶ οὐκ ἤθελεν ἵνα τις γνοῖ.*

This time there is no variation in our witnesses, and Matthew, too, retains the plural: Luke omits the whole clause, perhaps because he is going a few verses later to introduce his special story of the ascent to Jerusalem.

9. ix 33 *καὶ ἦλθον εἰς Καφαρναούμ· καὶ ἐν τῇ οἰκίᾳ γενόμενος ἐπηρώτα αὐτούς ...*

ἦλθον ℵ B D W *fam.* 1 the best Old Latins (*a b i k*) with Vulgate and Sahidic: *ἦλθεν* A C L Δ Θ etc. Matthew and Luke both omit the details of the arrival at Capernaum and entry into the house. Once more there is no doubt about the reading.

10. x 32 *ἦσαν δὲ ἐν τῇ ὁδῷ ἀναβαίνοντες εἰς Ἱεροσόλυμα, καὶ ἦν προάγων αὐτοὺς ὁ Ἰησους ... καὶ παραλαβὼν πάλιν τοὺς δώδεκα ...*

The form of the sentence precluded any temptation to scribes of Mark to evade the plural: but Matthew changes *ἀναβαίνοντες* to *ἀναβαίνων* and goes straight on with *παρέλαβεν τοὺς δώδεκα*, while Luke omits everything which precedes *παραλαβών*. Thus in both of them the plural entirely disappears.

---

[7] From vii 24 to vii 37 — the visit to Tyre, and return from Tyre to the sea of Galilee — the story is told throughout in the singular. May not our Lord have made this excursion alone and unaccompanied?

11. x 46 *καὶ ἔρχονται εἰς Ἰερειχώ. καὶ ἐκπορευομένου αὐτοῦ ἀπὸ Ἰερειχὼ ...*

ἔρχεται D with most of the Old Latins (but not *c k*) syr-sin and Origen. Matthew keeps the plural: Luke replaces the plural by the singular.

12. xi 1 *καὶ ὅτε ἐγγίζουσιν εἰς Ἰεροσόλυμα ... ἀποστέλλει δύο τῶν μαθητῶν αὐτοῦ.*

A very limited group, D and the Old Latins (with the exception of *a*), substitutes the singular, at the same time changing the present to a past tense: *k*, for the first time since it has come to our assistance (from no. **7** onwards), deserts the plural. As in no. **11**, Matthew retains the plural, while Luke gives *ἤγγισεν*.

13. xi 11 *καὶ εἰσῆλθον εἰς Ἰεροσόλυμα εἰς τὸ ἱερόν. καὶ περιβλεψάμενος πάντα ...*

Here I read the plural with a very small group, Θ *i* (cum introissent) *k* (et introiuerunt): syr-sin as in nos. **2** and **7**, combines plural and singular 'and they entered Jerusalem, and he entered the Temple'. All our other authorities, with Matthew and Luke, have the singular. But on the strength of 'Marcan usage', I venture to believe that the three authorities which give the plural are right.

14. xi 12 *καὶ τῇ ἐπαύριον ἐξελθόντων αὐτῶν ἀπὸ Βηθανίας ἐπείνασεν.*

The only recalcitrant witnesses here are D *b c ff* — not however *a d i k*. Thus the older Old Latins go with our Greek authorities: the ungrammatical *ἐξελθόντα* of D, where d has cum exissent, may safely be neglected. Matthew has the singular: Luke has no parallel.

15. xi 15 *καὶ ἔρχονται εἰς Ἰεροσόλυμα. καὶ εἰσελθὼν εἰς τὸ ἱερὸν ἤρξατο ἐκβάλλειν ...*

The singular is only offered by D (again against its Latin column intrauerunt) *b i* and syr-sin. Matthew and Luke both omit the first clause, and therewith the plural, entirely.

16. xi 19, 20, 21 *ἐξεπορεύοντο ἔξω τῆς πόλεως· καὶ παραπορευόμενοι πρωῒ εἶδον τὴν συκῆν ... καὶ ἀναμνησθεὶς ὁ Πέτρος λέγει αὐτῷ ...*

ἐξεπορεύοντο A B W Δ Ψ 124 565 *c d* arm W-H text: *ἐξεπορεύετο* the rest (with Θ *k* sah syr-sin). There is no parallel in the other Synoptists to account for the singular: and as *παραπορευόμενοι εἶδον* is quite certain, it is just possible that *ἐξεπορεύοντο* is a scribal assimilation to this following plural, and that *ἐξεπορεύετο* is original here. Decision is therefore less easy than usual.

17. xi 27 *καὶ ἔρχονται πάλιν εἰς Ἰεροσόλυμα. καὶ ἐν τῷ ἱερῷ περιπατοῦντος αὐτοῦ ...*

ἔρχεται only D with all the older Old Latins (*b e ff i k*) except *a*: compare no.**12** above. Matthew has the singular: Luke omits the first phrase, and so retains only the singular.

18. xiv 18 *καὶ ἀνακειμένων αὐτῶν καὶ ἐσθιόντων ὁ ᾿Ιησοῦς*[8] *εἶπεν* ...

Matthew retains (omitting *ἀνακειμένων καί*), Luke puts *ἀνέπεσεν* (singular) into a previous verse, and thus gets rid again of the plural.

19. xiv 22 *καὶ ἐσθιόντων αὐτῶν* λαβὼν *ἄρτον* ...

Matthew retains plural and singular: Luke again omits the phrase containing the plural.

20. xiv 26, 27 *καὶ ὑμνῆσαντες ἐξῆλθον* ... *καὶ* λέγει *αὐτοῦς ὁ* ᾿Ιησοῦς ...

Matthew again retains unchanged: Luke again omits *ὑμνήσαντες* and, instead of 'they went out', writes 'he went out and they followed'.

21. xiv 32 *καὶ ἔρχονται εἰς τὸ χωρίον οὗ τὸ ὄνομα* Γεθσημανεί· *καὶ* λέγει *τοῖς μαθηταῖς αὐτοῦ* ...

No variation in the text of Mark: but both Matthew and Luke change plural into singular.

Of the fourteen passages where our authorities differ, B is right in 12, ℵ in 11, W in 10, Θ in 9, sah in 11, *a* in 8, *d* in 8: *k* in six out of nine where it is extant. D and syr.sin have the worst record: on three occasions running, **14 15 16**, *d* is right where D is wrong.

ii. The singular followed by mention of the disciples (or the Twelve)

1. i 35, 36 *καὶ πρωῒ ἔννυχα λίαν ἀναστὰς ἐξῆλθεν* ... *καὶ κατεδίωξεν αὐτὸν Σίμων καὶ οἱ μετ' αὐτοῦ*. They are not yet 'the disciples', still less 'the Twelve', but 'Simon and his companions'. Peter takes the first place — or it was Peter who told the story, 'I and my companions'. There is no parallel in Matthew, while in Luke (iv 42) *οἱ ὄχλοι* take the place of *Σίμων καὶ οἱ μετ' αὐτοῦ*.

2. ii 15 *καὶ γίνεται κατακεῖσθαι αὐτὸν ἐν τῇ οἰκίᾳ αὐτοῦ, καὶ πολλοὶ τελῶναι καὶ ἁμαρτωλοὶ συνανέκειντο τῷ* ᾿Ιησοῦ *καὶ τοῖς μαθηταῖς αὐτοῦ*.

Matthew repeats Mark's statement: Luke omits the mention of the disciples.

3. ii 23 *καὶ ἐγένετο αὐτὸν* ... *παραπορεύεσθαι διὰ τῶν σπορίμων, καὶ οἱ μαθηταὶ αὐτοῦ ἤρξαντο* ...

The mention of the disciples at this point is necessary to the story, and is repeated by both the other Synoptists.

---

[8] ὁ ᾿Ιησοῦς is omitted by *a e ff* syr-sin, and the place of the words varies in our other authorities.

4. iii 7 *καὶ ὁ Ἰησοῦς μετὰ τῶν μαθητῶν αὐτοῦ ἀνεχώρησεν ...*
It is Matthew on this occasion who omits mention of the disciples, while Luke follows Mark by retaining it.

5. vi 1 *καὶ ἐξῆλθεν ἐκεῖθεν καὶ ἔρχεται εἰς τὴν πατρίδα αὐτοῦ καὶ ἀκολουθοῦσιν αὐτῷ οἱ μαθηταὶ αὐτοῦ.*
Matthew is wholly silent about the disciples here, because they play no part in the episode. Luke too, omits them, and necessarily, for he transfers this visit to Nazareth to a point in his history (iv 16) before the call of any of the disciples.

6. viii 27 *καὶ ἐξῆλθεν ὁ Ἰησοῦς καὶ οἱ μαθηταὶ αὐτοῦ εἰς τὰς κώμας Καισαρίας τῆς Φιλίππου.*
The question to the disciples 'Whom do men say that I am?' is of course an integral part of this story, and all three Evangelists mention them in that connexion: but in the introductory phrase Matthew drops the allusion to them.

7. x 13 *καὶ προσέφερον αὐτῷ παιδία ... οἱ δὲ μαθηταὶ ἐπετίμησαν αὐτοῖς. .*
The rebuke by the disciples being necessary to the episode, it is retained by both the derivative accounts.

8. xiv 12, 13 *καὶ τῇ πρώτῃ ἡμέρᾳ τῶν ἀζύμων ... λέγουσιν αὐτῷ οἱ μαθηταὶ αὐτοῦ· Ποῦ θέλεις ἀπελθόντες ἑτοιμάσωμεν ...*
Strictly speaking, this passage does not fulfil the requirement of singular before plural: but I include it here for purposes of comparison with St Luke, for it illustrates again the underlying principle that Mark tells the story from the point of view of the disciples. While Matthew exactly reproduces, Luke omits the initiative of the disciples, and writes (xxii 7, 8) *ἦλθεν δὲ ἡ ἡμέρα τῶν ἀζύμων ... καὶ ἀπέστειλεν ...*

9. xiv 17 *καὶ ὀψίας γενομένης ἔρχεται μετὰ τῶν δώδεκα ...*
The other two Synoptists agree, save that for 'the Twelve' Matthew substitutes 'the twelve disciples', Luke 'the apostles'.

These variations are instructive. Mark uses *οἱ δώδεκα* ten times: iii 14, 16 *ἐποίησεν [τοὺς] δώδεκα*, iv 10 *οἱ περὶ αὐτὸν σὺν τοῖς δώδεκα*, vi 7 *προσκαλεῖται τοὺς δώδεκα*, ix 35 *καθίσας ἐφώνησεν τοὺς δώδεκα*, x 32 *παραλαβὼν πάλιν τοὺς δώδεκα*, xi 11 *ἐξῆλθεν εἰς Βηθανίαν μετὰ τῶν δώδεκα*, xiv 10 *Ἰούδας Ἰσκαριὼθ ὁ εἷς τῶν δώδεκα*, xiv 17 (the passage under discussion), xiv 20 *εἷς τῶν δώδεκα ὁ ἐμβαπτόμενος μετ' ἐμοῦ*, xiv 43 *παραγίνεται ὁ Ἰούδας, εἷς τῶν δώδεκα* — and only once [9] *οἱ*

[9] In Mark iii 14 the words *οὓς καὶ ἀποστόλους ὠνόμασεν*, in spite of the strong authority for them (ℵ B Δ Θ 28 Ferrar group sah), are in my judgement nothing but an insertion borrowed from Lk. vi 13. They are omitted by Tischendorf with A D L W 1 33 all latins (O.L. and Vulg) syr-sin arm.

ἀπόστολοι, and that on the special occasion when they returned from the Missionary Journey, vi 30, where the noun corresponds to the *ἤρξατο αὐτοὺς ἀποστέλλειν δύο δύο* of vi 7 (cf. iii 15, of the purpose of the call of the Twelve, *ἵνα ἀποστέλλῃ αὐτοὺς κηρύσσειν* ...): neither *οἱ δώδεκα μαθηταί* nor *οἱ δώδεκα ἀπόστολοι* occurs in his Gospel. In other words *ἀπόστολος* has not lost with him its original sense of 'missionary', and there were other qualified 'missionaries' in the early Church besides the Twelve, while *οἱ δώδεκα* 'the Twelve' is the special phrase which in the latter part of his Gospel (side by side with *οἱ μαθηταὶ αὐτοῦ*) denotes the small company of those whom the Master had singled out for closest intimacy and training as his representatives. Here the Pauline epistles are the best commentary on Marcan usage. St Paul does not use *οἱ δώδεκα* himself: but we find the phrase in the Creed-summary of 1 Cor. xv 5, which he had 'received' from, and shared with, those who were in Christ before him. Similarly St Paul recognizes the original sense of *ἀπόστολος* as a 'missionary' 'one formally sent' (2 Cor. viii 23, Phil. ii 25), and can even write, in the additions which he makes in 1 Cor. xv 6-8 to the inherited Creed-form, *τοῖς ἀποστόλοις πᾶσιν* (verse 7) in contrast to *τοῖς δώδεκα* of verse 5.

On the other hand Matthew never uses the phrase *οἱ δώδεκα* (save in the phrase *εἷς τῶν δώδεκα* xxvi 14 = Mk. xiv 10, and xxvi 47 = Mk. xiv 43), but always *οἱ δώδεκα μαθηταί*, Matt. x 1, xi 1, xx 17 [10], xxvi 20, or *οἱ δώδεκα ἀπόστολοι*, Matt. x 2: in Matt. x 5 *τούτους τοὺς δώδεκα* may seem an exception, but it takes up *οἱ δώδεκα ἀπόστολοι* of verse 2. That is to say, though Matthew can say *εἷς τῶν δώδεκα* or *οὗτοι οἱ δώδεκα*, he never says *οἱ δώδεκα simpliciter*. Like Mark, he only uses *ἀπόστολος* once, but it is significant that on that one occasion (x 2) it is in reference to the call of 'the twelve apostles': cf. Rev. xxi 14 'the twelve apostles of the Lamb'.

Luke does not share Matthew's avoidance of the phrase 'the Twelve': Lk. viii 1, ix 1 [11], ix 12, xviii 31, xxii 3, xxii 47. But he is the first evangelist to introduce, as an alternative to 'the disciples' or 'the Twelve' the additional phrase 'the Apostles' — which in the Acts he uses of course quite regularly and consistently — Lk. ix 10 [= Mk. vi 30], xvii 5, xxii

---

[10] *τοὺς δώδεκα μαθητάς* B C W 28 33 Ferrar group latins (O.L. and Vulg.) sah and W-H margin. The authority would be preponderant, even without the argument from Matthaean usage. Omission of *μαθητάς* is due to the influence of the parallel texts in Luke and Mark.

[11] There is good, and perhaps sufficient, authority for adding *ἀποστόλους*, ℵ C L Θ 33 Ferrar group *a c e* Vulg.

14, xxiv 10. Like Matthew, but unlike Mark, he uses the noun 'apostles' in connexion with the Calling of the Twelve, vi 13.

Our passage, Mk. xiv 17 = Matt. xxvi 20 = Lk. xxii 14, is therefore of special interest as indicating characteristic usages of the three Synoptists, *οἱ δώδεκα, οἱ δώδεκα μαθηταί, οἱ ἀπόστολοι.*

iii. The Lord, the disciples, and the multitude.

1. iii 9 *καὶ εἶπεν τοῖς μαθηταῖς αὐτοῦ ἵνα πλοιάριον προσκαρτερῇ αὐτῷ διὰ τὸν ὄχλον, ἵνα μὴ θλίβωσιν αὐτόν.*

Mention of the disciples at this moment disappears entirely from Matthew and Luke. It had, in fact, no point save as a personal reminiscence.

2. iv 1, 2, 10 *καὶ συνάγεται πρὸς αὐτὸν ὄχλος πλεῖστος ...καὶ πᾶς ὁ ὄχλος πρὸς τὴν θάλασσαν ἐπὶ τῆς γῆς ἦσαν. καὶ ἐδίδασκεν αὐτοὺς ἐν παραβολαῖς πολλά ... καὶ ὅτε ἐγένετο κατὰ μόνας, ἠρώτων αὐτὸν οἱ περὶ αὐτὸν σὺν τοῖς δώδεκα τὰς παραβολάς.*

Here in Mark we have four elements, the Lord, the Twelve, the disciples outside the Twelve, and lastly the multitude. The intermediate elements distinguished by Mark — the Twelve are now a group by themselves among the disciples, but they are not yet isolated into a separate company — are massed together both by Matthew ('the disciples') and Luke ('his disciples'). All three share mention of the 'crowd', but Luke suppresses all details, and even in Matthew the detail disappears that the crowd was unusually big, *πλεῖστος*. *Ὄχλοι πολλοί* is a sort of standing phrase with him (Matt. iv 25, viii 1, xiii 2 [our passage], xv 30, xix 2), though he does employ *ὁ πλεῖστος ὄχλος* in xxi 8.

3. iv 34 *χωρὶς δὲ παραβολῆς οὐκ ἐλάλει αὐτοῖς, κατ' ἰδίαν δὲ τοῖς ἰδίοις μαθηταῖς ἐπέλυεν πάντα.*

Luke is not parallel here: Matthew retains the first or negative part of the sentence and caps it with a prophecy (Ps. lxxviii [lxxvii] 2), but says nothing of the interpretation to the disciples.

4. iv 35, 36 *καὶ λέγει αὐτοῖς ... Διέλθωμεν εἰς τὸ πέραν. καὶ ἀφέντες τὸν ὄχλον παραλαμβάνουσιν αὐτὸν ὡς ἦν ἐν τῷ πλοίῳ.*

Both Matthew and Luke are silent as to the action of the disciples; *ἀφέντες* and *παραλαμβάνουσιν* alike disappear. In Luke the 'crowd' drops out as well.

5. vii 17 *καὶ ὅτε εἰσῆλθεν εἰς [τὸν] οἶκον ἀπὸ τοῦ ὄχλου, ἐπηρώτων αὐτὸν οἱ μαθηταὶ αὐτοῦ τὴν παραβολήν.*

We have reached the long lacuna in Luke: Matthew, who has inserted additional matter since the mention of the summoning of the crowd (Mk. vii 14 = Matt. xv 10) has no place here for the crowd, and loses the characteristic Marcan contrast of *ὄχλος* and *μαθηταί*.

6. viii 1 *πάλιν πολλοῦ ὄχλου ὄντος καὶ μὴ ἐχόντων τί φάγωσιν, προσκαλεσάμενος τοὺς μαθητὰς λέγει αὐτοῖς* ...

There is, as before, no Luke: Matthew retains the substance, but by compressing misses Mark's juxtaposition of 'crowd' and 'disciples'.

7. viii 9, 10 *ἦσαν δὲ ὡς τετρακισχίλιοι· καὶ ἀπέλυσεν αὐτούς. ·καὶ εὐθὺς ἐμβὰς [αὐτὸς] εἰς τὸ πλοῖον μετὰ τῶν μαθητῶν αὐτοῦ ἦλθεν* ...

Matthew for the rest copies Mark meticulously, but he omits the disciples altogether and emphasizes his concentration on the Lord and the multitude by repeating the noun *ὄχλος* (*τοὺς ὄχλους* for *αὐτούς*).

8. viii 34 *καὶ προσκαλεσάμενος τὸν ὄχλον σὺν τοῖς μαθηταῖς αὐτοῦ εἶπεν αὐτοῖς* ...

Mark's characteristic combination of the crowd and the disciples fails as usual to find full echo in the other two Synoptists: for Matthew here omits the crowd, and Luke groups both elements together under the common heading *πάντας*.

9. ix 14 *καὶ ἐλθόντες πρὸς τοὺς μαθητὰς εἶδον ὄχλον πολὺν περὶ αὐτούς* ...

Mark is careful to note that Jesus, who had selected three of the disciples to accompany him on the Mount of the Transfiguration, now once more reunited the company. That does not in itself interest the other Synoptists: both of them note the crowd, neither of them says anything at this stage of the disciples.

10. x 46 *καὶ ἐκπορευομένου αὐτοῦ ἀπὸ Ἰερειχὼ καὶ τῶν μαθητῶν αὐτοῦ καὶ ὄχλου ἱκανοῦ* ...

Matthew (xx 29) avoids the separate mention of 'disciples' by the use of the plural participle *ἐκπορευομένων αὐτῶν*, and connects the 'crowd' by the expedient of his favourite word *ἀκολουθέω*.[12] Luke concentrates attention on the principal actors, Jesus and the blind beggar, leaves out the disciples altogether, but skilfully introduces the crowd when the blind man hears it passing by.

11. xii 41-43 *καὶ καθίσας κατέναντι τοῦ γαζοφυλακίου ἐθεώρει πῶς ὁ ὄχλος βάλλει χαλκὸν ... καὶ ἐλθοῦσα μία χήρα πτωχὴ ἔβαλεν ... καὶ προσκαλεσάμενος τοὺς μαθητὰς αὐτοῦ εἶπεν* ...

---

[12]On *ἀκολουθεῖν* see below.

Matthew omits the whole story. Luke tells it without any specific reference to the disciples.

iv. 'His disciples' 'the disciples' (οἱ μαθηταὶ αὐτοῦ, οἱ μαθηταί).†

Very early in the history of the Christian Society, μαθητής, οἱ μαθηταί, became the regular term for an individual follower of Jesus of Nazareth or for the members of the Society generally: and it is so used throughout the Acts. It is earlier than the word 'Christian', which, being of Latin or Greek coinage, belongs only to the period when Christianity began to establish itself in Gentile centres: Acts xi 26 ἐγένετο ... χρηματίσαι πρώτως ἐν Ἀντιοχείᾳ τοὺς μαθητὰς Χριστιανούς. As contrasted with 'Nazarene', it is the term which the followers of Jesus used of themselves, while to the Jews they were 'the Nazarenes', Acts xxiv 5 πρωτοστάτην τῆς τῶν Ναζωραίων[13] αἱρέσεως.

But originally, when 'disciples' collected first round Jesus of Nazareth, his were not the only disciples. There were 'disciples of John', there were 'disciples of the Pharisees', Mk. ii 18, Lk. v 33, vii 18, xi 1, Jo. i 35, iii 25; and therefore the followers of Jesus in his Ministry were not 'the disciples' but 'his disciples', not οἱ μαθηταί but οἱ μαθηταὶ αὐτοῦ.

This was of course the phraseology of the Jews[14]: 'Why are the disciples of John and the disciples of the Pharisees fasting, but thy disciples are not fasting?' 'Why do not thy disciples walk according to the tradition of the elders?' 'I said to thy disciples that they should cast it out'; Mk. ii 18, vii 5, ix 18. It is that of Jesus himself: 'Where is the guest-chamber where I may eat the passover with my disciples?' (Mk. xiv 14 and parallels): 'he cannot be my disciple,' Lk. xiv 26. But it also the phraseology of the earliest stratum of the evangelic narrative. Mark writes οἱ μαθηταὶ αὐτοῦ some thirty-two times out of about forty: Luke has οἱ μαθηταὶ αὐτοῦ rather oftener than οἱ μαθηταί, of which the first independent occurrence is Lk. ix 18: Matthew too, though his divergence

[13]Ναζωραῖος is the only form known to Matthew, John, and Acts: Ναζαρηνός the only form in Mark: Luke in his Gospel uses Ναζαρηνός iv 34 (= Mk. i 24), Ναζωραῖος xviii 37 (= Ναζαρηνός Mark x 47), while in xxiv 19 the authorities are divided between the two forms. As we know, Ναζαρηνός Nazarenus was the form which established itself in Greek and Latin usage. It looks as though Ναζωραῖος was the word used in the early period in Jewish circles, in place of which Mark, writing for Roman and Gentile readers, substituted the form intelligible to them.

[14]It is hardly credible that Matthew can have made Jews say (xxvii 64) to Pilate 'lest *the* disciples come and steal him away', in spite of ℵ B (unsupported indeed here by any other authorities), Tischendorf and W-H text, though not their margin; and we must certainly read with all other witnesses οἱ μαθηταὶ αὐτοῦ.

from Marcan usage is much greater, uses *οἱ μαθηταὶ αὐτοῦ* consistently until Matt. xiii 10: and even in the latest of the Gospels *οἱ μαθηταί* without *αὐτοῦ* is not found in St John till xi 7. That is to say, at one end of the evangelic tradition St Mark's Gospel distinguishes itself by its close adherence to the archaic phrase, at the other St Matthew's is the only Gospel where *οἱ μαθηταί* without *αὐτοῦ* becomes preponderant, especially in the nominative (Matt. xiii 10, xiv 15, 19 (*bis*), 22, xv 12, 33, 36 (*bis*), xvi 5, xvii 6, 10, 13, 19, xviii 1, xix 10, 13, 25, xxi 6, 20, xxiv 3, xxvi 8, 17, 35, 56).

It may be worth while just to examine the few exceptions in St Mark, for some of them are not really exceptions at all.

iv 34 *κατ' ἰδίαν δὲ τοῖς ἰδίοις μαθηταῖς ἐπέλυεν πάντα.* Here obviously *ἰδίοις* takes the place of *αὐτοῦ*.

vi 41 *ἐδίδου τοῖς μαθηταῖς.* In the middle of the story of the Feeding of the Five Thousand, the full phrase occurring just before, vi 35, and just after, vi 45.

viii 1. *προσκαλεσάμενος τοὺς μαθητάς.* Add probably *αὐτοῦ* with A B W Θ sah syr-sin (African Latin is defective).

ix 14 *ἐλθόντες πρὸς τοὺς μαθητάς.* Here the omission of *αὐτοῦ* is really natural, because three of the apostles were already with our Lord.

x 10, 13 are certainly exceptions to the ordinary usage. Like the other evangelists, Mark it would seem tired of the repetition of *αὐτοῦ*. Perhaps we may also take into account the consideration that *οἱ μαθηταί* at this point of the Gospel has become simply equivalent to 'the Twelve': Mark would never have written, like Luke at the Entry into Jerusalem (xix 37), *ἅπαν τὸ πλῆθος τῶν μαθητῶν*.

x 24 *οἱ δὲ μαθηταί* may simply take up *τοῖς μαθηταῖς αὐτοῦ* of verse 23: but some good authorities actually add *αὐτοῦ*, D Θ 1 Old Latins (including k).

xiv 16 *ἐξῆλθον οἱ μαθηταὶ καὶ ἦλθον.* Not 'the disciples' generally, but the two particular disciples who had been commissioned for the purpose.

v. 'The crowd', or 'the multitudes'. †

ὄχλος (ὄχλοι) is found thirty-seven times in Mark, forty-eight times in Matthew, thirty-nine times in Luke. Allowing for the relative lengths of the three Gospels, the preponderance is clearly with Mark. Thus in the story of Jairus's daughter he uses ὄχλος five times (v 21-31): 'a big crowd gathered', 'a big crowd followed', the woman 'came in the crowd', Jesus 'turned about in the crowd', the disciples remonstrate 'You see the crowd, and yet ... ' Luke reduces the five occasions to three, Matthew (whose compression of the whole episode is unusual even for him) has the word only once.

In Mark the noun is with one exception used in the singular: the crowd is visualized as one, and an ascending scale of adjectives πολύς, ἱκανός, πλεῖστος, defines on occasion its size. The single exception, x 1 συνπορεύονται πάλιν ὄχλοι, perhaps emphasizes the numbers who collected from different directions on the journey through Peraea, where our Lord was known by report but not personally. Matthew, on the other hand, prefers the vaguer and more general plural (thirty-one plural to seventeen singular): Luke uses both indifferently.

Of Mark's adjectives πολύς is of course the commonest, 'a big crowd' (v 21, 24, vi 34, viii 1, ix 14). Matthew, too, has both ὄχλος πολύς and, more commonly, ὄχλοι πολλοί. Luke like Mark prefers the singular, having ὄχλοι πολλοί only with a συν-verb (v 15 συνήρχοντο, xiv 25 [= apparently Mk. x 1] συνεπορεύοντο).

Mark has once ὁ πολὺς ὄχλος, xii 37, where the rendering 'the common people heard him gladly' (A.V.) is probably just what Mark meant.[15]

πλεῖστος ὄχλος once, iv 1, with ℵ B C L Δ : Matthew once (xxi 8) ὁ πλεῖστος ὄχλος.

ὄχλος ἱκανός once, x 46. It is a favourite epithet with Luke, and he employs it with ὄχλος Lk. vii 12, Acts xi 24, 26, xix 26.

πᾶς ὁ ὄχλος ii 13, iv 1, ix 15, xi 18. Matt. xiii 2 (= Mk. iv 1), Lk. vi 19, xiii 17. Note the idiom by which this phrase governs a plural verb, Mk. iv 1 ἦσαν ℵ B C L Δ Θ 33 *d*, ix 15 ἰδόντες ἐξεθάμβησαν ℵ B C D L W Δ (Θ ἰδὼν ἐξεθάμβησαν) *fam.* 1 and *fam.* 13, 28, 33, *a b c d ff i*[16]sah

---

[15]L.S. quote ὁ λεὼς ὁ πολύς from Lucian *Rhet.Praec.* 17.

[16]Vulg. codd. opt. (A F H* Y St Gall) 'stupefactus est expauerunt'. That is to say, either St Jerome had not made up his mind between the two alternatives, or more probably he meant to correct the O.L. expauerunt into the singular stupefactus est, and his amanuensis failed to make his intention clear.

syr-sin, xi 18 *ἐξεπλήσσοντο* ℵ Δ *c* sah syr-sin, Lk. vi 19 ℵ B L W *b e* (1) vulg. sah: i.e. Mark 2 (3) out of 4, Luke 1 out of 2.

For other instances of the same idiom see iii 7, 8 *καὶ πολὺ πλῆθος* ...[17] *πλῆθος πολύ, ἀκούοντες ὅσα ἐποίει, ἦλθον πρὸς αὐτόν* : and perhaps xv 1 where I suspect that a stop should be put after *γραμματέων*, and a fresh clause begin *καὶ ὅλον τὸ συνέδριον δήσαντες τὸν Ἰησοῦν ἀπήνεγκαν*. Luke can use *ὄχλος* or *πλῆθος* of disciples (Lk. vi 17, xix 37): Mark never does. 'Disciples' are always to Mark a limited company.

vi. The word 'to follow', *ἀκολουθεῖν*.†

Ἀκολουθεῖν has of course in all the Gospels the possibility of a metaphorical or spiritual sense, in which the literal sense tends almost to be forgotten. Instances in St Mark are the call of the apostles Simon and Andrew i 18, the call of the rich young man x 21, the summons of Jesus to all who would 'follow him' that they should take up the cross viii 34, the profession of St Peter that he and his fellow-apostles had 'left all and followed him' x 28.

But the notable points about the 'Marcan usage' of *ἀκολουθεῖν* appear to be (i) that the literal sense is in some passages obviously the only one; (ii) that it is not obscurely present in the background in the instances of the metaphorical use — 'to follow about'; (iii) that, with one possible exception in the earlier half of the Gospel, it is not used in narrative of or to the apostles, who did not 'follow' but rather accompanied their Master.

(i) In v 24 'a big crowd followed' Jesus: followed in the literal sense, and when the woman came in the crowd and touched him, she was behind, *ὄπισθεν*. In xi 9 part of the crowd 'goes in front', the other part 'follows behind', *οἱ προάγοντες καὶ οἱ ἀκολουθοῦντες*. In xiv 54 Peter 'followed a long way behind' to the high priest's residence. The verb is once used of the apostles on the journey to Jerusalem, x 32, and there anything but a literal meaning is excluded. Jesus went on ahead, the disciples 'followed' at a distance, and then he took them up again into his company: *ἦσαν ἐν τῇ ὁδῷ ... καὶ ἦν προάγων αὐτοὺς ὁ Ἰησοῦς ... οἱ δὲ ἀκολουθοῦντες ἐφοβοῦντο· καὶ παραλαβὼν πάλιν τοὺς δώδεκα* ... That is

[17] *ἠκολούθησεν* (-*av*) in the editions is I think an insertion from Matthew iv 25 (xii 15): see below. But even if it is genuine, some of the oldest authorities who give the word (ℵ C, followed by Tischendorf) give it in the plural. Luke, who is fond of *πλῆθος*, rarely uses the plural with it (Lk. xix 37), though on two occasions he appears to combine plural and singular, Lk. xxiii 1 *καὶ ἀναστὰν ἅπαν τὸ πλῆθος αὐτῶν ἤγαγον αὐτὸν ἐπὶ τὸν Πειλᾶτον*, Acts xxi 36 *ἠκολούθει τὸ πλῆθος τοῦ λαοῦ κράζοντες*.

to say, their normal position was at his side, he in the midst of them: it was exceptional that they should be behind him.

(ii) Even in the metaphorical use of 'following' Christ as his disciple, the literal sense is often, in St Mark, not far off. When Simon and Andrew are called to 'follow' in i 18, the parallel phrase in i 20 of James and John is *ἀπῆλθον ὀπίσω αὐτοῦ*. If in viii 34 *ὀπίσω μου ἀκολουθείν* (C* D W Θ a b i, against ℵ B c k syr-sin *ὀπίσω μου ἐλθεῖν* with Matthew) is taken as the true text, Mark preserves an indication of the literal meaning in *ὀπίσω μου*. When Bartimaeus was healed of his blindness at the gates of Jericho, x 52, a similar touch of the literal sense is given in the addition 'on the road', *ἀνέβλεψεν καὶ ἠκολούθει αὐτῷ ἐν τῇ ὁδῷ*, a touch omitted by both Matthew and Luke. Negatively it is most instructive to note that Mark never uses *ἀκολουθέω* in the intermediate sense of the crowds 'following' Jesus, more or less as his disciples: for in iii 7 the word *ἠκολούθησεν* (or *ἠκολούθησαν* or *ἠκολούθουν* — the very variations in form, and in the position of the word in the verse, are suspicious) is derived from Matt. iv 25 (xii 15) and is omitted by D 28 124 Old Latins and syr-sin. It was borrowed to ease the construction of the lengthy sentence. On the other hand, Matthew regularly uses *ἀκολουθεῖν* of the multitudes, iv 25, viii 1, (xii 15), xiv 13, xix 2, xx 29; Luke preserves something of the literal sense, vii 9, ix 11, xxiii 29.

(iii) As has been said above, Mark avoids the word *ἀκολουθεῖν* in relation to the apostolic company throughout the latter part of the Gospel: the disciples who were with Jesus were by that time not merely his followers but his companions and friends. *'Ακολουθεῖν* is in fact only used twice of the disciples: in ii 15, on the first mention of *μαθηταί*, we are told that they were now many, and that they were beginning to 'follow him about', *ἦσαν γὰρ πολλοί, καὶ ἠκολούθουν αὐτῷ*; and in vi 1 Jesus *ἔρχεται εἰς τὴν πατρίδα αὐτοῦ καὶ ἀκολουθοῦσιν αὐτῷ οἱ μαθηταὶ αὐτοῦ* — though I do not feel sure that we should not rather here interpret literally, in the sense that they 'followed' at an interval. However that may be, certain it is that in the Gospel as a whole the disciples and their Master are treated as a unit much more definitely than in the other two Synoptists. Mk. iv 36 illustrates this in comparison with Matthew, Mk. ix 38 in comparison with Luke.

In iv 36 it is the disciples who leave (or dismiss) the crowd and take up Jesus into their boat, *ἀφέντες τὸν ὄχλον παραλαμβάνουσιν αὐτὸν* (the same verb as in x 33, 'take into company with them') *ὡς ἦν ἐν τῷ πλοίῳ*. Matthew on the other hand makes Jesus himself dismiss the multitudes, xiii 36 ἀφεὶς τοὺς ὄχλους,[18] and the disciples follow him into the boat, viii 23 ἐμβάντι αὐτῷ εἰς πλοῖον ἠκολούθησαν αὐτῷ οἱ μαθηταὶ αὐτοῦ. And in ix 38 Mark writes that John said 'Master, we saw a man who does not follow us casting out devils in thy name, and we forbade him, because he does not follow us'[19]: but Luke (ix 49) does not like this identification of the 'following' of the disciples with the 'following' of Jesus, and substitutes μεθ' ἡμῶν 'follow with us'. Similar, though in itself less significant, is the change from Mk. xiv 26 ὑμνήσαντες ἐξῆλθον into Lk. xxii 39 ἐξελθὼν ἐπορεύθη ... ἠκολούθησαν δὲ αὐτῷ καὶ οἱ μαθηταί.

Note finally in illustration of St Mark's consistent use of ἀκολουθεῖν that, though it is never used of the apostles (or at any rate never after vi 1), it is used of the holy women in xv 41. While all the apostles 'left him and fled' (xiv 50), there were women watching the Crucifixion from afar, who 'when he was in Galilee used to follow him about and minister to him'. Their 'following' belonged, that is, to the Galilean period of the Ministry: they had not been in his company on the long circuitous journey up to Jerusalem: but they had doubtless come up to the feast in the hope or expectation of seeing him again.

---

[18] Though Huck in his *Synopsis* does not so print it, it is clear that, as Matt. xiii 34, 35 depends on Mk. iv 33, 34, so this opening phrase of Matt. xiii 36 depends on the opening phrase of Mk. iv 36.

[19] The variations of reading in this verse are puzzling (though in itself the repetition of the words οὐκ ἀκολουθεῖ ἡμῖν is quite after Marcan usage), but they do not affect the substantial point, which is that Mark writes 'follow *us*'. That is certain, in spite of the defection of D *a k* sah.

VI – The use of numbers in St Mark's Gospel.

It my firm conviction that the Mark which lay before the later Synoptists, St Matthew and St Luke, was no other than the Mark which we possess. Abstraction has indeed to be made of *various readings* which in the natural course of transmission by scribes may have crept into the text of Mark between its original publication and the particular copies which, ten or twenty years later, lay before the other two evangelists: or again it is conceivable (though not very probable) that the true reading of Mark might in individual cases survive only in Matthew, or in Luke, or in Matthew and Luke, and have been lost in all the direct tradition of manuscripts and versions. But various readings are one thing, recensions are another. And the evidence for an *Ur-Marcus* — that is to say, for an original Mark of which the Gospel we have is a *recension* or new edition — crumbles on examination into nothing.

In the book which is the starting-point of all detailed criticism of the Synoptic problem, Sir John Hawkins's *Horae Synopticae* (ed. 2p. 152) this conclusion is nearly but not quite reached. 'The Petrine source used by the two later Synoptists was not an *Ur-Marcus*, but St Mark's Gospel almost as we have it now. Almost; but not quite. For instance, a later editor's hand is very probably to be seen in ... ' and Sir John proceeds to enumerate nine passages. Now of these nine, three are cases of large numbers, 2,000 (v 13), 200 (vi 37), 300 (xiv 5), all three omitted by both Matthew and Luke, two of them found in St John: and it seems to be suggested that these two may owe their place in our present Mark to the influence of the 'Johannine tradition'.[1]

Therefore it may be useful, so far as these three passages are concerned, to lay the ghost once for all, and to show that it is Marcan usage to note numbers, and Matthaean and Lucan usage to tend to omit them. As we should expect, there is no universal rule to be laid down: sometimes both the two later evangelists retain the detail, but sometimes one omits, sometimes the other, and sometimes both. It is entirely in line with what happens in similar cases that there should be a proportion of

---

[1] I should reverse the argument, and see here proof of the dependence of the Fourth Gospel upon the Second: the numbers are not the only points of contact, and on Sir John's argument ἀγοράσωμεν and φαγεῖν (vi 37 = Jo. vi 5), ἀνέπεσαν and ἄνδρες (vi 40, 44 = Jo. vi 10) ought all to have come into Mark from the 'Johannine tradition'. It must always be borne in mind that for fifty years after its composition St Mark's Gospel was the standard source of the evangelic history. Not only Matthew and Luke but John and Pseudo-Peter as well depend on him.

instances in which their observed habit of omission of numbers should lead both to omit on the same occasion.

That Mark is fond of numerals is then a matter of fact which this instalment of my Notes is intended to prove: and if it is proved, the presumption is that the three doubtful or disputed numbers are genuine also.[2] But that is only one side of the argument. The other side is that the natural tendency of an educated writer of ancient times would be to omit numbers. For that assertion I am glad to be able to base myself on the testimony of Père Hippolyte Delehaye, written down without any reference to the Gospels but therefore the more impartial (I have quoted it once in print, but it will bear quoting again): 'Les procédés de la rhétorique des anciens les amenaient à ne point multiplier les noms de personnes et de lieux, à éviter de donner des chiffres exacts'.[3] Persons, places, numbers: Mark is no rhetorician and is full of all three, Matthew and Luke are in nearer touch with the literary habits and presuppositions of their time, and tend, irregularly no doubt and so in a sense capriciously, to improve on their exemplar by omitting them.

There are certain numbers which refer to significant periods or events of our Lord's life, and these naturally recur in the other Synoptic Gospels:

1. Mark i 13 the 'forty days' of the Temptation: Luke iv 1, 2, Matt. iv 2 (Matthew, however, makes it 'forty days and forty nights' of fasting).

2. Mark viii 31, ix 31, x 34, the prophecies of the Resurrection 'after three days': Matthew and Luke, however (with the Creed-form of St Paul 1 Cor. xv 4), prefer the phrase 'on the third day', Matt. xvi 21, xvii 23, xx 19, Luke ix 22 (in ix 44, parallel to Mark ix 31, he omits all details), xviii 33; just as the printed texts make them, save in Luke xviii 33, prefer *ἐγερθῆναι* (*ἐγερθήσεται*) to Mark's *ἀναστῆναι* (*ἀναστήσεται*).[4]

3. Mark ix 5, the 'three tabernacles' of the Transfiguration, is repeated in Matt. xvii 4, Luke ix 33.

There are also certain numbers which enhance the wonder of the miracles wrought by Christ, and probably for that reason, are retained by Matthew and Luke:

---

[2] I venture here to cite the final sentence of a letter from Sir John Hawkins to myself (under date June 1, 1920): 'What you say about Mark's *constant* fondness for numerals is a weighty argument for the genuineness of the 200 and 300 and 2,000 about which I was doubtful'.

[3] *Saint Martin et Sulpice Sévère* p. 82 (*Analecta Bollandiana* vol. xxxviii, 1920).

[4] B in Matthew ⅔ gives *ἀναστήσεται*. And D latt. in Matt. ⅔ give or represent *μετὰ τρεῖς ἡμέρας*.

4. Mark v 25 the woman who had had 'an issue of blood twelve years': repeated in Matt. ix 20, Luke viii 43.

5. Mark vi 38, 41, 43, 44: viii 2, 5, 6, 8, 9: viii 19, 20. The two accounts of the feeding of the multitude, and the summary reference to them by Christ, are incorporated by Matthew without the omission of any of the numbers which point either to the size of the multitudes (five thousand; four thousand), their long fast on the second occasion (three days), the small amount of provision (five loaves and two fishes; seven loaves and a few tiny fishes) and the large amount that remained over (twelve *κόφινοι*; seven *σπυρίδες*): indeed he adds on each occasion that the numbers of the multitude exclude 'women and children'.[5] Luke of course has only the first account of the feeding: but there he, like Matthew, repeats the five loaves and two fishes, the twelve basketsful, and the five thousand 'men'.

6. The references to 'the Twelve', common in St Mark (iii 14, [15], iv 10, vi 7, ix 35, x 32, xi 11, xiv 10, 17, 20, 43), are rarer in Matthew and Luke, and form a transitional use to their treatment of other numbers given in St Mark. As I discussed this point fully in the last instalment of Notes on Marcan usage (V ii), no more need to be said here than that Matthew never says *οἱ δώδεκα* but only *εἷς τῶν δώδεκα* (twice), *οὗτοι οἱ δώδεκα* (once), *οἱ δώδεκα μαθηταί* (four times), *οἱ δώδεκα ἀπόστολοι* (once), while Luke has *οἱ δώδεκα* five times, *οἱ ἀπόστολοι* four times — in Luke ix 1 it is not certain whether we should read 'the Twelve' or 'the twelve apostles'. In any case 'the Twelve' is characteristically Marcan.

From this point onwards I record Mark's mention of figures in the order in which they are found in his Gospel, including two instances (**8**, **28**: iv 4-8, xiii 35) which illustrate his passion for precision though no actual figures are given.

7. ii 3 *παραλυτικὸν αἰρόμενον ὑπὸ τεσσάρων*. Omitted by both Matthew and Luke, who doubtless considered that it was sufficient to say that the paralytic was brought 'on a bed'.

8. iv 4-8 *ὃ μὲν ἔπεσεν παρὰ τὴν ὁδὸν ... καὶ ἄλλο ἔπεσεν ἐπὶ τὸ πετρῶδες ... καὶ ἄλλο ἔπεσεν εἰς τὰς ἀκάνθας ... καὶ ἄλλα ἔπεσεν εἰς τὴν γῆν τὴν καλὴν ... καὶ ἔφερεν εἰς τριάκοντα καὶ εἰς ἑξήκοντα καὶ εἰς ἑκατόν*. Mark, that is, is careful to make a parallelism between three classes of seed that did not germinate at all, and three that did — that is the meaning of the change from singular to plural — producing respec-

[5] Presumably because Mark vi 44 (cf. John. vi 10) speaks of *πεντακισχίλιοι ἄνδρες*. In Matt. xvi 9, 10 the precise numbers of the *κόφινοι* and *σφυρίδες* are omitted.

tively thirtyfold, sixtyfold, and a hundredfold. Both Matthew and Luke miss the parallelism, and the one gives the plural all through, the other the singular, so that in both the implication is that only one class out of four came to any good, an implication that is definitely absent from St Mark's account.

9. iv 8, 20 *εἰς τριάκοντα καὶ εἰς ἑξήκοντα καὶ εἰς ἑκατόν ... ἐν τριάκοντα καὶ ἐν ἑξήκοντα καὶ ἐν ἑκατόν*.[6] Matt. xiii 8, 23, retains the numbers on both occasions, though on both he inverts their order, 'a hundred', 'sixty', 'thirty': Luke drops all distinction between the three numbers, giving in the parable only 'a hundredfold' and no number at all in the interpretation, viii 8, 15.

10. v 11, 13 *ἀγέλη χοίρων μεγάλη ... ὡς δισχίλιοι*, 'a great herd of swine ... about two thousand'. The number disappears from both the other accounts, Matthew being content with *ἀγέλη χοίρων πολλῶν*, Luke similarly with *ἀγέλη χοίρων ἱκανῶν*. Probably both of them — Luke at any rate — felt that the figure might be thought exaggerated. In fact all Mark's larger cyphers are dropped (apart from those of the miracles of Feeding, see **5** above), such as the 200 *δηνάρια* of **14**, vi 37, or the 300 of **30**, xiv 5, and it is only the smaller ones that have a chance of surviving.

11. v 42 *ἦν γὰρ ἐτῶν δώδεκα*, of the daughter of Jairus. Luke retains the note, but transfers it to the beginning of the story (viii 42), adding that she was an only daughter, *θυγάτηρ μονογενής*. Matthew who reduces the whole episode, like the preceding episode of the demoniac, to the smallest possible compass, omits.

12. vi 7 *ἤρξατο αὐτοὺς ἀποστέλλειν δύο δύο*. Both Matthew and Luke omit the 'two and two': Luke, however, has an equivalent statement in his record of the Mission of the Seventy (or Seventy-two) x 1 *ἀπέστειλεν αὐτοὺς ἀνὰ δύο*, and it might be thought that he has simply transferred it from the one place to the other. But it would seem that it was our Lord's constant habit to send his disciples in pairs: see **22** (xi 1) and **31** (xiv 13) below, and compare the lists of the Twelve in Matt. x 2, Acts i 13. The balance of probability suggests therefore that Luke derived his *ἀνὰ δύο* of the Seventy from his special source at that place: there are other instances where he suppresses in what he borrows from Mark features which he retains in non-Marcan portions of his Gospel. If Dr Streeter is right in his thesis that Luke came across Mark's Gospel when he had already composed the first draft of his own, it is not really surprising that in order to

---

[6] On the reading and interpretation of *εις*, *εν* in these verses, see Note III (9).

provide room for the new material he had to make excisions on a rather drastic scale. One may go further and conjecture that, just because Mark's non-literary Greek offered so many stumbling-blocks to his sense of style, he treated it throughout in a more ruthless temper and altered things that in a source presenting fewer solecisms he might have let pass.

13. vi 9 *μὴ ἐνδύσησθε δύο χιτῶνας*. The detail goes to heighten the ascetic character impressed by our Lord on the preparations for the Missionary journey of the Twelve: and Matthew and Luke, who emphasize this aspect to a still further point than Mark — they agree, according to the critical texts, in refusing the staff which Mark allows[7] — naturally repeat it.

14. vi 37 *ἀπελθόντες ἀγοράσωμεν δηναρίων διακοσίων ἄρτους*; 'Are we to go and spend ten pounds on bread for them?' The naïve question of the disciples seemed a reflection on their faith, and the whole clause disappears in both Matthew and Luke. But the Fourth Evangelist (Jo. vi 7) took it over from Mark , turning it into a statement of fact 'Ten pounds' worth of loaves would not be enough', and putting it into the mouth of Philip. Compare the case of the three hundred *δηνάρια*, **30** below.

15. vi 40 *κατὰ ἑκατὸν καὶ κατὰ πεντήκοντα*. Matthew omits entirely: Luke characteristically omits the higher number and contents himself (ix 14) with *ἀνὰ πεντήκοντα*. It is curious that in the story of Obadiah's hiding the prophets 'by fifties' in the cave, 3 Reg. xviii 4, 13, verse 4 gives the *κατὰ πεντήκοντα* of Mark, verse 13 the *ἀνὰ πεντήκοντα* of Luke.

16. vi 48 *περὶ τετάρτην φυλακὴν τῆς νυκτός*. Matthew keeps the phrase: Lucan parallels fail us till chapter ix of Mark, but see below on no. **28**.

17. viii 14 *εἰ μὴ ἕνα ἄρτον*. 'They had forgotten to bring loaves, and had not more than one loaf with them in the boat.' As so often in the case of Mark's dittographies, Matthew is content with one half of the double phrase, and omits the 'one loaf'.

18. ix 2 *μετὰ ἡμέρας ἕξ*, 'five days after' [i.e. after the Great Confession of viii 29] 'Jesus takes with him Peter and James and John'. Matthew retains the precise date: Luke ix 28 turns it into a round number, 'about a week', *ὡσεὶ ἡμέραι ὀκτώ*.

19. ix 43, 45 *τὰς δύο χεῖρας ... τοὺς δὺο πόδας*. There is no parallel in Luke: in Matthew's abbreviated account (xviii 8) the numerals remain,

---

[7] There is some authority in both Matt. x 10 and Luke ix 3 for *ῥάβδους* in place of *ῥάβδον*. In Luke it is quite inadequate: but in Matthew it includes C L W Δ *a k* and may possibly be right.

the articles disappear; Mark's phrase, however, is good Greek for 'your two hands', 'your two feet'.

20. x 30 *ἑκατονταπλασίονα νῦν ἐν τῷ καιρῷ τούτῳ*. To the other two Synoptists the phrase had a touch of exaggeration about it, and Matthew (xix 29) reduces it to *πολλαπλασίονα*, Luke (xviii 30) to *ἑπταπλασίονα*.[8]

21. x 35, 41 *οἱ δύο ... οἱ δέκα*. The reading *οἱ δύο* is only given by B C 579 and the Egyptian versions: but it is in accordance with 'Marcan usage', and *οἱ δύο ... οἱ δέκα*, 'the two ... the ten', mutually support one another. There is no Lucan parallel: Matthew has 'the ten', but has only 'the sons of Zebedee' without 'two'.

22. xi 1 *ἀποστέλλει δύο τῶν μαθητῶν αὐτοῦ*. So Matthew and Luke: but contrast Matthew in no. **31**. As I have suggested on no. **12** above, it seems to have been our Lord's regular custom to send out his disciples in pairs.

23. xii 20, 21 *ἑπτὰ ἀδελφοὶ ἦσαν· καὶ ὁ πρῶτος ἔλαβεν γυναῖκα ...καὶ ὁ δεύτερος ἔλαβεν ...καὶ ὁ τρίτος ὡσαύτως· καὶ οἱ ἑπτὰ οὐκ ἀφῆκαν σπέρμα*. The numerals are an integral element of the point of the problem put to our Lord, and so both the other accounts retain them all.

[24]. xii 42 *μία χήρα πτωχὴ ἔβαλεν* ... Matthew omits the episode: Luke substitutes *τινὰ χήραν πενιχράν*. I have put this instance in brackets, because Luke clearly regarded *μία* not as the numeral but as in effect the indefinite article: and in this I believe he interpreted Mark correctly. Mark's style is so naMve that it is not probable that he meant to emphasize any contrast between *πολλοί πλούσιοι* and *μία πτωχή*, any more than between *μία χήρα* and *λεπτὰ δύο*. There were 'plenty of rich people', and then there was 'a poor widow'. Mark is fond of *εἷς* (generally with a following genitive [9]), and Luke almost invariably changes it to *τις*. Just as in late Latin and in the Romance languages, so in Greek also (in the *κοινή* and in modern Greek), the place of an indefinite article came gradually to be supplied by the numeral 'one'.

---

[8] I follow Burkitt (*Gospel History and its Transmission* p. 50) in reading 'sevenfold' in Luke with D Old Latins (including St Cyprian and Jovinian) and perhaps the Diatessaron. St Jerome *adv. Jovin.* ii 19, 26 asserted that Jovinian, for reading *septies*, 'aut falsarii aut imperitiae reum teneri': the question now is whether the tables should not be turned.

[9] In two or three cases Mark has *εἷς ἐκ*, ix 17 *εἷς ἐκ τοῦ ὄχλου*, xiv 18 *εἷς ἐξ ὑμῶν*, and according to some authorities in xiv 20 *εἷς [ἐκ] τῶν δώδεκα*. I think this is one of Mark's latinisms: and as *unus ex (de)* is the only possible rendering in Latin of *εἷς* with a following genitive, it is futile of editors to cite the Latins, where *ἐκ* is doubtful in the Greek.

25. xii 42 *ἔβαλεν λεπτὰ δύο, ὅ ἐστιν κοδράντης*. Luke xxi 2 keeps the 'two mites' (omitting Mark's parenthetical explanation for his Roman readers, 'which are a farthing'), because the story turns on it.

[26]. xiii 2 *καὶ διὰ τριῶν ἡμερῶν ἄλλος ἀναστήσεται ἄνευ χειρῶν*. A 'Western' reading of D W and O.L., depending on xiv 58 xv 29: hardly genuine, or why should both Matthew and Luke have omitted it?

27. xiii 27 *ἐπισυνάξει ... ἐκ τῶν τεσσάρων ἀνέμων*. The 'four winds' are simply a variation of the proverbial 'four quarters' of the earth, north, south, east and west. The phrase is taken from Zach. ii 6 (10) and is copied by Matthew xxiv 31: Luke omits the whole verse.

28. xiii 35 *ἢ ὀψὲ ἢ μεσονύκτιον ἢ ἀλεκτοροφωνίας ἢ πρωΐ*. A popular way of representing the four watches (cf.'the fourth watch', no. **16** above), into which Roman usage divided the twelve hours of the night, so as to secure that no guard should be on watch for more than three hours: Vegetius *de re militari* p. 83, quoted by Blass (I owe the ref. to Swete *ad loc.*) on Acts xii 4. Matthew omits the details: when Luke writes (xii 38) 'whether in the second or in the third watch', he may be meaning to suggest the two central watches, i.e. the darkest hours, or he may be reproducing the Jewish terminology of three watches, the second being *φυλακὴ μέση* (Judges vii 19), the third *φυλακὴ πρωΐα* (Ps. cxxix [cxxx] 6).

29. xiv 1 *ἦν δὲ τὸ πάσχα καὶ τὰ ἄζυμα μετὰ δύο ἡμέρας*. Matthew retains the phrase: Luke paraphrases with *ἤγγιζεν*. If *μετὰ τρεῖς ἡμέρας* means — see Field's admirable note on Matt. xvi 21 — nothing else than *τῇ τρίτῃ ἡμέρᾳ*, i.e. as we should say 'after two days', it follows that *μετὰ δύο ἡμέρας* must be equivalent to *τῇ δευτέρᾳ ἡμέρᾳ* (if that phrase were used), and mean 'next day'. The only exact parallel appears to be Hosea vi 2 *ὑγιάσει ἡμᾶς μετὰ δύο ἡμέρας, ἐν τῇ ἡμέρᾳ τῇ τρίτῃ ἐξαναστησόμεθα* (quoted by Tertullian *adv. Marcionem* iv 43); for if, as Field assumes, the healing and the rising up refer to successive days, *μετὰ δύο ἡμέρας* must there again mean 'next day'. I do not feel entirely clear about this: but there is no real doubt as to the day of the week which Mark intends in this passage to identify. For in verse 12 the day before the Crucifixion, that is the Thursday, is called 'the first day of unleavened bread, when they sacrificed the Passover': by Roman reckoning the lambs were slain on the same day that they were eaten, and on that day the leavened bread would be cleared away and unleavened bread substituted, and it is Roman reckoning which Mark follows — by Jewish reckoning the lambs were slain on the afternoon of the 13th Nisan, and, a new day beginning at sunset, they were eaten on the evening of the 14th. But if the events of Thursday commence with xiv 12, then xiv 1-11 are the events of Wednesday at latest. But of Wednesday too at earliest, if tradition following the Fourth Gospel rightly places the Triumphal Entry on Palm Sunday: for xi 12 refers then to the morning of Monday, and xi 20 to the morning of Tuesday. The new day of xiv 1 can therefore only be Wednesday.

30. xiv 5 *ἠδύνατο τοῦτο τὸ μύρον πραθῆναι ἐπάνω δηναρίων τριακοσίων*. The figure was large, £12 or so, and no doubt seemed exaggerated: Matthew omits it, and there is nothing to correspond to it in Luke's account of an anointing (vii 36-50). But the Fourth Gospel (John xii 5) — just as with the 200 *δηνάρια* at the Feeding of the multitude, no.**14** above — follows Mark and retains it.

31. xiv 13 *ἀποστέλλει δύο τῶν μαθητῶν αὐτοῦ*. Mark once more notes (see nos. **12** and **22** above) that disciples were sent in pairs: Matthew, as in no. **12**, omits, Luke xxii 8, presumably from independent knowledge, inserts the names, Peter and John.

[32]. xiv 20 *ὁ ἐμβαπτόμενος μετ᾽ ἐμοῦ εἰς τὸ ἓν τρύβλιον*. So B C* ? Θ 565: the rest omit *εν*, and I think it may represent a marginal variant *ἐν* for *εἰς* (from Matthew xxvi 23 *ἐν τῷ τρυβλίῳ*). Therefore I have put it within brackets, for in that case it has no bearing on our problem, not being a numeral. But if *ἕν* is right, Matthew omits it: Luke has nothing strictly parallel.

33. xiv 30, 68, 72*a*, 72*b* (the two cock-crowings and three denials) *σήμερον ταύτῃ τῇ νυκτὶ πρὶν ἢ δὶς ἀλέκτορα φωνῆσαι τρίς με ἀπαρνήσῃ ... καὶ ἐξῆλθεν ἔξω εἰς τὸ προαύλιον* [*καὶ ἀλέκτωρ ἐφώνησεν*] *...καὶ εὐθὺς ἐκ δευτέρου ἀλέκτωρ ἐφώνησεν· καὶ ἀνεμνήσθη ὁ Πέτρος τὸ ῥῆμα ...ὅτι Πρὶν ἀλέκτορα δὶς φωνῆσαι τρίς με ἀπαρνήσῃ*. Admittedly all three Synoptists record a triple denial: admittedly Mark, and Mark only, speaks of a second cock-crowing. But so strong was the reciprocal influence exerted by the later accounts on the text of Mark that not many authorities in St Mark other than the Syrian recension (the *Textus Receptus*) give all four references to the second crowing, and one first class authority, ℵ (with 579 and *c*) omits it on all four occasions. (1) Verse 30: *om δίς* ℵ C* D W 579 *a c ff i k* arm aeth. (2) verse 68: *om καὶ ἀλέκτωρ ἐφώνησεν* ℵ B L W Ψ* 579 *c* syr-sin sah. (3) verse 72*a*: *om ἐκ δευτέρου* ℵ L 579 *c*. (4) verse 72*b*: *om δίς* ℵ C* W Δ Σ 579 *c* aeth. Our best authorities (B D the chief Old Latins syr-sin sah) all give three out of the four references: but they differ as to the one they omit, for B syr-sin sah have the first, third, and fourth, D and the Old Latins give the second, third, and fourth. Thus the third and fourth references are above cavil: the first is implied by the fourth, and it is further an observed rule[10] that scribes are more prone to the influence of their prejudices — in this case to the influence of the parallel accounts — on a first occasion, but defer to the authority of their exemplar if the reading they have tampered with recurs once again or oftener: only about the second can there be any doubt. Here ℵ B omit, and Westcott and Hort do not even give *καὶ ἀλέκτωρ ἐφώνησεν* a place in the margin. Tischendorf, against ℵ B, puts the words in the text, and I am sure he is right. The evidence of ℵ L W 579 *c* — five witnesses for omission out of the nine — is nearly worthless, since they omit on one or more of the other occasions: the documents of the Sahidic version are divided, see Horner *ad loc.*: so that B Ψ* syr-sin are the only unimpeachable authorities for omission. But it must not be forgotten that the influence of the parallel accounts, in the case of a complete statement like *καὶ ἀλέκτωρ ἐφώνησεν*, which could be simply dropped without apparent injury to the context, would be powerful for omission. And if ever internal evidence is allowed the decisive word, it guarantees (as I think) the genuineness of the phrase in dispute. I cannot believe that any other than the Evangelist put in the dramatic touch which is needed for the development of the story.

34. xiv 41 *καὶ ἔρχεται τὸ τρίτον*. Mark does not mention that our Lord went away and prayed a third time, though of course he implies it; but because his story is told, here as elsewhere, from the point of view of the disciples' experience he does mention his third coming to the disciples. Matthew xxvi 44 fills up what Mark implies, and transfers 'the third time' to Christ's prayer. Luke omits the repeated coming and going, and concentrates the whole story into one withdrawal and one return.

35. xiv 58 *ἠκούσαμεν αὐτοῦ λέγοντος ὅτι Ἐγὼ καταλύσω τὸν ναὸν τοῦτον τὸν χειροποίητον καὶ διὰ τριῶν ἡμερῶν ἄλλον ἀχειροποίητον οἰκοδομήσω*, and xv 29 *Οὐὰ ὁ καταλύων τὸν ναὸν καὶ οἰκοδομῶν* [*ἐν*] *τρισὶν ἡμέραις* (cf. xiii 2, no. **26** above, if the reading were genuine) Matthew retains, both at the trial and at the Crucifixion, doubtless because of the reference to the Resurrection: Luke omits the whole episode of the 'false witness'.

36. xv 1, 25, 33, 34 *πρωὶ συμβούλιον ποιήσαντες ...ἦν δὲ ὥρα τρίτη καὶ ἐσταύρωσαν αὐτόν ...καὶ γενομένης ὥρας ἕκτης σκότος ἐγένετο ἐφ' ὅλην τὴν γῆν ἕως ὥρας ἐνάτης. καὶ τῇ ἐνάτῃ ὥρᾳ ἐβόησεν ὁ Ἰησοῦς φωνῇ μεγάλῃ.* Only Mark enumerates the synchronisms of all the four

---

[10] See Wordsworth in the *Epilogus* to the Vulgate Gospels, p. 727 'saepe enim scribae quod primo loco pro mendo habebant, secundo pro nero agnoscunt'.

watches of Good Friday: both Matthew and Luke omit the notice of the third hour.[11]

Of these thirty cases (nos. **7** to **36**) I put aside three, nos. **24**, **26**, and **32**: there remain twenty-seven. Three times only out of this total, **13**, **22**, **23**, do both Matthew and Luke retain the numbers; but in order to be scrupulously fair I add on the same side the three occasions on which Matthew retains when there is no Lucan parallel, **16**, **19**, **27**, and the one occasion where Luke retains when there is no Matthaean parallel, **25**. Against these we have to set seven passages where both omit numbers, **7**, (**8**), **10**, **12**, **14**, **33**, **36**, and one where both bring the number down, **20**, as well as three passages where Matthew omits but there is no parallel in Luke, **17**, **21**, **30**. In the nine remaining instances one or other of the later Synoptists fails to reproduce the precision of Mark: in four, **11**, **15**, **28**, **31**, Matthew omits while Luke retains, in four more, **9**, **29**, **34**, **35**, Luke omits while Matthew retains, and in one, **18**, Luke changes a precise number to a round one.

That is to say, it is more common for both of them to omit than for both of them to retain a number given in Mark: and it is vastly more common (about three times in four) for one or other of them to omit a number than for both of them to retain it.

This clear and decisive result (as I think) tallies with a feature noticed in the last section of the Notes on Marcan usage (V), namely the ascending scale of adjectives with which Mark is careful on different occasions to estimate the size of the crowd.

As a result of our enquiry, it is not too much to say that the suggestion that some of the numbers in Mark are not original because both Matthew and Luke omit them cannot maintain itself in face of the argument from Marcan usage. One more nail has been driven into the coffin of that old acquaintance of our youth, *Ur-Marcus*. He did enough harm in his time, but he is dead and gone: let no attempts be made to disinter his skeleton.

---

[11] The Fourth Gospel has *ἦν δὲ πρωί* xviii 28, *ὥρα ἦν ὡς ἕκτη* xix 14, but I forbear to discuss the difficulty here

VII - Particles

(1) Ὅτι interrogative.†

1. ii 7 *διαλογιζόμενοι ἐν ταῖς καρδίαις αὐτῶν Ὅτι οὗτος οὕτως λαλεῖ; βλασφημεῖ.*

Matthew gives simply *οὗτος βλασφημεῖ*, and so probably read *ὅτι* in Mark, understanding it as = 'that'. So B Θ and W-H margin: *τί* the rest.

2. ii 16 *ἔλεγον τοῖς μαθηταῖς αὐτοῦ Ὅτι μετὰ τῶν τελωνῶν καὶ ἁμαρτωλῶν ἐσθίει;*

τί ὅτι A C Δ etc., *διὰ τί* ℵ D W with Matthew and Luke. Both these readings are obvious attempts to get rid of the difficulty of *ὅτι* interrogative. The modern editors give *ὅτι*.

3. viii 12 *καὶ ἀναστενάξας τῷ πνεύματι αὐτοῦ λέγει Ὅτι ἡ γενεὰ αὕτη ζητεῖ σημεῖον;*

So C, and Origen *Selecta in Ezech.* xiv 20[1] (Delarue iii p. 429) *ὁ Κύριος ἐν τῷ κατὰ Μάρκον εὐαγγελίῳ Ὅτι ἡ γενεὰ αὕτη σημεῖον ἐπιζητεῖ;* The rest have *τί*. Matthew and Luke both make it a statement, not a question, and if they drew on Mark must have read *ὅτι*: but if, as is probable, they drew here from Q, no argument of course can be drawn from their phraseology.

4. ix 11 *καὶ ἐπηρώτων αὐτὸν λέγοντες Ὅτι λέγουσιν οἱ γραμματεῖς ὅτι Ἠλείαν δεῖ ἐλθεῖν πρῶτον;*

The Ferrar group for *ὅτι* substitutes *πῶς οὖν*: the Ethiopic omits. The Old Latin MSS vary between *quare, quid, quia*, but all imply *ὅτι*. Matthew has *τί οὖν*;

5. ix 28 *οἱ μαθηταὶ αὐτοῦ κατ' ἰδίαν ἐπηρώτων αὐτόν Ὅτι ἡμεῖς οὐκ ἠδυνήθημεν ἐκβαλεῖν αὐτό;*

Matthew has *διὰ τί* (Luke has no parallel), and *διὰ τί* is read in Mark by A D and others, while a few authorities have *ὅτι διὰ τί* and a few *τί ὅτι*. There can be no doubt that *ὅτι* is original in Mark.

Here are three certain cases of *ὅτι* as the direct interrogative, and two more probable ones — probable because in each case there are two good authorities in support, and the tendency to get rid of the construction was so obvious (neither Matthew nor Luke ever accepts it), and the change so easy, that I have no hesitation in accepting the evidence of B Θ and C Origen respectively on those two occasions.

I add two instances of what I take to be a similar employment of *ὅτι* as the *indirect* interrogative in Mark.

---

[1] In *Nouum Testamentum S. Irenaei* p. clxxiii (on Rom. iv 3) the reference is wrongly given as xv 20.

6. viii 16, 17 *καὶ διελογίζοντο πρὸς ἀλλήλους ὅτι ἄρτους οὐκ ἔχουσιν; καὶ γνοὺς λέγει αὐτοῖς Τί διαλογίζεσθε ὅτι ἄρτους οὐκ ἔχετε;*

I think this means 'they discussed with another why they had no loaves': after *διαλογίζομαι* we expect a reference to the question discussed. Matthew, who dislikes (as we have seen) *ὅτι interrogativum,* has to insert *λέγοντες* to make it *ὅτι recitativum.*

7. xiv 60 *καὶ ἀναστὰς ὁ ἀρχιερεὺς εἰς μέσον ἐπηρώτησεν τὸν Ἰησοῦν λέγων Οὐκ ἀποκρίνῃ οὐδὲν ὅτι οὗτοί σου καταμαρτυροῦσιν;*

Ὅτι is read by L W Ψ and (according to Buttmann's edition of B and Huck's *Synopsis* [2]) by B also. It is supported by the Latins *a c ff k q* Vulg., who make no break after *οὐδέν* but construct the whole of the high priest's words as one question and not two. In that case *ὅτι* can only be the indirect interrogative.

Now *ὅτι* as indirect interrogative can be supported by good classical authority, as Field shews (*Notes on the Translation of N.T.* p. 33) on Mark ix 11; and therefore the last two passages are only cited here to shew that the construction was familiar to, and used by, Mark. It is otherwise with the direct interrogative: and the Revised Version makes a bold attempt to get rid of it, in the three passages (**2**, **4**, **5** above) where external evidence compels us to read *ὅτι*, by translating *ὅτι* 'that'. It needs only to cite their renderings to shew their futility.[3]

2. ii 16 'The scribes of the Pharisees ... said unto his disciples He eateth and drinketh with publicans and sinners'.

4. ix 11 'And they asked him, saying, The scribes say that Elijah must first come'.

5. ix 28 'His disciples asked him privately, *saying,* We could not cast it out'.

Of these three renderings in the text of R.V. (there is a relative return to sanity in the margin in each case) the first makes just tolerable sense, the other two are quite impossible, or in Field's language 'simply intolerable'. Classical prepossessions must be frankly thrown overboard when they lead us to such an *impasse*. Even if no authority could be found outside St Mark for the direct interrogative use of *ὅτι*, Field is certainly right that 'these two instances, occurring in the same chapter of

---

[2] I have taken the opportunity to verify the point by reference to the photographic edition of cod. Vaticanus: the reading *ὅτι* is quite clear, and Tischendorf is wrong (how rarely, all things considered, that happens!) in omitting its testimony. W-H read *τί* in the text, *ὅτι* in the margin.

[3] It should be noted that all three passages are rightly punctuated as interrogative in Westcott and Hort.

St Mark, must be held mutually to support and sanction each other'. [Cf. A. T. Robertson *Grammar of the Greek N.T.* p. 729, J. H. Moulton *Prolegomena* p. 94 l. 3.]

But it is the main object of this instalment of my Notes to produce outside authority. The first of the following citations comes from Field. LXX. 1 Chron. xvii 6 *εἰ λαλῶν ἐλάλησα πρὸς μίαν φυλὴν τοῦ Ἰσραὴλ τοῦ ποιμαίνειν τὸν λαόν μου λέγων Ὅτι οὐκ ᾠκοδομήκατέ μοι οἶκον κέδρινον*: So both A.V. and R.V. 'Why ... ', so too Lagarde's Lucianic text, *Διὰ τί ...* ; So Tischendorf's LXX: and it can only be considered another freak of judgement if the Cambridge small LXX text prints *λέγων ὅτι Οὐκ ...*

1. *Hermas* Similitudes

Of the four passages which follow the first two are from the printed texts, the last two depend on the testimony of the newly discovered papyrus (said to be of the third century) belonging to the University of Ann Arbor, Michigan. I am indebted to the generosity of Prof.Campbell Bonner of that University, who is in charge of the publication of the text, for my knowledge of the readings of this most important witness: in his article in the *Harvard Theological Review* for April 1925 he has himself called attention to the passage where the interrogative *ὅτι* is direct, *Sim.* VIII 6. 2.

Sim. II 10 *μακάριοι οἱ ... συνιέντες ὅτι παρὰ τοῦ κυρίου πλουτίζονται.* In the Palatine version 'felices qui ... sentiunt quomodo a domino locupletantur': though the older 'vulgate' version mistranslates it 'sentiunt se locupletari'.

Sim. V 6.4 *ὅτι δὲ ὁ κύριος σύμβουλον ἔλαβε τὸν υἱὸν αὐτοῦ καὶ τοὺς ἐνδόξους ἀγγέλους ... ἄκουε*: rightly rendered by both Latin versions 'quare autem dominus in consilio adhibuerit ('in consilium adhibuit' Pal.) filium honestosque nuntios ... audi'.[4]

Sim. VIII 1.4 (according to the new papyrus) *ἀφὲς δέ, φησί, πάντα ἴδῃς, καὶ δηλωθήσεταί σοι ὅτι ἐστίν.* Latin versions 'exspecta et [+ 'cum uniuersa uideris' Pal.] tunc demonstrabitur tibi quid significet'. Our other Greek authority, the late and bad Athos MS, has *τὸ τί* for *ὅτι*.

Sim. VIII 6. 2 (according to the new papyrus) *Ὅτι οὖν, φημί, κύριε, πάντες οὐ μετενόησαν;* Latins 'Quare ergo, domine, [+ 'inquam' Pal.] non omnes egerunt paenitentiam?' The Athos MS has corrupted *ὅτι* into

---

[4] In the printed texts of the Vulgate version of Hermas the sentence is hopelessly confused and corrupt: I give the reading of the best MS, Bodl. Laud. misc. 488.

οὗτοι, doubtless because the scribe of the MS or its exemplar was puzzled by *ὅτι interrogativum.*

Hermas then in a corrected text comes to the support of St Mark, and the Latin translator understood him rightly. It might be a profitable topic to compare the Greek of Hermas with the Greek of Mark in some detail: on the present occasion it must suffice to call attention to the parallel between the *συμπόσια συμπόσια* of Mark vi 39 and the *τάγματα τάγματα* (supported by both the Athos MS and the new papyrus) of *Sim.* VIII 2.8 *ἦλθον τάγματα τάγματα, καὶ ἐπεδίδουν τὰς ῥάβδους τῷ ποιμένι.* Shall we be told that 'the construction' in Hermas 'is Hebraistic'?

2. *Barnabas* Epistle.

To Tischendorf's note on Mark ii 16 I owe three references to Barnabas for the construction of *ὅτι* interrogative.

vii 9 *προσέχετε· Τὸν μὲν ἕνα ἐπὶ τὸ θυσιαστήριον, τὸν δὲ ἕνα ἐπικατάρατον. καὶ ὅτι τὸν ἐπικατάρατον ἐστεφανωμένον; ἐπειδὴ ὄψονται αὐτὸν* ... The editors do not mark a question: but the old Latin version has 'et quare is qui maledictus coronatus?'

viii 5 *ὅτι δὲ τὸ ἔριον ἐπὶ τὸ ξύλον; ὅτι ἡ βασιλεία Ἰησοῦ ἐπὶ ξύλου.* Latin 'quare ergo et lana in ligno est?'

x 1 *ὅτι δὲ Μωϋσῆς εἶπεν· Οὐ φάγεσθε χοῖρον* ...; *τρία ἔλαβεν ἐν τῇ συνέσει δόγματα.* Latin 'quare autem Moyses dicit ... ?'

Of these three passages only the second is quite certainly interrogative: but it establishes Barnabas' use of the construction, and the translator's witness is clear.

But Barnabas and Hermas are not the only early Christian authors whose translators were familiar with the construction of *ὅτι* interrogative, and indeed it has been introduced into contexts where it is probably or certainly alien to the intention of the original writer. The evidence to be cited is, however, valid as shewing that in the circles in which early translators moved — possibly we ought to paraphrase this as 'in early Roman Christian circles' — the construction belonged to the Greek with which they were familiar.

3. The earliest Latin version of the Gospels.

The earliest version known to us is that represented by *k* and St Cyprian. It emerges, that is to say, in Africa about A.D. 250: but it was doubtless half a century older than that, and it may well have been brought to Africa from Rome.

Matt. vii 13, 14 ap.Cypr.*Testimonia* iii 6 (Hartel i p. 119): 'De hoc ipso cata Mattheum Quid lata et spatiosa uia est quae ducit ad interitum ... quid arta et angusta uia est quae ducit ad uitam?' The reading *quid* is guaranteed by the best manuscripts, V L P B R T U (Bodl. Laud. misc. 105, s. x ineunt.) X* (Rylands-Crawford MS s. viii). It corresponds to the Greek *ὅτι πλατεῖα καὶ εὐρύχωρος ἡ ὁδὸς ἡ ἀπάγουσα εἰς τὴν ἀπώλειαν, ... ὅτι στενὴ καὶ τεθλιμμένη ἡ ὁδὸς ἡ ἀπάγουσα εἰς τὴν ζωήν*, and the only possible explanation is that the translator, however mistakenly, took the sentence as interrogative, and *ὅτι* as a particle of interrogation.[5]

4. *St Irenaeus* adv.hereses.

In two passages the Latin translator has used *quid* where the Greek had either certainly, as in the first of the two, or possibly, as in the second of the two, *ὅτι*. In the second passage, the Greek, whether *τί* or *ὅτι*, was intended to be interrogative; in the first the interrogation is a misrendering by the translator.

III xxxi [xxii] 2 *'Nec dixisset Quid tristis est anima mea*?' Matt. xxvi 38 (Ps. xli [xlii] 5). The Greek happens to be preserved in Theodoret's Dialogue *Ἄτρεπτος*: *Οὐδ' ἂν εἰρήκει ὅτι περίλυπός ἐστιν ἡ ψυχή μου*. There is no *ὅτι* in the text of St Matthew, but in the Psalm we have *ἵνα τί περίλυπος* ... and so the translator was led to render *εἰρήκει ὅτι* by 'said why' rather than by 'said that'. For though the Latin MSS are divided between *quid, quia, quod,* the best MS (C) has *quid*, and *quid* best explains the genesis of the other two, *quia* and *quod*: it must therefore be presumed that the Latin translator took *Ὅτι περίλυπός ἐστιν*; as a question, and *ὅτι* as the interrogative particle.

IV x 1 [v 3] 'Quid enim *credidit Abraham Deo et deputatem est ei ad iustitiam*? Primum quidem quoniam ipse est factor caeli et terrae, solus Deus: deinde autem quoniam faciet semen eius quasi stellas caeli'. Here St Irenaeus' meaning is clearly 'What was it that Abraham believed and it was counted to him for righteousness?' And the answer he gives appears to shew that he is thinking not of Rom. iv 3 at all (as the editors of Irenaeus followed by the *N.T.S. Irenaei* have assumed) but directly of Gen. xv 6, and that therefore the *Quid enim* that introduces the quotation has nothing to do with the *τί γὰρ ἡ γραφὴ λέγει*; of Rom. iv 3. But the Armenian version of Irenaeus has, corresponding to *Quid enim,* 'And that'. Since we have found reason to think that the Latin translator was

---

[5] I have no doubt that the reading of *k* 'quia data' is a corruption of 'quid lata'

acquainted with the idiom ὅτι = 'why?', it is natural to reconcile the apparent discrepancy between the two versions by supposing that Irenaeus wrote ὅτι ἐπίστευσεν and that one translator rendered 'what?', and the other 'that'. If so, as the sentence is certainly interrogative, St Irenaeus himself must have employed the interrogative ὅτι. But while I have no sort of doubt that Mark and Barnabas and Hermas and Latin translators of early Greek Christian writings used (or rendered) that construction, I should hesitate to place Irenaeus in the same category, and I think it more likely that the ὅτι which lay before the Armenian translator was a corruption of τί.

Ὅτι interrogative belongs to a different stratum of society, not to the writers of literary Greek, but to less cultivated Christian circles such as those which in the first and second centuries after Christ still talked Greek in the capital. Is it an accident that of the writings cited in this note Mark and Hermas certainly, in all probability the first translations of the Gospels and of Hermas, and posssibly the translations of Barnabas and Irenaeus, were produced in the Church of Rome?

(2) Ὅτι recitative (after λέγειν or similar verbs).

Much more common in St Mark than the odd use of ὅτι interrogative, is the idiom of a superfluous ὅτι after the verb 'to say' or the like, introducing not the *oratio obliqua*, as we should expect, but the *oratio recta*. In the large majority of cases, as will be seen, Matthew and (where a parallel is extant) Luke, drop the particle.

I proceed to catalogue some forty instances.

1. i 14, 15 *κηρύσσων τὸ εὐαγγέλιον τοῦ θεοῦ [καὶ] λέγων ὅτι Πεπλήρωται ὁ καιρὸς ... μετανοεῖτε καὶ πιστεύετε ...* Ὅτι is undisputed in Mark, and disappears in Matthew: there is no Lucan parallel. What is doubtful in Mark is λέγων which is omitted by Tischendorf and by W-H margin. But the authorities for omission are quite inadequate (א* Origen *c* syr-sin), and the constant use of λέγων in the passages to be cited in this list is practically decisive of Marcan usage.

2. i 37 *καί εὗρον αὐτὸν καὶ λέγουσιν αὐτῷ ὅτι Πάντες ζητοῦσίν σε.* No parallel in Matthew or Luke.

3. i 40 *λέγων αὐτῷ ὅτι Ἐὰν θέλῃς, δύνασαί με καθαρίσαι.* Is dropped by both the other Synoptists. Their influence has caused it to disappear from many authorities in Mark, including C D L W Θ 28 and most Latins: but it has rightly survived in א A B Δ *a*.

4. ii 12 *ὥστε ἐξίστασθαι πάντας καὶ δοξάζειν τὸν θεὸν λέγοντας ὅτι Οὕτως οὐδέποτε εἴδαμεν.* Matthew alters the last half of the clause and omits ὅτι: Luke retains. In Mark λέγοντας is omitted by B W *b*: but the combined evidence of Luke and of Marcan usage is too strong to be overthrown even by B.

5. ii 17 λέγει αὐτοῖς ὅτι Οὐ χρείαν ἔχουσιν οἱ ἰσχύοντες ἰατροῦ ... οὐκ ἦλθον καλέσαι δικαίους. Both Matthew and Luke omit ὅτι: and in this familiar saying of our Lord their texts have exercised even more than their usual disintegrating influence on the authorities for Mark: but ὅτι is rightly retained by B Δ Θ 565.

6. iii 11 τὰ πνεύματα τὰ ἀκάθαρτα ... ἔκραζον λέγοντες ὅτι Σὺ εἶ ὁ υἱὸς τοῦ θεοῦ. No parallel in Matthew: Luke, as in **4**, retains λέγοντα ὅτι (iv 41), though λέγοντες, not λέγοντα, must I think be right in Mark. There is the same mixture of masculine and neuter in the story of the demoniac in Mark v 10-13: and the change by scribes of λέγοντες to λέγοντα is far more probable than the converse one. λέγοντες is read only by ℵ D W 69 and a very few others, followed by Tischendorf and W-H margin.

***7**. iii 21 ἔλεγον γὰρ ὅτι Ἐξέστη. There is no parallel in the other Synoptists. But for Marcan usage, we could of course treat ἐξέστη as *oratio obliqua*. [I mark with an asterisk this single instance of past tense after λέγειν ὅτι].

8. iii 22 ἔλεγον ὅτι Βεελζεβοὺλ ἔχει, καὶ ὅτι Ἐν τῷ ἄρχοντι τῶν δαιμονίων ἐκβάλλει τὰ δαιμόνια. Both Matthew and Luke have εἶπον without ὅτι: in Mark only D omits.

[**9**. iii 28 ἀμὴν λέγω ὑμῖν ὅτι Πάντα ἀφεθήσεται τοῖς υἱοῖς τῶν ἀνθρώπων ... Matthew omits ὅτι: Luke has no parallel. No authorities omit in Mark . I place within square brackets those instances where ὅτι follows ἀμὴν λέγω ὑμῖν, since Matthew towards the end of his Gospel not infrequently retains ὅτι in this connexion, see on **34**: so too Luke in **32**, **34**.]

10. iv 21 καὶ ἔλεγεν αὐτοῖς ὅτι Μήτι ἔρχεται ὁ λύχνος ἵνα ὑπὸ τὸν μόδιον τεθῇ, No parallel in Matthew: and the introductory words as far as ὅτι are dropped in Luke. Most authorities in Mark omit ὅτι: the Ferrar group substitutes ἴδετε: for ὅτι we have B L 892 sah and Marcan usage.

11. v 23 καὶ παρακαλεῖ αὐτὸν πολλὰ, λέγων ὅτι Τὸ θυγάτριόν μου ἐσχάτως ἔχει. Matthew omits ὅτι: Luke changes the construction. In Mark some westerns — D and the Ferrar group: so too the best Old Latins, but in such cases versions must be cited with caution, or perhaps not at all, because the earliest translators rendered with some regard to the genius of their own language — wrongly omit ὅτι.

12. v 28 ἔλεγεν γὰρ ὅτι Ἐὰν ἅψωμαι κἂν τῶν ἱματίων αὐτοῦ, σωθήσομαι. Matthew omits ὅτι: Luke is not strictly parallel. In Mark only 28 and 33 of Greek MSS omit.

13. v 35 *ἔρχονται ἀπὸ τοῦ ἀρχισυναγώγου λέγοντες ὅτι Ἡ θυγάτηρ σου ἀπέθανεν.* Matthew has no parallel: Luke retains the *ὅτι*, as do all our authorities in Mark.

14. vi 4 *καὶ ἔλεγεν αὐτοῖς ὁ Ἰησοῦς ὅτι Οὐκ ἔστιν προφήτης ἄτιμος εἰ μὴ ἐν τῇ πατρίδι αὐτοῦ.* Matthew again omits: no Lucan parallel. In Mark only Δ and the Ferrar group, with a few others, omit.

15. vi 14, 15 *ἔλεγον ὅτι Ἰωάνης ὁ βαπτίζων ἐγήγερται ἐκ νεκρῶν ... ἄλλοι δὲ ἔλεγον ὅτι Ἠλείας ἐστίν· ἄλλοι δὲ ἔλεγον ὅτι Προφήτης ...* Matthew has no parallel to verses 14 and 15: Luke, as in **13**, retains *ὅτι*, but in each case he has aorist tenses after *ὅτι*, so that *oratio obliqua* is more easily suggested than by the present tenses of Mark. There is no variation in Mark.

16. vi 18 *ἔλεγεν γὰρ ὁ Ἰωάννης τῷ Ἡρῴδῃ ὅτι Οὐκ ἔξεστίν σοι ἔχειν τὴν γυναῖκα τοῦ ἀδελφοῦ σου.* Once more Matthew drops, and there is no Lucan parallel. Omission in Mark is supported only by D 28 and a very few others.

17. vi 23 *καὶ ὤμοσεν αὐτῇ ὅτι Ὃ ἐάν με αἰτήσῃς δώσω σοι.* No Lucan parallel, and in Matthew a change of construction. In Mark we have dissident witnesses in B Δ *ὅτι ἐάν*, and D *εἶ τι ἂν*.

18. vi 35 *προσελθόντες [αὐτῷ] οἱ μαθηταὶ αὐτοῦ ἔλεγον ὅτι Ἔρημός ἐστιν ὁ τόπος ... ἀπόλυσον αὐτούς.* Both Matthew and Luke omit the *ὅτι*: but the authorities in Mark are unanimous for it.

19. vii 6*a* *εἶπεν αὐτοῖς ὅτι Καλῶς ἐπροφήτευσεν περὶ ὑμῶν ...* The construction is changed, and *ὅτι* omitted, in Matt. In Mark the authorities are divided: those who retain *ὅτι* here omit it later in the sentence (see no. **20**), and *vice versa*, save that Δ Θ 33 omit in both places. No witness gives it in both places: yet Marcan usage suggests that it is right in both. A D W etc. give it here.

20. vii 6*b* Καλῶς *ἐπροφήτευσεν Ἠσαΐας περὶ ὑμῶν τῶν ὑποκριτῶν, ὡς γέγραπται ὅτι Οὗτος ὁ λαὸς τοῖς χείλεσίν με τιμᾷ...* Matthew drops *ὅτι*: Luke ceases to offer any parallels till no.23. In Mark only three witnesses support *ὅτι*, ℵ B L (syr-sin): but Marcan usage puts aside any doubt of their being right.

21. vii 20 *ἔλεγεν δὲ ὅτι Τὸ ἐκ τοῦ ἀνθρώπου ἐκπορευόμενον ἐκεῖνο κοινοῖ τὸν ἄνθρωπον.* Matthew drops the introductory words *ἔλεγεν δὲ ὅτι* altogether, so offers no real parallel. No variant in Mark.

22. viii 4 *καὶ ἀπεκρίθησαν αὐτῷ οἱ μαθηταὶ αὐτοῦ ὅτι Πόθεν τούτους δυνήσεταί τις ὧδε χορτάσαι ἄρτων ἐπ᾿ ἐρημίας;* Matthew, as we should guess he would, omits the *ὅτι*: even in Mark it is found in only three authorities B L Δ, but Marcan usage of course proves it right, and both Tischendorf and W-H accept it.

23. viii 28 *οἱ δὲ εἶπαν αὐτῷ λέγοντες ὅτι Ἰωάνην τὸν βαπτιστήν ... ἄλλοι δὲ ὅτι εἷς τῶν προφητῶν*. Small wonder that this strange phrase with its tautology *εἶπαν λέγοντες* is not reproduced by either Matthew or Luke — both drop *ὅτι*, Matthew drops *λέγοντες*, and Luke changes it to *ἀποκριθέντες*. In Mark ℵ* B (syr-sin) are the only witnesses to give *ὅτι*, of course rightly.[6]

24. ix 31 *καὶ ἔλεγεν ὅτι Ὁ υἱὸς τοῦ ἀνθρώπου παραδίδοται εἰς χεῖρας ἀνθρώπων*. Matthew omits *ὅτι*: Luke changes the construction, and so gets rid of it. All authorities retain it in Mark.

[**25.** ix 41 *ἀμὴν λέγω ὑμῖν ὅτι Οὐ μὴ ἀπολέσῃ τὸν μισθὸν αὐτοῦ*. There are no parallels in the other Synoptists: in the text of Mark *ὅτι* is supported by ℵ B C* D L W Δ Θ syr-sin and, exceptionally, by several Latins including *k*.]

26. x 32, 33 *ἤρξατο αὐτοῖς λέγειν τὰ μέλλοντα αὐτῷ συμβαίνειν, ὅτι Ἰδοὺ ἀναβαίνομεν εἰς Ἱεροσόλυμα* ... Both Matthew and Luke omit *ὅτι*: but there is no variant in Mark.

27. xi 17 Οὐ *γέγραπται ὅτι Ὁ οἶκός μου οἶκος προσευχῆς κληθήσεται πᾶσιν τοῖς ἔθνεσιν*; Both Matthew and Luke turn the question into a statement of fact, and both omit the *ὅτι*. Omission of *ὅτι* in Mark is confined to a small group including C D 69.

28. xii 7 *ἐκεῖνοι δὲ οἱ γεωργοὶ πρὸς ἑαυτοὺς εἶπαν ὅτι* Οὗτός *ἐστιν ὁ κληρονόμος· δεῦτε ἀποκτείνωμεν αὐτόν*. Again both the other Synoptists drop the *ὅτι*: and again the omitting group in Mark is small, D Θ 1 28 565 being the only Greek authorities on that side.

29. xii 19 Διδάσκαλε, Μωυσῆς *ἔγραψεν ἡμῖν ὅτι* Ἐάν *τινος ἀδελφὸς ἀποθάνῃ* ... Once more *ὅτι* disappears in Matthew and Luke: but in Mark it is only absent from D 69 108 of Greek MSS.

30. xii 28, 29 Ποία *ἐστὶν ἐντολὴ πρώτη πάντων; ἀπεκρίθη ὁ* Ἰησοῦς *ὅτι* Πρώτη *ἐστίν*, Ἄκουε Ἰσραήλ ... Matthew and Luke both abbreviate here, and both drop not only *ὅτι* but the words that immediately follow. The omitting group in Mark tends to be stereotyped: here it is D W Θ 1 28 565 with three other cursives.

31. xii 32 Καλῶς, *διδάσκαλε· ἐπ' ἀληθείας εἶπες ὅτι* Εἷς *ἐστὶν καὶ οὐκ ἔστιν ἄλλος πλὴν αὐτοῦ*. There are no parallels in Matthew or Luke: and no dissentient voices in Mark.

[**32.** xii 43 Ἀμὴν *λέγω ὑμῖν ὅτι* Ἡ *χήρα αὕτη ἡ πτωχὴ πλεῖον πάντων ἔβαλεν*. Ὅτι is retained by Luke (there is no Matthaean parallel) and is

---

[6] It may be noted here that *k* faithfully reproduces *εἶπαν λέγοντες* by *dixerunt dicentes*: for *dicentes* and not *omnes* is the true reading of the MS.

found without variant in Mark. As often, the phrase λέγω ὑμῖν ὅτι passes unchallenged.]

33. xiii 6 *πολλοὶ ἐλεύσονται ἐπὶ τῷ ὀνόματί μου λέγοντες ὅτι Ἐγώ εἰμι*. A striking instance, where the agreement of Matthew and Luke against Mark in the omission of ὅτι well reflects the 'usage' of the three writers. In Mark D Θ 33 omit.

[**34**. xiii 30 *ἀμὴν λέγω ὑμῖν ὅτι Οὐ μὴ παρέλθῃ ἡ γενεὰ αὕτη* ... Ὅτι is read by all authorities in Mark and almost all in Luke: in Matt. xxiv 34 the reading is doubtful, but B D L Θ *fam.* 1 *fam.* 13 give ὅτι and they outweigh ℵ. The phrase λέγω ὑμῖν ὅτι is not so unusual or so repellent to the sense of style as the ordinary Marcan λέγει ὅτι in narrative: and towards the end of the Gospel, as will be seen, Matthew who consistently rejects the latter, not infrequently accepts the former, see nos. **36**, **37**, **39**.]

35. xiv 14 *εἴπατε τῷ οἰκοδεσπότῃ ὅτι Ὁ διδάσκαλος λέγει· ποῦ ἐστιν τὸ κατάλυμά μου;* In Mark some twenty MSS (but none of importance) omit, influenced no doubt by omission in both Matthew and Luke.

[**36**. xiv 18 *Ἀμὴν λέγω ὑμῖν ὅτι Εἷς ἐξ ὑμῶν παραδώσει με*. ὅτι is without variant in Mark and Matthew, cf. no. **34**: in Luke there is no parallel.]

[**37**. xiv 25 *ἀμὴν λέγω ὑμῖν ὅτι Οὐκέτι οὐ μὴ πίω ἐκ τοῦ γενήματος τῆς ἀμπέλου* ... Again no parallel in Luke: again no variant in Mark, but as in **34** authorities are divided over ὅτι in Matt.xxvi 29. For omission are ℵ D Z Θ 1 33 and half a dozen others: for insertion A B C L Δ W and the rest. It is rather surprising that W-H omit without even a marginal variant.]

38. xiv 27 *Καὶ λέγει αὐτοῖς ὁ Ἰησοῦς ὅτι Πάντες σκανδαλισθήσεσθε*. Ὅτι is without variant in Mark, and omission is without variant in Matthew: no parallel in Luke.

[**39**. xiv 30 *Ἀμὴν λέγω σοι ὅτι Σὺ σήμερον ταύτῃ τῇ νυκτὶ ... τρίς με ἀπαρνήσῃ*. Ὅτι is without variant in Mark and Matthew: but omission is without variant in Luke.]

40. xiv 57, 58 *ἐψευδομαρτύρουν κατ' αὐτοῦ λέγοντες ὅτι Ἡμεῖς ἠκούσαμεν αὐτοῦ* ... Ὅτι without variant in Mark: omission without variant in Matthew: no Lucan parallel.

41. xiv 58 *ἠκούσαμεν αὐτοῦ λέγοντος ὅτι Ἐγὼ καταλύσω τὸν ναὸν τοῦτον τὸν χειροποίητον* ... The details are the same exactly as in the last case, Matthew omitting ὅτι.

42. xiv 69 *ἰδοῦσα αὐτὸν ἤρξατο πάλιν λέγειν τοῖς παρεστῶσιν ὅτι Οὗτος ἐξ αὐτῶν ἐστιν*. Ὅτι is omitted by both Matthew and Luke, but is without variant in Mark.

43. xiv 71 *ὁ δὲ ἤρξατο ... ὀμνύναι ὅτι Οὐκ οἶδα τὸν ἄνθρωπον*. Transferred without change by Matthew to his own Gospel. Luke, not liking to say that Peter 'cursed and swore', abbreviates the sentence, and in the process drops *ὅτι*.

44. xiv 72 *καὶ ἀνεμνήσθη ὁ Πέτρος τὸ ῥῆμα ὡς εἶπεν αὐτῷ ὁ Ἰησοῦς ὅτι Πρὶν ... τρίς με ἀπαρνήσῃ*. *Ὅτι* is given by all three Synoptists on the practically unanimous testimony of all Greek MSS other than D.

45. xvi 7 *εἴπατε τοῖς μαθηταῖς αὐτοῦ καὶ τῷ Πέτρῳ ὅτι Προάγει ὑμᾶς εἰς τὴν Γαλιλαίαν*. *Ὅτι* is retained by Matthew, but the whole sentence undergoes drastic rearrangement in Luke and *ὅτι* disappears in the process. Did Matthew, towards the end of the Gospel, tire of making as many changes as in the earlier part in the process of making the Marcan material his own? He retains *ἀμὴν λέγω ὑμῖν ὅτι* first in **34** (Matt. xxiv 34), and *ὅτι* in other connexions only in **43**, **44**, **45** (Matt. xxvi 74, 75, xxviii 7).

What are the results to be gathered from this long enumeration?

In the first place, that in all forty-five instances not more than four verbs are employed in introducing the *ὅτι* clause. Three times *γράφειν γραφεσθαι* (of Scripture), **20**, **27**, **29**: twice *ὀμνύναι*, **17**, **43**: twice *ἀποκρίνεσθαι*, **22**, **30**: but thirty-eight times *λέγειν* (*εἰπεῖν*). The mere statement of 'Marcan usage' is enough to prove that in one case where our authorities differ, **1**, *λέγων* must be right. Nothing emerges, I think, more decisively from the whole series of notes on 'Marcan usage' than the immense superiority in Mark of the text of B to the text of ℵ. The edition of Tischendorf (and to a less extent that of W-H) is vitiated by the too great deference shown to the latter MS.

In the second place, if we classify our forty-five instances according to the type of the *ὅτι* clause, we find

(a) that seven times it occurs not in narrative but in direct statements of our Lord, **9**, **25**, **32**, **34**, **36**, **37**, **39**, *ἀμὴν λέγω ὑμῖν ὅτι* ..., and that the other two Synoptists retain *ὅτι* in these cases much oftener than in the rest: Matthew accepts it in **34** (probably), **36**, **37** (probably), **39** — he has no parallel to **25** and **32**; Luke has no parallel to **9**, **25**, **36**, **37**, but retains *ὅτι* in **32** and **34**. That is to say, Matthew only drops *ὅτι* once, in **9**, Luke only once, in **39**. Clearly, then, in dealing with *ὅτι recitativum*, we must isolate these cases from the rest: and indeed they are not strictly 'recitative' at all.

(b) that, of the remaining thirty-eight cases, (i) three introduce quotations from Scripture, **20**, **27**, **29**; (ii) two introduce questions, **10** and **22**;

(iii) ten[7] introduce statements in the third person which, if they stood alone, might be treated as *oratio obliqua*, **7**, **8**, **14**, **15**, **19**, **21**, **24**, **30**, **31**, **42**; (iv) in the other twenty-three cases ὅτι is followed by a first or second person, so that these are necessarily in *oratio recta*. Now of all these cases, Luke omits ὅτι in all but five (**4**, **6**, **13**, **15**, **44**), Matthew in all but three (**43**, **44**, **45**), sometimes of course by changing the construction, more often by simply dropping the particle. As there are many more parallels in Matthew (thirty-one) than in Luke (twenty-two), the proportion varies as between the two, Luke retaining ὅτι five times out of twenty-two, or nearly one in four, Matthew only three times out of thirty-one, or one in ten.

On twelve occasions Matthew and Luke agree in simply dropping the ὅτι of Mark, **3**, **5**, **8**, **18**, **23**, **26**, **27**, **28**, **29**, **33**, **35**, **42**. Twelve agreements, then, of the two later Synoptists against Mark are cleared off the ground on examination of 'Marcan usage'.

(3) Asyndeta or absence of particles in Mark†

The following rough list is probably not at all exhaustive,[8] but it is sufficient to illustrate my point, and it is reinforced (see §4 below) by the special cases of *ναί*, *οὖν*, and *ἰδού*.

1. i 8 *ἐγὼ ἐβάπτισα ὑμᾶς ὕδατι*. So ℵ B L Θ 33 69 Origen *b c* Aug: the rest add *μέν* with Matthew and Luke.

2. i 22 *ὡς ἐξουσίαν ἔχων, οὐχ ὡς οἱ γραμματεῖς*. So D Θ *b c d e*: the rest read *καὶ οὐχ* with Matthew: Luke omits the last half of the phrase.

3. i 27 *τί ἐστιν τοῦτο; διδαχὴ καινή*. So ℵ B L 33 (*fam*.1). Not in Matthew: Luke *τίς ὁ λόγος οὗτος, ὅτι ἐν ἐξουσίᾳ* ... The remaining authorities in Mark prefix *τίς ἡ*.

4. ii 8, 9 *τί ταῦτα διαλογίζεσθε ...; τί ἐστιν εὐκοπώτερον ...;* So Luke: Matthew *τί γάρ ἐστιν εὐκοπώτερον ...;*

5. ii 17 *οὐ χρείαν ἔχουσιν οἱ ἰσχύοντες ἰατροῦ ... οὐκ ἦλθον καλέσαι δικαίους* ... As in the last case Luke follows Mark, and Matthew inserts *γάρ*, *οὐ γάρ ἦλθον καλέσαι* ...

6. ii 21 *οὐδεὶς ἐπίβλημα ῥάκους ἀγνάφου ἐπιράπτει*. *οὐδεὶς δέ* Matthew (followed by D and a few Latins in Mark): *ὅτι οὐδείς* Luke.

7. ii 25, 26 *οὐδέποτε ἀνέγνωτε τί ἐποίησεν Δαυείδ ...; εἰσῆλθεν εἰς τὸν οἶκον τοῦ θεοῦ* ... So B D (and *a* 'et'): the remainder *πῶς εἰσῆλθεν*

---

[7] But in only one of these, **7**, is the statement in the past tense.

[8] I have omitted all instances where there is no parallel in Matthew or Luke.

with Matt.: *ὡς εἰσῆλθεν* Luke, though B D omit as in Mark, perhaps rightly.

8. iii 27 *οὐ δύναται οὐδεὶς εἰς τὴν οἰκίαν τοῦ ἰσχυροῦ εἰσελθὼν...* So A D W and most Greek MSS, *e* and most Latins, and syr-sin: ℵ B and a few other good authorities prefix *ἀλλά*, but *ἀλλά* at the beginning of a sentence is extraordinarily rare in Mark, xiii 24 being the only other example. Luke is not strictly parallel: Matthew has *ἢ πῶς* ...

9. iii 34,35 *ἴδε ἡ μήτηρ μου καὶ οἱ ἀδελφοί μου. ὃς ἂν ποιήσῃ τὸ θέλημα τοῦ θεοῦ* ... So B *b e* (and 'et' *a c* Aug): the rest read *ὃς γὰρ ἂν ποιήσῃ*. Matthew *ὅστις γὰρ ἂν ποιήσῃ*: Luke again has no exact parallel.

10. iv 24 *Βλέπετε τί ἀκούετε· ἐν ᾧ μέτρῳ μετρεῖτε μετρηθήσεται ὑμῖν.* In what are practically the parallels, Matt. vii 2, Luke vi 38, *γάρ* is added by both the other Synoptists.

11. viii 15 *ὁρᾶτε, βλέπετε ἀπὸ τῆς ζύμης τῶν Φαρισαίων* ... Matthew *ὁρᾶτε καὶ προσέχετε ἀπό*, Luke *προσέχετε ἑαυτοῖς ἀπο*: *βλέπετε ἀπὸ* in the sense 'to beware of' is a Marcan vulgarism (cf. xii 38), which the other Synoptists instinctively avoid. In Mark the reading is not doubtful: but three separate attempts are made in different authorities to emend the text and get rid of the asyndeton or of the double verb: D Θ *fam.*1 565 omit *ὁρᾶτε*, Δ omits *βλέπετε*, C *fam.*13 insert *καί* between the verbs.

12. ix 38 *ἔφη αὐτῷ ὁ Ἰωάνης.* No parallel in Matthew: Luke *ἀποκριθεὶς δὲ ὁ Ἰωάνησ εἶπεν.* In Mark all authorities but ℵ B D Δ Θ sah and a few of the best Old Latins including *k*, with syr-sin, avoid the asyndeton, either by adding *δέ* or by prefixing *καί*.

13. x 9 *ὃ ὁ θεὸς συνέζευξεν, ἄνθρωπος μὴ χωριζέτω.* No parallel in Luke: Matthew *ὃ οὖν ὁ θεὸς* ..., and from Matthew most MSS of Mark. The true reading without *οὖν* is preserved only in D and *k*.

14. x 14 *ἄφετε τὰ παιδία ἔρχεσθαι πρός με, μὴ κωλύετε αὐτά.* Both Matthew and Luke alter to *καὶ μὴ κωλύετε αὐτά*, and they have drawn after them a large majority of the MSS of Mark. But the shorter reading has for it B W Δ, a dozen more uncials and some eighty cursives.

15. x 24, 25 *πῶς δύσκολόν ἐστιν εἰς τὴν βασιλείαν τοῦ θεοῦ εἰσελθεῖν· εὐκοπώτερόν ἐστιν κάμηλον...* Matthew *ὅτι εὐκοπώτερόν*, Luke *εὐκοπώτερόν γάρ*. Evidence for the asyndeton in Mark is only qualified by *δέ* in A, and *γάρ* in a few others.

16. x 27 *ἐμβλέψας αὐτοῖς ὁ Ἰησοῦς* ... *ἐμβλέψας δέ* Matthew, *ὁ δὲ εἶπεν* Luke. Most MSS of Mark follow Matthew: the true reading survives in ℵ B C* Δ 1 syr-sin.

17. x 28 *ἤρξατο λέγειν ὁ Πέτρος αὐτῷ. τότε ἤρξατο* Matthew, *εἶπεν δέ* Luke. In Mark we find *καὶ ἤρξατο, ἤρξατο δέ, τότε ἤρξατο, ἤρξατο* οὖν: but ἤρξατο without connecting particle in ℵ A B C W Δ Θ syr-sin, and a good many others.

18. x 29 (the fourth asyndeton in five verses) ἔφη ὁ Ἰησοῦς. Matthew ὁ δὲ Ἰησοῦς εἶπεν αὐτοῖς: Luke ὁ δὲ εἶπεν αὐτοῖς. In Mark only ℵ B Δ give ἔφη alone, and it is possible that with the rest we ought to prefix ἀποκριθείς: but even so most of them retain the asyndeton.

19. xii 9 τί ποιήσει ὁ κύριος τοῦ ἀμπελῶνος; τί οὖν ποιήσει Luke, and similarly Matthew ὅταν οὖν ἔλθῃ ὁ κύριος τοῦ ἀμπελῶνος, τί ποιήσει ... In Mark only B L (syr-sin sah) give the shorter reading without οὖν: but they are certainly right.

20. xii 17 ὁ δὲ Ἰησοῦς εἶπεν· Τὰ Καίσαρος ἀπόδοτε (al. Ἀπόδοτε τὰ Καίσαρος) Καίσαρι. Matthew ἀπόδοτε οὖν τὰ Καίσαρος, Luke τοίνυν ἀπόδοτε τὰ Καίσαρος. This time only a few authorities in Mark insert οὖν.

21. xii 20 ἑπτὰ ἀδελφοὶ ἦσαν. Luke ἑπτὰ οὖν ἀδελφοὶ ἦσαν, Matthew ἦσαν δὲ παρ' ἡμῖν ἑπτὰ ἀδελφοί. In Mark ℵ A B C* L W Δ Θ, the great majority of Greek MSS, syr-sin and *k*, read as above.

22. xii 23 ἐν τῇ ἀναστάσει ... τίνος αὐτῶν ἔσται γυνή; Both Matthew and Luke insert οὖν: omitted in Mark by ℵ B C* L Δ, many other Greek MSS, and *k*.

23. xii 24 ἔφη αὐτοῖς ὁ Ἰησοῦς. So in Mark ℵ B C L Δ 33 *k*, much as in **21** and **22**, but without support from later MSS: καὶ εἶπεν Luke, ἀποκριθεὶς δὲ ... εἶπεν Matthew.

24. xii 36 αὐτὸς Δαυεὶδ εἶπεν. So without particle ℵ B L W Δ *fam.*13 28 565 *a k* sah: the other MSS mostly αὐτὸς γάρ with Luke, Matthew πῶς οὖν ...

24. bis. xii 37 αὐτὸς Δαυεὶδ λέγει αὐτὸν κύριον. So in Mark ℵ B D L W Δ Θ 28 565 *a i k* sah (syr-sin). The rest add οὖν after αὐτὸς with Luke Δαυεὶδ οὖν: Matthew εἰ οὖν Δαυεὶδ καλεῖ ...

25. xiii 5, 6 βλέπετε μή τις ὑμᾶς πλανήσῃ· πολλοὶ ἐλεύσονται ἐπὶ τῷ ὀνόματί μου ... So ℵ B L W: the rest add γάρ with Matt. and Luke.

26. xiii 7 μὴ θροεῖσθε· δεῖ γενέσθαι. So only ℵ B W and the Egyptian versions: the rest have δεῖ γάρ after Matthew and Luke.

27. xiii 8*a* ἐγερθήσεται γὰρ ἔθνος ἐπ' ἔθνος καὶ βασιλεία ἐπὶ βασιλείαν, ἔσονται σεισμοὶ κατὰ τόπους, ἔσονται λιμοί. The first ἔσονται with ℵ B D L W 28 124 and the Egyptian versions, the second ἔσονται with ℵ^c B L (W) 28 sah: the rest in each case prefix καί. Matthew and Luke combine the two ἔσονται clauses into one, Matthew connecting with the ἐγερθήσεται clause by καί, Luke by τε.

28. xiii 8*b* ἀρχὴ ὠδίνων ταῦτα. So without connecting particle Mark: but Matt. πάντα δὲ ταῦτα ἀρχὴ ὠδίνων: no parallel in Luke.

29. xiii 23 *ὑμεῖς δὲ βλέπετε· προείρηκα ὑμῖν πάντα*. So B L W 28 *a*: the rest follow Matthew's *ἰδοὺ προείρηκα* ... No parallel in Luke.

30. xiii 34 *ὡς ἄνθρωπος ἀπόδημος ἀφεὶς τὴν οἰκίαν αὐτοῦ καὶ δοὺς τοῖς δούλοις αὐτοῦ τὴν ἐξουσίαν* ... So all the best authorities in Mark: but many MSS borrow *γάρ* from Matthew *ὥσπερ γὰρ ἄνθρωπος ἀποδημῶν* ... No parallel again in Luke.

31. xiv 3 *ἦλθεν γυνὴ ἔχουσα ἀλάβαστρον μύρου νάρδου πιστικῆς πολυτελοῦς· συντρίψασα τὴν ἀλάβαστρον κατέχεεν αὐτοῦ τῆς κεφαλῆς*. So only ℵ B L: the rest prefix *καί* to *συντρίψασα*. Matthew, omitting *συντρίψασα τὴν ἀ.*, gives *καὶ κατέχεεν*. Luke omits the whole incident, having related a parallel story in vii 36-50: this covers also **32**, **33**.

32. xiv 6 *τί αὐτῇ κόπους παρέχετε; καλὸν ἔργον ἠργάσατο ἐν ἐμοί*. So all but a few MSS of Mark : ℵ W *fam.*13 28 have *καλὸν γὰρ ἔργον* with Matthew's *ἔργον γὰρ καλὸν* ...

33. xiv 8 *ὃ ἔσχεν ἐποίησεν· προέλαβεν μυρίσαι μου τὸ σῶμα εἰς τὸν ἐνταφιασμόν*. The asyndeton is without variant in Mark: Matthew adds *γάρ*, *βαλοῦσα γὰρ αὕτη τὸ μύρον τοῦτο ἐπὶ τοῦ σώματός μου*.

34. xiv 19 *ἤρξαντο λυπεῖσθαι καὶ λέγειν αὐτῷ εἷς κατὰ εἷς, Μήτι ἐγώ;* So ℵ B L Origen in Mark: nearly all the rest avoid the asyndeton by *οἱ δὲ ἤρξαντο* ..., not on this occasion following Matthew's *καὶ λυπούμενοι σφόδρα ἤρξαντο λέγειν* ... There is therefore somewhat less certainty in this case: yet Marcan usage, combined with the excellent record of B in the whole series of passages here enumerated, is I think decisive. Luke, as so often in the Passion narrative (cf.**35**), has no parallel.

35. xiv 41 *καθεύδετε τὸ λοιπὸν καὶ ἀναπαύεσθε· ἀπέχει· ἦλθεν ἡ ὥρα, ἰδοὺ παραδίδοται ὁ υἱὸς τοῦ ἀνθρώπου* ... So with few exceptions (D W and Old Latins) the texts of Mark: Matthew omits the difficult *ἀπέχει*, and substitutes *ἰδοὺ ἤγγικεν ἡ ὥρα καὶ ὁ υἱὸς τοῦ ἀνθρώπου παραδίδοται*...

36. xiv 63, 64 *τί ἔτι χρείαν ἔχομεν μαρτύρων; ἠκούσατε τῆς βλασφημίας*.[9] No important witness differs in Mark save ℵ, which follows Matthew *ἴδε νῦν ἠκούσατε* ... Luke *αὐτοὶ γὰρ ἠκούσαμεν* ...

37. xvi 6*a* *μὴ ἐκθαμβεῖσθε· Ἰησοῦν ζητεῖτε τὸν Ναζαρηνὸν τὸν ἐσταυρωμένον*. Mark leaves us in doubt whether the second clause is a statement or a question: Matthew with *οἶδα γὰρ ὅτι* ... *ζητεῖτε* interprets in the former sense, Luke with *τί ζητεῖτε* in the latter.

---

[9] I think 'Marcan usage' is decisive against W-H's punctuation *ἠκούσατε τῆς βλασφημίας*; Compare e.g. ii 7, the statement *βλασφημεῖ* between two questions.

38. xvi 6*b* ἠγέρθη, οὐκ ἔστιν ὧδε. So Mark without variant: Matthew οὐκ ἔστιν ὧδε, ἠγέρθη γάρ. Luke οὐκ ἔστιν ὧδε, ἀλλὰ ἠγέρθη.

These passages are enough to prove to demonstration, in the first place, Mark's fondness for asyndeta — it corresponds to his rough unliterary style — and, in the second place, the constant tendency in Matthew and Luke to remove the asyndeta by providing particles to supply some sort of connection with what precedes. Sometimes, as we should expect, they provide the same particles, sometimes different ones. Out of some twenty-five cases where both Matthew and Luke have parallels to the Marcan text, Luke retains the asyndeton twice (**4** and **5**)[10], Matthew never: in twelve cases they give different supplements, in ten cases the same, namely **1** μέν, **10** γάρ, **14** καί, **16** δέ, **18** δέ, **19** οὖν, **22** οὖν, **24** *bis* οὖν, **25** γάρ, **26** γάρ. Ten cases may seem a large proportion: but the supplements are always natural ones, or indeed the most natural ones, and the agreements against Mark — side by side with a rather larger number of divergent supplements — mean no more than that the two later Synoptists, editing the text of the earlier Gospel, often hit independently on the same obvious improvements.

But further we learn of course something of the relative value of our authorities for the text of St Mark. In this particular section of our enquiry, the excellence of B stands out unchallenged: in eight instances the asyndeton is practically without variant, at any rate in all the older authorities, but in the remaining thirty-one B is right — on the assumption that an 'asyndeton' reading is to be preferred — in no less than twenty-eight, the exceptions being **2**, **8**, and **13**. א is right in twenty-one cases; the exceptions (besides the three just mentioned, which it shares with B) are **7**, **9**, **14**, **19**, **29**, **32**, **36**. D is right in only nine cases, though it should be noted that in **2**, **7**, **12**, **13**, **28**, it gives the shorter reading with only a few companions. But *k*, for the part of the Gospel for which it is extant (from 12 onwards), has a better record than D of asyndeta: **12**, **13**, **21**, **22**, **23**, **24**, **24** bis, four times against D. In **13**, a quite certain case, D *k* stand out alone with the right reading.

(4) Particles absent from Mark.

i. ναί

ναί is found eight times in Matthew, v 37, ix 28, xi 9, xi 26, xiii 51, xv 27, xvii 25, xxi 16: four times in Luke, vii 26, x 21, xi 51, xii 5. On two occasions the passages in Matthew and Luke are parallel, Matt. xi 9

---

[10] Possibly also in 7

= Luke vii 26 *ναί λέγω ὑμῖν, καὶ περισσότερον προφήτου*, Matt. xi 26 = Luke x 21 *ναί ὁ πατήρ, ὅτι οὕτως εὐδοκία ἐγένετο ἔμπροσθέν σου*: both passages presumably come from Q. But further the two other occasions where *ναί* is found in Luke belong also it would seem to Q sections: Luke xi 51 *ναί λέγω ὑμῖν* (Matthew *ἀμὴν λέγω ὑμῖν*), xii 5 *ναί λέγω ὑμῖν* (omitted by Matthew). It is possible therefore that Luke never uses *ναί* except where he is following Q.

Of the other six instances in Matthew, five occur in matter not found in Mark: the sixth, Matt. xv 27, is parallel to Mark vii 28. The printed texts give *ναί* in both Gospels as introducing the answer of the Syrophoenician woman to our Lord's objection about throwing the children's bread to dogs. There is no other case of the use of *ναί* in St Mark: and 'Marcan usage' is reinforced by the testimony of witnesses who omit it even here.

These witnesses are D W Δ *fam.*13 565 *b c ff i* syr-sin: all 'Western' indeed, but Western of very varied types. It is noteworthy that W-H gave the omission of *ναί* a place in the margin of their edition before the evidence of either W or Θ or the Sinai Syriac was available: and obviously, whatever was to be said on internal grounds before the new witnesses were known, the external evidence is now very strongly reinforced. The ℵ B group, in fact, have suffered assimilation to Matthew: and the solitary instance of *ναί* in St Mark disappears.[11]

ii. *οὖν*.†

οὖν is found in Matthew nearly sixty times, in Luke some thirty times — i.e. in proportion to the length of his Gospel about half as often as in Matthew — in Mark at the outside seven times: but on three of these seven W-H omit *οὖν* entirely, and on a fourth they bracket it. The weight of 'Marcan usage' is so strong that omission is presumably right where there is even a small body of good witnesses in support of it; and possibly right, where a parallel in Matthew will account for its insertion, without any external evidence at all.

1. x 9 *ὃ οὖν ὁ θεὸς συνέζευξεν ἄνθρωπος μὴ χωριζέτω*. So word for word Matthew, and so the critical editions of Mark with the vast majority of MSS. But D *k* omit *οὖν*: and the omission is so like Mark's style, while the correction from Matthew would be so easily and so obviously made, in a terse familiar saying, that I accept the shorter reading without hesitation. See Asyndeta **13**.

---

[11] I have dealt with this reading, more briefly in my *Study of the New Testament* (ed.2,1924) p.70.

2. xi 31 *ἐὰν εἴπωμεν· Ἐξ οὐρανοῦ, ἐρεῖ· Διὰ τί οὖν οὐκ ἐπιστεύσατε αὐτῷ;* Here Matthew has *οὖν*, but it is important to note that it is absent from Luke: and omission in Mark has for it A C* L W *a b c d ff i k* syr-sin. W-H give omission a place in the margin; but where Marcan usage, Lucan parallel, and good Greek and Latin evidence, all coincide, omission is, I think, incontestably right.

3. xii 8, 9 *καὶ λαβόντες ἀπέκτειναν αὐτόν, καὶ ἐξέβαλον αὐτὸν ἔξω τοῦ ἀμπελῶνος. τί οὖν ποιήσει ὁ κύριος τοῦ ἀμπελῶνος;* So all MSS of Mark, except B L (syr-sin) sah. But both Luke and Matthew have *οὖν*, Luke following Mark closely *τί οὖν ποιήσει* ..., Matthew inserting it into an introductory clause *ὅταν οὖν ἔλθῃ ὁ κύριος τοῦ ἀμπελῶνος, τί ποιήσει*... We shall have therefore no hesitation in accepting, with Tischendorf and W-H, the evidence of B, and in ejecting once more the particle *οὖν* from the text of Mark.

4. xii 23 *ἐν τῇ ἀναστάσει οὖν* ... So (or *ἐν τῇ οὖν ἀναστάσει*) many MSS of Mark, including A D W Θ 1 28 565 and most Latins, with Matthew *ἐν τῇ ἀναστάσει οὖν* ... and Luke *ἡ γυνὴ οὖν ἐν τῇ ἀναστάσει* ... Omit *οὖν* in Mark with ℵ B C* L Δ, very many Greek MSS, and *k*: so also Tischendorf and W-H. See under Asyndeta **22**.

5. xii 37 *αὐτὸς οὖν Δαυεὶδ λέγει αὐτὸν κύριον*. So in Mark A and the great majority of Greek MSS, compare Luke *Δαυεὶδ οὖν κύριον αὐτὸν καλεῖ*, and Matthew *εἰ οὖν Δαυεὶδ καλεῖ αὐτὸν κύριον* ... Again omit *οὖν* in Mark with ℵ B D L W Δ Θ 28 565 *a i k*, the Egyptian versions (syr-sin), and the critical editions. See Asyndeta **24** bis.

6. xiii 35 *γρηγορεῖτε οὖν· οὐκ οἴδατε γὰρ πότε ὁ κύριος τῆς οἰκίας ἔρχεται*. No variant in Mark: and though *οὖν* may conceivably have been borrowed by the scribes of Mark from Matt. xxiv 42 (there is no parallel in Luke), it would be hazardous to question it without any MS support, the more so that there is another instance to follow where our authorities are unanimous for the word.

7. xv 12 *ὁ δὲ Πειλᾶτος πάλιν ἀποκριθεὶς ἔλεγεν αὐτοῖς, Τί οὖν θέλετε*[12] *ποιήσω ὃν λέγετε τὸν βασιλέα τῶν Ἰουδαίων;* Again no variant in Mark, *τί οὖν* in Matthew, and no parallel in Luke. The same considerations apply as in the last case: I am not sure that *οὖν* in Mark is right, but I should not venture to remove it from the text.

Thus out of seven instances *οὖν* should be banished from Mark in five. In three of these both Matthew and Luke have the particle: that is to say,

[12] W-H omit *θέλετε* with ℵ B C Δ *fam.*1 *fam.*13 33 and the Egyptian versions: but the omission I believe to be due either to assimilation to Matt. xxvii 22 or to a desire to get rid of the construction *θέλετε ποίησω*. Tischendorf retains *θέλετε*.

three instances of agreement between the two other Synoptists against Mark are seen to be meaningless, because we have once more the key to the solution in 'Marcan usage'.

iii. ἰδού in narrative.

Neither Mark nor John ever uses ἰδού in narrative: Luke employs it fairly often (sixteen times), Matthew twice as often (thirty-two times) as Luke. In Luke it is regularly in the form καὶ ἰδού: that is also the predominant form in Matthew, but ἰδού is also found in this Gospel with a genitive absolute preceding it as often as nine times. In both Matthew and Luke the usage is found alike in portions that are parallel to Mark and portions that are not — about three-quarters of the instances in Matthew and something over half of the instances in Luke belonging to the 'triple tradition'.

There are in fact some twenty-five passages where one or other of the later Synoptists grafts ἰδού on to the Marcan stock, three of these being peculiar to Luke, sixteen being peculiar to Matthew, and six common to both. Again it may be asked, Is not this a high percentage of agreement?

In two out of every three cases where Luke uses it Matthew has it too, and can this be due to chance? The answer is twofold.

In the first place Matthew uses the phrase so commonly, when a new character or new element in the story is introduced, that it is not wonderful that Luke, using it much more sparingly, should be found to coincide with Matthew in a high proportion of his relatively few cases. If ἰδού were to be introduced at all, certain occasions would stand out as specially calling for it. The six occasions common to Matthew and Luke are in fact *(a)* the commencement of three stories of miracles, Mark i 40, ii 3, v 22: *(b)* the appearance of Moses and Elias at the Transfiguration, Mark ix 4: *(c)* the appearance of Judas in the Garden, Mark xiv 43: *(d)* the appearance of the angel or angels who announced the Resurrection, Mark xvi 5.

In the second place, as Mark is *never* found to use the phrase in narrative, we can hardly explain any coincidences of Matthew and Luke against Mark as pointing back to a more original text of Mark. It was not Mark, but much more probably the Old Testament, that taught Matthew, and to a less degree Luke, the value of the employment of ἰδού to give vigour and movement to the narrative.[13]

---

[13] It is worth noting that in several of the cases where Matthew and Luke have ἰδού, it replaces an ἔρχεται of St Mark: Mark i 40, ii 3, v 22.

VIII – 'The disciples' and 'the Twelve'.[1]

Eduard Meyer, in his important work *Ursprung und Anfänge des Christentums* (3 vols., Stuttgart and Berlin, 1921-3), attempts to analyse the sources of St Mark and assumes a distinction between a 'disciples' source and a 'Twelve' source according as *οἱ μαθηταί* or *οἱ δώδεκα* is the phrase employed (i pp. 133-147).

These 'Notes on Marcan Usage' are being put together primarily as a contribution to the examination of the history of the text and of the Synoptic problem. But it is also part of their purpose to test, and if the evidence tends that way to establish the truth of, my own working hypothesis that the authority of St Peter stands, as tradition has always indicated, very closely behind the authority of the Evangelist.

Of course it goes without saying that the hypothesis applies especially to the period between St Peter's call (i 16) and the flight of the disciples (xiv 50). For the story of the Baptism[2] and Temptation the ultimate authority must be that of Jesus himself, though it must have reached the Evangelist through the medium of some personal disciple to whom Jesus had confided it — naturally, in this case, St Peter. For the story of the Crucifixion and (so far as the extant part of the Gospel extends) the Resurrection one primary authority is presumably that of the holy women or one of them — if one must select, that one whose name is otherwise unknown to us, Mary the mother of James and Joses.

But it does not follow that, even if the authority of St Peter stands in the main behind the narrative i 16-xiv 50, it stands in equal degree behind every part of it. Distinction must be made in the first place between that part of the story where we may presume that he was spectator or auditor, and those exceptional passages where the contrary was certainly or probably the case. There is the story of Herod and John the Baptist, vi 14-29:

---

[1] The following pages were originally written as an appendix to Marcan Usage: V. The movements of Jesus and his disciples and the crowd' (*JTS* April 1925, xxvi 225-240 = Note V), where I tried to emphasize the indications in Mark, as contrasted with Matthew and Luke, of the evidence of an eye-witness, indications which appear to be spread over practically the whole story of the Ministry. It seems simpler now to print this examination of a rival theory as an independent section of my Notes.

[2] Note that in St Mark's Gospel, and in his Gospel only, the Baptism is related throughout as our Lord's experience: i 10 *ἀναβαίνων ... εἶδεν*, i 11 *σὺ εἶ ὁ υἱός μου ὁ ἀγαπητός*. Matthew changes the latter part, and, as in the Transfiguration where the Voice from heaven is addressed to the three apostles (Mk. ix 7 = Matt. xvii 5 = Lk. ix 35), writes *οὗτός ἐστιν ὁ υἱός μου ...*, while Luke changes the former part into a historical statement, *ἐγένετο ... ἀνεῳχθῆναι τὸν οὐρανὸν ... καὶ φωνὴν ... γενέσθαι*: Matt. iii 17, Lk. iii 21, 22.

there is perhaps the journey of our Lord to Tyre and back, vii 24-37, where from the absence of any allusion to disciples it may not improbably be deduced that the journey was undertaken without companions.

Even in these passages the information may still have reached the Evangelist by way of St Peter. But I should not want to exclude the possibility that there may be episodes which the Evangelist derived from other sources and has interwoven into the Petrine tradition. Such in particular might be the second account of miraculous feeding, viii 1-9, of which the most probable explanation seems to me to be that it is a variant, derived by Mark from another source, of the first (Petrine) account in vi 34-44.[3]

But returning, with the reserves indicated, to the working hypothesis that the account of the Ministry is a homogeneous whole depending on the Petrine tradition, let us see whether the actual use or interchange of the phrases 'the disciples' and 'the Twelve' suggests an actual interchange of sources or whether it grows naturally out of the situation in the process of development described in St Mark's Gospel. That is the first test of all theories of partition of sources, whether in this or any other document.

Μαθηταί are first mentioned in ii 15, when we are told that they were now 'many' and were beginning to collect around him and 'follow' him: before that we have only (1) the call of four disciples who came 'after him' (*ὀπίσω*, i 17,20) — these form at once a group of four (i 29): it may be only these four, it may already be others, who are included in the 'Simon and his companions' of i 36 — and (2) the call of a fifth personally named disciple[4], with the summons 'Follow me', in ii 14. Then

---

[3] See Dr Headlam's *Jesus the Christ* (1923), p.14. As Dr Headlam points out, the second distinguishes itself from the first by the absence of those vivid details which we are accustomed to call 'Marcan touches'. But if these details are found in the Petrine, and are absent from the non-Petrine account, the important conclusion results that the vivid touches of the Evangelist go back in the main to the apostle. It does not follow, of course, that the disciple and 'interpreter' has not caught something of the style and spirit of his master.

[4] Levi, son of Alpheus, who is not identified either by Mark, or by Luke who follows Mark (Luke v 27-29), with Matthew. On the other hand we should naturally suppose that one whose call is thus given in detail was in fact one of the Twelve, as his brother 'James son of Alpheus' (Mark iii 18) certainly was. The Western text solves the difficulty by reading 'James [not Levi] son of Alpheus' in Mark ii 14; but St Luke's support of 'Levi' seems to disprove this otherwise attractive solution. We may either suppose that *Λεββαῖον* of the Western text is right in the list of the Apostles iii 18 — *Θαδδαῖον* would then have come in from Matt. x 3 — and that *Λεββαῖος* is a variant form of *Λευείν* (Origen has *ὁ Λεβὴς τελώνης*); or alternatively that we should read in iii 18 *Ἰάκωβον* [*καὶ Λευείν*] *τὸν Ἁλφαίου*. If the mention of Levi had accidentally dropped out from a very early copy, we could understand both the presence of the variants *Θαδδαῖος* and *Λεββαῖος* in Mark and Matthew and the appearance in Luke of a new name *Ἰούδας Ἰακώβου*. The number of the

we hear (in the next verse) of the 'many disciples' who were 'following' Jesus. From this point onwards begins the regular usage of the word, perhaps 'thy disciples'[5] ii 18, at any rate 'his disciples' in ii 23, iii 7, 9.

Obviously the term 'the Twelve' cannot be used till the formal separation of an inner group among the disciples, iii 13 ff, and obviously at that point the use of some such phrase was imperative to express what was happening, and all three Synoptists agree so far. Luke (vi 13-17), unlike Matthew, keeps close to the order of Mark, but inverts the call of the twelve apostles and the notice of the wide districts from which hearers were now being attracted. In Mark it may be supposed that it was just the extension of the work which caused our Lord to create the first rudiments of organization in selecting the Twelve to be his companions and his delegates. Of the actual call Luke's account is limpid in its clearness, 'He called his disciples, and chose out of them twelve, whom he named "apostles", Simon, whom he named Peter, and...' Doubtless Luke understands himself to be giving the sum of Mark's rather involved account, 'He called whom he would and they came to him and he appointed twelve to be' his companions and apostolic delegates; 'and he appointed the Twelve and gave Simon the name Peter, and James ...': and it is just this involved character of Mark's account which prompts Meyer to see in it, quite unnecessarily as I think, a conflation of two separate strata of tradition.

In the first place, then, when Mark says 'he called whom he would and they came to him and he appointed twelve', I do not think he means to describe two acts, as Luke thought, but one. 'He summoned whom he would' is in fact the selection of the Twelve: and so Matthew appears to understand him when writing 'He summoned his twelve disciples' Matt. x 1 — odd as is the phrase *τοὺς δώδεκα μαθητάς αὐτοῦ*, when we have so far heard nothing about the disciples being twelve. Mark's *καὶ ἐποίησεν δώδεκα* is a characteristic piece of redundancy, due to his desire to emphasize the formal nature of the act, and should not be separated from the preceding verse by more than a comma.

Twelve had somehow to be filled up.

5 Probably B is right in omitting *μαθηταί* and reading *οἱ δὲ σοὶ οὐ νηστεύουσιν*: for (1) Luke has not got the word, which a little suggests that he did not find it in Mark, (2) the MSS which give it differ among themselves as to the place where they put it. I think it has come in from Matt. ix 14; and, if so, the reason of Mark's phrase may be that Jews hardly recognised the new Teacher's followers yet as organized 'disciples' in the same sense as those of the Baptist and of the Pharisees — it is something like 'Your people'.

So far any difficulty has been removed by exegesis and punctuation: for the next problems textual evidence must be called in to assist. Modern critics seem fairly unanimous in following Tischendorf, as against Westcott and Hort, and ejecting the words *οὓς καὶ ἀποστόλους ὠνόμασεν* from verse 14 as a plain contamination from Luke vi 13. Decision is not quite so simple as to the opening words of verse 16, *καὶ ἐποίησεν τοὺς δώδεκα*: but the omitting and inserting groups are so nearly the same as in the last case that, if there is anything in the principle *noscitur a sociis*, this phrase is naturally treated as a companion interpolation and should also disappear.[6] The names in the accusative, verses 17-19, will then depend directly on *ἐποίησεν* of verse 14, an awkwardness which Matthew removes by commencing a new sentence, 'Now the names of the Twelve Apostles were these'. Meyer's mountain has by now crumbled down to the rather ungrammatical parenthesis 'and he gave Simon the name Peter'.[7]

Our Lord had thus formed an inner circle, for intimate companionship and for missionary work, out of the whole number of his disciples. That is exactly the situation reflected in the two next mentions of the Twelve. In iv 10 'those who were round him with the Twelve' *οἱ περὶ αὐτὸν σὺν τοῖς δώδεκα*, ask of him the meaning of the parables. In vi 7 he summons the Twelve, and sends them out in pairs on a missionary tour, *προσκαλεῖται τοὺς δώδεκα καὶ ἤρξατο αὐτοὺς ἀποστέλλειν δύο δύο* : in vi 30 the 'apostles' or 'missionaries' return and report to him the results, and he retires with them privately to the wilder country across the lake.

That is to say, he is from now onwards more and more concentrating himself on the training of a select few, more and more withdrawing himself from his public ministry in Galilee. It was not done at any definite moment. There is a transition period, during which he reappears from time to time in Capernaum and its neighbourhood. 'His disciples' is a general term describing those who were associated with him at any particular moment. It becomes therefore a synonym for the Twelve, just in proportion as he journeys about more and more exclusively with them. Only the Twelve were with him in the desert place to which he retired for

---

6 *οὓς καὶ ἀποστόλους ὠνόμασεν* absent from A C^2 D L W all Latins syr-sin and Armenian: found in ℵ B C^* (*ut vid*) Δ Θ Ferrar group 28 sah. *καὶ ἐποίησεν τοὺς δώδεκα*, absent from A C^2 D L W Θ *fam.*1 *fam.*13 all Latins syr-sin sah and Armenian: found in ℵ B C^* Δ 565 700. The latter insertion may have been a marginal gloss to *καὶ ἐποίησεν δώδεκα* of verse 14: the glossator wanted to substitute 'the Twelve' for 'twelve', and fearing that a mere *τοὺς* would not make his meaning clear, wrote the phrase in full.

7 If with the Ferrar group and sah we could for *ἐποίησεν τοὺς δώδεκα* read *πρῶτον Σίμωνα*, the last difficulty would go. But the evidence is far too slight, I am afraid.

privacy, so that *οἱ μαθηταί αὐτοῦ* in the episode of the feeding of the multitudes who had followed him there (vi 35-41) are naturally the Twelve. On the other hand when he returned to the west of the lake and the neighbourhood of Capernaum, 'his disciples' (vii 2) may reassume the larger meaning, though it should be noted that 'his disciples' who enter the house with him (vii 17) cannot have been an indefinitely large company.

From vii 24 to vii 37 there is no mention either of the Twelve or of the disciples: Jesus was, it would seem, alone. The succeeding verses, viii 1-10 are probably a variant tradition of vi 35-45. In the continuous narrative 'his disciples' first therefore reappear at viii 27 on the road to Caesarea Philippi, on the occasion of the great confession of faith which forms the climax of the earlier part of the Ministry. If I read the Gospel rightly, the 'disciples' are from this point onwards practically identical with the Twelve, and I do not think that the Evangelist or his authority intended to make distinction between them. Perhaps the summoning of 'the crowd with his disciples', viii 34, may denote the older and larger body of followers. But the interval, if it was an interval, was a brief one, for less than a week (ix 2) separates the Confession from the Transfiguration, and the disciples of viii 27 are presumably also the disciples of ix 14. From Caesarea Philippi to Jerusalem the record is one of almost continuous movement. Once indeed Jesus revisited the scene of his earlier preaching, but it was, if one may use the phrase, incognito: 'they passed along through Galilee, and he would not that any should know,' for the subject-matter of his teaching was appropriate to a narrower circle only, ix 30, 31. Three times the Evangelist reiterates the prophecy of the Passion, viii 31, ix 31, x 33. On the first occasion the recipients were apparently the group of disciples who accompanied Jesus on the way to Caesarea Philippi, since when Peter was shocked by what was told him and burst into vehement protest, Jesus 'turned round and saw his disciples', viii 32, 33. On the second occasion the teaching was again addressed to 'his disciples', ix 31; on the third to the Twelve, x 32-34. There is an increasing definiteness of detail in the prophecy, but there seems to be no suggestion that those to whom it is addressed are other than before.

No other interpretation of the later chapters of the Gospel, viii 27 onwards (with the possible exception of viii 34), is so simple and so satisfactory as that which treats the phrases 'the disciples' and 'the Twelve', *οἱ μαθηταὶ αὐτοῦ* and *οἱ δώδεκα*, as practically synonyms.

'He was teaching his disciples ... and they came to Capernaum, and after going indoors he asked them what they had been talking about ...

and he called the Twelve ... and set a child in the middle of them,' ix 31-35. Is it reasonable to think that one set of persons had been discussing who was greatest, and that the moral was pointed to a different set?

The next two examples of the use of 'the disciples' tell us just the same tale. 'And when he was in the house the disciples again put questions to him about' the teaching he had been giving on divorce, x 10. Again we remind ourselves that those 'in the house' must have been a limited number, as in vii 17 and ix 33. And when 'the disciples' rebuked the forwardness of the mothers who brought children for his blessing, our Lord expressed his indignation in similar words and with the same action, *ἐναγκαλισάμενος*, as he had employed on the last occasion of the mention of the Twelve, x 13-16, cf ix 36, 37.[8]

After the episode of the rich young man, 'Jesus looked round on his disciples' with the saying 'How hard it will be for those with possessions to enter into the Kingdom of God,' x 23. But immediately after, x 24, the disciples are addressed as *τέκνα* — here only in the Gospels, save for John xiii 33, *τεκνία, ἔτι μικρὸν μεθ' ὑμῶν εἰμί* — a term indicative of affection and intimacy such as could not be applied outside a very narrow circle. Those to whom he spoke had given up home and everything to follow him (x 28). That need not mean the Twelve only: but it must mean a very few.

'And they were on the road going up to Jerusalem: and Jesus went on ahead ... and they followed him in fear. And he took the Twelve again into his company', and he repeated to them the prophecy of the Passion, connecting it now definitely with the very journey on which they had set out, x 32-34. It is an unnatural exegesis to distinguish between those from whom Jesus for the moment separated himself, and those whom he took 'again' into his company.

Precisely the same conclusion is suggested by the request of the brothers James and John, x 35 ff. It created grave indignation — among whom? among 'the disciples'? No, but among the remaining members of the Twelve, *οἱ δέκα*, x 41. There may have been some few others with him: but it is the Twelve who fill the foreground throughout the journey.

---

[8] If these two episodes stood alone, there would no doubt be something to be said for Meyer's hypothesis: the 'Twelve' source and the 'disciples' source had each, it might be suggested with some reason, an episode which emphasized by an appropriate action the necessity of the childlike spirit, the two stories being really variant accounts of the same thing. But they do not stand alone. We have in fact abundant evidence for the repetition by Jesus of the same teaching on different occasions, and also for the indifferent use by Mark, in the later chapters of his Gospel (ix 31, 35; xi 11, 14; xiv 12, 17), of the two phrases 'his disciples' and 'the Twelve' in reference to the same occasions.

Once more 'his disciples' leave Jericho with Jesus and the crowd, x 46: 'they draw near Jerusalem', and at the Mount of Olives he sends on 'two of his disciples' to prepare for the triumphal entry, xi 1: he entered the city, went into the Temple, swept his glance round over everything, but it was late and he did no more that night, but went out to Bethany — with the Twelve, *μετὰ τῶν δώδεκα*, xi 11. Next day on his return he pronounced the doom of the barren fig-tree 'and his disciples heard it' xi 14. Were the Twelve, then, who went out with him to Bethany in the evening, different from the 'disciples' who came back with him in the morning?

From xi 27 to xii 34 the narrative is occupied by the public debates, if we may so put it, with the authorities at large, with the different parties separately, and with an individual scribe. The crisis is approaching: the breach is complete: for the last time Jesus teaches the crowd, and forces the situation by direct denunciation of the religious leaders of the people. If they give largely to the treasury, their income is extracted from helpless widows: and one such widow, he tells 'his disciples', had given more than any of them, xii 35-44.

As he left the Temple, 'one of his disciples' called his attention to its magnificence: he answered with a prophecy of its destruction. They ascended the Mount of Olives: and the four leading apostles — the only apostles, unless Levi was one, who are mentioned by name (apart from Judas Iscariot) in the Gospel — asked him to explain himself further. It was apparently in answer to their request, and to them only, that he imparted his teaching about the End, xiii 5-37.

So far then in these chapters there seems no valid reason for distinguishing between 'the disciples' and 'the Twelve': and now we come immediately[9] to a very clear case for identification in xiv 12-17, where 'his disciples say to him Where do you want us to go and prepare for your passover? and he sends two of his disciples [Peter and John, according to Luke xxii 8] ... and the disciples went out and ... found just what he told them and prepared the passover: and in the evening he came with the Twelve'. Once more we ask, were the disciples who spoke about the passover in the morning a separate set from the Twelve who kept it with Jesus in the evening?

---

[9] The reading of D and some Latins (not k) in xiv 4 *οἱ δὲ μαθηταὶ αὐτοῦ* is a mere assimilation to Matt. xxvi 8.

After this the phrase *οἱ δώδεκα* is not used again, save as a definition of Judas Iscariot, xiv 10[10], 20, 43: nor *οἱ μαθηταί*, save in the Garden of Gethsemane, xiv 32, where it must mean those who were at the Last Supper, and in the angelic message, xvi 7, where it is in close connexion with Peter, *εἴπατε τοῖς μαθηταῖς αὐτοῦ καὶ τῷ Πέτρῳ*. 'His disciples' are a group of which Peter is head. It is impossible not to be reminded of the apostolic Creed-form in 1 Cor. xv 3-5 *παρέλαβον* ... *ὅτι ὤφθη Κηφᾷ εἶτα τοῖς δώδεκα*.

The argument here developed does not imply an absolute identification of the phrases 'the disciples' 'the Twelve' in the latter part of St Mark's Gospel. There may have been a few in the band that accompanied Jesus on his last journey who were on the fringe of the Twelve but not actually belonging to it. What is asserted is that for practical purposes the phrases come to the same thing, and that the Evangelist neither meant a sharp distinction himself between the two nor composed his narrative out of two sources each of which used one, and one only, of them. The discrimination of sources in the case of secondary documents like Matthew and Luke is of course one of the principal tasks of the critic. That every document is constructed on the basis of different literary sources is an assumption and an unjustifiable one. That Mark in particular used a 'disciple' source and a 'Twelve' source is in my judgement pure fantasy — or rather it could only be due to fantasy if it were not in fact due rather to *Tendenz*.

Meyer has made up his mind that Jesus cannot have foreseen the continuity of the movement which he called into being so far as to have equipped it with the rudiments of authority, and in that sense of organization, in the persons of the Twelve. That conclusion can only be established by a ruthless undermining of the evidence of St Mark's Gospel as it stands: and Meyer does not shrink from this. I have tried to show on the other hand, firstly, that this Gospel represents a natural development in the Ministry of Jesus by which he gradually restricted his teaching, as it became more advanced and faced more and more clearly the apparent failure of the movement, to a limited number of his followers; and secondly, that the 'disciples' who receive this later teaching being in effect the 'Twelve', the Evangelist uses one or other phrase indifferently to describe them, and that any analysis which attempts to separate the two uses as indicating two rival sources raises so many difficulties that it can only be called, even on literary grounds, a failure.

---

10 xiv 10 *ὁ εἷς τῶν δώδεκα* ℵ B C* L. The reading is too strange to be an invention. I take it to mean 'the Judas who was one of the Twelve' as opposed to the Judas who was, according to St Mark's list, not of the Twelve.

VIII – Auxiliary and quasi-auxiliary verbs.

i. The past tense of the substantive verb ἦν ἦσαν with present active, present or perfect passive, participle as auxiliary; exactly equivalent to our English 'was' 'were' *with present and past participle (rare in Matthew: frequent in Mark and Luke)*†

1. i 6 *ἦν ὁ Ἰωάνης ἐνδεδυμένος τρίχας καμήλου ... καὶ ἔσθων ἀκρίδας*. No parallel in Luke: altered by Matthew. In classical Greek this construction would be quite regular, but the tense would be pluperfect and the meaning 'had been clothed'. Mark means 'was clothed'.

2. i 13 *ἦν ἐν τῇ ἐρήμῳ ... πειραζόμενος ὑπὸ τοῦ Σατανᾶ*, 'was ... being tempted', though both A.V. and R.V. have, less exactly, 'was ... tempted'. Neither Matthew nor Luke is strictly parallel. Present passive participle only once again, in **17**.

3. i 22 *ἦν γὰρ διδάσκων αὐτοὺς ὡς ἐξουσίαν ἔχων*, 'was teaching'. The only case where both Matthew and Luke retain Marcan construction.

4. i 33 *ἦν ὅλη ἡ πόλις ἐπισυνηγμένη πρὸς τὴν θύραν*. Not (of course) 'had been gathered', but 'was gathered'. No Synoptic parallel.

5. i 39 *ἦν κηρύσσων εἰς τὰς συναγωγὰς αὐτῶν*, 'was preaching'. As pointed out in ch. III of these Notes W-H give a wrong reading here with ℵ B L *ἦλθεν*, due to the desire to find a construction for *εἰς*. Not only does the Lucan parallel (iv 44) support *ἦν*, but Mark i 14 is decisive on the same side: Jesus 'came into Galilee preaching', at the outset of His ministry, here He 'continued preaching'. Luke retains the construction, Matthew alters it.

6. ii 6 *ἦσαν δέ τινες τῶν γραμματέων ἐκεῖ καθήμενοι καὶ διαλογιζόμενοι*, 'were sitting there and discussing'. Matthew alters: Luke retains *ἦσαν καθήμενοι*, but removes it to the opening of the story, v 17.

7. ii 18 *ἦσαν οἱ μαθηταὶ Ἰωάνου καὶ οἱ Φαρισαῖοι νηστεύοντες*. The statement is dropped at this point by both Matthew and Luke.

8. iv 38 *αὐτὸς ἦν ἐν τῇ πρύμνῃ ... καθεύδων*. Again altered by both, by Matthew to the imperfect, by Luke to an aorist.

9. v 5 *ἦν κράζων καὶ κατακόπτων ἑαυτὸν λίθοις*, 'continually, night and day ... he was crying out and cutting himself ...' The verse is dropped in both derivative accounts.

10. v 11 *ἦν δέ ἐκεῖ ... ἀγέλη χοίρων μεγάλη βοσκομένη*. Retained by Matthew, probably because the verb need not go with the participle: 'there was there a great herd feeding', rather than 'a great herd was feeding there'. Luke makes that clearer by altering to *βοσκομένων*.[1]

---

[1] *βοσκομένη* in Luke viii 32, in spite of the strong authority of ℵ B D (not *d*) Θ *a*,

11. vi 52 *ἦν αὐτῶν ἡ καρδία πεπωρωμένη*. No parallels.

12. ix 4 *καὶ ἦσαν συνλαλοῦντες τῷ Ἰησοῦ*. Both Matthew and Luke alter, Luke to the imperfect *συνελάλουν*, Matthew by suppressing *ἦσαν* and connecting the participle with the preceding verb.

13. x 22 *ἦν γὰρ ἔχων χρήματα* [*v.l.* *κτήματα*] *πολλά*. Here it is Matthew who retains the Marcan construction, Luke who alters it (*ἦν πλούσιος*): but see further, on this verse and context, § v 15 below.

14. x 32*a* *ἦσαν δὲ ἐν τῇ ὁδῷ ἀναβαίνοντες εἰς Ἱεροσόλυμα*. Luke omits the verse, Matthew quite alters the construction.

15. x 32*b*. *καὶ ἦν προάγων αὐτοὺς ὁ Ἰησοῦς*. No parallels.

16. xiv 4 *ἦσαν δέ τινες ἀγανακτοῦντες πρὸς ἑαυτούς*. No parallel in Luke: Matthew alters to the aorist.

17. xiv 40 *ἦσαν γὰρ αὐτῶν οἱ ὀφθαλμοὶ καταβαρυνόμενοι*. Matthew retains the construction but alters the present to the perfect participle: by so doing he may keep the letter of grammatical rule, but it is to the havoc of the sense, for the pluperfect is quite out of place. Their eyes 'were being weighed down', not 'had been weighed down'. There is no parallel in Luke.

18. xiv 49 *καθ' ἡμέραν ἤμην πρὸς ὑμᾶς ἐν τῷ ἱερῷ διδάσκων*. Altered by Luke to a participle, *ὄντος μου* (avoiding two verbs connected with *καὶ*), by Matthew, because he disliked the construction, to *ἐκαθεζόμην*.

19. xiv 54 *ἦν συνκαθήμενος μετὰ τῶν ὑπηρετῶν*. Here for the first time both Matthew and Luke make the same alteration, substituting *ἐκάθητο* for *ἦν συνκαθήμενος* — though one has *μετὰ τῶν* with Mark and the other *μέσος αὐτῶν*. But it is not beyond the ordinary doctrine of chances that in this solitary case out of a list of twenty-four passages the two later Evangelists should independently hit on so simple a change.

20. xv 7 *ἦν δὲ ὁ λεγόμενος Βαραββᾶς μετὰ τῶν στασιαστῶν δεδεμένος*. 'Now the fellow called Barabbas was ... lying in prison'. A.V. wrongly separates *ἦν* from *δεδεμένος*, rendering 'there was one ... Barabbas which lay bound'; R.V. is ambiguous. Mark's whole reference to Barabbas is so awkwardly expressed, that it is not to be wondered at that the story is re-drafted by the other two Evangelists.

21. xv 26 *ἦν ἡ ἐπιγραφὴ τῆς αἰτίας αὐτοῦ ἐπιγεγραμμένη*. Both the others change, partly perhaps because the brevity of the Marcan account seemed to call for expansion: Mark e.g. does not tell us where the inscription was put.

---

looks like an assimilation to Matthew (and Mark).

22. xv 40 *ἦσαν δὲ καὶ γυναῖκες ἀπὸ μακρόθεν θεωροῦσαι*. Retained by Matthew, probably for the reason suggested on no. **10** above: altered by Luke.

23. xv 43 *ὅς καὶ αὐτὸς ἦν προσδεχόμενος τὴν βασιλείαν τοῦ θεοῦ*. Altered by both, by Luke to the imperfect of the same verb, by Matthew to the aorist of another verb.

24. xv 46 *ἐν μνήματι ὃ ἦν λελατομημένον ἐκ πέτρας*, 'which was hewn out' A.V. rightly: R.V. which had rendered the idiom rightly in **1**, **4**, **11**, **21**, at last found a chance to hark back to the classical pluperfect, 'which had been hewn out'. But Marcan usage is clear. Matthew changes to the active *ὃ ἐλατόμησεν ἐν τῇ πέτρᾳ*, Luke to the shorter but perhaps more ambiguous phrase *ἐν μνήματι λαξευτῷ*.

The number of instances cited shews that we have here a favourite locution of Mark. No difference has been made in the list between instances of the present active (or passive **2**, **17**) participle and instances of the perfect passive participle, because it does not appear that Mark made any. But his most characteristic usage is with the present participle, ([**2**], **3**, **5**, **6**, **7**, **8**, **9**, **10**, **12**, **13**, **14**, **15**, **16**, [**17**], **18**, **19**, **22**, **23**, or three out of every four cases), and it is exactly equivalent to our own use of the auxiliary verb and participle for the imperfect 'he was teaching' 'they were fasting' 'he was in the stern sleeping'. Similarly the construction with the perfect passive participle corresponds closely enough to our 'he was clothed'. Matthew very rarely uses any form of the construction; never with the present participle, except in the few cases he takes over unaltered from Mark, **3**, **10**, **13**, **22**. Luke on the other hand is not averse to it in the rest of his Gospel, but he prunes it away drastically from his Marcan material, leaving it only in the three first cases of his meeting with it, **3**, **5**, **6**.

It might almost be said that this construction with the auxiliary verb is for Mark, as for us, the real imperfect: for his use of the proper imperfect is little, if at all, removed from his use of the aorist. In cases such as ii 27 *ἔλεγεν αὐτοῖς* Τὸ *σάββατον διὰ τὸν ἄνθρωπον κτλ*, or v 30 *ἐπιστραφεὶς ἐν τῷ ὄχλῳ ἔλεγεν* Τίς *μου ἥψατο*; it seems quite impossible to read into *ἔλεγεν* any sense different from that of *εἶπεν*. When Mark wants to give the continuous sense of the imperfect, he uses *ἦν* with the present participle: just as when he wants to give another shade of the imperfect, the inchoative sense, 'began to do' a thing, he uses what is in effect another auxiliary verb, as we shall now see.[2]

[2] Both uses, *ἦν* with present participle and *ἤρξατο* with present infinitive, reflect Aramaic use, cf. G.Dalman, *Die Worte Jesu* pp. 28, 21.

ii. The verb ἄρχομαι (ἤρξατο ἤρξαντο) with present infinitive as auxiliary for the imperfect (Matthew 10 times, Mark 26, Luke 18).†

1. i 45 *ὁ δὲ ἐξελθὼν ἤρξατο κηρύσσειν* ... Matthew omits the verse: Luke has a (roughly parallel) imperfect.

2. ii 23 *οἱ μαθηταὶ αὐτοῦ ἤρξαντο ὁδὸν ποιεῖν τίλλοντες* ... Matthew retains *ἤρξαντο*: Luke again substitutes an imperfect.

3. iv 1 *καὶ πάλιν ἤρξατο διδάσκειν παρὰ τὴν θάλασσαν.* Both Matthew and Luke omit the phrase.

4. v 17 *καὶ ἤρξαντο παρακαλεῖν αὐτὸν ἀπελθεῖν* ... Both the other Synoptists change into an aorist.

5. v 20 *καὶ ἀπῆλθεν καὶ ἤρξατο κηρύσσειν* ... No parallel in Matthew: Luke substitutes a participle, *ἀπῆλθεν κηρύσσων.*

6. vi 2 *καὶ γενομένου σαββάτου ἤρξατο διδάσκειν ἐν τῇ συναγωγῇ.* No parallel in Luke: Matthew gives the imperfect.

7. vi 7 *ἤρξατο αὐτοὺς ἀποστέλλειν δύο δύο, καὶ ἐδίδου αὐτοῖς ἐξουσίαν*... No strict parallel in either Synoptist: but for the imperfect *ἐδίδου* both substitute the aorist *ἔδωκεν*. Here, and often in Mark, *ἤρξατο* marks a 'beginning' in the sense of a new departure rather than a continuous process.

8. vi 34 *καὶ ἤρξατο διδάσκειν αὐτοὺς πολλά.* The whole phrase disappears from both the other accounts: but in the next verse Luke ix 12 has *ἡ δὲ ἡμέρα ἤρξατο κλίνειν*. That is to say, he borrows Mark's *ἤρξατο*, but transfers it to something to which 'beginning' was strictly appropriate: 'the sun began to get low'.

9. vi 55 *καὶ ἤρξαντο ἐπὶ τοῖς κραβάττοις τοὺς κακῶς ἔχοντας περιφέρειν.* The whole paragraph is absent from Luke: Matthew substitutes an aorist, *προσήνεγκαν.*

10. viii 11 *καὶ ἐξῆλθον οἱ Φαρισαῖοι καὶ ἤρξαντο συνζητεῖν αὐτῷ.* Matthew has an imperfect: Luke has the Q account of the demand for a sign (xi 29), and therefore leaves out Mark's account.

11. viii 31 *καὶ ἤρξατο διδάσκειν αὐτοὺς ὅτι δεῖ* ... Retained by Matthew: Luke has an aorist participle.

12. viii 32 *καὶ προσλαβόμενος ὁ Πέτρος αὐτὸν ἤρξατο ἐπιτιμᾶν αὐτῷ.* So also Matthew: Luke omits the episode.

13. x 28 *ἤρξατο λέγειν ὁ Πέτρος αὐτῷ.* In both the other accounts *εἶπεν.*

14. x 32 *ἤρξατο αὐτοῖς λέγειν τὰ μέλλοντα αὐτῷ συμβαίνειν*: just as viii 31, no. **11**. Once more both Matthew and Luke have simply *εἶπεν*.

15. x 41 *καὶ ἀκούσαντες οἱ δέκα ἤρξαντο ἀγανακτεῖν* ... Luke, to save the credit of two leading apostles, omits all personal references in this episode: Matthew leaves the main story untouched, but for *ἤρξαντο ἀγανακτεῖν* substitutes the aorist *ἠγανάκτησαν*.

16. x 47 (of Bartimaeus) *ἤρξατο κράζειν καὶ λέγειν* ... Very probably he did begin and go on with repeated cries: but both Matthew and Luke are, as usual, content with an aorist.

17. xi 15 *ἤρξατο ἐκβάλλειν τοὺς πωλοῦντας*. Matthew again has the aorist: Luke by exception (and so in no. **18**) retains the Marcan phrase.

18. xii 1 *καὶ ἤρξατο αὐτοῖς ἐν παραβολαῖς λαλεῖν Ἀμπελῶνα* ... Matthew, having just inserted in the Marcan framework the parable of the Two Sons, naturally omits the whole phrase: Luke follows Mark again, as in the last preceding case.

19. xiii 5 *ἤρξατο λέγειν αὐτοῖς Βλέπετε μή τις ὑμᾶς πλανήσῃ*. As in no. 11, it is a real commencement of new matter, the eschatological discourse. Notwithstanding, both the other Synoptists prefer to treat our Lord's words simply as an answer to the question put to Him, 'When shall these things be?' and so introduce them with an aorist.

20. xiv 19 *ἤρξαντο λυπεῖσθαι καὶ λέγειν αὐτῷ* ... Matthew retains *ἤρξαντο*: Luke omits this and the following verse. perhaps because it seemed impossible that any but the actual traitor could have needed to put the question 'Is it I?'

21. xiv 33 *ἤρξατο ἐκθαμβεῖσθαι καὶ ἀδημονεῖν*. Matthew once more retains *ἤρξατο*: Luke omits the whole verse.

22. xiv 65 *καὶ ἤρξαντό τινες ἐμπτύειν αὐτῷ*. For this Matthew has an aorist, Luke (better) an imperfect.

23. xiv 69 *καὶ ἡ παιδίσκη ἰδοῦσα αὐτὸν ἤρξατο πάλιν λέγειν*. For this Matthew has a present tense, Luke an aorist. B and the Sahidic, moved by just the same considerations as the two Evangelists, substitute *εἶπεν* in St. Mark for the characteristic language of the author.

24. xiv 71 *ὁ δὲ ἤρξατο ἀναθεματίζειν*. So too Matthew: Luke, not liking to attribute oaths or curses to the apostle, contents himself with the statement of fact 'Peter said'.

25. xv 8 *ὁ ὄχλος ἤρξατο αἰτεῖσθαι* ... The verse has nothing corresponding to it in the other two accounts.

26. xv 18 *καὶ ἤρξαντο ἀσπάζεσθαι αὐτόν*. Cf. no. **22**: there, as here, Matthew has, instead of *ἤρξαντο*, an aorist. No parallel in Luke.

Out of these twenty-six instances, there are parallels in Matthew to nineteen, in Luke to fifteen: Matthew gets rid of *ἤρξα(ν)το* thirteen times, or twice in every three, Luke twelve times, or four times out of every five. As with regard to the substantive verb and participle, so here Matthew is averse to the construction himself, and where he does use it it is more often than not (six times out of ten: see **2**, **11**, **12**, **20**, **21**, **24**) taken over straight from Mark; while conversely Luke is again not so disinclined to the usage on his own account, but leaves it unaltered in Mark less often than Matthew, **17**, **18**, and see on **8**.

iii. The verb δύναμαι as auxiliary (altogether Matthew 27 times, Mark 33, Luke 26).†

Not only is the verb *δύναμαι* more common in Mark than in either Matthew or Luke, but in many cases its force is so weakened that it becomes almost an auxiliary verb, and corresponds to our 'can' 'could' or even 'may' 'might'. Translation of this shade of meaning is therefore easy in English, and the Authorized Version uses ordinarily 'can' and 'could', but in iv 32 'may', in xiv 5 'might have been sold', and in iv 33 'as they were able'. In about half the cases of the use of *δύναμαι* in St. Mark, there is nothing remarkable about it, and they will not be cited here: where there are parallels in the other Synoptists, they do not shrink from repeating Mark's phraseology; where, as in the majority of cases, a negative is expressed or implied, we could paraphrase 'it is impossible'. But in the other half Mark's usage of *δύναμαι* is tending towards an auxiliary sense, and any rendering like 'it is not possible' would exaggerate his meaning: R.V. (though it may be right in substituting 'are able' for the 'can' of A.V. in Mark x 38, 39) goes wrong when it tries to represent the future *δυνήσεται* (iii 25, viii 4, ix 39) by 'will (shall) be able': for the 'can' of A.V. all that is necessary is to put 'could'.

The cases that follow are those where the weakened or auxiliary use is probable or at least possible.

1. i 45 *ὥστε μηκέτι αὐτὸν δύνασθαι εἰς πόλιν φανερῶς εἰσελθεῖν*. There was no physical impossibility: A.V., R.V., rightly 'could no more'. No parallel in Matthew or Luke.

2. iii 20 *ὥστε μὴ δύνασθαι αὐτοὺς μηδὲ ἄρτον φαγεῖν*. No parallels: but cf. Mark vi 31 *οὐδὲ φαγεῖν εὐκαίρουν* where the sense is practically the same as in iii 20 'They could not even get a meal'. Again no question of physical impossibility.

3. iii 23, 24, 25, 26 *πῶς δύναται Σατανᾶς Σατανᾶν ἐκβάλλειν; ... οὐ δύναται σταθῆναι ... οὐ δυνήσεται στῆναι ... οὐ δύναται στῆναι*. Probably Matthew and Luke take the passage from Q: in any case they avoid the use of *δύναμαι* right through. (But Matthew follows Mark iii 27 in using it of the entry into the strong man's house.)

4. iv 32 *ὥστε δύνασθαι ὑπὸ τὴν σκιὰν αὐτοῦ τὰ πετεινὰ τοῦ οὐρανοῦ κατασκηνοῦν*. Matthew retains Mark's construction but substitutes *ἐλθεῖν* for *δύνασθαι*: Luke turns the clause into a statement of fact *καὶ ... κατεσκήνωσεν*. Q may once more have affected Matthew and Luke: but anyhow they have in fact both avoided Mark's *δύνασθαι*, which A.V. very well renders 'may'.

5. iv 33. He spoke the word to them in parables *καθὼς ἠδύναντο ἀκούειν*. No parallel in Luke: Matthew omits the phrase. A.V. and R.V. 'as they were able to hear it', but I suspect that Mark does not mean more than 'in proportion to their capacity' 'as they could hear'.

6. vi 5 *οὐκ ἐδύνατο ἐκεῖ ποιῆσαι οὐδεμίαν δύναμιν*. No parallel: but obviously Mark means that it was a moral impossibility for Christ to work miracles where there was not faith to correspond. Both our versions rightly 'could there do'.

7. vii 15 *ὃ δύναται κοινῶσαι αὐτόν* (cf. *v*. 18). No parallel in Luke: Matthew substitutes the simple *κοινοῖ*, because 'can defile' hardly means more here than 'does defile'.

8. ix 39 *οὐδεὶς γάρ ἐστιν ὃς ποιήσει δύναμιν ἐπὶ τῷ ὀνόματί μου καὶ δυνήσεται ταχὺ κακολογῆσαί με*. 'Could easily revile me' is surely the right shade of the meaning, rather than 'shall be able to' of R.V. No parallel in Matthew or Luke.

9. xiv 5 *ἠδύνατο γὰρ τοῦτο τὸ μύρον πραθῆναι ...* So Matthew: no parallel in Luke. 'Might have been sold' A.V. and R.V., rightly.

10. xiv 7 *ὅταν θέλητε δύνασθε ... εὖ ποιῆσαι*. Matthew omits: Luke again has no parallel. A.V. 'whensoever ye will ye may do them good' is exactly right: 'can do them good' of R.V. is unnecessary, and 'are able to do them good' would be an exaggeration of emphasis.

Consideration of Mark's use of *δύναμαι* does not perhaps at first sight compel us to conclusions so clear as those of the two preceding sections of this paper. But it cannot be without significance that Mark uses this verb, in proportion to the length of his Gospel, about twice as often as the other two Synoptists: and that being so, I think it is legitimate to apply the presumption to be drawn from his use of auxiliary verbs in general to this particular case. The parallel of our own language shows us how a verb like 'can' has tended to lose something of its original force: 'can you come to lunch to-morrow?' is intermediate between 'will you come?' and 'are you able to come?' Verbs like *ἰσχύω* begin to replace the stricter meaning of *δύναμαι* in later Greek. In Mark ix 18 'I said to thy disciples that they should cast it out' *καὶ οὐκ ἴσχυσαν*, both the other Synoptists substitute *οὐκ ἠδυνήθησαν*, perhaps from *οὐκ ἠδυνήθημεν* of Mark ix 28. Did the father use a stronger word than the apostles?

iv. The verb θέλω as auxiliary (altogether Matthew 39 times, Mark 25, Luke 28).†

Θέλω is even more definitely an auxiliary in Mark than *δύναμαι*. It cannot indeed be distinguished from *βούλομαι*, since the latter word has almost dropped out from the language of the Gospels, and *θέλω* has replaced it. But *θέλω* itself hardly expresses the idea of a strong definite wish: for that sense other words have to be found, and *θέλω* in Mark can almost always be rendered by our own auxiliary verbs 'will' (in the present tense) and 'would' (in the past). Since, however, we use 'shall' and not 'will' as the auxiliary verb in the first person (singular and plural), the rule does not apply to the forms *θέλω θέλομεν*: Mark vi 25 *θέλω ἵνα ἐξαυτῆς δῷς μοι* is really mistranslated by the 'I will' of both A.V. and R.V.: x 35 *θέλομεν ἵνα ὃ ἐὰν αἰτήσωμέν σε ποιήσῃς ἡμῖν* is better rendered by them 'we would'; 'I want' or 'I should like' would be the most exact equivalents, and so indeed also, though the existing rendering has too sacred associations to be replaced by any other, in xiv 36.

It is interesting to note further how often in Mark the verbs *θέλω* and *δύναμαι*, our 'would' and 'could', stand in context and contrast with one another: i 40 *ἐὰν θέλῃς δύνασαί με καθαρίσαι*, 'if you would, you could make me clean'; vi 19 *ἤθελεν αὐτὸν ἀποκτεῖναι καὶ οὐκ ἠδύνατο*, 'she would have killed him, but could not' (A.V. is right: R.V. 'desired to kill him' is wrong); vii 24 *οὐδένα ἤθελεν γνῶναι καὶ οὐκ ἠδυνάσθη λαθεῖν*, 'he would have remained incognito, but could not'; xiv 7 *ὅταν θέλητε δύνασθε αὐτοῖς πάντοτε εὖ ποιῆσαι*, 'if you would, you could be benefiting them continually'.

That *θέλω* must not be translated 'wish' or 'desire' in St. Mark is made abundantly clear by vi 48 *ἤθελεν παρελθεῖν αὐτούς*, which of course does not mean 'He desired to pass them by', but exactly what we express by 'He would have passed them by' — if they had not noticed Him and stopped Him.

Now let us take some other passages in order, and see how they fit in with the principles of rendering just enunciated.

iii 13 *προσκαλεῖται οὓς ἤθελεν αὐτός*. Here we approach nearer than anywhere else in the Gospel to the sense of 'choice', and it is possible that this is just what is suggested by the otherwise inexplicable *αὐτός*. For obviously it cannot mean 'whom he himself selected and not somebody else', so that R.V.'s 'whom he himself would' is pure nonsense: and though St Mark wrote a Greek of his own and not that of the grammars, he meant something by it. *Faute de mieux,* it may therefore not be too bold to suggest that what he did mean by *αὐτός* was to add the element of personal choice to the colourless word *ἤθελεν*, and so for A.V. 'whom he would' I would substitute 'whom he willed'.

vi 26 *οὐκ ἠθέλησεν ἀθετῆσαι αὐτήν.* For 'he would not reject her' I should be inclined to write 'he did not want to reject her'. That is, I think, the best rendering where a negative precedes *θέλω*.

viii 34 *εἴ τις θέλει ὀπίσω μου ἐλθεῖν.* A.V. is right with 'will come after me', rather than R.V. with 'would come after me'. Note that in the next verse *ὃς ἐὰν θέλῃ σῶσαι* is strictly parallel to *ὃς δ' ἂν ἀπολέσει* — for it will hardly be suggested that a 'will to save life' is contrasted with an accidental or involuntary loss of it. No instances could show more clearly that *θέλω* is *practically* an auxiliary verb, and nothing else.

So ix 35, x 43.

ix 13 *ἐποίησαν αὐτῷ ὅσα ἤθελον.* Both A.V. and R.V. 'what they listed': that is, in modern English, 'what they liked'. Not 'what they willed'.

x 36 *τί θέλετε ποιήσω ὑμῖν;* Our authorities vary a good deal in these words, but the reading is borne out by x 51 *τί σοι θέλεις ποιήσω;* xiv 12 *ποῦ θέλεις ἀπελθόντες ἑτοιμάσωμεν;* xv 9 *θέλετε ἀπολύσω ὑμῖν;* and possibly xv 12 *τί οὖν [θέλετε] ποιήσω;* 'What would ye I should do?' or in more modernized English 'what do you want me to do?'[3] The extraordinary reading of ℵ^c B Ψ in x 36 *τί θέλετέ με ποιήσω ὑμῖν;* is relegated to the margin of W-H, and must presumably be a conflation between two readings *ποιήσω* and *με ποιῆσαι*.

xii 38 *τῶν γραμματέων τῶν θελόντων ἐν στολαῖς περιπατεῖν.* A.V. 'love' is a shade too strong: but it is nearer the mark than R.V. 'desire'. Our exact equivalent is 'like' to walk in their best clothes.

One remaining word, and it is an important one, must be said about the construction *θέλω ἵνα*.[4] It is found three times in Mark, vi 25 *θέλω ἵνα ἐξαυτῆς δῷς μοι ἐπὶ πίνακι τὴν κεφαλὴν Ἰωάνου,* ix 30 *καὶ οὐκ ἤθελεν ἵνα τις γνοῖ,* x 35 *θέλομεν ἵνα ὃ ἐὰν αἰτήσωμέν σε ποιήσῃς ἡμῖν,* where the idiomatic rendering is, I think, 'I want you to give me' 'He did not

[3] In ix 5 the ordinary texts give *καὶ ποιήσωμεν τρεῖς σκηνάς*, and Luke too has *καὶ ποιήσωμεν*: but Matthew has *εἰ θέλεις ποιήσω*, and whence did he derive *εἰ θέλεις*, unless he read in Mark either *θέλεις ποιήσω* with D *b ff i*, or *θέλεις ποιήσωμεν* with Θ *fam* 13 565? 'would you like us to make three tabernacles?'

[4] The use of *ἵνα* in Mark demands special treatment. It is found 58 times in Mark, as against 33 and 37 times respectively in the longer Gospels of Matthew and Luke.

want any one to know' 'We want you to give us': once apiece in Matthew and Luke but in the same phrase, Matt. vii 12 = Luke vi 31 *ὅσα ἐὰν θέλητε (καθὼς θέλετε) ἵνα ποιῶσιν ὑμῖν οἱ ἄνθρωποι*, where perhaps the phrase of Q was already so ingrained in Christian use as not to permit of change: once in John, xvii 24. Now *θέλω νά* is the modern Greek for the future tense: obviously the *κοινή* of the first century A.D. was already moving in that direction, and Mark of all the Evangelists most nearly represents the *κοινή* unaffected by literary tradition. The usage of auxiliary verbs was already beginning to establish itself.

v. The verb ἔχω (73 times in Matthew, 68 in Mark, 76 in Luke).

The account of auxiliary and quasi-auxiliary verbs would be incomplete without some treatment of the verb *ἔχω*, which shares with the words hitherto treated a disproportionate frequency of usage in Mark as compared with Matthew and Luke, though it is not strictly auxiliary. Only in two passages is there anything like an echo of the low-Latin idiom of *habeo* with the past participle passive which has as we know established itself in the languages of Western Europe: iii 1 *ἄνθρωπος ἐξηραμμένην ἔχων τὴν χεῖρα*, viii 17 *πεπωρωμένην ἔχετε τὴν καρδίαν ὑμῶν*; That does a little bit suggest *arefactam habens manum,* and Matthew and Luke both instinctively substitute the adjective *ξηρά* for the participle *ἐξηραμμένη*: they have nothing parallel to viii 17. The papyri and modern Greek, I am told, show that Greek as well as Latin developed along the lines of the auxiliary use of 'have' with the perfect participle; and that would account for the two instances in Mark.

But Mark's fondness for *ἔχειν* goes much farther than this, and the tendency of the two other Synoptists, and especially Luke, to modify Mark's language on many of the occasions of its use, is worth recording. I do not propose to examine all, or anything like all, of the sixty-eight instances where *ἔχω* occurs: any Greek writer, literary or not, will of course be found to make regular use of the word: what is peculiar to Mark is partly just his fondness for it, partly certain characteristic methods of employing it where a better trained writer like Luke will generally avoid it.

1. i 22 *ὡς ἐξουσίαν ἔχων*. So Matthew: but Luke gets rid of *ἔχων* by writing *ἦν ἐν ἐξουσίᾳ ὁ λόγος αὐτοῦ*. In ii 10, iii 15, the same phrase is followed by an infinitive, which makes all the difference.

2. i 32 *τοὺς κακῶς ἔχοντας*, cf. i 34, ii 17, vi 55. In classical Greek this would be *κακῶς πράσσοντας* or *κακῶς πάσχοντας*: and therefore, though Matthew has no objection to the phrase, Luke avoids it here,

though he does not alter it where our Lord is the speaker, ii 17 *χρείαν ἔχουσιν ... ἰατροῦ ... οἱ κακῶς ἔχοντες* — probably a proverbial phrase, and for that reason also more difficult of change.

3. ii 19 *ὅσον χρόνον ἔχουσιν τὸν νυμφίον μετ' αὐτῶν*, cf. xiv 7 *πάντοτε τοὺς πτωχοὺς ἔχετε μεθ' ἑαυτῶν*. In ii 19 both Matthew and Luke omit the phrase, primarily no doubt because it is redundant after *ἐν ᾧ ὁ νυμφίος μετ' αὐτῶν ἐστίν*. But the use with *εἶναι* is the use satisfactory to Luke, cf. **1**, **5**, **9**, **13**.

4. ii 25 *χρείαν ἔσχεν*. Omitted by Matthew and Luke, and characteristically Marcan: but quite classical with a genitive following, ii 17, xi 3, xiv 63, and retained on each occasion by both Matthew and Luke.

5. iii 1, 3 *ἐξηραμμένην ἔχων τὴν χεῖρα* (see above), *τῷ τὴν χεῖρα ἔχοντι ξηράν*: on the first of the two occasions Luke vi 6 substitutes *ἡ χεὶρ αὐτοῦ ἡ δεξιὰ ἦν ξηρά*, cf, **1**, **3**. See the next note.

6. iii 10 *ὅσοι εἶχον μάστιγας*, cf. iii 22 *Βεεζεβοὺλ ἔχει*, iii 30 *πνεῦμα ἀκάθαρτον ἔχει*, v 15 *τὸν ἐσχηκότα τὸν λεγιῶνα*, vii 25 *εἶχεν τὸ θυγάτριον αὐτῆς πνεῦμα ἀκάθαρτον*, ix 17 *ἔχοντα πνεῦμα ἄλαλον*. Of these six cases of *ἔχειν* neither Matthew nor Luke (where they have parallels at all) retains any one. Luke paraphrases with *οἱ ἐνοχλούμενοι ὑπὸ ... ἀφ' οὗ τὰ δαιμόνια ἐξῆλθεν* (but in viii 27 he writes *ἔχων δαιμόνια*), Matthew with *κακῶς ἔχοντες*, *κακῶς δαιμονίζεται*, *κακῶς πάσχει*. Mark's use would seem to be sort of colloquial idiom, somewhat resembling our own 'a man with an unclean spirit' and the like.

7. iii 29 *οὐκ ἔχει ἄφεσιν*. Both Matthew and Luke substitute the cognate verb *ἀφίεσθαι*. Mark's use is very un-Greek — 'to have forgiveness' instead of 'to be forgiven' — and no better example of his exaggerated use of *ἔχειν* could be found.

8. iv 5, 5, 6, 17 *οὐκ εἶχεν γῆν πολλήν*, *διὰ τὸ μὴ ἔχειν βάθος γῆς*, *διὰ τὸ μὴ ἔχειν ῥίζαν*, *οὐκ ἔχουσιν ῥίζαν*. There is nothing wrong in these phrases, but they do illustrate the limitations of Mark's vocabulary and his fondness for an elementary verb like *ἔχειν*. Precisely similar is his repeated usage, for instance, of *ἔρχεσθαι*.

9. iv 40 *οὔπω ἔχετε πίστιν*; cf. xi 22 *ἔχετε πίστιν θεοῦ*. Again nothing absolutely incorrect, and Matthew has the construction three times, the Epistle of James twice. But common as *πίστις* is in St Paul's Epistles, *ἔχειν πίστιν* only occurs three times. Luke viii 25 changes to *ποῦ ἡ πίστις ὑμῶν*;

10. v 3 *κατοίκησιν εἶχεν ἐν τοῖς μνήμασιν*. Again Luke changes noun with *ἔχειν* to verb *ἔμενεν*, viii 27.

11. v 23 *ἐσχάτως ἔχει*. A colloquial phrase, unique in N.T., and condemned by purists as not found in Attic writers: see Rutherford *The New Phrynichus* p. 481. Both Matthew and Luke alter it.

12. vi 34 *ὡς πρόβατα μὴ ἔχοντα ποιμένα*, 'as sheep without a shepherd', see on **6** above. The phrase is adopted by Matthew in another context, Matt. ix 36. The idea is frequent in O.T., but the LXX (cf. Luke's usage, see on **3** above) always renders *οἷς οὐκ ἔστιν ποιμήν* (Swete).

13. vi 38, viii 5 *πόσους ἄρτους ἔχετε*; Matthew on both occasions has the same construction as Mark: Luke here (no parallel to viii 5) changes once more to the construction with *εἶναι*, see on **3**, *οὐκ εἰσὶν ἡμῖν πλεῖον ἢ* ... But in viii 16, 17 *ὅτι ἄρτους οὐκ ἔχουσιν*, *ὅτι ἄρτους οὐκ ἔχετε* (no Lucan parallel), Matthew substitutes *ἐλάβομεν*, *ἐλάβετε*.

14. ix 50 *ἔχετε ἐν ἑαυτοῖς ἅλα*. No parallel: but perhaps Matthew's *ὑμεῖς ἐστὲ τὸ ἅλας τῆς γῆς* (Matt. v 13) represents the Q form of the same Saying.

15. x 21 *ὅσα ἔχεις πώλησον*, 22 *ἦν γὰρ ἔχων χρήματα πολλά*, 23 *οἱ τὰ χρήματα ἔχοντες*. It is curious that Luke retains the first and third of these contiguous phrases, and changes the second to *ἦν γὰρ πλούσιος σφόδρα*, while Matthew retains in substance the second (with *κτήματα* for *χρήματα*) but changes the first to *πώλησόν σου τὰ ὑπάρχοντα* and the third to *πλούσιος*. Obviously the common instinct of both was to modify at some point or another Mark's superabundant use of *ἔχειν* in this context.

16. xi 13 *συκῆν* ... *ἔχουσαν φύλλα*, 'a fig-tree in leaf' 'with leaves'. Luke omits the whole episode because of its difficulty, Matthew omits *ἔχουσαν φύλλα*, perhaps simply because the phrase immediately following 'nothing but leaves' sufficiently implies that there were leaves.

17. xii 6 *ἔτι ἕνα εἶχεν υἱὸν ἀγαπητόν*. Both Matthew and Luke reconstruct the phrase, perhaps just in order to get rid of *ἔχω* in this connexion. A Greek would naturally have written not *εἶχεν υἱόν*, but *ἦν αὐτῷ υἱός*.

18. xiv 8 *ὃ ἔσχεν ἐποίησεν*, 'what she could she did'. Luke omits the episode, because he has already given a similar story in vii 37 ff: Matthew omits this sentence, it may be only to get rid of the collocation *ἐμὲ οὐ πάντοτε ἔχετε ὃ ἔσχεν* ... But the parallels which Swete quotes from Luke to this use of *ἔχω* (Luke vii 42, xii 4, xiv 14, Acts iv 14) are not strictly in point, for in each of them a negative precedes, and that makes a real difference.

Nothing was said above of i 38 *τὰς ἐχομένας κωμοπόλεις*, because this use of the participle of the middle voice is not *in pari materia* with the rest of the passages enumerated, and moreover it is quite good Greek.

APPENDIX

εἰδέναι, γινώσκειν, ἐπιγινώσκειν, substantially identical in sense in Mark.

We are all familiar with the distinction in classical Greek between *εἰδέναι* 'to know by intuition' and *γινώσκω* 'to know by experience or learning', or in other words between 'knowing' and 'learning'. But does this distinction exist for St Mark? Does not the process of degeneration of the language of which we have been accumulating evidence extend to these two similar verbs as well?

1. iv 13 *οὐκ οἴδατε τὴν παραβολὴν ταύτην; καὶ πῶς πάσας τὰς παραβολὰς γνώσεσθε*; (no parallel in Matthew or Luke).

Both A.V. and R.V. translate both words 'know': but Swete *ad loc.* would draw the ordinary distinction between 'knowledge which comes from intuition or insight' and 'that which is gained by experience or acquaintance'. Our versions are right, if only for the reason that there is no future of *εἰδέναι* in N.T.: *εἰδήσω* is only once found (Heb. viii 11), and that in a quotation from the LXX. But if *γνώσομαι* is used as the future of *εἰδέναι* — as it certainly appears to be in this passage — a presumption is already created that in Mark at any rate the two verbs are not really distinguishable. That presumption appears to be borne out in the passages which follow.

2. v 29, 33 *ἔγνω τῷ σώματι ὅτι ἴαται ἀπὸ τῆς μάστιγος ... εἰδυῖα ὃ γέγονεν αὐτῇ*.

Our versions make the distinction of 'felt' and 'knowing': but I do not think there is any justification for this, beyond perhaps the consideration that *γινώσκω* may tend to be used where the sphere of knowledge, *σώματι* or *πνεύματι*, is expressed.

3. xiii 28, 29; 33, 35 *γινώσκεται ὅτι ἐγγὺς τὸ θέρος ἐστίν ... γινώσκετε ὅτι ἐγγύς ἐστιν ἐπὶ θύραις ... οὐκ οἴδατε γὰρ πότε ὁ καιρός [ἐστιν] ... οὐκ οἴδατε γὰρ πότε ὁ κύριος τῆς οἰκίας ἔρχεται.*

Here it is not easy to give any other rendering throughout than 'know'. All that can be said is that it is practically a rule with the negative to use *οἴδατε* rather than *γινώσκετε*: cf. iv 27, ix 6, x 38, xi 33, xii 24, xiii 32, xiv 40.

4. xii 12 *ἔγνωσαν γὰρ ὅτι πρὸς αὐτοὺς τὴν παραβολὴν εἶπεν*, and xv 10 *ἐγίνωσκεν γὰρ ὅτι διὰ φθόνον παραδεδώκεισαν αὐτόν* (where Matthew at any rate thought that *ᾔδει* was the proper word to use) contrasted with ii 10 *ἵνα δὲ εἰδῆτε ὅτι ἐξουσίαν ἔχει ὁ υἱὸς τοῦ ἀνθρώπου ἀφιέναι*

ἁμαρτίας and xi 32 *ἅπαντες γὰρ ᾔδεισαν τὸν Ἰωάνην ὄντως ὅτι προφήτης ἦν*. Here I read *ᾔδεισαν* confidently with D W Θ 565 700 and O.L. including *k*: for (i) the alternative reading *εἶχον* is easily explained as introduced from Matthew, (ii) *ᾔδεισαν* suits better than *εἶχον* with the word *ὄντως* — you can 'know of a surety', but how can you 'regard of a surety'?

Does Mark mean to distinguish in these two sets of passages between two sorts of knowledge as predicated on these different occasions of Scribes and Pharisees, of Pilate, and of the crowd? I think the words are synonymous.

5. ii 8, v 30, viii 17, xii 15: the participles *γνούς*, *ἐπιγνούς*, *εἰδὼς*, as used of our Lord.

ii 8 *καὶ εὐθὺς ἐπιγνοὺς ὁ Ἰησοῦς τῷ πνεύματι αὐτοῦ ὅτι οὕτως διαλογίζονται* ... For this and the next case see on 2 above.

v 30 *καὶ εὐθὺς ὁ Ἰησοῦς ἐπιγνοὺς ἐν ἑαυτῷ τὴν ἐξ αὐτοῦ δύναμιν ἐξελθοῦσαν* ...

viii 17 *καὶ γνοὺς λέγει αὐτοῖς* Τί *διαλογίζεσθε ὅτι ἄρτους οὐκ ἔχετε;*

xii 15 *ὁ δὲ εἰδὼς αὐτῶν τὴν ὑπόκρισιν εἶπεν αὐτοῖς* Τί *με πειράζετε;* So B C L Δ Δ Ψ *a k* Vulg. Syriac and Egyptian versions against *ἰδών* of the rest: and in spite of xii 34 (and xii 28?) the preponderance of authority for *εἰδώς* here seems decisive.[5]

It does not seem possible to distinguish any difference of meaning between the three verbs as used of our Lord's knowledge in these four passages. What distinction there is is perhaps one of tense — *εἰδώς* being the present, *γνούς* and *ἐπιγνούς* the aorist: *γινώσκων*, *ἐπιγινώσκων*, are not found in Mark. In other words, when Mark wanted to write a present participle, he used that of *οἶδα*: when he was writing an aorist, he turned to *γινώσκω* or *ἐπιγινώσκω*. Just as with *οἴδατε* and *γνώσεσθε*, so with *εἰδώς* and *γνούς*, we construct the complete paradigm only by the help of the two verbs.

The practical identity of *γινώσκω* and *ἐπιγινώσκω* seems to be borne out by a comparison of vi 33 *καὶ ἔγνωσαν πολλοί* (if we read *ἔγνωσαν* with B D and *fam*. 1) *καὶ πεζῇ* ... *συνέδραμον* and vi 54 *εὐθὺς ἐπιγνόντες αὐτὸν περιέδραμον* ...

---

[5] Even if *εἰδώς* is not the correct reading in this passage, the participle reappears in v 33 (quoted above) and vi 20 of Herod *ἐφοβεῖτο τὸν Ἰωάνην, εἰδὼς αὐτὸν ἄνδρα δίκαιον καὶ ἅγιον*. So for the other two verbs cf. vi 54 *εὐθὺς ἐπιγνόντες αὐτόν* and xv 45 *γνοὺς ἀπὸ τοῦ κεντυρίωνος*.

IX. Lexical notes on (1) some ἅπαξ λεγόμενα: words used once in Mark, and nowhere else in the Gospels: (2) some words or phrases of common occurrence in Mark but rare in Matthew or Luke.

(1)

ἀποστερεῖν.†

Mark x 19 *μὴ ἀποστερήσῃς*. The word occurs among the list of the Commandments, and is clearly intended to be one of them: but because it does not in terms correspond to the Old Testament lists, it is dropped by both Matthew and Luke. It is quite certainly genuine, and is indeed presumably the source of the inclusion of 'fraud' among irremissible sins in the penitential discipline of the early Western Church. If *μὴ πορνεύσῃς* (after *μὴ μοιχεύσῃς*) at the beginning of the Marcan list is, as I suspect, genuine, then just as the Seventh Commandment is extended to include fornication, so here we may suppose the Eighth is extended to include fraud as well as literal theft.

For the use of *ἀποστερεῖν* in non-Christian writers I need do no more than refer to Field's admirable note *ad loc.* (*Notes on the Translation of the New Testament* p. 33): its technical meaning is that of holding back 'money or goods deposited with another for safe keeping'. But it is, I think, worth while to add some references from Christian writers, or in one case from a non-Christian writer in relation to Christian ethics; and with that object I begin by shewing that the earliest Latin rendering of *ἀποστερεῖν* is *abnegare.*

Mark x 19 'ne abnegaueris' *k,* 'non abnegabis' *a c.* Hermas *Mand.* iii 2 *ἀποστερηταὶ τοῦ Κυρίου*, lat. 'abnegant Dominum': *Mand.* viii 5 *ἀποστέρησις*, lat. 'ab abnegantia'. We can therefore confidently assume that where we find 'abnegare' in an appropriate context, it corresponds to *ἀποστερεῖν.*

Pliny *ep. ad Traianum 96*(Lightfoot, *S. Ignatius* i pp. 50-53: the well known letter about the Christians) 'seque sacramento non in scelus aliquod obstringere, sed ne furta, ne latrocinia, ne adulteria commiterent, ne fidem fallerent, ne depositum appellati abnegarent'.

Hermas *Mand.* iii 2 *οἱ οὖν ψευδόμενοι ἀθετοῦσι τὸν Κύριον, καὶ γίνονται ἀποστερηταὶ τοῦ Κυρίου, μὴ παραδίδοντες αὐτῷ τὴν παρακαταθήκην ἣν ἔλαβον. ἔλαβον γὰρ πνεῦμα ἄψευστον· τοῦτο ἐαν ψευδὲς ἀποδώσωσιν, ἐμίαναν τὴν ἐντολὴν τοῦ Κυρίου καὶ ἐγένοντο ἀποστερηταί.*

Id. *Mand.* viii 5 *καί γε πολλά, φησίν, ἔστιν ἀφ' ὧν δεῖ τὸν δοῦλον τοῦ Θεοῦ ἐγκρατεύεσθαι· κλέμμα, ψεῦσμα, ἀποστέρησις, ψευδομαρτυρία, πλεονεξία κτλ.*

Id. *Sim.* vi 5. 5 *ὁ ὀξύχολος ... καὶ ὁ μοιχὸς καὶ ὁ μέθυσος καὶ ὁ κατάλαλος καὶ ὁ ψεύστης καὶ ὁ πλεονέκτης καὶ ὁ ἀποστερητὴς καὶ ὁ τούτοις τὰ ὅμοια ποιῶν κτλ.*

Cyprian *ep.* lii 1 (Hartel 617. 1) 'Nicostratum quoque diaconio sanctae administrationis amisso, ecclesiasticis pecuniis sacrilega fraude subtractis et uiduarum ac pupillorum depositis denegatis ...'

κεφαλιόω.†

Mark xii 4 *καὶ πάλιν ἀπέστειλεν πρὸς αὐτοὺς ἄλλον δοῦλον· κἀκεῖνον ἐκεφαλίωσαν καὶ ἠτίμασαν.*

Our authorities vary between *ἐκεφαλίωσαν* (ℵ B L Ψ) and *ἐκεφαλαίωσαν* (A C D Θ etc.): *κεφαλιόω* is not given in Liddell and Scott, *κεφαλαιόω* only — apart from this passage in Mark — in the sense 'to sum up'. The earliest Latin rendering is 'decollauerunt' *k*: but the injury implied must be something between the *ἔδειραν* of verse 3 and the *ἀπέκτειναν* of verse 5, and it must be on the same plane with *ἠτίμασαν*: in other words, it must be some sort of treatment which would degrade a man, or at any rate make him look ridiculous. I do not see that to 'knock on the head', even if we could get that sense out of the Greek word, which is all but impossible, satisfies this condition: and I see no alternative but conjectural emendation. Burkitt proposes *ἐκολάφισαν*: but how is 'slapped' a worse form of punishment than 'thrashed'? and why should a fairly familiar word have suffered so gross a corruption? Very tentatively I suggest, that a metathesis of the syllables *κε* and *φα* has taken place, such as might occur with an unfamiliar word, and that we should read *ἐφακελίωσαν* (or *ἐφακέλωσαν*), 'trussed him up in a bundle'. *φάκελος* is a classical word, and the verbal form *φακελόω* is quoted in L. S. from the Byzantine writer Nicetas. I notice too in Thumb that *φακιόλι* is modern Greek for a turban. If this were the true reading, the procedure indicated would be preparatory to some degrading process expressed by *ἠτίμασαν.*

προδοῦναι.

Mark xiv 10 *ἵνα αὐτὸν προδοῖ* (*or προδοῖ αὐτὸν*) *αὐτοῖς* is the reading of D *c i k* vulg (proderet), where the other texts have the verb elsewhere always used in the Gospels, *παραδοῖ* (traderet). In the next verse *πῶς αὐτὸν εὐκαίρως παραδοῖ* stands without variant. I suspect that the Western reading in verse 10 is correct. The contrast between *προδοῖ* and *παραδοῖ* is very much to the point, *προδοῦναι* meaning 'to betray', *παραδοῦναι* properly to 'hand over', 'deliver up' to the chief priests. And it seems much more likely that the normal *παραδοῦναι* should be introduced by scribes and editors in place of the unusual word, than that the unusual word should have been, on this one occasion, introduced at all.

On the assumption then that *προδοῖ* is genuine, it will be, with Luke vi 16 *Ἰούδαν Ἰσκαριὼθ ὃς ἐγένετο προδότης*, the only New Testament source of any usage of *προδοῦναι προδότης*, *prodere proditor,* in early Greek and Latin Christian literature. But while *proditor* is good Latin enough, there is no noun *παραδότης* in Greek, and therefore *προδότης* was inevitable (as well as *προδοσία*), but for the verb *παραδοῦναι tradere* is so all but universal in the Gospels in connexion with Judas that any evidence for the use of the alternative word in Christian antiquity seems worth collecting.

Martyrium Polycarpi vi 1, 2 *ὁ εἰρήναρχος ὁ κεκληρωμένος τὸ αὐτὸ ὄνομα, Ἡρώδης ἐπιλεγόμενος, ἔσπευδεν εἰς τὸ στάδιον αὐτὸν εἰσαγαγεῖν· ἵνα ἐκεῖνος μὲν τὸν ἴδιον κλῆρον ἀπαρτίσῃ Χριστοῦ κοινωνὸς γενόμενος, οἱ δὲ προδόντες αὐτὸν τὴν αὐτοῦ τοῦ Ἰούδα ὑπόσχοιεν τιμωρίαν.*

But this single example of *προδοῦναι* refers primarily to the betrayal of Polycarp by a domestic rather than to the betrayal of Christ by Judas. One cannot therefore, on the evidence so far available, establish any influence of the solitary instance of *προδοῦναι* in St Mark, even if it is genuine, on Greek Christian usage.

The case for *prodere* in Latin is more respectable. It is of course clear that *προδοῖ* in Mark xiv 10, whether or no it is original, was the word rendered by the earliest Latin version: and the two writers now to be cited may or may not have derived their use of *prodere* from its use in this one instance in their Latin Gospels.

Cyprian *de eccl. unit.* 22 (Hartel, 229. 23) 'nam et Iudam inter apostolos Dominus elegit, et tamen Dominum Iudas postmodum prodidit [prodidit R M* prodit G tradidit W M^2]. non tamen idcirco apostolorum firmitas et fides cecidit quia proditor Iudas ab eorum societate defecit'.

Id. *ep.* lix 2 (668. 2) 'cum uideamus ipsum Dominum... ab eo quem inter apostolos ipse delegerat proditum'.

Ps.-Cypr. ad *Nouatianum* 14 (Hartel, iii 64. 20) 'Iudas ille inter apostolos electus...ipse postmodum deum prodidit'.

Proditor occurs also in Iren. lat. I xxviii 9 [xxxi 1] and II xxxii 3 [xx 5], but in the latter passage *traditor* two lines farther on: and in ps.-Tert. *adv. omn. haer.* 2. But as with *προδότης* this does not perhaps take us very far; though in Latin *traditor* was a possible (and presumably the usual) equivalent for the 'traitor'.

πυγμῇ.†

vii 3 *οἱ γὰρ Φαρισαῖοι καὶ πάντες οἱ Ἰουδαῖοι ἐὰν μὴ πυγμῇ νίψωνται τὰς χεῖρας οὐκ ἐσθίουσιν.*

Beyond question *πυγμῇ* stands rightly in the text: so all Greek MSS except ℵ W: but the word was unfamiliar, as the varieties in rendering shew — the Sinai Syriac omits, while of the Latins *a* has momento, *b* subinde, *d* primo, *c ff i* (more correctly) pugillo — and ℵ (followed, as so often, by Jerome in the Vulgate) W emend to *πυκνά*, crebro. But no one would have thought of altering a known word giving apparently (though not really) a suitable sense to anything as obscure as *πυγμῇ*. Now *πυγμή* means 'fist'; but it was also used as a measure of length 'from the fist to the elbow', and the Greek commentators Euthymius and Theophylact in fact interpret it here to mean thrusting the arm into the water up to the elbow (Swete). More than twenty years ago I called attention in *JTS* (vi p. 353), when reviewing Dom Butler's edition of the *Lausiac History* of Palladius, to the phrase in chapter lv, p. 148, l. 21, *νίψασθαι τὰς χεῖρας καὶ τοὺς πόδας πυγμῇ ὕδατι ψυχροτάτῳ*. A certain young deacon Jovinus was a member of a party travelling from Jerusalem to Egypt, and one very hot day on arriving at their destination he got a washing-tub and plunged hands and feet *πυγμῇ* into ice-cold water. Whereupon an elderly lady of the party rebuked him for self-indulgence in so pampering himself in his youth: she herself, though in the sixtieth year of her age, never washed anything *ἐκτὸς τῶν ἄκρων τῶν χειρῶν*. Since *χείρ* in Greek means properly the forearm, *τὰ ἄκρα τῶν χειρῶν* may mean 'the fingers' or even as much as 'the hands' in the modern sense of the word, but not more: and in contrast with this, Jovinus' washing must have clearly have been 'up to the elbow'. That gives excellent sense also to the passage in Mark, and justifies the exegesis of Euthymius and Theophylact. We learn once more the value of the Greek Fathers, even the latest of them, as interpreters of the New Testament.

(2)

ἀλλά (Mark 46 times, Matthew 37 times, Luke 36 times).†

Obviously from these numbers the particle is a special favourite of Mark's: but obviously also there will be many instances where its use is normal, and offered no temptation to change. There are however some ten instances where Matthew does, apparently with intention, substitute another word, generally *δέ*: though as it happens in only three of these (**3**, **8**, **9**) have we a real parallel in Luke.

1. ix 8 *οὐδένα εἶδον ἀλλὰ τὸν Ἰησοῦν μόνον*: so A C L W Δ Θ 565 sah. arm. Matt. xvii 8 *οὐδένα εἶδον εἰ μὴ τὸν Ἰησοῦν μόνον*. In Mark ℵ B D have introduced *εἰ μή* from Matthew, but the Latins should not be quoted on this side, for they could hardly help rendering *ἀλλά* in this context by 'neminem nisi' — I suspect indeed that the *εἰ μή* of D may be due to assimilation to the 'nisi' of its Latin column. It is in the last degree unlikely that any scribe should have altered *εἰ μή* to the ungrammatical *ἀλλά*, while the converse change, supported by the parallel in Matthew, would be easy enough. Mark's usage is probably influenced by Aramaic, but Moulton-Milligan in their *Vocabulary of N.T.* cite from the papyri a close parallel *μὴ ἐξέστω Φιλίσκῳ γυναῖκα ἄλλην ἐπαγαγέσθαι ἀλλά Ἀπωλλωνίαν*.

2. ix 13 *ἀλλά λέγω ὑμῖν*. Matt. xvii 12 *λέγω δὲ ὑμῖν*.

3. xi 32 *ἀλλά εἴπωμεν Ἐξ ἀνθρώπων*; Matt. xxi 26, Luke xx 6, *ἐὰν δὲ εἴπωμεν Ἐξ ἀνθρώπων* ...

4. xiii 20 *οὐκ ἂν ἐσώθη πᾶσα σάρξ. ἀλλὰ διὰ τοὺς ἐκλεκτοὺς* ... Matt. xxiv 22 *διὰ δὲ τοὺς ἐκλεκτοὺς* ...

5. xiii 24 *ἀλλὰ ἐν ἐκείναις ταῖς ἡμέραις μετὰ τὴν θλίψιν ἐκείνην* ... Matt. xxiv 29 *εὐθέως δὲ μετὰ τὴν θλίψιν τῶν ἡμερῶν ἐκείνων* ...

6. xiv 28 *ἀλλὰ μετὰ τὸ ἐγερθῆναί με προάξω ὑμᾶς εἰς τὴν Γαλιλαίαν*. Matt. xxvi 32 *μετὰ δὲ τὸ ἐγερθῆναί με* ...

7. xiv 29 *ὁ δὲ Πέτρος ἔφη αὐτῷ, Εἰ καὶ πάντες σκανδαλισθήσονται, ἀλλ' οὐκ ἐγώ*. Matt. xxvi 33 omits the *ἀλλά* and writes *εἰ πάντες σκανδαλισθήσονται ἐν σοί, ἐγὼ οὐδέποτε σκανδαλισθήσομαι*.

8. xiv 36 *παρένεγκε τὸ ποτήριον τοῦτο ἀπ' ἐμοῦ· ἀλλ' οὐ τί ἐγὼ θέλω ἀλλὰ τί σύ*. Matt. xxvi 39, Luke xxii 42, agree in substituting *πλὴν* for *ἀλλά* 1°, possibly to avoid the double *ἀλλά* of Mark.

9. xiv 49 *ἀλλ' ἵνα πληρωθῶσιν αἱ γραφαί*. The sentence is of course incomplete: Matt. xxvi 56 completes it by dropping *ἀλλά* and substituting *τοῦτο δὲ ὅλον γέγονεν*. Luke xxii 53 on the other hand retains *ἀλλά* but gives it full construction, *ἀλλ' αὕτη ἐστὶν ὑμῶν ἡ ὥρα* ...

10. xvi 7 *ἀλλὰ ὑπάγετε εἴπατε τοῖς μαθηταῖς αὐτοῦ* ... Matthew once more drops *ἀλλά*, xxviii 7 *καὶ ταχὺ πορευθεῖσαι εἴπατε* ...

(πρὸς) ἑαυτοὺς

(Mark has *πρὸς ἑαυτούς* seven times, *πρὸς ἀλλήλους* four times: Luke *πρὸς ἑαυτούς* twice, *πρὸς ἀλλήλους* eight times: John *πρὸς ἑαυτούς* twice, *πρὸς ἀλλήλους* four times: Matthew never uses either phrase.)

There is of course no doubt about the meaning of *πρὸς ἀλλήλους* (Mark iv 41, viii 16, ix 34, xv 31): the problem to be resolved is the meaning of *πρὸς ἑαυτούς*.

1. i 27 *ὥστε συνζητεῖν πρὸς ἑαυτούς λέγοντας* ... I read *πρὸς ἑαυτούς* with A C D Θ W (*αὐτούς* 565) and Marcan usage, cf. **3** below: syr-sin 'to one another': *αὐτούς* ℵ B Tisch. W-H. I do not doubt that Alexandrian scholars disliked the phrase *πρὸς ἑαυτούς* if it was used — as *συνζητεῖν* shews it was here used — to mean 'with one another'. Luke's *συνελάλουν πρὸς ἀλλήλους* shews that he had *πρὸς ἑαυτούς*, not *αὐτούς*, before him in Mark. There is no parallel in Matthew.

2. ix 10 *καὶ τὸν λόγον ἐκράτησαν πρὸς ἑαυτούς συνζητοῦντες τί ἐστιν* ... The parallel of **1** suggests that, in spite of the unusual order of the words, *πρὸς ἑαυτούς* must be taken with *συνζητοῦντες* 'discussing with one another': for the absolute use of *τὸν λόγον κρατεῖν* 'keep in mind', cf. vii 3, 4, 8, 'observe the tradition'. There is no parallel in either Matthew or Luke.

3. x 26 *οἱ δὲ περισσῶς ἐξεπλήσσοντο λέγοντες πρὸς ἑαυτούς* ... Once more the Alexandrians avoided *πρὸς ἑαυτούς*, substituting *πρὸς αὐτόν·* so ℵ B C Δ Ψ and the Egyptian versions with W-H, against A D W latt. syr-sin and all other authorities with Tisch. But Mark's usage is quite decisive, for *λέγειν πρὸς αὐτόν* is never found in his Gospel, but always *λέγειν αὐτῷ*. Both Matthew and Luke have simply *λέγοντες* (*εἶπαν*)

4. xi 31 *καὶ διελογίζοντο πρὸς ἑαυτοὺς λέγοντες* ... Here Matthew alters to *παρ' ἑαυτοῖς* 'among themselves', and Luke, while retaining *πρὸς ἑαυτούς*, alters the verb to *συνελογίσαντο*, Luke xx 5, compare xxii 23 *συνζητεῖν πρὸς ἑαυτούς*

5. xii 7 *ἐκεῖνοι δὲ οἱ γεωργοὶ πρὸς ἑαυτοὺς εἶπαν ὅτι* ... Again Matthew alters to *εἶπον ἐν ἑαυτοῖς* ..., Luke, to *διελογίζοντο πρὸς ἀλλήλους λέγοντες* ... Luke, as in **1**, clearly understood Mark to mean 'said to one another'.

6. xiv 4 *ἦσαν δέ τινες ἀγανακτοῦντες πρὸς ἑαυτούς* ... Textual complications abound in this passage, and the usual conditions are reversed, for the Alexandrians and the mass of authorities with W syr sin give *πρὸς ἑαυτούς*, while D Θ 565 *c ff i k* omit *πρὸς ἑαυτούς* with Matthew (there is no parallel in Luke): but again Marcan usage must be the decisive factor.

7. xvi 3 *καὶ ἔλεγον πρὸς ἑαυτάς, Τίς ἀποκυλίσει* ... Neither Matthew nor Luke has anything parallel here.

Πρὸς ἑαυτούς 'with one another' is thus a Marcan usage, which Luke generally modifies, Matthew absolutely rejects. But Luke, wherever he is parallel to Mark, always retains the sense: it is a more difficult question whether Matthew, when he substitutes *παρ' ἑαυτοῖς* (**4** above), or *ἐν ἑαυτοῖς* (**5** above, and similarly for *πρὸς ἀλλήλους* of Mark viii 16), means the same thing as Mark or no, since *ἐν ἑαυτοῖς* might mean, what ἐν ἑαυτῷ must mean (Matt. ix 21, Mark v 30, Luke vii 39, xii 17, xvi 3, xviii 4), 'in their own hearts'.

ἐκ, ἀπό.

(Mark has ἐκ half as often again as ἀπό; Matthew and Luke have ἀπό rather more frequently than ἐκ; John has ἐκ more than three times as often as ἀπό. The actual numbers for ἐκ are roughly Mark 66, Matthew 82, Luke 87.)

On many occasions of course the other Synoptists take no offence at Mark's use of ἐκ: but some phrases they omit, and further in something over a dozen cases ἐκ of Mark is changed to ἀπό in one or both of them. Since ἐκ has given way to ἀπό in modern Greek, it does not seem likely that we can appeal to the κοινή to explain the preponderant use of ἐκ in Mark and John: and we seem thrown back on the Semitic atmosphere of the two Gospels.

1. i 10 *ἀναβαίνων ἐκ τοῦ ὕδατος*. Matthew *ἀνέβη ἀπὸ τοῦ ὕδατος*: no parallel in Luke.

2, 3. i 25, 26 *ἔξελθε ἐξ αὐτοῦ* [*ἐκ τοῦ ἀνθρώπου*] ... *ἐξῆλθεν ἐξ αὐτοῦ*. Luke *ἔξελθε ἀπ' αὐτοῦ* ... *ἐξελθεν ἀπ' αὐτοῦ*. The whole episode is absent from Matthew: but compare **9** below.

4. i 29 *καὶ εὐθὺς ἐκ τῆς συναγωγῆς ἐξελθόντες*. Luke *ἀναστὰς δὲ ἀπὸ τῆς συναγωγῆς*: no parallel in Matthew.

5. v 8 *ἔλεγεν γὰρ αὐτῷ, Ἔξελθε ... ἐκ τοῦ ἀνθρώπου*. Luke *παρήγγελλεν γὰρ τῷ πνεύματι τῷ ἀκαθάρτῳ ἐξελθεῖν ἀπο τοῦ ἀνθρώπου*. Matthew abbreviates at this point and omits the whole verse.

6. vi 14 *ἔλεγον ὅτι Ἰωάνης ὁ βαπτίζων ἐγήγερται ἐκ νεκρῶν*. Luke retains ἐκ, doubtless because in the phrase 'rose again from the dead' *ἐκ νεκρῶν* was almost universal (so Luke, John, Acts, Pauline epistles, Hebrews, 1 Peter): Matthew is the only N.T. writer who even here prefers ἀπό, *ἠγέρθη ἀπὸ τῶν νεκρῶν* xiv 2, cf. xxvii 64, xxviii 7 (xvii 9 *b* is the only exception).

7. ix 9*a* *καταβαινόντων αὐτῶν ἐκ τοῦ ὄρους*. So I read with B D 33 (and 'de monte' of latt. perhaps suggests ἐκ rather than ἀπό) W-H: if with the rest we read *ἀπὸ τοῦ ὄρους* the explanation of the preposition may be that *ἐκ νεκρῶν* follows immediately after. Luke *κατελθόντων αὐτῶν ἀπὸ τοῦ ὄρους*: in Matt. xvii 9*a* ℵ B C D W Θ and others agree with the ἐκ of Mark, and it is possible that the Lucan parallel is responsible for the intrusion of ἀπό into the majority of MSS of both Matthew and Mark. Of course ἀπό is the natural preposition to use with *καταβαίνειν*: so Matt. viii 1, xiv 29, xxvii 40, 42, Mark iii 22, xv 30, 32, Luke ix 54, x

30, Acts viii 26, xxv 7, 1 Thess. iv 6. The Gospel of John and the Apocalypse are alone in writing regularly *καταβαίνειν ἐκ*.

8. ix 17 *εἷς ἐκ τοῦ ὄχλου*. Matthew *ἄνθρωπος*: Luke *ἀνήρ ἀπὸ τοῦ ὄχλου*.

9. ix 25 *ἔξελθε ἐξ αὐτοῦ*. Matthew *ἐξῆλθεν ἀπ' αὐτοῦ*: no parallel in Luke. Conversely the same phrase in **2**, **3**, **5**, is altered to *ἀπό* in Luke, while there is no parallel in Matthew.

10. xi 8 *στιβάδας κόψαντες ἐκ τῶν δένδρων*. Matthew *ἔκοπτον κλάδους ἀπὸ τῶν δένδρων*. Luke omits the clause.

11. xiii 1 *καὶ ἐκπορευομένου αὐτοῦ ἐκ τοῦ ἱεροῦ*. Matthew *ἐξελθὼν ὁ Ἰησοῦς ἀπὸ τοῦ ἱεροῦ*: the whole clause is dropped by Luke.

12. xiv 25 *οὐκέτι οὐ μὴ πίω ἐκ τοῦ γενήματος τῆς ἀμπέλου*. So in effect Matthew: but Luke *ἀπὸ τοῦ γενήματος τῆς ἀμπέλου*.

13. xvi 3 *Τίς ἀποκυλίσει ἡμῖν τὸν λίθον ἐκ τῆς θύρας τοῦ μνημείου;* Luke *εὗρον δὲ τὸν λίθον ἀποκεκυλισμένον ἀπὸ τοῦ μνημείου*. No parallel in Matthew.

πάλιν (Mark 27 times, Matthew 16 times, Luke thrice, John 43 times).†

The mere enumeration of these numbers creates at once the suspicion that the preponderant use of the word in Mark and John, coupled with its practical absence from Luke, must be due *either* to the Aramaic background of the thought of the second and fourth evangelists, *or* to some characteristic of the *Κοινή* instinctively repugnant to the other two and especially to Luke. I do not propose here to choose between these two alternatives (they are indeed mutually exclusive), but I confine myself to the investigation of the meaning or meanings of the word in Mark and of the procedure of the other two Synoptists when they found the word before them. But the caution must be given *in limine* that since Mark most commonly uses *πάλιν* in cases of transition — as we should put it, at the beginning of a paragraph — and since it is just these introductory phrases which Matthew and Luke habitually drop in copying Mark, the proportion of cases where there is no actual parallelism between the three is much smaller than the number at first sight suggest. In fact out of twenty-seven instances in Mark, there are only nineteen where Matthew is strictly parallel, and for Luke only nine. Even so, the results are startling enough: Matthew retains *πάλιν* five times — twice with some modification — Luke retains it once.

Before giving the catalogue of the instances of *πάλιν* in Mark, it may be well to deal with, and dismiss, those cases where the textual evidence is divided for or against *πάλιν*. There are not many, and for the most part they reflect simply the same tendency, on the part of ancient scribes or editors, to dislike the word and therefore to remove it, which influenced Matthew and to a still greater degree Luke. But the textual problem is rather more complicated when it is a question of the place of *πάλιν* in the sentence, though it is probably a good general rule for Mark that in case of doubt the earlier place is the more likely to be genuine.

The most definite result that emerges is the bad record of the Textus Receptus: in vii 14 it substitutes *πάντα τὸν ὄχλον* for *πάλιν τὸν ὄχλον*, in viii 1 *παμπολλοῦ ὄχλου* for *πάλιν πολλοῦ ὄχλου*; in xi 3 it omits *πάλιν* entirely, and, as represented by cod. A, also in x 24; while in viii 13 and xiv 40 it moves *πάλιν* to a later position in the sentence. But again the record of the Western text is not wholly satisfactory, though it must of course not be forgotten, so far as the Latin witnesses are concerned, that either omission or transposition of so apparently unimportant a word may take place in the process of rendering into the vernacular, whatever was the form of the Greek before the translator: for omission compare ii 13 (D^{gr}, *fam* 13?), viii 13 (*b c*), x 1 (W *fam* 13 *b c ff i*), xi 3 (W 565 syr-sin latt.), xiv 40 (D W *a c ff k*), for transposition iv 1 *ἤρξατο πάλιν* and v 21 *εἰς τὸ πέραν πάλιν* (D 565 O.L., with the support on the second occasion of ℵ and on the first of W). On the other hand in ii 1 *πάλιν εἰσῆλθεν* of latt. (W) is a transposition in the right direction, and in xiv 69 *πάλιν ἰδοῦσα αὐτὸν ἡ παιδίσκη* of D Θ 565 *c k* syr-sin. I believe to be right against the rest. The solitary instance of a serious discrepancy in text is xiv 40, where *πάλιν ἐλθὼν εὗρεν αὐτούς* of ℵ B L (so syr-sin, but with *πάλιν* after *αὐτούς*, and D and O. L., but without *πάλιν*) must unquestionably be right against the *ὑποστρέψας* of W Θ 565 vulg. and the mass of Greek authorities, since *ὑποστρέφω*, while common in Luke and Acts, is never found (apart from this passage) in Matthew, Mark, or John: it is just an attempt to vary the construction of xiv 40 from that of xiv 39.

1. ii 1 *καὶ εἰσελθὼν πάλιν εἰς Καφαρναούμ...* 'Again', with reference back to i 39 *καὶ ἦλθεν κηρύσσων εἰς τὰς συναγωγὰς αὐτῶς εἰς ὅλην τὴν Γαλιλαίαν*. Matthew omits *πάλιν*: Luke is not parallel.

2. ii 13 *καί ἐξῆλθεν πάλιν παρὰ τὴν θάλασσαν...* 'And he left Capernaum again for the lake-side', with reference to ii 1. *Πάλιν* omitted by Luke: Matthew not parallel.

3. iii 1 *καὶ εἰσῆλθεν πάλιν εἰς συναγωγήν*. *Πάλιν* omitted by both the others: in Mark are we to interpret 'again', 'once more', with possibly a reference to i 21, 39? or if that is too distant, are we forced to render *πάλιν* by something like 'next'?

4. iii 20 *καὶ συνέρχεται πάλιν* [ὁ] *ὄχλος*. And again a [the] crowd collects': we can quite easily refer back, if need be, to iii 9 *διὰ τὸν ὄχλον*. No parallels in the other Synoptists.

5. iv 1 *καὶ πάλιν ἤρξατο διδάσκειν παρὰ τὴν θάλασσαν*. The lake-side had been mentioned in iii 7, and teaching by the lake-side in ii 13. But with each recurrence of *πάλιν* the impression seems to become clearer that Mark has not really got these elaborate cross-references in his mind, the more so that *πάλιν*, as the story proceeds, comes more frequently at the beginning of the sentence, and so corresponds more closely to our English use of 'Again' in the same position. Omitted by Matthew: no parallel in Luke.

6. v 21 *καὶ διαπεράσαντος ... πάλιν εἰς τὸ πέραν*. Here the idiomatic rendering would certainly be 'back to the other side': and viii 13, x 10, x 32, xi 3, xi 27, xiv 39, 40, are also other cases, where with verbs of motion, the same word 'back' may not be the right one. It appears to be the only meaning of *πάλιν* in Homer. Luke omits: no parallel in Matthew.

7. vii 14 *καὶ προσκαλεσάμενος πάλιν τὸν ὄχλον*. 'And summoning the crowd again'. The right rule for securing the equivalent sense in English seems to be to put 'again' into the most inconspicuous place. 'Once more' is certainly reading too much into Mark. Matthew omits: Luke is deficient as far as **11** inclusive.

8. vii 31 *καὶ πάλιν ἐξελθὼν ἐκ τῶν ὁρίων* Τύρου *ἦλθεν*. Omitted by Matthew. Conceivably we should render 'and on the return, leaving the district of Tyre, he came'.

9. viii 1 *ἐν ἐκείναις ταῖς ἡμέραις πάλιν πολλοῦ ὄχλου ὄντος*. It is here more attractive to see a definite intention to hark back to the other miracle of feeding, vi 34 *εἶδεν πολὺν ὄχλον*, and if so we must render 'there was again a great crowd', in the sense of 'once more'. Matthew has just mentioned 'crowds' twice over as present, and so omits the whole verse.

10. viii 13 *καὶ ἀφεὶς αὐτοὺς πάλιν ἐμβὰς ἀπῆλθεν εἰς τὸ πέραν*. Here again, comparing verse 10 *ἐμβὰς εἰς τὸ πλοῖον*, we must apparently render 'embarked again and went away to the other side'. Matthew again omits the word.

11. viii 25 *εἶτα πάλιν* [*ἐπ*]*έθηκεν τὰς χεῖρας ἐπὶ τοὺς ὀφθαλμοὺς αὐτοῦ*. *Πάλιν* obviously here refers back to the first imposition of hands in verse 23, 'again' in the sense of a second time, cf. xiv 39, 40, 69, 70. The whole story is absent from Matthew.

12, 13. x 1 *συνέρχεται πάλιν ὁ ὄχλος* (for the reading see on [*συν*]-*πορεύεσθαι* below) *πρὸς αὐτόν, και ὡς εἰώθει πάλιν ἐδίδασκεν αὐτούς*.

It is worth noting that the combination of 'crowd' and 'teaching' does occur before in vi 34; but the interval is so great that we can hardly suppose a direct reference, and must fall back on the indefinite 'again'. In neither clause does *πάλιν* reappear in Matthew: there is no parallel in Luke.

14. x 10 *καὶ εἰς τὴν οἰκίαν πάλιν οἱ μαθηταὶ περὶ τούτου ἐπηρώτων αὐτόν*. It is very tempting to render 'and when they were all back in the house his disciples asked him about it': see **6** above. Again no parallel in Luke: omission of the whole verse in Matthew.

15. x 24 *ὁ δὲ Ἰησοῦς πάλιν ἀποκριθεὶς λέγει*. Here the reference to verse 23 seems clear, 'but Jesus repeated his statement', 'said once more'. Luke omits the verse, no doubt because it is a repetition: Matthew, to avoid any break in our Lord's words, ingeniously alters to *πάλιν δὲ λέγω ὑμῖν*.

16. x 32 *καί παραλαβὼν πάλιν τοὺς δώδεκα*, 'taking the twelve back into company with him', because He had been walking on alone in front. See again **6** above.

17. xi 3 *καὶ εὐθὺς ἀποστέλλει αὐτὸν πάλιν ὧδε*. If (as I think) these words are part of the message the two disciples were to deliver, we could render 'The Lord needs the colt, and will send back again here (i.e. to the place from which it was taken) as soon as ever he has done with him'. The clause is omitted by Luke, the word by Matthew.

18. xi 27 *καὶ ἔρχονται πάλιν εἰς Ἱεροσόλυμα*. Comparing verse 19 'they left the city', I should once more render 'they come back to Jerusalem'. Both the other Evangelists omit the whole sentence.

19. xii 4 *καὶ πάλιν ἀπέστειλεν πρὸς αὐτοὺς ἄλλον δοῦλον*. The reference is to the first sending of a servant in verse 2, 'and again he sent them a second servant'. Matthew retains *πάλιν*, Luke retains the idea but avoids the word by *προσέθετο πέμψαι*.

20, 21. xiv 39, 40 (*καὶ προελθὼν μικρὸν ... καὶ ἔρχεται ...*) *καὶ πάλιν ἀπελθὼν...καὶ πάλιν ἐλθὼν*... It seems impossible here not to translate 'he went forward [*v*. 35]...and he came and found them asleep [*v*. 37]...and a second time he went away [*v*. 39]...and a second time he came and found them asleep [*v*. 40]... [Mark leaves us to understand the third departure, which Matthew supplies, xxvi 44 *καὶ ἀφεὶς αὐτοὺς πάλιν ἀπελθών*] ... and he came the third time and said unto them'. *πάλιν ... τὸ τρίτον* correspond, that is, to one another: Matthew makes this still clearer by writing *πάλιν ἐκ δευτέρου ... ἐκ τρίτου*. But Mark is content with the less emphatic *πάλιν*: it is only when the second time is important as such that he writes in xiv 72 *εὐθὺς ἐκ δευτέρου ἀλέκτωρ ἐφώνησεν*.

Luke has no parallel: Matthew to the double use of *πάλιν* in Mark adds a third of his own.

22. xiv 61 *καὶ πάλιν ὁ ἀρχιερεὺς ἐπηρώτα αὐτόν*: referring to a previous *ἐπηρώτησεν* of *v*. 60, cf. **26**. Matthew omits: Luke is not parallel.

23, 24, 25. xiv 69, 70 [*ἔρχεται μία τῶν παιδισκῶν ... καὶ ἰδοῦσα τὸν Πέτρον ... λέγει ... ὁ δὲ ἠρνήσατο λέγων ...*] *πάλιν ἰδοῦσα αὐτὸν ἡ παιδίσκη ἤρξατο λέγειν ... ὁ δὲ πάλιν ἠρνεῖτο. καὶ μετὰ μικρὸν πάλιν οἱ παρεστῶτες ἔλεγον ...* Here we have, as in **21, 22**, *πάλιν* for the second assertion and the second denial, but, in contrast to that passage, also of the third assertion. Of the three cases of *πάλιν* Luke retains none, Matthew only the second.

26. xv 4 *ὁ δὲ Πειλᾶτος πάλιν ἐπηρώτα αὐτόν*, referring to *v*. 2 *καὶ ἐπηρώτησεν αὐτὸν ὁ Πειλᾶτος*. 'Questioned him again ', exactly as in **22**. No parallel in Luke: Matthew substitutes his favourite *τότε*.

27. xv 12 *ὁ δὲ Πειλᾶτος πάλιν ἀποκριθεὶς ἔλεγεν αὐτοῖς*, referring back (as in **22** and **26**) to a previous contact of the same interlocutors, *v*. 9 *ὁ δὲ Πειλᾶτος ἀπεκρίθη αὐτοῖς λέγων*.

28. xv 13 *οἱ δὲ πάλιν ἔκραξαν Ἵταύρωσον αὐτόν*. A difficulty is raised (see Moulton and Milligan *Vocabulary* s.v.) by Souter, on the ground presumably that the crowd had not been said to have made the cry before. But it must be remembered that in the case of the high priest, and both times in the case of Pilate — **22, 26, 27** — Mark's *πάλιν* does not imply that the same question or statement was repeated, but only that 'he questioned him again' or 'he made answer to them again'. And we may well suppose that possibly *v*. 8 and more certainly *v*. 11 implies a previous *ἔκραξαν* on the part of the crowd. Luke at least so interpreted the words of *v*. 11 *ἀνέσεισαν τὸν ὄχλον ἵνα μᾶλλον τὸν Βαραββᾶν ἀπολύσῃ αὐτοῖς*, for he writes in xxiii 18 *ἀνέκραγον δὲ παμπληθεὶ λέγοντες· Αἶρε τοῦτον, ἀπόλυσον δὲ ἡμῖν τὸν Βαραββᾶν.*

What are the general results of this perhaps over long and over detailed enquiry? Primarily, I think, that *πάλιν* is in Mark a very light and unemphatic particle: and secondly that the original sense of 'back' seems clear in certain connexions, e.g. **6, 17**, and possible in **8, 14, 16, 18**. The vehement dislike of Luke for the word I should suppose to be due exactly to his Hellenic sense of the importance of definiteness and precision in the use of particles. In the first five instances of the list just given *πάλιν* is really almost otiose as used by Mark.

ὑπάγω and πορεύεσθαι (with its compounds).

A. *ὑπάγω.*

(Mark 15 times, Matthew 19 times, Luke 5 times, John 32 times, Apocalypse 6 times: not in Acts, Paul, or Hebrews.)

The first distinction that needs drawing about *ὑπάγω* is between its use in the imperative and its use in other moods: for while Matthew (17 times out of 19) and Mark (12 times out of 15) use it almost exclusively in the imperative, this was exactly what Luke most disliked. The imperative is found only twice in Luke, four times in John, and twice in the Apocalypse.

Imperative.

1. i 44 *ὕπαγε σεαυτὸν δεῖξον τῷ ἱερεῖ.* So Matthew: Luke *ἀπελθὼν δεῖξον* ...

[ii 9 *καὶ ἆρον τὸν κράβαττόν σου καὶ ὕπαγε* ℵ L Δ Tisch (and with the addition *εἰς τὸν οἶκόν σου* D 33 *a ff* arm.: this is perhaps the earlier form of the corruption) is certainly wrong, and has come in from *v.* 11. *περιπάτει* must be read with A B C W Θ 565 *b c e* vulg. sah.: and so Matthew and Luke.]

2. ii 11 *καὶ ὕπαγε εἰς τὸν οἶκόν σου.* So Matthew: Luke *πορεύου* ...

3. v 19 *Ὕπαγε εἰς τὸν οἶκόν σου.* Absent from Matthew: Luke *ὑπόστρεφε* ...

4. v 34 *Ὕπαγε εἰς εἰρήνην.* Again no parallel in Matthew: *πορεύου* Luke.

5. vi 38 *Πόσους ἄρτους ἔχετε; ὑπάγετε ἴδετε.* Matthew drops the verse: Luke recasts, using *πορευθέντες*.

6. vii 29 *Διὰ τοῦτον τὸν λόγον ὕπαγε.* Matthew recasts: Luke is defective.

7. viii 33 *Ὕπαγε ὀπίσω μου, Σατανᾶ.* So Matthew: Luke omits the episode.

8. x 21 *Ὕπαγε ὅσα ἔχεις πώλησον.* Matthew retains *ὕπαγε*, Luke omits it.

9. x 52 *Ὕπαγε, ἡ πίστις σου σέσωκέν σε.* Luke changes *ὕπαγε* to *ἀνάβλεψον*, Matthew omits the whole clause.

10. xi 2 *Ὑπάγετε εἰς τὴν κώμην τὴν κατέναντι ὑμῶν.* Here the usual conditions are reversed, for Matthew changes to *πορεύεσθε*, Luke on this one occasion retains *ὑπαγετε*.

11. xiv 13 *Ὑπάγετε εἰς τὴν πόλιν.* So Matthew: Luke *εἰσελθόντων ὑμῶν εἰς* ...

12. xvi 7 *ἀλλὰ ὑπάγετε, εἴπατε τοῖς μαθηταῖς αὐτοῦ*. Matthew substitutes *πορευθεῖσαι εἴπατε*, Luke omits the charge to deliver a message, probably because of the reference to Galilee.

Other moods (participle and indicative).

13. vi 31 *ἦσαν γὰρ οἱ ἐρχόμενοι καὶ οἱ ὑπάγοντες πολλοί*. Not in Matthew or Luke.

14. vi 33 *καὶ εἶδαν αὐτοὺς ὑπάγοντας*. Again not in either Matthew or Luke.

15. xiv 21 *ὁ μὲν υἱὸς τοῦ ἀνθρώπου ὑπάγει*. So Matthew: Luke *πορεύεται*.

On the whole then Matthew retains Mark's imperatives 5/7, but substitutes *πορεύεσθε* (*πορευθεῖσαι*) 2/7: in the other moods he retains *ὑπάγειν* only once, xiv 21 = Matt. xxvi 24. Luke never retains any form of the verb where he finds it in Mark, save only xi 2 = Luke xix 30: four times he substitutes *πορεύεσθαι*, once *ὑποστρέφειν*, and twice uses the participles *ἀπελθών*, *εἰσελθόντων*. It seems not unusual with Luke to deal more drastically than in the rest of his Gospel with a word which he finds often, and dislikes, in Mark.

ὑπάγειν must have been *κοινή* use, and appears to survive in modern Greek (Blass, *Grammatik des N.T. Griechisch* § 24 s.v.). The use probably had its origin in the want of a word to express 'go' as contrasted with 'come' (Mark vi 31 *οἱ ἐρχόμενοι καὶ οἱ ὑπάγοντες* is exactly our 'coming and going'), and for this purpose it is more expressive than the alternative *πορεύεσθαι*. Further it seems not unlikely that the colloquial imperative *ὕπαγε* 'go' is an echo of the similar, quite classical, *ἄγε* 'come': though it is not clear why the particular compound *ὕπαγε* was employed for the purpose.

B. *πορεύεσθαι* and its compounds.†

πορεύεσθαι (Matthew 28 times, Luke 50 times,: never in Mark).

[Mark ix 30 *κἀκεῖθεν ἐξελθόντες ἐπορεύοντο διὰ τῆς Γαλιλαίας* B D *c* W-H text. *παρεπορεύοντο* the rest, and Marcan usage — see below on *παραπορεύεσθαι* — is decisive in favour of this reading. 'Iter faciebant' of *a* should not be cited (as by Tischendorf) on the side of the simple verb: it would be an excellent rendering of *παραπορεύεσθαι*.]

In Luke *πορεύεσθαι* is three times substituted for *ἀπελθεῖν* of Mark, four times for *ὑπάγειν* of Mark.

διαπορεύεσθαι (Luke thrice: not Matthew or Mark at all).

[Mark ii 23 *καὶ ἐγένετο αὐτὸν ἐν τοῖς σάββασιν διαπορεύεσθαι διὰ τῶν σπορίμων* B C D W-H text: *πορεύεσθαι* W : *παραπορεύεσθαι* the rest, according to Marcan usage. *διαπορεύεσθαι* has clearly come in from Luke.]

ἐκπορεύεσθαι (Mark eleven times, Matthew four times [Mt.xvii 21 is not genuine], Luke three times).

Matthew twice substitutes the simple verb, twice *ἐξέρχεσθαι*, once *ἐκβάλλεσθαι*. Luke generally omits. Note that Mark three times uses the word in the genitive absolute of the present participle, *ἐκπορευομένου αὐτοῦ*, of our Lord's movements: x 17, x 46, xiii 1.

παραπορεύεσθαι (Mark four times, Matthew once, copying Mark xv 29, Luke never).

Apparently the compound verb *παραπορεύεσθαι* must have been unfamiliar or unpalatable, for, as we have seen, B D agree in altering it on two of the four occasions (ii 23, ix 30) when Mark uses it. *παράγειν* too is never used by Luke.

προσπορεύεσθαι (not in Matthew or Luke).

Mark x 35 *καὶ προσπορεύονται αὐτῷ Ἰάκωβος καὶ Ἰωάννης*. This compound is found in the LXX, but nowhere else in N.T.

συνπορεύεσθαι (Luke three times,: not in Matthew).

[Mark x 1 *καὶ συνπορεύονται πάλιν ὄχλοι πρὸς αὐτόν* ℵ B and the mass of Greek MSS, followed by Tischendorf and W-H. Marcan usage shews conclusively that *ὄχλος* is right against *ὄχλοι*, and I have no doubt that *συνέρχεται πάλιν ὁ ὄχλος* should be read with D 565 syr-sin *a b c ff i k* (*conuenit turba*). The other reading has come in from Luke xiv 25 *συνεπορεύοντο δὲ αὐτῷ ὄχλοι πολλοί*.]

The investigation leads to queer results as between the Gospels. The simple verb is common in Matthew, very common in Luke, but never occurs in Mark. Of the compounds Mark uses *ἐκπορεύεσθαι* rather often, and is not averse to *παραπορεύεσθαι*: but both are rarely or never found in the other two Synoptists. Luke on the other hand uses two compounds, *διαπορεύεσθαι* and *συνπορεύεσθαι*, which are never found in Matthew or Mark. Perhaps more curious still is the effort which scribes of Mark, and especially we may say the Alexandrian editor whose work is represented in B, have made to get rid of *παραπορεύεσθαι* and to introduce the forms preferred by Luke (in ii 23 *διαπορεύεσθαι*, in ix 30 *πορεύεσθαι*, cf. x 1 *συνπορεύεσθαι*): some similar instinct of Hellenic taste must, it would seem, have prompted both the evangelist and the Alexandrian scholar.

X – Usage of Mark: (1) Titles of address to Christ; (2) Diminutives; (3) The verb at the end of the sentence; (4) ἵνα not of purpose only; (5) absence of λέγων (λέγοντες) before a statement or question, where the main verb seems sufficient to imply it.

As this series of notes draws to a close, each separate instalment becomes, almost inevitably, more miscellaneous in character. As some feature of St Mark's Gospel in relation to the other Synoptists strikes me, I proceed to group instances together, and to consider what general induction, if any, can be drawn from them. Many of the points have emerged in the course of the investigation into the 'agreements of Matthew and Luke against Mark' on which I have been engaged in my Seminar for some years — an investigation now nearly complete.

One characteristic of the present notes I should specially wish to emphasize, though I claim no finality for the conclusions which I have suggested, and that is the possibility that the Greek of St Mark has owed something, through his residence at Rome, to the influence of Latin. We all know that he transliterates Latin words more frequently than the other evangelists: but I suspect that Latin influence goes much further than that, and I doubt whether writers on New Testament Greek have given adequate consideration to this side of their subject. I should like some one to treat systematically the Greek of Mark and of Hermas — both of them non-literary authors, both of them writing Greek in Rome — from this point of view.

My last instalment (IX) needs supplementing at two points.

i. Too late for insertion into my note on ἀποστερεῖν, I consulted the *Thesaurus Linguae Latinae* under *abnego*, and the reference there given to Wölfflin's article in his *Archiv für lateinische Lexicographie* iv (1887) pp. 574-577. Wölfflin did not, I think, fully grasp the relation between *abnego* and ἀποστερεῖν in early Christian writers: but his collection of examples of *abnego*, as used of the refusal to return a sum deposited, is admirably full, and I complete my own list by the following:

Irenaeus *adv. Haer.* II xxxii 1 (xlviii 4) 'non solum non abnegare quae sunt aliena, sed etiam si sua auferantur illis [?aliis] non expostulare'.

Tertullian *ad Scapulam* 4 'Praeter haec depositum non abnegamus, matrimonium nullius adulteramus, pupillos pie tractamus, indigentibus refrigeramus, nulli malum pro malo reddimus'.

de fuga 12 *ad fin.* 'Quid autem Deo debeo, sicut denarium Caesari, nisi sanguinem quem pro me filius fudit ipsius? quodsi Deo quidem hominem et sanguinem meum debeo, nunc uero in eo sum tempore ut quod Deo debeo expostuler. utique fraudem Deo facio, id agens ne quod debeo soluam: bene obseruaui praeceptum, Caesari reddens quae sunt Caesaris, Deo uero quae sunt Dei abnegans'.

ii. In dealing with the compounds of *πορεύεσθαι* I omitted *εἰσπορεύεσθαι* (Mark 8, Matthew 1, Luke 5). Mark i 21 (no parallels): iv 19 (Matthew omits, Luke substitutes *πορευόμενοι*, but also changes the sense): v 40 (no parallels): vi 56 (Matthew omits; no parallel in Luke): vii 15, 18, 19, of the things that 'go into ' a man (no parallel in Luke; Matt. 1° substitutes *εἰσερχόμενον*, 2° retains *εἰσπορευόμενον*, 3° omits): xi 2 (Matthew omits, Luke retains). Luke certainly does not dislike the form, for twice where Mark has *εἰσέρχεσθαι* (Mark x 23; xiv 14) he substitutes *εἰσπορεύεσθαι*. Matthew on the other hand, it seems, avoids very generally any compound of *πορεύεσθαι* (though he shows no reluctance to use *πορεύεσθαι* itself), preferring the compounds of *ἔρχεσθαι*, especially *εἰσέρχεσθαι* and *προσέρχεσθαι*.

(1) Titles used in addressing Christ.

i. Ῥαββεί (Ῥαββουνεί)

(Mark four times: Matthew once [by Judas]: Luke never).

1. ix 5 'Ῥαββεί, *καλόν ἐστιν ἡμᾶς ὧδε εἶναι*. Matthew *κύριε*, Luke *ἐπιστάτα*.

2. x 51 'Ῥαββουνεί, *ἵνα ἀναβλέψω*. Matthew and Luke *κύριε*.

3. xi 21 'Ῥαββεί, *ἴδε ἡ συκῆ ἣν κατηράσω ἐξήρανται*. Matthew changes the form of the sentence: no parallel in Luke.

4. xiv 45 'Ῥαββείκαὶ *κατεφίλησεν αὐτόν*. Luke omits the address of Judas: Matthew, here only, retains the vocative 'Ῥαββεί.

ii. Διδάσκαλε

(Mark ten times: Matthew six: Luke twelve).

5. iv 38 *Διδάσκαλε, οὐ μέλει σοι ὅτι ἀπολλύμεθα*. As in **1** above, Matthew has *κύριε*, Luke *ἐπιστάτα*.

6. ix 17 *Διδάσκαλε, ἤνεγκα τὸν υἱόν μου*. Again Matthew substitutes *κύριε*: Luke retains *διδάσκαλε*, as in **8**, **11**, **12**, **13**, in each case because it is not a disciple who is speaking.

7. ix 38 *Διδάσκαλε, εἴδαμέν τινα ἐν τῷ ὀνόματί σου* ... Luke *ἐπιστάτα*, for John is the speaker. No parallel in Matthew.

8. x 17 *Διδάσκαλε ἀγαθέ τί ποιήσω* ... Both Luke (see on **6**) and Matthew (as also in **11**, **12**) retain *διδάσκαλε*, for the reason given on **6** above.

9. x 20 Διδάσκαλε, ταῦτα πάντα ἐφυλαξάμην ... Omitted by the other two, no doubt because the formal address had been used only three verses before.

10. x 35 Διδάσκαλε, θέλομεν ἵνα ὃ ἐὰν αἰτήσωμεν ... Omitted by Matthew: no parallel in Luke.

11. xii 14 (Pharisees and Herodians) ἐλθόντές λέγουσιν αὐτῷ Διδάσκαλε ... So both the others: they had no objection to the word as used by other Jews than the disciples.

12. xii 19 (Sadducees) ἐπηρώτων αὐτὸν λέγοντες Διδάσκαλε ... So both the other two, for just the same reason as in the last case.

13. xii 32 εἶπεν αὐτῷ ὁ γραμματεύς Καλῶς, διδάσκαλε ... Retained by Luke again on the same principle as before: no parallel in Matthew.

14. xiii 1 Διδάσκαλε, ἴδε ποταποὶ λίθοι ... The exclamation came from disciples, or a disciple, and so διδάσκαλε is avoided by Matthew: Luke, quite exceptionally, retains it in effect, for he inserts it in two verses farther on.

iii. Κύριε

(Mark once, by a non-Jew: Matthew twenty-two times, of which four occur in our Lord's teaching about Himself: Luke eighteen times).

15. vii 28 Κύριε, καὶ τὰ κυνάρια ὑποκάτω τῆς τραπέζης ... And so, as we should expect, Matthew: there is no parallel in Luke. This unique occurrence of Κύριε in Mark is simply due to the fact that the woman was Ἑλληνίς, a heathen, and therefore used not the Jewish term 'Rabbi', but the ordinary title of respect 'Sir'.

Κύριε is inserted, where Mark has no title of address, at i 40 by both Matthew and Luke, at xiv 19 by Matthew, at xiv 29 by Luke.

iv. Ἰησοῦ

(Mark three times, but always with a further defining phrase, and twice in the mouth of evil spirits: Luke six times: Matthew never).

16. i 24 Τί ἡμῖν καὶ σοί, Ἰησοῦ Ναζαρηνέ; So Luke: no parallel in Matthew.

17. v 7 Τί ἐμοὶ καὶ σοί, Ἰησοῦ υἱὲ τοῦ θεοῦ τοῦ ὑψίστου; So again Luke: Matthew omits the personal name.

18. x 47 Υἱὲ Δαυεὶδ Ἰησοῦ, ἐλέησόν με. Again Luke follows Mark, though he inverts the personal and the official name: again Matthew retains the latter, but again omits Ἰησοῦ: according to many MSS he has Κύριε also. If an explanation is wanted of this isolated usage of the address 'Jesus' in Mark, it should perhaps be found in the setting of the episode as a whole. It is full of details that give it a place by itself in St Mark's Gospel: I believe it represents a story given *viva voce* by Bartimaeus to the evangelist, and therefore the phrase may well be that actually used by the man himself.

The deductions from the *data* here accumulated can be very briefly expressed. 'Rabbi', the Aramaic word, represented in Greek by *διδάσκαλος*, would have been in fact the form of address used to our Lord by any other Jew, whether a disciple or not: and so Mark uses it, reserving *κύριε* for the solitary case where the speaker was not a Jew at all. But while Mark, or rather Peter, thus represents to us the language actually used in the days of our Lord's Ministry, the writers of the second generation could not picture our Lord's own disciples as addressing Him in the same way as those Jews did who were not His disciples: and therefore Matthew and Luke, while they retain the address Rabbi (Teacher) in the mouth of others than disciples — and Luke more consistently than Matthew — never allow it with disciples, save that Matthew keeps it in the case of Judas, no. **4**, and Luke by exception in no. **14**. Where Matthew and Luke differ, is just in this, that Matthew, when he substitutes another word, regularly employs *κύριε* (**1**, **2**, **5**, **6**); Luke only once changes to *κύριε* (**2**), more often (**1**, **5**, **7**) to *ἐπιστάτα*. 'Επιστάτα is only Lucan (six times in all): but even in Luke *κύριε* is much more common, and no doubt both Matthew and Luke mean by *κύριε* in this connexion not 'Sir' but 'Lord'.

(2) Diminutives in Mark.†

i. *θυγάτριον*

(twice in Mark: never in Matthew or Luke).

1. v 23 *τὸ θυγάτριον μου ἐσχάτως ἔχει*, Both Matthew and Luke substitute *θυγάτηρ*.

2. vii 25 *ἧς εἶχεν τὸ θυγάτριον αὐτῆς πνεῦμα ἀκάθαρτον*. Matthew again *θυγατήρ*: no Lucan parallel.

ii. *ἰχθύδιον*

(Mark once, Matthew once).

3. viii 7 *καὶ εἶχον ἰχθύδια ὀλίγα*. Retained in Matthew : there is no Luke.

iii. *κοράσιον*

(Mark five times, Matthew thrice: never in Luke).

4, 5. v 41, 42 Τὸ *κοράσιον, σοὶ λέγω, ἔγειρε. καὶ εὐθὺς ἀνέστη τὸ κοράσιον.* Matthew omits the first, but retains the second, *κοράσιον*: but he also uses *κοράσιον* for the *παιδίον* of Mark v 39. Luke changes the first *κοράσιον* to 'Η *παῖς*, and omits the second.

6. vi 22 *ὁ δὲ βασιλεὺς εἶπεν τῷ κορασίῳ.* The episode is absent from Luke, the word from Matthew.

7, 8. vi 28 *ἔδωκεν αὐτὴν τῶ κορασίῳ· καὶ τὸ κοράσιον ἔδωκεν αὐτὴν τῇ μητρί.* Matthew retains the word on the first occasion, omits it on the second.

iv. *κυνάριον*

(Mark and Matthew twice each: not in Luke).

8,(*sic* ed.) **9.** vii 27, 28 *λαβεῖν τὸν ἄρτον τῶν τέκνων καὶ τοῖς κυναρίοις βαλεῖν. ἡ δὲ ἀπεκρίθη καὶ λέγει αὐτῷ* Κύριε, *καὶ τὰ κυνάρια ὑποκάτω τῆς τραπέζης* ... Not in Luke: Matthew has both the episode and the double mention of *κυνάρια*. Phrynichus (quoted by Wetstein: Rutherford *New Phrynichus* p. 268) says that *κυνίδιον*, not *κυνάριον*, is the correct form of the diminutive.

v. *σανδάλιον*

(once in Mark, but nowhere else in the Gospels).

10. vi 9 *ἀλλὰ ὑποδεδεμένους σανδάλια.* Not in either Matthew or Luke: Luke omits the item, perhaps because it breaks into the catalogue of things that the Apostles were *not* to take with them; Matthew more skilfully adapts it to the negative framework of the catalogue by substituting *μηδὲ ὑποδήματα* — if they were to wear 'little sandals', they were not to wear boots or shoes. The diminutive *σανδάλιον* is apparently commoner in Greek than the form *σάνδαλον*.

vi. *ψιχίον*

(once each in Mark and Matthew).

11. vii 28 *καὶ τὰ κυνάρια ... ἐσθίουσιν ἀπὸ τῶν ψιχίων τῶν παιδίων.* And similarly the parallel in Matthew. Both *ψίξ* and *ψιχίον* appear to be rare words, but Suidas recognizes both forms: cod. D has *ψιχων* in both Gospels.

vii. ὠτάριον

(once in Mark, followed by John : not in Matthew or Luke).

12. xiv 47 ἀφεῖλεν αὐτοῦ τὸ ὠτάριον. So ℵ B D 1; and in the parallel passage John xviii 10, ℵ B C* L W. The rest have ὠτίον, following Matthew. Luke has οὖς in xxii 50 without variant, in the next verse D (with the Old Latins) again gives οὖς, the other MSS ὠτίον. Of all examples of diminutives in Mark, this is the most instructive, for, in contrast to words like θυγάτριον κοράσιον παιδίον, ears of adults are more or less similar in size — we cannot suppose that Mark means that Malcus' ear was a particularly small one — and the diminutive must be due simply to the writer's fondness for that type of word. Moreover ὠτάριον is not only a diminutive, but a diminutive of a diminutive. οὖς is the classical form, and as such is used by Luke: ὠτίον is the first stage of change, occurs occasionally in the LXX, and was probably in common use in the κοινή (οὖς ἀττικῶς, ὠτίον ἑλληνικῶς is quoted from a grammarian by Wetstein on Matt. xxvi 51): ὠτάριον is a further stage of change, but is cited mainly from comic verse — it was doubtless only colloquial. It is typically Marcan, and John has followed Mark. The preservation of ὠτάριον in the Alexandrian text (with D in Mark, and W in John) is a striking testimony to their faithfulness, for it must have been just the word they would have liked to alter. Note that Matthew goes only one stage back in substituting ὠτίον, while Luke goes the whole way with οὖς.

One word, diminutive in form, is not included in the above list, namely παιδίον. All three Synoptists use it regularly,[1] but again there is a significant distinction to be drawn: παῖς is used, though less frequently than παιδίον, in both Matthew and Luke, but it nowhere found in Mark, and therefore παιδίον takes its place. Thus in the story of Jairus' daughter Mark has (besides θυγάτηρ, θυγάτριον, and κοράσιον) four instances of παιδίον, Matthew has θυγάτηρ and κοράσιον, Luke has θυγάτηρ and (twice) παῖς. The child was twelve years old, so that Luke made the dividing line between παῖς and παιδίον at an earlier point than twelve. Again in the miracle of ix 17-27 the boy healed had suffered ἐκ παιδιόθεν (*v.* 21), and therefore cannot have been a mere child: moreover he is brought to Christ, not carried (*vv.* 19, 20) — not to say that he is called by his father at the opening of the story (*v.* 17) 'my son': yet we have in

---

[1] Mark 12; Matthew 18, but chapter ii accounts for just half the instances; Luke 13, and again about half in chapters i and ii. Thus Mark is the one of the three who, apart from the Infancy narratives, uses the word most.

Mark (*v*. 24) ὁ πατὴρ τοῦ παιδίου. We are not surprised that both Matthew and Luke call the boy not παιδίον but παῖς. Clearly then there is no justification for translating the word in Mark 'little child', as R. V. in ix 36, 37, x 13, 14, 15: in ix 36, 37 A. V. rightly has 'child' 'children', and in x 13 'young children' of A. V. is less incorrect than R. V.'s 'little children'.[2]

In the result Mark's fondness for diminutive forms is well established; at least with ὠτάριον and παιδίον, perhaps with other words, he uses such forms without any necessarily diminutive sense about them. Luke uses none of Mark's diminutives at all except παιδίον, and then as we have just seen, as strictly diminutive in contrast with παῖς. Matthew, as so often, takes an intermediate place. Put in other words, Luke upholds a literary tradition stringently, Matthew makes some concession to popular usage, Mark reproduces whole-heartedly the colloquial talk of everyday life. The fondness for diminutives grows with the growth of the language. They are absent from Homer: they begin to abound in Aristophanes and the later comedians: in the first century after Christ it must have been a conscious literary archaism to avoid them.

(3) The verb at the end of the sentence, after noun or personal pronoun.

(a) with the verb ἅπτεσθαι

(Mark eleven, Matthew ten, Luke ten).

ἅπτεσθαι is thus a rather favourite word of Mark's, and his fondness for putting the verb after the pronoun (or noun) is specially noticeable in relation to it, so that I have treated it separately.

1. i 41 ἐκτείνας τὴν χεῖρα αὐτοῦ ἥψατο. Both Matthew and Luke ἐκτείνας τήν χεῖρα ἥψατο αὐτοῦ. Perhaps the caution should be given that in Mark αὐτοῦ goes of course with ἥψατο and not with τὴν χεῖρα, which according to Greek idiom (and Latin usage is similar) would mean 'his hand' without the addition of any pronoun.

2. iii 10 ὥστε ἐπιπίπτειν αὐτῷ ἵνα αὐτου ἅψωνται ὅσοι εἶχον μάστιγας. No parallel in Matthew: but Luke again changes the order πᾶς ὁ ὄχλος ἐζήτουν ἅπτεσθαι αὐτοῦ.

---

2 Luke, however, here (xviii 15) has βρέφη, interpreting Mark's παιδία — rightly or wrongly — in this sense. He also uses βρέφος four times in chapters i and ii, of the babe in the womb or newly born: his terms for age are more clearly articulated (as we should expect) than those of the other evangelists.

[v 27 *ἥψατο τοῦ ἱματίου αὐτοῦ*. So by exception (though the addition of *τοῦ ἱματίου* makes the exception less marked), and so naturally the other two Synoptists here retain the same order of words.]

3. v 28 *ἐὰν ἅψωμαι κἂν τῶν ἱματίων αὐτοῦ*. So the critical editions, and so Matthew (Luke drops the verse): but Marcan usage makes it more than probable that the Alexandrian reading — it is only found in ℵ B C L Δ Θ — is an assimilation to the previous verse or to Matthew, and that we ought to follow the rest of our authorities, including D and the Latins (it is true that Latins may be just following the idiom of their language), and invert the order *κἂν τῶν ἱματίων αὐτοῦ ἅψωμαι*.

4. v 30 *Τίς μου ἥψατο τῶν ἱματίων*; Luke substitutes *Τίς ὁ ἁψάμενός μου*; Matthew drops the verse.

5. v 31 *καὶ λέγεις Τίς μου ἥψατο*; Matthew again gives no parallel: Luke changes the interrogation to a statement, alters the order to *Ἥψατό μού τις*.

6. vi 56 *ἵνα κἂν τοῦ κρασπέδου τοῦ ἱματίου αὐτοῦ ἅψωνται*. No Luke: but Matthew makes the expected change *ἵνα μόνον ἅψωνται τοῦ κρασπέδου τοῦ ἱματίου αὐτοῦ*.

7. vi 56*b* *καὶ ὅσοι ἂν ἥψαντο αὐτοῦ διεσώθησαν*. But I suspect that with the Old Latins and Matthew (there is no Luke) we ought to omit *αὐτοῦ*. If Matthew had found *αὐτοῦ* in that position in his text of Mark, why in the world should he have omitted it?

[vii 33 *πτύσας ἥψατο τῆς γλώσσης αὐτοῦ*. Compare v 27 above: no parallel in either Matthew or Luke.]

8. viii 22 *παρακαλοῦσιν αὐτὸν ἵνα αὐτοῦ ἅψηται*. Again no parallels.

9. x 13 *προσέφερον αὐτῷ παιδία ἵνα αὐτῶν ἅψηται*. So W-H with ℵ B C L Δ Θ 124 and Luke: Matthew *ἵνα τὰς χεῖρας ἐπιθῇ αὐτοῖς*. But Tischendorf in Mark has *ἅψηται αὐτῶν* with the mass of authorities, including D W Old Latins and Origen. Decision is difficult: yet can we suppose that Luke found before him in Mark *ἅψηται αὐτῶν*, and altered it to *αὐτῶν ἅψηται*?

(b) Other instances in Mark of the verb placed last, after its object, or the noun after the pronoun depending on it.†

10. i 44 *σεαυτὸν δεῖξον τῷ ἱερεῖ*. So Matthew: but Luke *δεῖξον σεαυτόν*.

11. ii 5, 9 *ἀφίενταί σου αἱ ἁμαρτιαι*, with Matthew: Luke *ἀφέωνταί σοι αἱ ἁμαρτίαι σου*.

12. iii 11 *ὅταν αὐτὸν ἐθεώρουν*. No parallels.

13. iv 30 *ἐν τίνι αὐτὴν παραβολῇ θῶμεν*; No parallel in Matthew: Luke *τίνι ὁμοιώσω αὐτήν*;

14. iv 41 *ὁ ἄνεμος καὶ ἡ θάλασσα αὐτῷ ὑπακούει.* So in effect Matt.: Luke again inverts verb and personal pronoun, *ὑπακούουσιν αὐτῷ.*

15. v 4 *οὐδεὶς ἴσχυεν αὐτὸν δαμάσαι.* No parallels.

16. v 10 *ἵνα μὴ αὐτὰ ἀποστείλῃ ...* No parallel in Matthew: Luke *ἵνα μὴ ἐπιτάξῃ αὐτοῖς ...*

17. vi 17 *ὅτι αὐτὴν ἐγάμησεν.* No parallel.

18. vi 20 *ἡδέως αὐτοῦ ἤκουεν.* Matthew in effect retains the construction while he alters the sense, *ὡς προφήτην αὐτὸν εἶχον.* No Luke.

19. vii 18 *οὐ δύναται αὐτὸν κοινῶσαι.* No parallel.

20. ix 18*a* *ὅπου ἐὰν αὐτὸν καταλάβῃ.* Matthew omits: Luke, though with a change to the direct construction, *ἰδοὺ πνεῦμα λαμβάνει αὐτὸν.*

21. ix 18*b* *ἵνα αὐτὸ ἐκβάλωσιν.* Omitted by Matthew: Luke again transposes, *ἵνα ἐκβάλωσιν αὐτό.*

22. ix 19 *ἕως πότε πρὸς ὑμᾶς ἔσομαι;* So in effect Matthew: Luke *ἕως πότε ἔσομαι πρὸς ὑμᾶς;*

23. ix 32 *ἐφοβοῦντο αὐτὸν ἐπερωτῆσαι.* Matthew has another phrase: Luke transposes *ἐφοβοῦντο ἐρωτῆσαι αὐτόν.*

24. ix 37 *ὃς ἂν ἓν τῶν παιδίων τούτων δέξηται.* Here both the other Synoptists transpose, *ὃς ἐὰν δέξηται ἓν παιδίον τοιοῦτο* (Luke *τοῦτο τὸ παιδίον*).

25. x 2 *εἰ ἔξεστιν ἀνδρὶ γυναῖκα ἀπολῦσαι.* No Luke: but Matthew *ἀπολῦσαι τὴν γυναῖκα αὐτοῦ.*

26. x 32 *ἤρξατο αὐτοῖς λέγειν.* Matthew and Luke both omit *ἤρξατο*, but both put the personal pronoun last, *εἶπεν αὐτοῖς, εἶπεν πρὸς αὐτούς.*

27. xi 28 *τίς σοι τὴν ἐξουσίαν ταύτην ἔδωκεν ... ;* Both Matthew and Luke transfer *τὴν ἐξουσίαν ταύτην* to the end, after the verb.

28. xii 12*a* *ἐζήτουν αὐτὸν κρατῆσαι.* So Matthew: Luke *ἐζήτησαν ... ἐπιβαλεῖν ἐπ' αὐτὸν τὰς χεῖρας.*

29. xii 12*b* *ὅτι πρὸς αὐτοὺς τὴν παραβολὴν εἶπεν.* Matthew omits the noun, Luke transposes it *εἶπεν τὴν παραβολὴν ταύτην.*

30. xii 13 *ἵνα αὐτὸν ἀγρεύσωσιν λόγῳ.* So Matthew: but Luke *ἵνα ἐπιλάβωνται αὐτοῦ λόγου.*

31. (*cf* 23). xii 34 *οὐδείς οὐκέτι ἐτόλμα αὐτὸν ἐπερωτῆσαι.* Matthew *ἐπερωτῆσαι αὐτὸν οὐκέτι*, Luke *ἐπερωτᾶν αὐτὸν οὐδέν.*

32. xiv 1 *πῶς αὐτὸν ... ἀποκτείνωσιν.* So in substance Matthew, but with *τὸν Ἰησοῦν* for *αὐτόν*: Luke *τὸ πῶς ἀνέλωσιν αὐτόν.*

33. xiv 10 *ἵνα αὐτὸν προδοῖ [παραδοῖ] αὐτοῖς.* Both the others invert dative and accusative: Luke *τὸ πῶς αὐτοῖς παραδῷ αὐτόν*, Matthew *ἐγὼ ὑμῖν παραδώσω αὐτόν.*

34. xiv 11 *πῶς αὐτὸν εὐκαίρως παραδοῖ.* So Matthew *ἵνα αὐτὸν παραδῷ*: but Luke *εὐκαιρίαν τοῦ παραδοῦναι αὐτόν.*

35. xiv 12 *ὅτε τὸ πάσχα ἔθυον*. No parallel in Matthew: but Luke *ἐν ᾗ ἔδει θύεσθαι τὸ πάσχα*.

36. xiv 14 *ὅπου τὸ πάσχα ... φάγω*. Luke by exception agrees: it is here Matthew who inverts, *ποιῶ τὸ πάσχα*.

37. xiv 30 *τρίς με ἀπαρνήσῃ*. Both the other Synoptists invert: Matthew *τρὶς ἀπαρνήσῃ με*, Luke *τρὶς ἀπαρνήσῃ μὴ εἰδέναι με*.

38. xiv 42 *ὁ παραδιδούς με ἤγγικεν*. No parallel in Luke: Matthew *ἤγγικεν ὁ παραδιδούς με*. Strictly speaking this instance does not come under the heading of verb and object, as *ἤγγικεν* is intransitive; but the change of order in Matthew seems significant.

39. xiv 47 *ἀφεῖλεν αὐτοῦ τὸ ὠτάριον*. So Matthew: but Luke *ἀφεῖλεν τὸ οὖς αὐτοῦ τὸ δεξιόν*. Possibly Mark meant *αὐτοῦ* to depend upon *ἀφεῖλεν*, and if so his phrase would stand: but certainly Luke interpreted him in the other sense.

40. xiv 63 *τί ἔτι χρείαν ἔχομεν μαρτύρων*; with Matthew. Even here, where change seems less necessary, Luke alters to *τί ἔτι ἔχομεν μαρτυρίας χρείαν*;

41. xiv 65 *οἱ ὑπηρέται ῥαπίσμασιν αὐτὸν ἔβαλον*. No parallels.

42. xiv 72 *ἀλέκτωρ ἐφώνησεν*, and so Matthew: but Luke *ἐφώνησεν ἀλέκτωρ*.

43. xv 31 *ἄλλους ἔσωσεν, ἑαυτὸν οὐ δύναται σῶσαι*. So Matthew, and the emphasis on *ἄλλους ... ἑαυτόν* seems to justify the order: but again Luke's instinct is for change, *ἄλλους ἔσωσεν σωσάτω ἑαυτόν*.

44. xvi 7 *ἐκεῖ αὐτὸν ὄψεσθε*. Here, though Matthew follows Mark the order seems indefensible in Greek: but unfortunately there is no Lucan parallel.

It is not suggested that these instances are typical of Mark in the sense that this order of words is his normal usage: but they are not inconsiderable in number, and Luke's alteration of them in almost every case, whether instinctive or intentional, is certainly no mere accident — not even though the actual converse happens on occasion, as for instance (if our texts are correct) Mark xi 17 *πεποιήκατε αὐτὸν σπήλαιον λῃστῶν*, where the others give *αὐτὸν ἐποιεῖτε* (*ἐποιήσατε*) *σπήλαιον λῃστῶν*. In thirteen of our forty-four cases there is no Lucan parallel: of the remaining thirty-one, Luke makes the change to the normal Greek order of words in no less than twenty-nine, the exceptions being only **9**, **36**. Matthew, as so often, stands in between Mark and Luke, altering the Marcan order about as frequently as he leaves it unchanged; that is to say, out of twenty-eight cases where his text is parallel, he follows Mark in fourteen and diverges in thirteen (**7** being a doubtful reading in Mark).

Whence did Mark derive his occasional use of an order of words so fundamentally alien to the Greek language? Greek puts the emphatic words in the forefront of the sentence, and the verb therefore cannot be left to the last. Latin, on the other hand, habitually closes the sentence with the verb. The conclusion seems irresistible that — just as Jerome in the Vulgate introduces a Graecizing order, putting words like *eius*, for instance, at the end of the sentence — Mark introduces in the Greek of his Gospel a Latinizing order. The influence which Mark's years of residence in Rome exercised over the development of his literary Greek style (if one may use such a phrase about his Gospel at all) was doubtless not inconsiderable. The Greek he had picked up in his boyhood at Jerusalem was, we may assume, wholly non-literary and colloquial. That it came in a Latin-speaking city to such maturity as it attained, is suggested forcibly by the feature of it which we have now been examining.

(4) ἵνα (Mark 1½ columns, Matthew barely 1, Luke 1; John nearly 3). But in the following list ἵνα is only included when not used with its proper sense of purpose.

1. iii 9 *καὶ εἶπεν τοῖς μαθηταῖς αὐτοῦ ἵνα πλοιάριον προσκαρτερῇ αὐτῷ.* No parallels.

2. v 18 *παρεκάλει ὁ δαιμονισθεὶς ἵνα μετ' αὐτοῦ ᾖ.* Luke *ἐδέετο ... εἶναι σὺν αὐτῷ.* No parallel in Matthew.

3. v 23 *καὶ παρακαλεῖ αὐτὸν πολλὰ ... ἵνα ἐλθὼν ἐπιθῇς τὰς χεῖρας αὐτῇ* — so I think Mark means to construct the *ἵνα* (*cf.* **10**). Matthew turns the sentence into *oratio recta*, *ἀλλὰ ἐλθὼν ἐπίθες ...* Luke omits.

4. v 43 *καὶ διεστείλατο αὐτοῖς πολλὰ ἵνα μηδεὶς γνοῖ τοῦτο.* Nothing parallel in Matthew: Luke again has infinitive *παρήγγειλεν αὐτοῖς μηδενὶ εἰπεῖν τὸ γεγονός.*

5. vi 8 *καὶ παρήγγειλεν αὐτοῖς ἵνα μηδὲν αἴρωσιν εἰς ὁδόν.* Both the others substitute the *oratio recta*, *μὴ κτήσησθε, μηδὲν αἴρετε.*

6. vi 12 *καὶ ἐξελθόντες ἐκήρυξαν ἵνα μετανοῶσιν.* Luke omits the phrase: Matthew has no parallel.

7. vi 25 *θέλω ἵνα ἐξαυτῆς δῷς μοι ἐπὶ πίνακι ...* Matthew omits *θέλω ἵνα* and writes *δός μοι ὧδε ἐπὶ πίνακι.* Luke has no parallel for the six cases **7-12**.

8. vi 56 *καὶ παρεκάλουν αὐτὸν ἵνα κἂν τοῦ κρασπέδου τοῦ ἱματίου αὐτοῦ ἅψωνται.* Here for the first time Matthew follows Mark.

9. vii 26 *ἠρώτα αὐτὸν ἵνα τὸ δαιμόνιον ἐκβάλῃ ...* Matthew again substitutes the *oratio recta*.

10. vii 32 *καὶ παρακαλοῦσιν αὐτὸν ἵνα ἐπιθῇ αὐτῷ τὴν χεῖρα.* Matthew omits the whole clause.

11. vii 36 *καὶ διεστείλατο αὐτοῖς ἵνα μηδενὶ λέγωσιν.* No parallel.

12. viii 22 *καὶ παρακαλοῦσιν αὐτὸν ἵνα αὐτοῦ ἅψηται.* No parallel.

13. viii 30 *καὶ ἐπετίμησεν αὐτοῖς ἵνα μηδενὶ λέγωσιν περὶ αὐτοῦ.* Matthew for the second time agrees, *διεστείλατο τοῖς μαθηταῖς ἵνα μηδενὶ εἴπωσιν* ... Luke, as in **2** and **4**, substitutes the infinitive, *παρήγγειλεν μηδενὶ λέγειν τοῦτο.*

14. ix 9 *διεστείλατο αὐτοῖς ἵνα μηδενὶ ἃ εἶδον διηγήσωνται.* Matthew changes to a command in the *oratio recta*, *μηδενι εἴπητε τὸ ὅραμα*, Luke to a statement of fact, *οὐδενὶ ἀπήγγειλαν ... οὐδὲν ὧν ἑώρακαν.*

15. ix 12 *πῶς γέγραπται ἐπὶ τὸν υἱὸν τοῦ ἀνθρώπου ἵνα πολλὰ πάθῃ.* No parallel.

16. ix 18 *καὶ εἶπα τοῖς μαθηταῖς σου ἵνα αὐτὸ ἐκβάλωσιν.* Matthew omits the *ἵνα* clause, Luke (with *ἐδεήθη* for *εἶπα*) here retains it.

17. ix 30 *καὶ οὐκ ἤθελεν ἵνα τις γνοῖ.* Both the others omit the phrase.

18. x 35 *θέλομεν ἵνα ὃ ἐὰν αἰτήσωμέν σε ποιήσῃς ἡμῖν.* Matthew omits the clause, Luke the whole episode, including **19**.

19. x 37 *δὸς ἡμῖν ἵνα εἷς σου ἐκ δεξιῶν ... καθίσωμεν.* And so Matthew, *εἰπὲ ἵνα καθίσωσιν* ...

20. x 48 *καὶ ἐπετίμων αὐτῷ πολλοὶ ἵνα σιωπήσῃ.* So both Matthew and Luke, as in the next case.

21. x 51 *ὁ δὲ τυφλὸς εἶπεν αὐτῷ Ῥαββουνί, ἵνα ἀναβλέψω.* I believe that the construction with *ἵνα* depends (cf. no.**3**) on the verb of the preceding verse *θέλω ποιήσῃς.* Both Matthew and Luke follow Mark closely here, and presumably constructed *ἵνα* in the same way after *θέλειν.*

22. xi 16 *καὶ οὐκ ἤφιεν ἵνα τις διενέγκῃ σκεῦος διὰ τοῦ ἱεροῦ.* No parallels.

23. xi 28 *ἢ τίς σοι τὴν ἐξουσίαν ταύτην ἔδωκεν ἵνα ταῦτα ποιῇς;* The *ἵνα* clause is strictly superfluous after *ταύτην*, and both Matthew and Luke seize on so good an excuse for omitting it.

24. xii 19 Μωυσῆς *ἔγραψεν ἡμῖν ὅτι ἐὰν ... ἵνα λάβῃ* ... It would appear that *ἵνα*, which is not part of the O.T. quotation, must depend on *ἔγραψεν.* Matthew re-writes the quotation: Luke follows Mark, possibly supposing that *ἵνα λάβῃ* was from the LXX.

25. xiii 34 *καὶ τῷ θυρωρῷ ἐνετείλατο ἵνα γρηγορῇ.* No parallels.

26. xiv 12 *ποῦ θέλεις ἑτοιμάσωμεν ἵνα φάγῃς τὸ πάσχα;* Luke omits the *ἵνα* clause, Matthew substitutes the infinitive *φαγεῖν.*

27. xiv 35 *προσηύχετο ἵνα εἰ δυνατόν ἐστιν παρέλθῃ ἀπ᾽ αὐτοῦ ἡ ὥρα.* Where Mark as here, and occasionally elsewhere, makes a statement in *oratio obliqua* and follows it by the same thing *oratio recta*, Matthew and Luke do not repeat both of the two but prefer that in *oratio recta*; Matthew, however, has clearly taken εἰ δυνατόν ἐστιν παρελθάτω from Mark's ἵνα παρέλθῃ, so that in his case at least the ἵνα clause is turned into a direct prayer.

28. xv 11 οἱ δὲ ἀρχιερεῖς ἀνέσεισαν τὸν ὄχλον ἵνα μᾶλλον τὸν Βαραββᾶν ἀπολύσῃ αὐτοῖς. So in substance Matthew, with ἔπεισαν for ἀνέπεισαν: Luke has the *oratio recta*, ἀνέκραγον δὲ πανπληθεὶ λέγοντες Αἶρε τοῦτον ἀπόλυσον δὲ ἡμῖν Βαραββᾶν.

29. xv 15 καὶ παρέδωκεν τὸν Ἰ. φραγελλώσας ἵνα σταυρωθῇ. So Matthew: Luke παρέδωκεν τῷ θελήματι αὐτῶν.

30. xv 20 καὶ ἐξάγουσιν αὐτὸν ἵνα σταυρώσωσιν. Both **30** and **29** could be rendered 'in order that', but in both cases the meaning is just 'to be crucified' 'to crucify', and Matthew rightly interprets with εἰς τὸ σταυρῶσαι. There is no parallel in Luke.

31. xv 21 καὶ ἀγγαρεύουσιν ... Σίμωνα ... ἵνα ἄρῃ τὸν σταυρὸν αὐτοῦ. As in **29** Matthew follows Mark: Luke substitutes an infinitive, φέρειν.

Some of these instances of ἵνα, and perhaps especially the last three, are not so clearly non-purposive as the rest, and it is hardly surprising that Matthew here and there (**8**, **13**, **19**, **20**, **21**, **28**, **29**, **31**) accepts the construction, as even Luke, though more rarely, does sometimes (**16**, **20**, **21**, **24**). But the general instinct of both is to make a change, Matthew twelve times out of twenty, Luke thirteen times out of seventeen. Sometimes they merely omit: in other cases they substitute the *oratio recta* (so especially Matthew, five times: Luke twice) or an infinitive (so especially Luke, four times: Matthew once or twice).

But what then is the explanation of Mark's fondness for ἵνα after verbs like παρακαλεῖν διαστέλλεσθαι παραγγέλλειν ἐπιτιμᾶν ἐντέλλεσθαι and others? I cannot help thinking that we have here another illustration of the influence of the Latin of Rome on Mark's Greek: for in Latin we have *rogo ut, oro ut, impero ut, monco (admonco) ut, suadeo ut,* and so on.

No doubt ἵνα in the Κοινή generally was coming into much more general use than it had enjoyed in Attic Greek: any grammar of New Testament Greek will illustrate the point that ἵνα is no longer confined to the sense of purpose, and references need not be accumulated here. But writers on New Testament Greek are (naturally) inclined to exaggerate the extent to which it is a single self-contained whole: if these 'notes on Marcan usage' have done anything else, they have, I hope, established the result that the Greek of one of the three Synoptic writers does show broad, almost fundamental, differences from the Greek of the other two. And the more we emphasize the enlarged use of ἵνα throughout the range of the Κοινή, the more pressing, as it seems to me, is the need for accounting for the contrast in this respect between Mark and Luke. If Mark's extended use of ἵνα is not to be explained as a vulgarism, some other way of explaining it must be sought.

Now there are two or three directions in which recent investigations cited in Moulton's *Prolegomena* to the Grammar of N.T.Greek (1906) offer instructive parallels. Thumb (Moulton, p. 205) concludes that there were two rival tendencies, with a geographical dividing line between them, in this matter, Asiatic Greek leaning to a larger use of the infinitive, Western and European Greek to the universalizing of ἵνα (it will be noted that Luke, as pointed out above, sometimes replaces the ἵνα of Mark by an infinitive), the European use having in modern Greek ousted the other alternative. To a similar result are we led by Kälker's emphasis (Moulton, p. 206) on the frequency of ἵνα in Polybius — for Polybius spent a large proportion of the years of his adult life in Italy. Add to this that Mark has been shown, half a dozen pages back, to adopt, often enough to call for explanation, an order of words in his Greek which is not a Greek order but a Latin: and I submit that the thesis needs consideration that his exaggerated use of ἵνα should be traced back to the same source, his years of residence in Rome.[3]

These scholars who, like Moulton himself (p. 20) and Radermacher (*Neutestamentliche Grammatik* p. 11), restrain within very narrow limits the influence of Latin on Hellenistic and New Testament Greek have perhaps not sufficiently investigated the possibility of this influence being specially great in individual writers such as St Mark: and it is only with regard to St Mark in contrast to the other two Synoptists that I plead for a reconsideration of the case.

(5) Absence of λέγων (λέγοντες) after verbs introducing a statement or a question, where Matthew and Luke add or substitute it. †

i. ἀγανακτεῖν

1. xiv 4 ἦσαν δέ τινες ἀγανακτοῦντες πρὸς ἑαυτούς Εἰς τί ἡ ἀπώλεια αὕτη ...; Matthew ἠγανάκτησαν λέγοντες Εἰς τί ... No Luke.

[3] Moulton (p. 21 and p. 21 n.3) admits that some writers are more disposed than he is himself to allow some place to Latin influence, e.g. Blass *Grammatik des NTlichen Griechisch* p. 4; and on more general lines W. Schulze *Graeca Latina*.

ii. *ἀποκρίνεσθαι*

2. viii 4 *ἀπεκρίθησαν αὐτῷ οἱ μαθηταὶ αὐτοῦ ὅτι Πόθεν τούτους δυνήσεταί τις...* Matthew *λέγουσιν αὐτῷ οἱ μαθηταί Πόθεν ἡμῖν ...* No Luke.

3. ix 17 *ἀπεκρίθη αὐτῷ εἷς ἐκ τοῦ ὄχλου Διδάσκαλε, ἤνεγκα τὸν υἱόν μου.* Matthew *προσῆλθεν ... λέγων,* Luke *ἐβόησεν λέγων.*

4. xii 29 *ἀπεκρίθη ὁ Ἰησοῦς ὅτι Πρώτη ἐστίν ...* Matthew *ὁ δὲ ἔφη αὐτῷ ...* Luke *ὁ δὲ εἶπεν πρὸς αὐτόν ...*

iii. *βοᾶν*

5. xv 34 *ἐβόησεν ὁ Ἰησοῦς φωνῇ μεγάλῃ Ἠλεὶ Ἠλεὶ ...* Matthew *ἀνεβόησεν ὁ Ἰ. φωνῇ μεγάλῃ λέγων ...* No parallel in Luke: but cf. no. 3.

iv. *διαλογίζεσθαι*

6. ii 6 *διαλογιζόμενοι ἐν ταῖς καρδίαις αὐτῶν Τί οὗτος οὕτω λαλεῖ;* Luke *ἤρξαντο διαλογίζεσθαι λέγοντες Τίς ...* Matthew *εἶπον ἐν ἑαυτοῖς Οὗτος ...*

7. viii 16 *διελογίζοντο πρὸς ἀλλήλους ὅτι ἄρτους οὐκ ἔχουσιν.* Matthew *διελογίζοντο ἐν ἑαυτοῖς λέγοντες ὅτι Ἄρτους οὐκ ἐλάβομεν.* No Luke.

v. *διαστέλλεσθαι*

8. ix 9 *διεστείλατο αὐτοῖς ἵνα μηδένι ἃ εἶδον διηγήσωνται.* Matthew *ἐνετείλατο αὐτοῖς ὁ Ἰ. λέγων· Μηδενὶ εἴπητε τὸ ὅραμα.* No Luke.

vi. *ἐπερωτάω (ἐρωτάω)*†

9. v 9 *ἐπηρώτα αὐτόν Τί ὄνομά σοι;* Luke *ἐπερώτησεν αὐτὸν ὁ Ἰ. λέγων Τί σοι ὄνομά ἐστιν;* Nothing parallel in Matthew.

10. vii 26 *ἠρώτα αὐτὸν ἵνα τὸ δαιμόνιον ἐκβάλῃ ἐκ τῆς θυγατρὸς αὐτῆς.* Matthew *προσεκύνει αὐτῷ λέγουσα Κύριε, βοήθει μοι.* No Luke.

11. viii 5 *ἠρώτα αὐτούς Πόσους ἔχετε ἄρτους;* Matthew substitutes *λέγει* for *ἠρώτα.* There is no Luke.

12. viii 29 *ἐπηρώτα αὐτούς Ὑμεῖς δὲ τίνα με λέγετε εἶναι;* Matthew and Luke substitute *λέγει (εἶπεν)* for *ἐπηρώτα.*

13. ix 28 *κατ᾽ ἰδίαν ἐπηρώτων αὐτόν Ὅτι ἡμεῖς οὐκ ἐδυνήθημεν ἐκβαλεῖν αὐτό:* Once more Matthew *κατ᾽ ἰδίαν εἶπον· Διὰ τί ἡμεῖς ...* No parallel to this verse in Luke.

14. x 2 *ἐπηρώτων αὐτόν* Εἰ *ἔξεστιν ἀνδρὶ γυναῖκα ἀπολῦσαι; πειράζοντες αὐτόν*. Matthew *προσῆλθον αὐτῷ ... πειράζοντες αὐτὸν καὶ λέγοντες* Εἰ *ἔξεστιν* ... Again no Luke.

15. x 17 *προσδραμὼν εἷς καὶ γονυπετήσας αὐτὸν ἐπηρώτα αὐτόν* Διδάσκαλε ... Luke adds *λέγων* (*ἐπηρώτησέν τις αὐτὸν ἄρχων λέγων* Διδάσκαλε ...), Matthew as elsewhere substitutes *εἶπεν* (*εἷς προσελθὼν αὐτῷ εἶπεν* Διδάσκαλε ...)

16. xii 28 *ἐπηρώτησεν αὐτον* Ποία *ἐστὶν ἐντολὴ πρώτη* ... Matthew for once repeats Mark's phrase; Luke, in a more or less parallel passage, substitutes *ἀνέστη* ... *λέγων*.

17. xiii 3 *ἐπηρώτα αὐτὸν κατ' ἰδίαν* Πέτρος *καὶ* Ἰάκωβος ... Εἰπὸν *ἡμῖν πότε* ... Both Matthew and Luke add *λέγοντες*: Luke keeps *ἐπηρώτησαν*, for which Matthew has his favourite phrase *προσῆλθον αὐτῷ*.

18. xv 2 *ἐπηρώτησεν αὐτον ὁ* Πειλᾶτος Σὺ *εἶ ὁ βασιλεὺς τῶν* Ἰ.; Both the others retain the verb (Luke *ἠρώτησεν*), but both add *λέγων*.

[vii. *ἐπιτιμάω*

19. i 25 *ἐπετίμησεν αὐτῷ ὁ* Ἰησοῦς Φιμώθητι *καὶ ἔξελθε*. So Tischendorf with ℵ* A*, but the rest agree with Luke *ἐπετίμησεν αὐτῷ ὁ* Ἰ. *λέγων* ... , and that may probably be right: though the caution must be given that the Old Latins frequently add *dicens* where Mark's text is without it (so *k* in ix 29, x 17, xii 28, xv 2: not in x 2, xiii 3), presumably following the idiom of their language.]

viii. *κατακρίνειν*

20. xiv 64 *οἱ δὲ πάντες κατέκρινον αὐτὸν ἔνοχον εἶναι θανάτου*. Matthew turns it with *λέγειν* into the *oratio recta οἱ δὲ ἀποκριθέντες εἶπον*· Ἔνοχος *θανάτου ἐστίν*. No parallel in Luke.

[ix. *κηρύσσειν*

21. i 14, 15 *κηρύσσων τὸ εὐαγγέλιον* [*τῆς βασιλείας*] *τοῦ θεοῦ, ὅτι* Πεπλήρωται *ὁ καιρός* ... So again Tischendorf with ℵ* *c* Origen, against the rest, who add *λέγων* or *καὶ λέγων* before *ὅτι*; Matthew *ἤρξατο κηρύσσειν καὶ λέγειν*. Once more, as with *ἐπιτιμᾶν*, the want of clear Marcan parallels weights the balance against the reading of ℵ.]

x. *κράζω* (with *λέγειν*, however, 5/8)

22. xi 9 *ἔκραζον* Ὡσαννά. Matthew and Luke both add *λέγοντες*, and Luke substitutes *αἰνεῖν τὸν θεόν* for *κράζειν*.

23, 24. xv 13, 14 *ἔκραξαν Σταύρωσον αὐτόν ... περισσῶς ἔκραξον Σταύρωσον αὐτόν.* Here Matthew has λέγουσιν πάντες ... περισσῶς ἔκραξον λέγοντες; Luke has ἐπεφώνουν λέγοντες on the first occasion, and phrases the second differently.

xi. λαλεῖν

25. xiv 31 *ὁ δὲ ἐκπερισσῶς ἐλάλει Ἐάν δέῃ με συναποθανεῖν σοι ...* Matthew *λέγει αὐτῷ ὁ Πέτρος Κἂν δέῃ με ...* , and so Luke, though he has only a rougher parallel, *ὁ δὲ εἶπεν αὐτῷ*.

Perhaps no very striking results emerge. Nearly half the instances cited are in connexion with a single verb *ἐπερωτάω* (*ἐρωτάω*), and here we may safely say that Mark uses it without λέγω, the other two tend either to add λέγω (so Luke 4/6) or to substitute it (so Matt. 7/9). As to the remaining ten verbs, it is not meant to be suggested that Mark's normal usage is to employ them without λέγω: but even if the instances are exceptional, they are at the same time numerous enough to justify the impression that he can on occasion use any verb which implies 'saying' without adding the actual phrase 'saying', while with Matthew and Luke the rule is almost absolute the other way. And just as with Mark's *ἐπερωτάω*, so with the other verbs, Matthew prefers the substitution of λέγω, Luke the addition. Mark's omission of λέγω is no Latinism, but is probably just colloquial rather than literary language. But it accounts for some half-dozen of these agreements between Matthew and Luke against Mark which have disturbed the judgement of so many critics.

XI – Usage of Mark: ὁ Ἰησοῦς and Ἰησοῦς†

I am not here discussing St Mark's usage of ὁ Ἰησοῦς in general. In Note V I called attention to his comparatively infrequent use of the phrase in narrative (that is, at the head of a paragraph or sub-paragraph) as compared with his use of it "in the give and take of question and answer". It is also characteristic that he rather often introduces it in the middle or at the end of a sentence — in most of such cases one or the other of the later Synoptists omits it.[1] My purpose is limited to the presence or absence of the article with Ἰησοῦς, whether in the nominative or in the oblique cases. And I propose to extend the investigation to cover all four Gospels.

Abstraction must first be made of certain phrases, where the article before Ἰησοῦς is necessarily or normally absent. Such would be, apart from the vocative, the title Ἰησοῦς Χριστός (i 1) and the instances of addition to the name Ἰησοῦς of an adjective with article prefixed, Ἰησοῦς ὁ Ναζαρηνός, x 47, xvi 6 — though even in this phrase we have in xiv 67, if the W-H text is right, *μετὰ τοῦ Ναζαρηνοῦ ἦσθα τοῦ Ἰησοῦ*.

But with this qualification, the rule in Mark is practically absolute ὁ Ἰησοῦς not Ἰησοῦς. The concordance gives between sixty and seventy instances (of which all but some eighteen are in the nominative) and in only two is there any serious evidence for omission of the article. Occasionally indeed it may be a question whether the personal name should go altogether: but wherever Ἰησοῦς stands in the text ὁ stands also[2] except possibly in i 9 and i 14. In i 9 Ἰησοῦς is the reading of ℵ A B L and the great majority: in i 14 of A, several uncials and some forty minuscules. In the latter case the evidence for omission is obviously inadequate. In the former case we have to set a large preponderance of MS evidence against D Δ 28 *fam* 13 and Marcan usage.

At the most then we have only a single example in St. Mark of Ἰησοῦς alone. At the other end stands John where the usage Ἰησοῦς is not quite infrequent. In both Matthew and Luke we have a few cases where the evidence for omission of the article is overwhelming (Matt. xiv 1 *τὴν ἀκοὴν Ἰησοῦν*, Matt xx 30 *ὅτι Ἰησοῦς παράγει*, Luke ii 52 *καὶ Ἰησοῦς προέκοπτεν ἐν τῇ σοφίᾳ*, Luke iii 21 *καὶ Ἰησοῦν βαπτισθέντος*, Luke iv 1

---

[1] Mark ii 15, v 15, vi 30 (contrast Luke), ix 4 (contrast Matthew), x 50, xi 7 (contrast Matt.), xi 33 (contrast Luke), xiv 55, xiv 60 (contrast Matt.), xiv 67 (contrast Luke).

[2] Of course Latin evidence does not ordinarily count in questions of the article, though in the African Old Latin ὁ is sometimes represented by *ille*. But even there you would not find *ille Iesus* for ὁ Ἰησοῦς.

Ἰησοῦς δὲ πλήρης Πνεύματος Ἁγίου, Luke ix 36 εὑρέθη Ἰησοῦς μόνος), and more where our best or some of our best MSS are in favour of omission, though the total numbers for Ἰησοῦς would not rise to more than eight in all for Matthew and fourteen for Luke. What is remarkable is that B is in both Gospels the constant factor, whether alone or with a smaller or larger group of other MSS, in favour of omission. Matt. xxvi 51 is the solitary exception to the rule. It will also be noted that, while in Luke the clearest cases for omission occur for the most part at the beginning of the Gospel, in Matthew every single instance, whether of the supporting authorities are few or many, occurs in the second half of the Gospel.

Ἰησοῦς *in Matthew*

1. xiv 1 *τὴν ἀκοὴν Ἰησοῦ*. No variant.
2. xxvi 8[3] *εἰ μὴ αὐτὸν Ἰησοῦν* (ℵ *Ἰησοῦν αὐτόν*) *μόνον* B* ℵ. All others *τὸν Ἰησοῦν μόνον*
3. xx 17 *μέλλων δὲ ἀναβαίνειν Ἰησοῦς* B. All the rest *καὶ ἀναβαίνειν ὁ Ἰησοῦς* save 1 and Origen *μέλλων δὲ ὁ Ἰησοῦς ἀναβαίνειν*
4. xx 30 *ἀκούσαντες ὅτι Ἰησοῦς παράγει*, No variant.
5. xxi 1 *τότε Ἰησοῦς ἀπέστειλεν δύο μαθητὰς* B D 22* al mu.
6. xxi 12 *καὶ εἰσῆλθεν Ἰησοῦς εἰς τὸ ἱερὸν* B ℵ * C Δ al Orig ¾
7. xxvi 51 *εἷς τῶν μετὰ Ἰησοῦ*. All except (1) L and a few others *μετὰ τοῦ Ἰησοῦ*, (2) B *μετ' αὐτοῦ*.
8. xxviii 9 *καὶ ἰδοὺ Ἰησοῦς ὑπήντησεν αὐταῖς*. A B C D etc.

Ἰησοῦς *in Luke*

1. ii 52 *καὶ Ἰησοῦς προέκοπτεν ἐν τῇ σοφίᾳ* B ℵ^c A B C D L Δ and practically all others: ℵ* Orig ½ (note the agreement) *ὁ Ἰησοῦς*.
2. iii 21 *καὶ Ἰησοῦ βαπτισθέντος*. No variant.
3. iii 23 *καὶ αὐτὸς ἦν Ἰησοῦς ἀρχόμενος ὡσεὶ* ... B ℵ L 33 al aliq, and so, though otherwise with a different reading, D Clem Ath.
4. iv 1 *Ἰησοῦς δὲ πλήρης Πνεύματος Ἁγίου*. No variant.
5. iv 8 *καὶ ἀποκριθεὶς εἶπεν αὐτῷ Ἰησοῦς* B
6. v 8 *προσέπεσεν τοῖς γόνασιν Ἰησοῦ* B ℵ Δ and some eighty others.
7. v 10 *καὶ εἶπεν πρὸς τον Σίμονα Ἰησοῦς* B L
8. ix 36 *εὑρέθη Ἰησοῦς μόνος* B ℵ A C* D Δ and some fifty others. cf. Matt. xvii 8
9. ix 50 *εἶπεν δὲ πρὸς αὐτόν Ἰησοῦς* B *ℵ

---

[3] For omission after *αὐτός* cf. Luke iii. 23, xxiv. 15.

10. xviii 40[4] *σταθεὶς δὲ* 'Ιησοῦς B D
11. xxii 48 'Ιησοῦς *δὲ εἶπεν αὐτῷ*· 'Ιούδα B ℵ L T
12. xxii 52 *εἶπεν δὲ* 'Ιησοῦς *πρὸς τοὺς παραγενομένους* B ℵ A T
13. xxiii 28 *στραφεὶς δὲ πρὸς αὐτὰς* 'Ιησοῦς B ℵ L
14. xxiv 15 *καὶ αὐτὸς* 'Ιησοῦς *ἐγγίσας διεπορεύετο* B ℵ A L

---

[4] Note that the section ix 51 - xviii 14 contains no instance of 'Ιησοῦς, whereas there are examples just before and just after. But the personal name itself is rather markedly uncommon in the section.

ADDITIONAL NOTES

The following notes give added bibliographical information or further details about issues raised by Turner. The numerals preceding each note refer to the sections of Turner's Notes.

I See N.Turner, chapter 12 § 2

IV See N.Turner, chapter 12 § 5

IV 1 For a different punctuation of Mark i 1-4 and a discussion of *καθώς* in the New Testament see J.K.Elliott, "*καθώς* and *ὥσπερ* in the New Testament" *Filología Neotestamentaria* 7 (1991) pp. 55-8

V See Note VIII "The Disciples and the Twelve".

V (i) See N.Turner, chapter 12 § 2

V (iv) Further on *οἱ μαθηταί* (*αὐτοῦ*) see J.K.Elliott, "*μαθητής* with a Possessive in the New Testament" *TZ* 35 (1979) pp. 300-4 and in my "An Eclectic Textual Commentary on the Greek Text of Mark's Gospel" (chapter 10 below under vi 41). Both articles are reproduced in my *Essays and Studies in New Testament Textual Criticism* (Córdoba, 1991) pp. 139-145 and 159-170 (= *Estudios de Filología Neotestamentaria* 3)

V (v) Turner changed his mind on the occurrence of the plural of ὄχλος at x 1. See his "Western Readings in the Second Half of St. Mark's Gospel" *JTS* xxix (1927) esp. pp. 4f. We may add to Turner's Note on ὄχλος in several particulars. First regarding the use of the adjective with ὄχλος. Mark with one exception uses the article or an adjective, never both: the exception is πᾶς. (πᾶς ὁ ὄχλος occurs at ii 13, iv 1, ix 15, xi 18). At iii 32 *v.l.* adds ὁ and this should be accepted as original; it would have been easy to omit the article before ὄχλος, as may be seen in variants at iii 20, ix 25 and x 1 (where we should read the singular ὁ ὄχλος: the plural reading there is doubly against Mark's style both being an exceptional plural and being anarthrous. Another *v.l.* ὄχλος πολύς at x 1 would also be compatible with Mark's usage.) At iii 7 read πολὺς ὄχλος and thus increase Turner's total of occurrences of ὄχλος from 37 to 38 (*v.l.* πολὺ πλῆθος is likely to be a harmonization to the Lucan parallel [1]). At iv 1 read πολὺς not πλεῖστος. At xii 37 omit ὁ with ℵ D W etc. At xiv 43 add πολύς. If these *vv.ll* are accepted, Mark's pattern of using ὄχλος with either article or adjective (excluding πᾶς) may be maintained, and the adjectives are restricted to πολύς or ἱκανός.

The use of ὄχλος suggests that the word has a precise meaning in Mark. As Turner indicates, Mark does not use ὄχλος of the disciples. He keeps crowd and disciples distinct. This feature of his style has a bearing on v 24. Here ὄχλος πολύς is not the disciples and ἀκολουθεῖν (see Turner, Note V (vi)) is used of other than disciples. If we eliminate πλῆθος from Mark then the only apparent synonym is λαός. This is found in the quotation at vii 6 and xiv 2 where it may mean 'the people (Israel)' as in Luke. At xi 32 we may read *v.l.* ὄχλον (and thereby increase the total number of occurrences of ὄχλος to 39) but if λαός is read, again 'the people (Israel)' is likely to be the meaning.

Turner notes that πᾶς ὁ ὄχλος governs a plural verb three times out of four, although each of those three is not firm in the ms.tradition. The exception in his list is at ii 13 but there is a *v.l.* ἤρχοντο read by 157, 565, 1071 supported by some Old Latin witnesses. The plural is likely to be original throughout: scribes motivated by formal grammar could have altered these to singulars.

For ὄχλος without πᾶς (either with another adjective or with the definite article) the singular verb is used whether the verb precedes or not: the one exception to this is at iii 7 but this noun is some distance from its verb (ἠκολούθησαν is unlikely to be original at iii 7) and the unusual list of dependent phrases has doubtless influenced the use of ἀκούοντες ... ἦλθον. Again we note that iii 7 has been subjected to much scribal activity.

V (vi) Further on ἀκολουθέω see G.D.Kilpatrick, "Some Notes on Marcan Usage" (chapter 6 below).

VII See further G.D.Kilpatrick on particles (chapter 9 below).

---

[1] πλῆθος πολὺ in iii. 8 is also likely to be secondary.

VII 3 See N.Turner, chapter 12 § 2

VII 4 (ii) G.D.Kilpatrick supplements Turner on οὖν and on asyndeton in his "Matthew on Matthew" reprinted as chapter 33 in J.K.Elliott (ed.), *The Principles and Practice of New Testament Textual Criticism* (Leuven, 1990) pp. 250-8, esp. pp. 253 f. (=*BETL* 96).

VIII (i) See further G.D.Kilpatrick on periphrastic εἶναι and participle in "Some Notes on Marcan Usage" (chapter 6 below) and Nigel Turner (chapter 12 below) § 5.

VIII (ii) On ἤρξατο / ἤρξαντο with the present infinitive the following additional comments may be made. One is that this formula occurs as a variant at v 18, xiv 72 (both in D). As this is characteristic of Mark's usage (26 times) these variants present themselves as worthy of consideration as the original reading. The fact that, apart from one isolated example of the active, the verb occurs only in this stereotyped kind of phrase suggests that we are dealing with a precisely defined idiom. At several places the meaning, "began to" is inappropriate. Thus at x 28 Peter did not merely begin to say what follows, he said it. This applies to similar phrases with λέγειν as at x 32, 47, xii 1, xiii 5, xiv 69. Likewise in other passages the evangelist is not concerned to stress that Jesus or others began to do something as distinct from just doing it. For example, at v 20 it is not that the man "began to proclaim" which makes people marvel but what he "proclaimed".

At other places the context allows us to give ἤρξαντο the meaning "began" or not as we choose. For example, ii 23 we can translate ἤρξαντο ὁδὸν ποιεῖν "began to make their way" or "made their way" without harm to the sense. On the other hand there are no passages where the sense "began" is required.

These considerations, that in some verses the verb cannot be translated "began" without conflicting with the context, that elsewhere the rendering "began" is optional and that nowhere the meaning "began" is necessary, are in favour of the view that this kind of phrase in Mark is merely a periphrasis for a past tense.

This periphrasis has one noteworthy feature. It is the middle aorist of *ἄρχειν*, not the passive, that is used. The middle forms were going out of use in the ordinary Greek of this period and it may be that the evangelist in using the middle is using an older idiom.

The second point about this periphrasis is its meaning. For what kind of past tense does it serve? To this question we can give no clear answer. We cannot equate the tense exclusively with either imperfect or aorist. We have several instances of this kind *ἤρξατο λέγειν*, but correspondingly the evangelist uses *ἔλεγεν*, *εἶπεν* or *λέγει*.

See also N.Turner, chapter 12 § 4 "The Pleonastic Auxiliary"

VIII (iv) *θέλω*. See C.H.Turner, "Western Readings in the Second Half of St.Mark's Gospel" *JTS* xxix (1927) p. 3, no. 3 with reference to *θέλεις ποιήσωμεν*. Further comments may be made regarding *θέλειν* with the subjunctive: originally it consisted of a verb of wishing followed by a deliberative subjunctive and as such the subjunctive was confined mainly to the first person. The idiom survives with this limitation in Mark. *τί θέλεις* (or *θέλετε*) *ποιήσω* (or *ποιήσωμεν*) or the like occur at ix 5, x 36, 51, xiv 12, xv 9, 12. Unfortunately the idiom was unwelcome to scribes. At ix 5 for *θέλεις ποιήσωμεν* the printed text has *καὶ ποιήσωμεν*, at x 36 it has the conflation *τί θέλετέ με ποιήσω ὑμῖν*. At x 51, xiv 12, xv 9 the idiom has survived, but at xv 12 we should insert *θέλετε* after *οὖν*. The meaning throughout is clear and an English equivalent is "What would you have me do?" or the like. At x 35 *ἵνα* is left out by D 118 pc Lat.vt. *i k r*[1] vg(1). This gives us a sentence *θέλομεν ὃ ἐὰν αἰτήσωμέν σε ποιήσῃς ἡμῖν*. The difficulty is that this gives us a verb of wishing in the first person followed by a subjunctive in the second, an unparalleled conjunction. All Mark's examples have the verb of wishing in the second person and the subjunctive in the first. On the other hand we have an example of *θέλω ἵνα* etc. followed by a second person subjunctive at vi 25. In view of this *ἵνα* is best read at x 35.

IX (1) *ἀποστηρεῖν*. See also Note X Introduction.

IX (1) *κεφαλιόω*. For a different suggestion for the etymology see V.Taylor's commentary (*The Gospel According to St. Mark* (London, 1952)) *in loc.*

IX (1) *πυγμῇ* a recent discussion see T.C.Skeat, "A Note on *πυγμῇ* in Mark 7.3", *JTS* xli (1990) pp. 525-7.

IX (2) *ἀλλά*. See further G.D.Kilpatrick, "Particles" (chapter 9 below)

IX (2) *πάλιν*. For a full discussion see D.B.Peabody, *Mark as Composer* (Leuven and Macon, Georgia, 1987) *passim* and esp. table 70. See G.D. Kilpatrick, "Some Notes on Marcan Usage" (chapter 6 below).

IX (2B) Further see Note X Introduction, and G.D.Kilpatrick, "*πορεύεσθαι* and its Compounds" (Chapter 5 below) and J.K.Elliott, "The Text and Language of the Endings to Mark's Gospel" (chapter 11 below under verse 10).

X (2) See further J.K.Elliott, "Nouns with Diminutive Endings in the New Testament" *Novum Testamentum* 12 (1970) pp. 391-8.

X (3b) For a different view of the reason for the position of the verb at the end of its clause in Mark see M.Zerwick, *Untersuchungen zum Markus-Stil* (Rome, 1937) pp. 108-116.

The following may be said about Mark's word order in general: this supplements Turner's statement about the verb at the end of the sentence.

Unlike Greek and like formal Latin prose of the Classical period, Mark has a dominant word order. Its main characteristics are simple: first the verb, followed by subject, next the object and finally the rest of the predicate. There are certain modifications of this rule. For example, connecting particles come towards the beginning of their clauses, and it is noteworthy in this connexion how often *εὐθύς* is near the beginning of its sentence. Then again pronouns dependent on the verb follow it immediately. This is true not only of the simple accusative, genitive and dative but of phrases consisting of a preposition and pronoun such as *ἀπ' αὐτοῦ*. Similarly, words or phrases frequently follow the nouns on which they depend. Adjectives frequently follow their nouns and if one has the article the other has it also, thus *πνεῦμα ἀκάθαρτον* or *τὸ πνεῦμα τὸ ἀκάθαρτον*. Apart from adjectives, words are rarely inserted between the article and the noun. They usually follow. Thus *τῶν ἑστηκότων ὧδε* is preferable to *τῶν ὧδε ἑστηκότων*. Marcan usage seems to be against repeating the article with a phrase dependent as a noun. We should read *Ἰωσὴφ ἀπὸ Ἀριμαθαίας* not *ὁ ἀπὸ κτλ*.

There are exceptions to these rules however. These are due to a desire to emphasize a word or to avoid monotony. Where there is emphasis, apart from the position of the emphatic word at the beginning of its phrase, the word order seems to be normal. Where the word order is altered for variety, the alteration seems to be more far-reaching.

There are some passages whose interpretation is determined by Marcan word order. For example, the punctuation at ii 15f. is in dispute. Which is right? In one arrangement the subject, the noun phrase *οἱ γραμματεῖς τῶν Φαρισαίων* precedes the verbs *ἰδόντες* and *ἔλεγον*. In the other the noun phrase attaches to the previous verb *ἠκολούθουν*, and the following verbal forms begin their phrases or clauses. This is the Marcan order and in accordance with it we read and punctuate: *πολλοί· Καὶ ἠκολούθουν αὐτῷ καὶ οἱ γραμματεῖς τῶν Φαρισαίων καὶ ἰδόντες κτλ.*[2]

A dominant word order is alien to the Greek language and must have been a strong irritant to scribes and readers of the text. This is implied by the frequent changes of order we find in the apparatus to Mark, which look like attempts to get away from this irregularity. It seems in fact as though we may take it as a general principle, other things being equal, that the reading which conforms to Mark's dominant order is more likely to be right than the one which departs from it.

---

[2] N. Turner draws attention to this in his section 3 (see chapter 12 below)

X (5) See G.D.Kilpatrick, "Recitative λέγων" (chapter 7 below).

X (5 vi) ἐπερωτάω. See J.K.Elliott, "Ἐρωτᾶν and ἐπερωτᾶν in the New Testament" *Filología Neotestamentaria* 2 (1989) pp. 205-6.

XI See further R.C.Nevius, *The Divine Names in the Gospels* (Salt Lake City, 1967) (=*Studies and Documents* 30).

G.D.Kilpatrick

CHAPTER TWO

MARK i 45 AND THE MEANING OF λόγος

The word λόγος occurs in Mark twenty-three times,[1] and it is the purpose of this note to show that, with one exception, it is used only in certain closely related senses, and that this fact materially affects the interpretation of Mk i 45.

Λόγος (used thus in the singular only) may mean 'the message' of Jesus or the Church, as in ii 2, iv 14, 15 bis, 16, 17, 18, 19, 20, 33, viii 32. This meaning is common in the New Testament, but in Mark it is noticeable that it is never qualified, as it often is elsewhere, by such phrases as *τοῦ Θεοῦ, τῆς ἀληθείας* or *τοῦ σταυροῦ*. In the explanation of the parable of the sower it is intended for the Christian message, and in ii 2, iv 33, viii 32, it is the message of Jesus.

The second meaning is 'an utterance' or in the plural 'a body of utterances'. In this use in the singular it refers to an utterance or pronouncement in the context as in v 36, vii 29, ix 10, x 22, xi 29, xiv 39. In vii 13, *ἀκυροῦντες τὸν λόγον τοῦ Θεοῦ*, the reference is to a particular pronouncement of God quoted just before. In the plural, viii 38, x 24, xiii 31, it refers to the utterances of Jesus as a whole and in meaning approaches to the first use. In xii 13, *ἀγρεύσωσιν λόγῳ*, 'catch in speech', we have the one example of the word with a sense outside the above group of related meanings.

It will be noticed that Mk i 45 has not yet been treated. Here λόγος is usually translated 'the story'. To this there are two objections: firstly, as W.C. Allen pointed out, this translation involves an abrupt change of subject from Jesus to the healed leper, and secondly, as is shown above, Mark nowhere else has λόγος in this sense. In the parallel, Lk. v 15, it is true that λόγος is to be understood in this sense, but it is doubtful if,

---

[1] ADDENDUM: This statement needs correction. At Mk viii 38 λόγους is omitted by W *k* sah (cf. Tertullian). It cannot be divined from the spacing whether P^{45} had λόγους or not. The phrase *τὸν αὐτὸν λόγον εἰπών*, Mk xiv 39, is omitted by D *a b c ff k*. The omission cannot be explained as a palaeographical error. On the other hand the phrase may be a harmonistic addition from Mt xxvi 44. If these two omissions are thought to be correct, the references to Mk viii 38, xiv 39 disappear from the lists, but the argument of the note is not affected. [J.K.E.]

apart from this parallel, Mk i 45 would have ever been so understood. The only other places where λόγος means 'story' are Lk. vii 17 and Mt. xxviii 15.

It might be asked how, if the generally assumed meaning of the sentence were the intended one, St.Mark could have avoided using λόγος. It may be replied that, while they do not mean the same as λόγος, *δύναμις* as in vi 2, 5, *τὸ γεγονός* v 14, or even *ἔργον* xiv 6, would have been available had this general meeting of the sentence been intended.

In view of these facts it seems preferable to understand λόγος here as 'the message'. In this way the abrupt change of subject is avoided, Jesus being the subject both of λέγει, v.44, and of *ἤρξατο*, v.45, and a use of λόγος unparalleled in Mark is removed.

If we translate λόγον as 'message' how do we understand the verse? It is clear that it must be severed from the story of the leprous man so that we are not told whether the injunction to silence was kept or not. Positively the sentence proves to be a summarizing verse between two stories such as we have in i 14, 39, vi 56.

CHAPTER THREE

MARK i 45

My note on 'Mark i 45 and the meaning of λόγος' has been criticised by the Rev. T. Nicklin on p.252 of the *Expository Times* for February 1940. He condemns my interpretation of the verse for the following reasons. First he cites 'the use of ὁ δὲ which indicates a change in the subject from that in v.44'. This at first sight appeared an argument of great weight, and both Dr Howard, who kindly allowed me to consult him, and I have been unable to find a parallel for this exception. Indeed, it is surprising that neither Klostermann nor W.C. Allen notices the difficulty[1], though they agree with me in their explanation of the verse. As soon, however, as the context of vv.40-45 is examined the difficulty appears much smaller. V.45 picks up v.39 and vv.40-44 are an intrusion which breaks the connexion. To get back from the leper to Jesus' main activity, Mark writes in v.45 ὁ δὲ, contrasting Jesus with the leper of v.40, *καὶ ἔρχεται πρὸς αὐτὸν λεπρὸς κτλ.* We have indeed something very like the parentheses[2] of which Mark is so fond. This connexion is supported by the parallelism between v.45 and vv.38f., especially in the words *εἰς τοῦτο γὰρ ἐξῆλθον. καὶ ἦν κηρύσσων*, a parallelism which also favours my general interpretation of v.45.

Secondly, Mr. Nicklin argues from 'the insertion of *αὐτὸν* in the final clause which shows that the subject of the previous verb must be a leper, thus distinguished from Him who could not enter a town'. As it happens the *αὐτόν* in which Mr. Nicklin trusts is omitted by DW 478 and inserted after *δύνασθαι* in ℵΦ 245, 349, 700, 1071.[3] Even if *αὐτόν* be original, in this construction it lacks the requisite force to indicate a change of subject. Of course such abrupt changes do occasionally occur, but it was this difficulty which led W.C. Allen to interpret the verse as he did. For an abrupt change of subject Luke xv 15 may be cited, but to show that *αὐτός*

---

[1] E.Klostermann, *Des Markusevangelium* (Tubingen,[2] 1926).

[2] C.H.Turner, Note IV.

[3] C.H.Turner, *JTS* xxviii (1926) p. 158.

need not indicate a change of person it is enough to refer to Mark i 27 (if the reading be right) and Matt.xiii 4.

Further, Mr. Nicklin underestimates the weight of the evidence on the use of λόγος. Its importance must lie in the marked regularity of usage over the last twenty-two instances. Commentators who take the same line as Mr. Nicklin usually are much more ready than he to acknowledge the difficulty that this regularity constitutes for them. Lagrange may be referred to in this connexion. Mr Nicklin does not explicitly reassert the translation 'story' for λόγος; but, as I pointed out, that sense is extremely rare in the New Testament, nor do Moulton and Milligan or Bauer provide other parallels from contemporary sources.

Additional Note

Further on this verse see J.K.Elliott, "The Conclusion of the Pericope of the Healing of the Leper and Mark i 45" *JTS* xxii(1971) pp. 153-7; *id.*, "Is λόγος a Title for Jesus in Mark i 45?" *JTS* xxvii(1976) pp. 402-5; *id.*, "The Healing of the Leper in the Synoptic Parallels" *TZ* 34(1978) pp. 175-6 and chapter 6 below.

CHAPTER FOUR

Ἐπάνω Mark xiv 5

In this verse, though ἐπάνω has not been questioned by the commentators, there appear to be several grounds for suspicion. Of these the first is linguistic. Ἐπάνω occurs here only in the Gospel, and it can be seen from the use of πλεῖον at xii 43 that other expressions were available for the evangelist to convey this meaning. We must, of course, remember that linguistic peculiarity is not alone a sufficient reason for ejecting the word. Some support for this step is found in the fact that according to Legg's apparatus ἐπάνω is omitted by *c k syr.sin, Geo. I.* To these authorities von Soden adds the three cursives, 517, 954, 1675, all members of his $I\phi^a$ group, part of the fam. 1424 which is known to be related to the Caesarean family. From a textual point of view the evidence for omission is small in numbers but imposing.

While, however, the linguistic and textual evidence taken together would render the word suspect, no reason can be derived from it to explain the tradition. Here we may find enlightenment from the events of our own times. During the last forty or so years the purchasing power of the pound has noticeably decreased. A like depreciation of currency took place in the first and second centuries of our era. During this period the standard of living remained constant, but while under Augustus the legionary was paid 150 denarii a year, under Tiberius this became 225 denarii; under Domitian 300 denarii, under Commodus 375, under Severus 500, and under Caracalla 750 denarii. There was a certain debasement of coinage too, and the denarius which under Nero contained 93 per cent of silver, under Commodus contained only 71 per cent. We may accordingly assume that three denarii under Nero could purchase as much as five denarii about A.D. 180, and a jar of ointment costing 300 denarii about A.D. 60 would cost about 500 denarii one hundred and twenty years later. The textual evidence for its presence in the verse suggests that ἐπάνω is a second-century addition, and once such a depreciation had taken place the interpolation of ἐπάνω or something similar would be called for. Subsequent and far greater depreciations would make a mere 300 denarii seem a trifle and would encourage the acceptance of the addition in the majority of our texts.

If these lines of reasoning are correct, we have an example, such as C.H. Turner loved, of a few eastern and western witnesses preserving the true text against the evidence of the bulk of the tradition, as well as an example how, in details, research in different fields may converge on the same conclusion.

Mark xiv 5, AN ADDENDUM

Jerome can now be added to the authorities which omit ἐπάνω. In the *Tractatus in Marc. xiii 32-33 et xiiii 3-6* (G.Morin, *Anecdota Maredsolana*, III, pars ii, pp. 368f.) he quotes once 'potuit uenumdari trecentis', and once 'potuit trecentis denariis uenumdari'. The exposition supports the absence of any equivalent of ἐπάνω.

CHAPTER FIVE

ΠΟΡΕΥΕΣΘΑΙ AND ITS COMPOUNDS

In Note IX C.H.Turner gave a short discussion of 'πορεύεσθαι and its compounds'. This may be supplemented in two directions.

A. Compounds of πορεύεσθαι.

εἰσπορεύεσθαι (Mark 8, Luke 5, Acts 4).

Matt. xv 17 εἰσπορευόμενον] εἰσερχόμενον B Θ 1279, 1305, Orig. We cannot expect evidence from the versions on such a point as this and there seems no reason to reject the reading of B, for in Matthew εἰσέρχεσθαι occurs frequently, but εἰσπορεύεσθαι nowhere else.

ἐκπορεύεσθαι (Mark 11, Matt. 4, Luke 3).

This word seems to be absent from the true text of Matt. iv 4 as well as from that of xvii 20 f. To the evidence for omitting iv 4 ἐκπορευομένῳ διὰ στόματος, given at *JTS* xlv p. 176 should be added *Passio Bartholomaei* (*Acta Apostolorum Apocrypha*, Bonnet, ii, vol. I p.136) and also *Opus Imperfectum in Matthaeum V.*

προσπορεύεσθαι (Only at Mark x 35 in NT).

It perhaps ought to be mentioned that παραπορεύονται is read in ℵ *eth* (2 MSS.) *boh*. παραπορεύεσθαι occurs elsewhere four times in Mark and at Matt. xxvii 39 from Mark xv 29.

B. πορεύεσθαι and ἔρχεσθαι in Mark

Turner's statement that the simple πορεύεσθαι does not occur in Mark may be developed. It seems that where the evangelist used a verbal form of πορεύεσθαι or its compounds he avoided the corresponding form of ἔρχεσθαι or its compounds. This may be illustrated by the table overleaf.

The terms, present, future, etc., include these tenses and their derivative forms such as the participle and the infinitive. The fact that the first person singular is given indicates only that one or more form of the principal tense or its derivatives are found. Thus διῆλθον itself is not found, but διέλθωμεν and διελθεῖν are.

Present	Future	Aorist	Perfect
ἔρχομαι	ἐλεύσομαι	ἦλθον	ἐλήλυθα
		ἀπῆλθον	
		διῆλθον	
εἰσπορεύομαι	εἰσελεύσομαι	εἰσῆλθον	
ἐκπορεύομαι		ἐξῆλθον	ἐξελήλυθα
παραπορεύομαι	παρελεύσομαι	παρῆλθον	
		προῆλθον	
προσπορεύομαι		προσῆλθον	

The evidence for *συνέρχεσθαι* and *συμπορεύεσθαι* is uncertain. *συνέρχονται*, or *συνέρχεται*, seems beyond question at Mark iii 20. At x 1 we must read *ὄχλος* and the singular verb (cf. C.H.Turner, "Western Readings in the Second Half of St Mark's Gospel" *JTS* xxix pp. 4f.). This gives us a choice between *συμπορεύεται* W f1 f13 (exc. 124), 28, 91, 299, 433 and *συνέρχεται* D Θ 700. *συνέρχονται* is read by 565 and *συμπορεύονται* by the remaining Greek authorities. At xiv 53 *συμπορεύονται* is supported by W 1542 and *συνέρχονται* by the rest. At vi 33 *προῆλθον* seems the most likely reading, but we can trace three other readings, *προσῆλθον*, *συνῆλθον*, *ἦλθον*. This variety shows that the form *συνῆλθον* which occurs nowhere else in Mark is far from certain. We can conclude from these passages that *συνέρχομαι* is sure in Mark, *συμπορεύομαι* is doubtful, and *συνῆλθον* most unlikely. But as we have seen above the evangelist does not draw elsewhere on both *ἔρχεσθαι* and *πορεύεσθαι* for the same part of the verb. This fact favours *συνέρχεται* at Mark x 1 and *συνέρχονται* at xiv 53.

We may now add some further rules for the use of these two groups of words in Mark. *ἔρχομαι* and its compounds alone supply the future, aorist, and perfect and, except for *ἔρχεσθαι* itself and *συνέρχεσθαι*, the compounds of *πορεύεσθαι* regularly provide the present and forms derived from it. It is hard to see the reason for this usage but the facts are clear and it may be that we have another example of Mark's peculiar regularity in the use of terms such as can be seen in his employment of *ὄχλος* and *λόγος*. This regularity in the use of *ἔρχεσθαι* and *πορεύεσθαι* does not obtain in Q and the later evangelists themselves do not observe it. Many of the forms from the two groups of verbs in Matthew conform to the rule but there are many exceptions while in Luke almost all traces of the rule have vanished.

CHAPTER SIX

SOME NOTES ON MARCAN USAGE

(i)

Ὡς

Ὡς in Mark has lost many of its classical uses, but has also acquired new ones. It is used primarily to make a comparison. Where the comparison is with a noun or nominal expression the English translation is 'like': i 10, 22; iv 31; vi 15, 34; viii 24; x 15; xii 25, 31, 33; xiii 34. At ix 3 there are in some manuscripts the words *ὡς χιών*. Were this longer text right, it would provide another example of this idiom. In the use with numerals, v 13 'they were like two thousand', viii 9 'they were like four thousand' and, according to some manuscripts, vi 44 'they were like five thousand', would be possible interpretations, but this idiom is classical and is probably a survival in Mark. In several of these passages there is a participle in the nominal expression as at i 22; vi 34. At xiii 34 this is carried further. We have two participles followed by a finite verb which in English we would render consistently with relative clauses, 'like a man going on a journey who left his house, assigned his servants their responsibilities and ordered the porter to watch'. The change is probably not as harsh in Greek as it would be in English. Greek, unlike English, does not sustain its relative clauses but quickly returns to main clauses. If in xiii 34 the participles may be regarded as equivalent to relative clauses, with *ἐνετείλατο* the evangelist returns to a main clause. Though *ὥσπερ*, *ὡσεί* occur several times as variants to *ὡς* introducing a comparison, *ὥσπερ* nowhere occurs in our printed text of Mark, and *ὡσεί* only at ix 26 where however *ὡς* is read by D supported by most of the Latin witnesses. This is probably right.

The evangelist carries this use of *ὡς* to the point where *ὅμοιος* would be more natural as at iv 31 where there is a variant *ὁμοία ἐστιν*. Revelation, which uses *ὡς* very much as it is used in Mark, also uses *ὅμοιος* in the sense of *ὡς* and at Revelation i 13; xiv 14 *ὅμοιος* is construed like *ὡς* as well. Compare Charles, *Revelation*, I pp. 35-7.

Ὡς is also used to introduce clauses. At xiv 48 the meaning is 'You have come out as you would come out against a thief', though the verb occurs only once and that in the main clause. At iv 26 *οὕτως ... ὡς ἐὰν ἄνθρωπος βαλῇ*, *ὡς* makes a comparison as is clearly shown by the preceding *οὕτως*. 'Εάν (ἄν), which is absent from some manuscripts and could easily be dropped out before *ἄνθρωπος*, must be read as the following subjunctives indicate. This is the only example of *ὡς ἐάν* in Mark. As we saw, *ὡσεί* probably never occurs in the Gospel. Another example of *ὡς* introducing a comparison is at x 1 'he taught them as he was accustomed'. iv 27 can be also understood in this way: the seed grows in such a way "as he does not know", meaning "he knows not how".

Another group of uses of *ὡς*, the temporal, is indicated by the Latin versions iv 27 which, except for *k*, render *ὡς* by '*dum*'. Now *ὡς* does mean 'while' sometimes in the New Testament, cf. John xii 35, 36 and Blass-Debrunner, *Grammatik* para. 455.3 (and the Appendix). We may think that the Latin is mistaken at iv 27, but it is worth considering whether *ὡς* can be used for 'while' elsewhere in Mark. First, how does the evangelist represent the meaning 'while'. There is one example of *ἕως* and the present indicative with this sense at vi 45 and one of *ἐν ᾧ* at ii 19. From this it seems as though he had no one conjunction for 'while'. If 'while' appears inapplicable at iv 27, it gives a reasonable translation at iv 36 'while he was in the boat'. A temporal sense is required at ix 21 'how long a time is it since this happened to him?' In this last rendering *γέγονεν* would indicate that the fits started at some point in the past and have continued to the present. 'When', a meaning for *ὡς* that occurs in John, for example at ii 9, is not right here, but is possible at xiv 72 'and Peter remembered the saying when Jesus said to him'. The difficulty about this suggestion is that Mark normally uses *ὅτε* or *ὅταν* for 'when'.

There are one or two residual problems. *Ὡς γέγραπται* at Mk i 2 is a stylistic correction of *καθώς γέγραπται*. Phrynichus condemns *καθώς*. vii 6 *ὡς γέγραπται* is probably a false reading for *καὶ εἶπεν*. The evangelist seems not to use the formula *ὡς γέγραπται*. At xii 26 *ὡς* and *πῶς* are confused. "Have you not read in the book of Moses ... when God said to him". Here *πῶς* may be a correction of *ὡς*.

From this examination it appears that whereas the evangelist uses *ὡς* with nouns consistently to introduce a comparison, his use of *ὡς* introducing a clause is not so consistent, and sometimes at any rate he uses it as a temporal conjunction.

The Perfect

This examination follows closely the treatment in Chantraine, *Histoire du Parfait Grec* (Paris, 1907) chapter IX. The details of his discussion have been checked, textual evidence has been supplied and some comments have been added. In particular his lists of instances have been closely followed.

Five kinds of perfect can be detected in Mark. First comes "the perfect with intransitive meaning and active endings, often corresponding to a middle present" (Chantraine p. 215). Γέγονα appears at v 33; ix 21; xiii 19; xiv 4 and the participle at v 14. At xiii 19 for *οἵα οὐ γέγονεν τοιαύτη* there is a variant *οἵαι οὐκ ἐγένοντο τοιαῦται* in D 299 565 *l*184 lat vt. vg Aug Arm. The parallel, Matthew xxiv 21, *οἵα οὐ γέγονεν* has a variant *οἵα οὐκ ἐγένετο* in ℵ D Θ 700 *e* Geo[1], Eus Hipp (2). At Mark xiv 4 *γέγονεν* is omitted by D 64 Lat *a ff i* Syr s. It is absent from Matthew xxvi 8, the corresponding passage. The participle *τὸ γεγονός* occurs at Mark v 14, *ἕστηκα* and its compounds are absent from Mark, but the participle appears perhaps three times, ix 1 (*ἑστηκότων*), xi 5 (*ἑστηκότων*, *v.l.* *ἑστώτων*) and xiii 14 (*ἑστηκότα*, *v.l.* *ἑστός* and *στῆκον*).

At iii 31 the true reading is *στήκοντες* and not *ἑστῶτες*. Some manuscripts add *τούς πεποιθότας ἐπὶ χρήμασιν* at x 24, but the modern printed texts rightly omit the phrase. There is no other example of *πέποιθα* in Mark. From *ἐλήλυθα* we have ix 1 *ἐληλυθυῖαν*, ix 13 *ἐλήλυθε* (*v.l.* *ἦλθεν* or *ἤδη ἦλθεν*), and from its compound vii 29 *ἐξελήλυθεν* and vii 30 *ἐξεληλυθός*. At viii 3 *ἥκασιν* and *ἥκουσιν* occur as variants to *εἰσίν*, *ἥκουσιν* being probably an Atticist correction to *ἥκασιν*. The printed texts rightly read *εἰσίν*.

This kind of perfect is going out of use in the *Koine*. It is uncommon not only in Mark but also in the New Testament as a whole. The participle *ἑστηκώς* is indistinguishable in meaning from the present participle, *στήκων*. On the other hand, *ἐλήλυθα* and its derived forms do not seem to differ in sense from some instances of the aorist in Mark. The participle at ix 1 *ἐληλυθυῖαν* has no more the force of the resultative perfect than has *ἐλθοῦσα* at v 26 or v 30 *ἐξελθοῦσαν*. ix 13 Ἠλίας *ἐλήλυθεν* should be compared with i 38 *ἐξῆλθον*. Does vii 29 *ἐξελήλυθεν* differ in meaning from ix 26 *ἐξῆλθεν* or vii 30 *ἐξεληλυθός* from v 13 *ἐξελθόντα*? Likewise how does *τὸ γεγονός* v 14 differ from *τὸ γενόμενον* Luke xxiii 47? At Mark xiii 19 the perfect *γέγονεν* has a variant, the aorist *ἐγένετο*, which suggests that the two tenses were felt to be near each other in meaning. Thus there are two tenses toward which this kind of perfect approximates in Mark, the aorist and the present. The present meaning appears only in the participle and the aorist in both indicative and participle. It is noteworthy how many verbs which could form a perfect of this kind do without a perfect at all. Thus it would have been possible to use the perfect of *ἀνιστάναι* at ix. 9f. but instead we find an aorist.

The second class of perfects is similar to the first and consists of intransitive active perfects from verbs with an intransitive active present (Chantraine p. 218). From *ἐγγίζειν* we have *ἤγγικεν* i 15 and xiv 42 (*ἤγγισεν* ℵ C). To *ἐκάθισεν* xi 2 there is the variant *κεκάθικεν* A (W) X Y Π Φ ω. *Τέθνηκεν* occurs at xv 44. In this group we may also take *εἰώθει* x 1. In meaning these forms vary. At xv 44 it is hard to see any difference between *ἤδη τέθνηκεν* and *πάλαι ἀπέθανεν*. The evangelist seems to use the two phrases as alternative ways of saying the same thing. Either can be translated 'he is already' or 'he has already died'. *Εἰώθει* at x i is the equivalent of an imperfect so that we may assume that the evangelist regarded *εἴωθα* as having a present tense. The variant at xi 2 we may disregard. We can take *ἤγγικεν* at i 15 and xiv 42 in two ways. If we stress the present reference as the true one, the meaning is 'here is the kingdom of God' and 'look here is he who arrests me'. On the other hand if we prefer the past reference the rendering is 'the kingdom of God is at hand' and 'look, he who arrests me is at hand'. Decision here is difficult but important and our conclusion must be determined in part by other considerations, as well as by Mark's use of the perfect.

This perhaps is the point at which to mention *οἶδα*. It had long been a perfect with the present meaning in Greek and this usage has been accepted by Mark as by other New Testament writers. *Κεῖμαι* too was probably regarded as a kind of present with a few infunctional peculiarities.

The next class of perfects, the resultative, was greatly developed in Attic Greek but is again rare in Mark. Chantraine lists the following: v 15 *ἐσχηκότα* (the whole phrase is omitted by D 17* 27 Lat vt vg pl Syr s Bo$^{pt.}$; v 19 *πεποίηκεν* (*ἐποίησεν* D K Φ f1 517 565 700 *al*); vii 37 *πεποίηκεν*; xi 17 *πεποιήκατε* (so B L Δ Ψ 892 1342 Orig: *ἐποιήσατε ceteri*); xv 7 *πεποιήκεισαν* (*πεποιήκασιν* Γ (Θ) Ψ *pc*); v 34, x 32 *σέσωκεν*; xiv 44 *δέδωκει* (*δέδωκεν* Θ, *ἔδωκεν* D *a c k r*^{1} vg (1)); xv 10 *παραδεδώκεισαν* (*παρέδωκαν* D H S W Θ f13 1 5 17 565 700 *pc* Lat *a c* vg (1)). At v 33 *διὸ πεποιήκει λάθρᾳ* is added by D Θ 28 565 700 *pc* Lat *a ff ir*^{1} Geo Arm, but *διό* and *λάθρᾳ* occur nowhere else in Mark. It is possible to read the resultative meaning into *σέσωκεν* v 34; x 32. For *ἐσχηκότα* the aorist participle would have been a fair equivalent as the participle describes something that is past. Two of the instances of *πεποίηκα* are not certain but at vii 36 we have an unquestioned perfect and at xv 7 either a pluperfect or less probably a perfect. At vii 37 there is no necessary difference in meaning from an aorist and at xv 7 the pluperfect seems to have the same sense as the Latin pluperfect, a use normally carried by the aorist in Greek. Consequently the fluctuation between aorist and perfect in the manuscripts at v 19; xi 17 is not surprising. At xiv 44; xv 10 there is a similar variation between aorist and pluperfect. It may be that Mark's use of the pluperfect, rare as it is, to serve a purpose like that of the Latin pluperfect seemed odd to scribes. To conclude, we may have one true resultative perfect. The remainder are indistinguishable from aorists. The pluperfects are strangely like Latin pluperfects.

The fourth and fifth classes of verb have middle endings and are much larger than the previous ones. First come middle perfects apart from the participles (Chantraine pp. 219f.). Ἀνακεκύλισται xvi 4 (ἀποκεκυλισμένον (א) D Θ 565 Lat *c d ff k l n q* vg Eus); γέγραπται i 2, vii 6 (καὶ εἶπεν D *i z*, ὅς εἶπεν Θ *a b*, ὡς εἶπεν fl 565 Arm), ix 12, 13, xi 17, xiv 21 (ἐστιν γεγραμμένον D), 27; δεδέσθαι v 4 (δεδεμένον D omit 565 700); δέδοται iv 11; ἐγήγερται vi 14 (א B D L Δ 33 565 700 892: ἀνέστη A Π *pc*: ἠγέρθη *ceteri*); ἡτοίμασται x 40; πεπλήρωται i 15; διεσπάσθαι v 4 (διεσπακέναι D W 565 700 vt^{pt} vg); συντετρίφθαι v 4 (συντετριφέναι D W 565 700 Lat vt^{pt} vg); τέθειται xv 47 (τίθεται W Y Θ ω fl 22 124 543 28 157 565 *pl*); πεφίμωσο iv 39 (φιμώθητι D W); ἐξήρανται xi 21 (ἐξηράνθη D L N Δ Θ Σ Ψ fl 22 33 517 565 579 700 1342 *pc* Or). Most of these instances seem sound despite the variants. Those at v 4 for example can be dismissed. On the other hand ὡς γέγραπται at vii 6 is against Marcan idiom which prefers καθώς. It is also easier to explain ὡς γέγραπται as a correction of καὶ εἶπεν to an expression found elsewhere, Luke iii 4, Acts xiii 33. Ἀνέστη vi 14 may seem preferable to ἐγήγερται despite vi 16. There are six examples of ἀνιστάναι in the sense of 'raise from the dead' in Mark against three of ἐγείρειν apart from the present passage. At xv 47 τίθεται is right against τέθειται. It is noteworthy that three readings, xvi 4; xiv 21; v 4, involve the substitution of the middle participle for some other part of the perfect.

These perfects are all passive in sense. It is noteworthy that, though there are a number of variants, only at three places, iv 39; vi 14; xii 21, is an aorist an alternative reading, apart from vii 6 where εἶπεν is probably right. Further only at xv 47 is a present (apparently the right reading) a variant to the perfect. From this we may infer that there is less confusion between these perfects, passive in meaning, and the present or aorist passive. This suggests that we are dealing with forms that have a distinctive meaning of their own, just as in English 'Warsaw is taken' does not mean the same as 'Warsaw has been taken' or 'Warsaw is being taken'. This is in keeping with the fact that these forms are more numerous than those in the preceding classes and most of them survive criticism of the text. Even they, however, are not numerous and the only verb at all common is γέγραπται which is formulary.

The last class consists of perfect participles with middle endings and is as numerous as the fourth. The examples are as follows: ἐνδεδύμενος i 6; ἐπισυνηγμένη i 33; εὐλογημένος xi 9; εὐλογημένη xi 10; ἱματισμένον v 15; λελατομημένον xv 46; ἐξηραμμένην iii 1 (ξηράν D W); ἐξηραμμένην iii 3 (ξήραν ℵ B C L W Δ Θ 28 33 124 565 892); ἐξηραμμένην xi 20; πεπωρωμένη vi 52; πεπωρωμένην viii 17; ἐσμυρισμένον xv 23; ἐσπαρμένον iv 15; ἐσταυρωμένον xvi 6; ἐστρωμένον xiv 15. Perhaps the readings ἀποκεκυλισμένον xvi 4 and γεγραμμένον xiv 21 should be added. One thing is immediately noticeable in this list, the scarcity of variants. The periphrasis ἦν with the participle, occurs at i 6, 33; xv 46; vi 52, four examples. Here would belong γεγραμμένον D xiv 21. With these we may take xi 9, 10 where the participle forms the whole of the predicate in a species of wish. Next are iii 1, possibly iii 3 and viii 17 where we have ἔχειν with a noun and participle in the accusative, a construction which can easily develop into a compound tense, and has done so in Modern Greek. Another example of the dependent accusative and participle occurs at v 15, with which we may take the variant ἀποκεκυλισμένον at xvi 4. The remaining instances, xv 23; iv 15; xvi 6; xiv 15 are best classified as adjectival participles. In all occurrences the participle has passive and not middle meaning.

Our analysis of the perfect has left us with two problems, the problem of meaning, and the problem of text. The problem of meaning is best taken first.

The oldest use of the perfect is to describe a state and to begin with the resultative meaning is excluded. In keeping with this the perfect is intransitive and outside the distinction of active and middle. Already in Homer, however, we can see the beginnings of two developments. First there are two instances of the resultative perfect in -κα and secondly the middle perfect is coming into being. With these developments there is soon a third. Transitive perfects appear and correspondingly perfects with passive meaning. We see the fruits of these developments in classical Greek when the perfect is integrated into the conjugations that the users of the language evolved.

In Attic prose, especially in the orators, it is the resultative perfect which is predominant, for example ἠδίκηκα 'I have done wrong and my wrong doing remains'. This use continues frequent in the Ptolemaic Koine and in literary and especially Atticizing Greek. On the other hand, in Mark it is rare and in Later Greek it survives only where literary influences are strong enough to maintain it. It implies a past act and a present state resulting from it. If the emphasis is on the past act the perfect differs little from an aorist, if on the present state it differs as little from a present. Usually by this time it is equivalent to an aorist (E.Schwyzer, *Grammatik*, ii. (Munich, 1950) p. 287, 'So in the Hellenistic period the perfect indicative becomes equivalent to the aorist indicative for which it is making way in the beginning of the Christian period'.). What is true for the resultative perfects is no less true for the old intransitive perfects. They are very rare in Mark and can usually be rendered like an aorist.

The middle perfects with passive meaning show a little more vitality. Their nearest English equivalent is the participle with the verb 'to be', for example 'is seen', 'is known'. Here there is little or no confusion in the text with the aorist. We can detect the beginnings of periphrastic tenses which were to develop more widely in later Greek. Already it appears as though the perfect passive participle has the best chances of survival. Its descendant is used in Modern Greek to help in forming several compound tenses.

We may notice separately a very few pluperfects. If the perfect is equivalent to the aorist, the pluperfect seems to be equivalent to the Latin or English pluperfect. This is understandable. The pluperfect was the past of the old perfect. The perfect has disappeared or become largely equivalent to the aorist. Consequently the pluperfect either retains its old meaning as an isolated survival or serves as the past of the aorist. As a past to the aorist it corresponds most nearly to the Latin pluperfect.

The text remains to be discussed. Most of the variants to the perfect are aorists and in view of the fact that the two tenses have come together in meaning this is not surprising. One problem does remain. Are these aorists interpretative substitutions for original perfects or are the perfects attempts to introduce a more Attic character into the style at the expense of the aorist? There is little evidence to enable us to give a conclusive answer to this question. Probably both influences, the interpretative and the Atticizing, were at work. In any case we cannot eliminate any of our classes of perfect from the Marcan text, and, from what we have seen, the variations between aorist and perfect probably make no difference to the sense.

(ii)

Δόγος[1]

Δόγος occurs in the printed text of Mark at the following places: i 45; ii 2; iv 14, 15 (*bis*), 16, 17, 18, 19, 20, 33; v 36; vii 13, 29; viii 32, 38; ix 10; x 22, 24; xi 29; xii 13; xiii 31; xiv 39. At viii 38 λόγους is interpolated (cf. C.H.Turner "Western Readings in the Second Half of St Mark's Gospel" *JTS* xxix pp. 1-16) and at xiv 39 *τὸν αὐτὸν λόγον εἰπών* is a harmonizing addition from Matthew xxvi 44. In both places the text with λόγος conflicts with Marcan idiom. If we omit these two occurrences and xvi 20 in the Longer Ending, the word occurs in Mark twenty-one times.

How is it used? In Mark iv and at ii 2 it means 'the message', whether of Jesus or the Christian Church, and is a technical term similar to *εὐαγγέλιον*. In keeping with this, it is always used absolutely without an attributive adjective or a dependent phrase and always has the article.

A second meaning occurs at v 36, *ἀκούσας τὸν λόγον λαλούμενον*. Here λόγος refers to a particular utterance occurring just before the statement to Jairus about his daughter. This use of λόγος for a saying or utterance in the context accounts for several passages in Mark, vii 29; ix 10; x 22. Ῥῆμα is used similarly twice in Mark, ix 32; xiv 72. Probably in vii 13, *ἀκυροῦντες τὸν λόγον τοῦ Θεοῦ*, we should understand the phrase in this way: the particular utterance or pronouncement of God just mentioned, namely 'thou shalt honour thy father and thy mother'. We may at first sight be inclined to take *ὁ λόγος τοῦ Θεοῦ* here in the sense of 'Holy Scripture' but this significance does not occur in the New Testament. At xi 29; xii 13 the utterance is still to come, λόγος in the first passage referring to a question which is about to be put, and in the second either to a question with which the Pharisees and Herodians would entrap Jesus or to a dangerous utterance which he might be lured into making. The use of λόγος in the plural at x. 24; xiii. 31 to mean a body of utterances or sayings is similar to that of the singular for an utterance.

If we consider these passages as a whole, we find that as far as Mark iv λόγος means 'Message', but in v-xiii 'utterance'. This difference is suggestive and has a bearing on our interpretation of the two outstanding passages, i 45 and viii 32.

Though i 45 immediately follows an utterance of Jesus, no one has suggested that λόγος here refers to this utterance and there is no reason why

[1] Earlier discussions occur in Chapters 2 and 3.

the healed leper should proclaim Jesus' command to him to shew himself to the priest and make the accustomed offering. With this possibility rejected, we have either to understand λόγος of the Message which would agree with its use elsewhere up to Mark iv inclusive, or else go outside the range of Mark's use of the word.

Let us consider the former use of the word in its context. First, to whom does λόγος refer? It has been suggested, for example by Klostermann, that it refers to Jesus, but Marcan usage is against this. The nominative article with *δέ* in Mark always indicates a change of subject. So *ὁ δέ* must be the leper. At first it seems odd that we should have to consider the suggestion that this man "going out preached much and proclaimed the Message": we expect him to proclaim the fact that he has been healed by Jesus. This, however, may be due to our less theological approach to the matter. What the man may be thought of as saying is 'God has visited and redeemed his people in Jesus and by him has healed me of my leprosy'. On this exegesis the man proclaimed his healing not as an isolated piece of good luck but as an expression of God's deliverance in the Messiah, as integral to the message. If this interpretation is accepted, there is no need to go outside the demonstrable meanings of λόγος elsewhere in Mark and in particular to treat it as the equivalent of *τὸ γενόμενον*, the 'event', or as signifying 'narration' or 'story', usages for which it would be hard to find parallels in the Gospels.

At viii 32, *τὸν λόγον* is either 'the saying' or 'the Message'. The evangelist's practice elsewhere in the latter part of the Gospel is in favour of 'saying' and there is a particular saying in the context to which λόγος can refer, Jesus' statement about his Passion and Resurrection. On the other hand, 'Message' does not fit into the passage so easily. If Jesus merely spoke the Message, why did Peter rebuke him? Thus, 'saying' or 'utterance' seems to suit the situation better. If this conclusion is right, then Jesus spoke about his Passion *παρρησίᾳ* and whatever *παρρησίᾳ* means here, it is hard to maintain that it implies secrecy or concealment.

To sum up our enquiry we find that λόγος in Mark is apparently used in two senses. First it means 'saying' or 'utterance', a meaning which occurs at v 36 and nine subsequent passages, among them vii 13; viii 32, where it has not always been understood. Secondly it means 'the Word' or 'the Message' eleven times, eight of them in the explanation of the parable of the Sower. Only at i 45 has this meaning not been apprehended. This consistency in the use of the word is in keeping with Mark's style as a whole. We may compare his treatment of ὄχλος and *πορεύεσθαι*. The most significant feature about Mark's use of λόγος is not that the twenty-one instances of the word can be brought under two heads, but that they are two and not one. Does this indicate a twofold source for the Evangelist's vocabulary, one usage coming from current Greek and the other, the use of the word as 'Message', from the peculiar terminology of early Christianity?

Εὐθύς

There are probably forty-seven instances of *εὐθύς* in Mark: i 10, 12, 18, 20, 21, 23, 28, 29, 30, 31, 42, 43; ii 2, 8, 12; iii 6; iv 5, 15, 16, 17, 29; v 2, 13, 29, 30, 36, 42 *bis*; vi 25, 27, 45, 50, 54; vii 25, 35; viii 10; ix 8, 15, 20, 24; x 52; xi 2, 3; xiv 43, 45, 72; xv 1.

Of these forty-seven, twenty-nine instances and two variant readings appear in the phrase *καὶ εὐθύς* at the beginning of their clause. We have one example of *ἀλλ' εὐθύς* in the same position at vii 25. Where there is a preceding subordinate clause or a participle equivalent to a clause, *εὐθύς* begins the main clause at i 43; iv 15, 16, 17, 29; v 2; vi 54; ix 20, 24; xiv 45, in all ten instances. There remain five exceptions to the initial position, i 28; v 13, 36, 42; vi 25; vii 25 and the two variant readings at i 31; iii 6. v 36 is hardly an exception. The subject is put first out of order and the rest of the sentence is quite regular. i 28 and the variant reading at iii 6 give us this arrangement: *καὶ*, verb, subject, *εὐθύς*, rest of predicate. At v 42; vi 25 we have *καὶ*, verb, *εὐθύς*, rest of predicate, and at v 13 *καὶ*, verb, *εὐθύς*, subject, and at i 31 *καὶ*, verb, subject, *εὐθύς*. In these analyses pronoun objects, direct or indirect, which follow their verbs are not taken into account.

This analysis of the position of *εὐθύς* clearly indicates the evangelist's dominant practice. Εὐθύς normally comes at the beginning of its clause. The exceptions are few and indicate no uniform alternative, nor is there any reason for thinking that difference in position indicates any difference in meaning. The evidence suggests that we are dealing not with an adverb of time but with a connecting particle. Εὐθύς or *εὐθέως* occurs in Matthew eighteen times, Luke seven, John six, Acts ten. There may be traces of the use of the word as a particle in Matthew and Acts.

Πάλιν

Like *εὐθύς*, *πάλιν* occurs frequently in Mark. There is, however, one feature which prevents us from treating it like *εὐθύς* as a connecting particle and that is its place in the sentence. Εὐθύς is usually placed at the beginning of its clause or phrase but this is not true of *πάλιν*. Of twenty-nine instances, only eight occur at the beginning of this clause. On the other hand, the commonest position for *πάλιν* is immediately before or after its verb. We have the order *πάλιν*, verb, rest of sentence, at iv 1; vii 31; viii 25; x 1; xii 4; xiv 39, 40; seven examples. In addition there is the order, subject, *πάλιν*, verb, rest of sentence at x 24; xiv 70 *bis*; xv 4, 12, 13; six instances. Verb, *πάλιν*, rest of sentence, occurs at ii 1, 13; iii 1, 20; vii 14; viii 13; x 1, 32; xi 27; xiv 69; ten times. This leaves six exceptions out of twenty-nine appearances, v 21; viii 1; x 10; xi 3; xii 5; xiv 61. The fact that for nearly four fifths of its occurrences *πάλιν* is placed next to its verb is very much in favour of its being an adverb as distinct from a connecting particle.

This is in contrast to the use of *πάλιν* in a writer of *Koine* like Hero of Alexandria. He uses the word very frequently where the Atticists employed *αὖ* and *αὖθις*. In his writings it usually occurs at the beginning of the sentence, often in the place of an enclitic and may fairly be regarded as a connecting particle, cf. Reinhardt, *De Heronis Alexandrini Dictione Quaestiones Selectae* (1930) pp. 126, 132.

The evidence about the position of *πάλιν* enables us to decide a question of text. At v 21 manuscripts which read *πάλιν* have before *συνήχθη* either *πάλιν εἰς τὸ πέραν* or *εἰς τὸ πέραν πάλιν*. The second reading brings *πάλιν* next to a verb and so conforms to Mark's dominant order.

This use of *πάλιν* was unwelcome to the scribes. It is absent from our printed texts at xii 5. Scribes have tried to get rid of it at vii 14; viii 1; xi 3; xii 5; xiv 40. The word is frequent in John, and some manuscripts eliminate it at ix 20; x 31; xi 7.

Οἶκος and οἰκία

In Attic Greek *οἰκία* is commoner than *οἶκος* and although both words occur in the New Testament the Attic preference is maintained at any rate in Mark. There seems, however, to be no trace of the Attic legal distinction between *οἶκος* 'property, estate' and *οἰκία* 'dwelling house'.

Οἶκος is used in Mark at ii 1, 11, 26; iii 20; v 19, 38; vii 17, 30; viii 3, 26; ix 28; xi 17; twelve times in all. It occurs only in the accusative singular with *εἰς*, except in the quotation at xi 17.

At ii 11, 26; v 19, 38; vii 30; viii 3, 26 (*v.l.*) it has the article and a dependent genitive, except at viii 3, where it is used generically, and the article is absent. Only at v 38 is Jesus described as entering the house of the ruler of the synagogue and in none of these passages is the house described as being that of Jesus. In view of the fact that *οἶκος* is in all of them someone's house, the nearest English equivalent seems to be 'home'. Only at ii 26 *τὸν οἶκον τοῦ θεοῦ* and the quotation at xi 17, does 'home' sound unnatural in English, perhaps because we are used to the phrase 'house of God' as a description of the Tabernacle or Temple. Ὁ *οἶκος τοῦ θεοῦ* seems to be the conventional phrase, and *ἡ οἰκία τοῦ θεοῦ* does not occur.

Οἶκος is employed absolutely without the article at ii 1; iii 20; vii 17; ix 28, in all four passages with reference to Jesus, though at iii 20 *ἔρχονται* (so we should read) includes the disciples. At ii 1 the translation 'a house' would be wrong. The crowd could gather only at a known house. Here too the rendering 'home' would be in place. It is heard that Jesus is at his home, and all interested know where to go. The translation 'home' will suit the other three passages admirably and there is nothing against the inference that in all four places Jesus' 'home' in Capernaum is meant. The context of iii 20 favours this. At iii 7 Jesus is by the sea, at iii 13 he ascends the mountain and at iv 1 he is by the sea again. The same is true for vii 17. At vi 53 Jesus lands at Gennesaret and at vii 24 he leaves for the neighbourhood of Tyre and Sidon. At ix 28 he has come down from the mountain of transfiguration and at ix 30 sets out through Galilee.

If *οἶκος* in Mark is 'home', *οἰκία* seems to be 'house'. It occurs nineteen times in the Gospel and everywhere 'house' is an acceptable translation. At iii 25; xiii 35; for example, 'home' is impossible. However, just as in English, there are passages where 'house' and 'home' are interchangeable, so in Mark it is sometimes possible to render *οἰκία* by 'home'. Thus it is probable that in ii 15 *ἐν τῇ οἰκίᾳ αὐτοῦ* refers to the same place as is described in ii 1 as *εἰς οἶκον*. We too would find no difficulty in English in referring to the same dwelling place sometimes as 'house' and sometimes as 'home'. Further, we must remember that while *οἶκος* is restricted in Mark to one kind of phrase, *οἰκία* occurs in the plural as well as in all cases of the singular.

Ἐπιτιμᾶν

At first sight this verb seems to be used in two senses in Mark, 'to rebuke' and 'to charge strictly', as a verb of censure and as one of command. It is less common for words to be used in a variety of senses in this Gospel than in others and an examination of the occurrences of our word suggests that its meaning is more coherent. The verb in Classical Greek can mean 'to inflict a *τιμή*, a fine or penalty upon someone'. Next it comes to mean 'to censure'. One form of censure is to tell someone that they ought not to have done something. It differs little from this to tell someone that they ought not to do it. This again is very close to a straight prohibition not to do something.

These last senses seem to be characteristic of the verb in Mark. It is used in this Gospel in three ways. First, it is used twice absolutely. At x 13 they were bringing their children to Jesus and the disciples told them not to, *ἐπετίμησαν*. At viii 32 Jesus had been foretelling his passion and Peter *ἤρξατο ἐπιτμᾶν αὐτῷ* 'told him not to', 'told him to desist'. Next we have three examples with *ἵνα*, iii 12, *ἵνα μή*, viii 30, *ἵνα μηδένι*, and x 48 *ἵνα σιωπήσῃ*. Two of these are prohibitions and the third which means 'stop his shouting' is very near to one.

In four remaining instances of the word, it is followed by a verb of saying and direct speech. At i 25 *φιμώθητι* and iv 39 *σιώπα* are tantamount to prohibitions. viii 33 *ὕπαγε ὀπίσω μου, Σατανᾶ,* is also an order to desist. ix 25 *τὸ πνεῦμα τὸ ἄλαλον καὶ κωφὸν, ἐγὼ ἐπιτάσσω σοι, ἔξελθε ἐξ αὐτοῦ καὶ μηκέτι εἰσέλθῃς εἰς αὐτόν*. Here we have two commands, one an incontrovertible prohibition and the other implies one, 'beset him no longer'. It is noteworthy that the commands in this verse are reinforced by *ἐπιτάσσω*, a verb of positive meaning.

From this examination it appears that the meaning of *ἐπιτιμᾶν* is much more unified than appeared at first sight. Everywhere it means or is near to meaning 'desist from an action being performed' whether it is shouting or bringing children to Jesus, or speaking a prophecy or dissuading.

Ἀκολουθεῖν

The verb occurs at Mark i 18; ii 14 (2), 15; v 24; vi 1; viii 34 (2?); ix 38 (2?); x 21, 28, 32, 52; xi 9; xiv 13, 54; xv 41. It is also in the printed texts at iii 7, but C.H.Turner[2] and Vincent Taylor have given good reasons for following the manuscripts which omit it here.

It is used in the literal sense of physical following, as at xi 9; xiv 54, and also in the derived sense of being a disciple, for example at viii 34. When the word has the derived sense the literal sense is not always absent. Thus at i 18 *ἠκολούθουν* (so read with B) implies discipleship, but at i 20 *ἀπῆλθον ὀπίσω αὐτοῦ* is used with the same suggestion. To this extent there is agreement among interpreters.

It is when we consider the subjects of the verb in its various senses that agreement fails, and yet the conclusion we reach about Mark's usage at this point is important for our interpretation of passages like ii 15. The idea of discipleship, with or without the sense of physical following as

---

[2] Note V (vi) above.

well, is present at i 18 (subject, Peter and Andrew), ii 14 (Levi), viii 34 (general), ix 38 (general), x 21 (the rich man), x 28 (Peter and the disciples), xv 41 (women from Galilee). From this it appears that the subject of *ἀκολουθεῖν* with the meaning of discipleship may be any who can or do become disciples. This does not agree with Turner's third conclusion about the use of the word: 'that, with one possible exception in the earlier half of the Gospel, it is not used in narrative of or to the apostles, who did not 'follow' but rather accompanied their Master'. (*JTS* xxvi pp.238f. Note V (vi) above.).

The physical sense may be uppermost at v 24 (subject, the crowd), vi 1 (the disciples), x 32 (the twelve), x 52 (Bartimaeus), xi 9 (the crowd), xiv 13 (two disciples), xiv 54 (Peter). Here too the variety of subjects excludes any limitation of the word in this sense to one class. We may note that at xiv 13 Jesus is not the object.

Probably the evangelist used the word for any who accompanied Jesus in this way. Nor does there seem to be any reason why scribes and Pharisees should not follow him on occasion in the physical sense. As a class they were certainly not his disciples and for part of the ministry at least were opposed to him, but they are found in close contact with him for example at ii 6, 24; iii 22f.; vii 1. Sometimes they are discussing with him in the same room, sometimes out in the open. If there is no objection in principle to the Pharisees following Jesus in the literal sense, then the one argument against punctuating at ii 15f. *πολλοί. Καὶ ἠκολούθουν αυτῷ καὶ οἱ γραμματεῖς τῶς Φαρισαίων* collapses, namely the argument that the Pharisees did not follow Jesus. We, of course, need not suppose that in following they were doing more than holding a watching brief.

We may notice that, except at viii 34; xi 9 and the spurious iii 7, *ἀκολουθεῖν* is followed by a dative. At viii 34 *ὀπίσω μου* serves instead of the dative and in this passage we should probably read *ἐλθεῖν* instead of *ἀκολουθεῖν*. Thus it follows that xi 9 is the only passage in Mark where *ἀκολουθεῖν* is not followed for certain by a dative.

Πολλά

Unlike *οὕτως* which precedes the verb in Mark except at iv 41, adverbial *πολλά* regularly follows it (i 45; iv 2; v 10, 23, 38, 43; vi 23, 34; xv 3). There is a clear and incontrovertible exception at iii 12 *πολλά ἐπετίμα αὐτοῖς* and three instances of *πολλά παθεῖν*, v 26; viii 31; ix 12.

These are the only examples of *πάσχειν* in Mark and we seem to have here a stereotyped phrase. This is supported by the fact that where in the Gospels the aorist *παθεῖν* is accompanied by an accusative or an adverb, the verb comes in the second place: Matthew *xvi 21 (=Mark viii 31); *xxvii 19; Luke *ix 22 (=Mark viii 31); xiii 2; *xvii 25; xxiv 26, 46. *πολλά* occurs in the instances marked with an asterisk. At Matthew xvii 15 we may have the present, *κακῶς πάσχει*

Mark's practice bears on the interpretation of two passages. At Mark vi 20 it is said of Herod *ἀκουσας αὐτοῦ πολλά ἠπόρει* (*v.l.* *ἐποίει*). Mark's order is definitely in favour of taking *πολλά* with *ἀκούσας*. This, however, enables us to decide in favour of *ἠπόρει* against *ἐποίει*, because, while *ἠπόρει* makes sense standing alone, *ἐποίει* alone does not, whatever *πολλά ἐποίει* might have been taken to mean.

At Mark ix 26 we have two readings, *κράξας καὶ πολλὰ σπαράξας* and in far fewer manuscripts *κράξας πολλὰ καὶ σπαράξας* (Δ Θ Ψ fl 565 *pc*). The second reading is in keeping with Mark's placing of *πολλά* and is probably original.

Scribes did not like *πολλά* as an adverb and tried to get rid of it at i 45; iii 12; iv 2; v 10, 23, 38, 43; vi 23; ix 25. It is not in the printed texts at vi 23 and Dr Vincent Taylor has rightly restored it.

Periphrastic Εἶναι *and Participle*

In addition to the discussions in the grammars, there are two studies: C.H.Turner, *Marcan Usage* viii, *JTS* xxviii pp. 349-351 Note VIII above, and G.Björck, HN ΔΙΔΑΣΚΩΝ (Uppsala, 1940). Björck takes account only of *εἶναι* with the present and aorist participles and Turner of the present and perfect passive participles. Chantraine, *Histoire du Parfait Grec,* chapter IX, has some important remarks on the use of the perfect passive participle in periphrastic tenses in the New Testament.

Before we consider the commonest periphrases with *εἶναι* in Mark we must distinguish between tense periphrases and other uses of *εἶναι* with the participle. First we may refer to instances where *εἶναι* is the copula and the participle is an adjective or noun. We can distinguish in English between 'he was amusing the baby' and 'the book was amusing'. In the latter example the participle is adjectival. Likewise in Greek, *ἦν ἄρχων* can mean 'he was a magistrate' as distinct from 'he was ruling'. The second use to be distinguished is that of the supplementary predicate. There is an example with *γίνεσθαι* at Mark i 4, *ἐγένετο Ἰωάννης ὁ βαπτίζων ἐν τῇ ἐρήμῳ κηρύσσων κτλ.* Here *ἐγένετο ... κηρύσσων* is not our tense but a main verb with a supplementary participle which could be replaced by *καὶ* and a second main verb thus: *ἐγένετο .... καὶ ἐκήρυσσεν.*

In Mark εἶναι, usually in the imperfect, and the present participle may be presumed to form a single tense, and the same is probably true for Luke at least. On the other hand, where γίνεσθαι is joined with a participle, Mark i 4; ix 3, 7,(cf. Björck p. 62) no true periphrastic tense is constituted. Consequently we shall translate ἦν etc. with the present participle as an imperfect but not so γίνεσθαι and the participle.

The periphrasis for the imperfect was not popular with scribes and it has not survived in the printed text at Mark i 39; ii 4; v 40. There are variant readings which suppressed it at iii 1; v 11; ix 4; xiii 25; xiv 4; xv 26. Periphrasis occurs at i 6, 13, 22, 33, 39; ii 4, 6, 18; iii 1; iv 38; v 5, 11, 40; vi 52; vii 15; ix 4; x 22, 32 (*bis*); xiii 13, 25; xiv 4, 40, 49, 54; xv 7, 26, 40, 43; twenty-nine instances in all. Of these only vii 15; xiii 13, 25 are not examples of the participle with the imperfect of εἶναι.

In English we are used to the participle following the verb 'to be' immediately in compound tenses. The fact that the two are usually separated in Mark has probably inclined translators not to treat them as forming a single tense. In Mark apart from particles like καὶ and relatives, the copula comes first in its clause. The exceptions are v 5; vii 15; xiii 25; xiv 49; four instances out of twenty-nine. Again the subject where it is separately expressed comes between the copula and the participle as at i 6, 33; ii 4, 6, 18; iii 1; iv 38; v 11, 40; vi 52; xiv 4, 40; xv 7, 26, 40, 43; sixteen examples against three exceptions, vii 15; x 32; xiii 25. The rest of the predicate is usually put between the copula and the participle or after the participle. This practice conforms with Mark's word order, verb, subject, rest of predicate, where εἶναι provides the verb and the participle is treated as part of the predicate. It does not, however, determine which part of the predicate the participle is, and so constitutes no obstacle to treating the verb and participle as a compound tense.

CHAPTER SEVEN

RECITATIVE λέγων

The use of λέγων to introduce oratio recta or obliqua has certain features that deserve examination. The participle appears in this construction in the nominative forms, λέγων, λέγουσα, λέγοντες for certain. The accusative λέγοντας appears at i 27 with λέγοντες as a variant, and at ii 12 where the alternative reading *καὶ* λέγειν meets another difficulty in this passage. We may therefore regard these two instances as highly doubtful.

λέγων and the other forms are sometimes followed by recitative ὅτι and sometimes not. Can we discover any rule for this?

First we must isolate the examples of interrogative ὅτι. This occurs with διελογίζεσθαι ii 6, viii 16, 17. At xi 31 we should probably read διελογίζοντο πρὸς ἑαυτοὺς λέγοντες· τί εἴπωμεν; ἐαν εἴπωμεν κτλ., which would give us another example of a question with διαλογίζεσθαι λέγων. Another occurrence of interrogative ὅτι is ix 11 after ἐπηρώτων αὐτὸν λέγοντες.

Recitative ὅτι with λέγων regularly follows verbs of motion: ἦλθεν i 15, ἔρχεται i 40, ἔρχονται v 35, ἐλεύσονται xiii 6, προσπορεύονται x 35, ἀπέστειλεν xii 6. At viii 26 ἀπέστειλεν αὐτὸν εἰς τὸν οἶκον αὐτοῦ λέγων· μηδὲ κτλ. lacks ὅτι. There is however to λέγων a variant καὶ λέγει αὐτῷ D Lat.vt *d* Geo (ms.) Syr s (p) Eth. This would remove our one irregularity.

κράζειν xi 9, ἀνακράζειν i 24, φωνεῖν x 49, xv 34 (*v.l.*), φωνή ix 7 lack ὅτι but it is read at iii 11 after ἔκραζον λέγοντες. Here it is omitted by D W Lat.vt *a b c d e ff*^{2} *i g*^{2} *t gat* vg. Syr Geo Arm Eth and the omission may well be right.

There is a similar problem at ii 12 δοξάζειν τὸν θεὸν λέγοντας ὅτι κτλ. λέγοντας is omitted by B W *b* and D *d* read καὶ λέγειν, but ὅτι is omitted by 124 565 579 Lat.vt. *a*. Of these readings that in D is intrinsically most probable and that in B W least. In any case we cannot regard this instance as certain.

ἀποκρίνεσθαι λέγων, a formula which occurs in John also, normally dispenses with recitative ὅτι, iii 33 *v.l.*, v 9, ix 38 *v.l.*, xv 9, but at viii

28 ὅτι occurs twice, itself an unusual feature. On the first occasion it is read only by ℵ* B 0143^vid 1342 Syr p, and on the second ὅτι εἷς appears in ℵ B C* L 579 892 1342 Syr sin p (1 ms.) Copt bo.(*pl.*) but other manuscripts read ἕνα. We may regard these instances as improbable.

Finally xiv 57f. *ἐψευδομαρτύρουν κατ' αὐτοῦ λέγοντες ὅτι* stands alone. The text again is confused. Homoioteleuton or some form of *ὁμ* seems to have been at work. We have *κατ' αὐτοῦ λέγοντες ὅτι* and later *αὐτοῦ λέγοντος ὅτι*. Some of the Latin renderings seem to assume an omission resulting from this: et dicebant *k* seems parallel to D's *καὶ ἔλεγον*. *καὶ ἔλεγον ὅτι* would correspond to the renderings of Syr sin p Geo Eth. We must allow for the possibility that either *ἐψευδομαρτύρουν κατ' αὐτοῦ καὶ ἔλεγον ὅτι* is the right reading, or, perhaps less likely, *ἐψευδομαρτύρουν καὶ ἔλεγον κατ' αὐτοῦ ὅτι* with D.

This examination suggests that there is no certain example of λέγων and recitative ὅτι except where they are associated with verbs of motion. In all instances where the contrary appears to be true the text is in doubt.

Two features may seem to require comment. Except for the verbs of motion all the verbs associated with this construction are verbs of communicating information except *ποτίζειν* xv 36. We would not have been surprised if recitative ὅτι had been present here but it is not.

Tautology occurs at xii 26 *εἶπεν ... λέγων*. Legg's apparatus notes λέγων *om.* 28 Syr sin p.

APPENDIX: A LIST OF VERBS FOLLOWED BY λέγων

(a) verbs of motion λέγων + ὅτι
ἔρχεται i 40, *ἔρχονται* v 35 *ἐλεύσονται* xiii 6
ἦλθεν i 15 *προσπορεύονται* x 35 *ἀπέστειλεν* xii 6
(n.b. *ἀπέστειλεν* + λέγων + ὅτι viii 26 *v.l.*)

(b) verbs of crying and the like + λέγων
κράζειν iii 11 (+ ὅτι *v.l.*), xi 9 *ἀνακράζειν* i 24
φωνεῖν x 49, xv. 34 (*v.l.*) *φωνή* ix 7

(c) other verbs + λέγων
αἰτεῖσθαι vi 25
ἀποκρίνεσθαι iii 33 (*v.l.*), v 9 *v.l.*, viii 28 + ὅτι (*bis v.l.*), ix 38, xv 9
ἀρνεῖσθαι xiv 68
βλασφημεῖν xv 29
διαλογίζεσθαι ii 6 + ὅτι interrogative, viii 16, 17 + ὅτι interrogative, xi 31 + *τί*

διαστέλλειν viii 15
διδόναι σύνσημον xiv 44
δοξάζειν ii 12 (+ *ὅτι v.l.*)
εἰπεῖν xii 26
ἐκπλήσσεσθαι vi 2, vii 37, x 26
ἐπερωτᾶν viii 27, ix 11 + *ὅτι* interrogative, xii 18, xiv 60, xv 4 *contra* v 9, viii 29, ix 16, 21, 28, 33 etc.
ἐπιτιμᾶν i 25, ix 25
κηρύσσειν i 7 *v.l.*
παρακαλεῖν v 12, 23
ποτίζειν xv 36
συνζητεῖν i 27
ψευδομαρτυρεῖν xiv 57 (+ *ὅτι v.l.*)

CHAPTER EIGHT

VERBS OF SEEING

If we analyse Mark's use of these verbs we can construct the following table:

Present/Impf.	*Future*	*Aorist*
θεωρεῖν (7)		
ὁρᾶν (3)	ὄψεσθαι (3)	ὀφθῆναι (1)
βλέπειν (14)		
		ἀναβλέψαι (6)
		διαβλέψαι (1)
ἐμβλέπειν (1)		ἐμβλέψαι (3)
περιβλέπεσθαι (1)		περιβλέψασθαι (5)
		ἰδεῖν (32)

Numerals in brackets indicate the number of times a tense occurs. The analysis reveals certain features at once. In the present three verbs share the work between them. The future is rare and has only one form. In the active and middle aorist ἰδεῖν does most of the work and other forms are used with particular meanings. There is one passive aorist. No perfect forms occur.

First we notice that θεωρεῖν (iii 11; v 15, 38; xii 41; xv 40, 47; xvi 4) depends on the other verbs for a future and aorist. Its meaning presents no problems. ὁρᾶν which we would expect to be the present to ὄψεσθαι, ἰδεῖν and ὀφθῆναι does not seem to do so: at i 44 and viii 15 it has a cautionary meaning and at viii 24 its sense is uncertain, possibly being synonymous with βλέπεῖν. ὄψεσθαι (xiii 26; xiv 62; xvi 7) may have an eschatological suggestion. ὀφθῆναι (ix 4) is used of a vision.

βλέπειν is used in the present only. At iv 24; viii 15; xii 38; xiii 5, 9, 23, 33 it is cautionary in sense. At viii 15; xii 38 it is followed by ἀπὸ and at xiii 5 by μή. In these passages it means "beware". At iv 24; xiii 9 it is followed by the accusative and we can render "look to". At xiii 23, 33 it is used absolutely and the equivalent may be "look out". At iv 12 βλέπειν and ἰδεῖν are contrasted and at viii 18 ὀφθαλμοὺς ἔχοντες and *βλέπετε* stand together. At v 31; viii 23, 24; xiii 2 *βλέπειν* means "see". A development of this occurs at xii 14 *βλέπεις εἰς πρόσωπον*.

If *βλέπειν* occurs only in the present, its compounds are never found in that tense and with one or two exceptions only in the aorist active. *ἀναβλέψαι* has two meanings, "to look up" vi 41; vii 34; xvi 4, and "to recover sight" viii 24; x 51, 52. At xvi 4 *ἀναβλέψασαι θεωροῦσιν* there is a clear distinction between the two verbs. *διαβλέψαι* occurs only at viii 25 apparently with the sense "see clearly". *ἐμβλέψαι* has the meaning "look on (an object)" at x 21, 27; xiv 67 and this may be the meaning of *ἐνέβλεπεν*, viii 25, if it is the right reading.

The certain exception among the compounds of *βλέπειν* is *περιβλέπεσθαι*. It occurs only in the middle, five times in the aorist participle (iii 5, 34; ix 8, x 23; xi 11) and once in the imperfect, *περιεβλέπετο ἰδεῖν* at v 32 where there is a difference between looking *περιεβλέπετο* and seeing *ἰδεῖν*. The same difference appears at ix 8 *περιβλέψάμενοι εἶδον*.

CHAPTER NINE

PARTICLES

δέ

In Classical Greek δέ has a wide range of use (cf. J.D.Denniston, *Greek Particles* (Oxford, 1934) *sub voc.* and p. 582). It is not current in Modern Greek (A.Thumb, *Handbook of the Modern Greek Vernacular* (Edinburgh, 1912) p. 185) and seems to have disappeared from non-literary Greek in the period A.D. 600-1000 (A.N.Jannaris, *An Historical Greek Grammar*, (London 1897) pp. 400, 402). This disappearance was encouraged by two factors. First, δέ shared with other particles which could not begin their clause or phrase the tendency to make way for particles which could, such as καί and ἀλλά.

Secondly, as its meaning weakened it overlapped more and more with καί and ἀλλά and so became otiose. In Mark its use is already becoming restricted. In this Gospel it occurs about 122 times for certain, about as frequently in proportion as in John where there are some 150 certain instances.

The clearest survival from the Classical language is the use of δέ in contrast. μέν ... δέ is rare, xii 5; xiv 21, 38, but the contrast is present when δέ alone is used at ii 18; iv 11, 34; vi 15; vii 6, 11; viii 29, 35; x 6, 40; xi 8, 17; xii 44; xiii 23, 31; and perhaps at vi 16; vii 20.

From the use of δέ in contrasts seems to develop another use. Where the contrast is between two nouns or pronouns in the nominative, the second being conjoined with δέ, there is inevitably at this point a change of subject. In Mark this is universal with the article, pronouns and nouns, in all for some ninety instances. It is also the rule for δέ conjoined with other words: verbs 17/19, conjunctions 3/5, prepositional phrases 4/6, οὐαί 1/1 but μάτην 0/1, μέν ... δέ 2/2. This gives a total 27/34, a very high proportion. This use of δέ where a change of subject takes place is much commoner than the contrastive use in Mark.

This use has an effect on Mark's word order. Usually in Mark the verb comes first in its clause, but in nearly four fifths of the instances of contrastive δέ the subject comes first constituting a large proportion of the exceptions to Mark's normal order. We may therefore regard Mark's use of δέ with a nominative as bringing the change of subject clearly before the reader's notice.

Are there any other uses of δέ in Mark? If we look at some of the categories of words where the change of subject with δέ is not universal we may detect other usages. Conjoined with verbs it often seems to introduce a fresh event or circumstance. Thus at x 32 (pr.); xiii 9, 18?; xiv 1; xv 40 we have a fresh paragraph or section. At ii 6; v 11; x 14; xiii 22 *v.l.*; xiv 4 *v.l.*; xv 39 a fresh feature is introduced into the story. At xii 26; viii 9; xiv 44; xv 7, 25, this becomes an aside. Similar examples with conjunctions, prepositional phrases and the like occur at ii 10; xii 26; xiii 14, 17, 28, 32; xv 6.

Sometimes the fresh item is a correction as at vii 7; ix 50; x 6, a use that comes near to the adversative. There are no certain examples of the adversative use of δέ in Mark and it may be that the evangelist never used the particle in this sense.

It is noticeable that only the strictly contrastive use of δέ is not paralleled by καί or ἀλλά. Already in Mark this is the less common use. The fact that καί would have served in many passages where we have δέ helps to explain why already in this Gospel δέ is passing out of use.

In drawing up this note no account has been taken of the passages where δέ is textually in doubt. There are nearly sixty of them, and it seems possible that scribes added δέ frequently in order to improve the style and modify the excessive use of καί.

γάρ

γάρ, occurring some sixty-three times, is the third commonest particle in Mark. There is little remarkable in its use in Mark. It occurs in discourse thirty-one times, half its total occurrence.

It introduces answers to questions at iv 22; viii 38; xii 23, 25; xiv 5. At iv 22 the sense is "yes, for". At viii 38 the connexion is very loose. At xii 23 we may enlarge thus, "we cannot tell, for", and at xii 25 "there is no real difficulty, for". xiv 5 may be "for nothing, for". At each the connexion is clearer with some such expansion. γάρ introduces questions at viii 36, 37; xv 14.

καὶ γάρ occurs at x 45; xiv 70. At both places each particle seems to retain its full force.

Again scribes tend to add this particle. It occurs about fourteen times in our printed texts where it is open to question. In several of these its insertion removes hiatus. It is confused with δέ at v 42 and xiii 22. At xi 18(sec.) scribes substitute it for ὅτι.

γάρ disturbs Marcan order. In γάρ clauses verbs come first only 25/63, nouns and pronouns 20/63, the negative οὐ 7/63. There are several clusters of the particle as at vi 17, 18, 20; viii 35-8; ix 6(*bis*), 39-41.

ἀλλά

ἀλλά occurs in Mark at i 44, 45; ii 17(*bis*), 22; iii 26, 27?, 29; iv 17, 22; v 19, 26, 39; vi 9, 52; vii 5, 15, 19, 25; viii 33; ix 8, 13, 22, 37; x 8, 27, 40, 43, 45; xi 23, 32; xii 14, 25, 27; xiii 7, 11(*bis*), 20, 24; xiv 28, 29, 36(*bis*), 49; xvi 7, in all forty-five times compared with Matthew's thirty-seven, Luke thirty-six and Acts thirty. ἀλλά is commoner in John and the Epistles.

The text is rarely in question. The particle should be read at ii 22; ix 8. There is room for doubt at iii 27.

ἀλλά is the adversative particle. It normally follows a negative clause, i 44, 45; ii 17(sec.); iii 26, 29; iv 17, 22; v 19, 39; vi 52; vii 5, 15, 25; viii 33; x 27, 40, 43; xi 23; xii 14, 25; xiii 11(sec), 20; xiv 49, or phrase, ii 17(pr.), 22; v 26; vi 9; vii 19; ix 8, 37; x 8, 45; xii 27; xiii 11; xiv 36(sec.).

Rarely the preceding clause is positive and the ἀλλά clause negative, xiii 7; xiv 29, 36(pr.).

The remaining instances, iii 27; ix 13, 22; xi 32; xiii 24; xiv 28; xvi 7, must be examined separately. At several of these, iii 27; ix 13, 22; xiv 28; xvi 7, the connexion is broken and a fresh line of thought begun. At xiii 24 this amounts to the beginning of a fresh paragraph. At xi 32 there may be an implied negative: "We cannot say 'from heaven', but if we say 'from men'..."

Causal ὅτι[1]

This occurs at i 27, 34; iii 30; iv 29; v 9; vi 2, 17, 34; vii 19; viii 2, 24, 33; ix 38, 41?; xiv 21, 27. The scribes did not like this usage and tried to eliminate it at i 27; vi 2; ix 38.

At i 27; vi 2; vii 19 it introduces the answer to a question.

---

[1] See J.K. Elliott, "The Position of Causal ὅτι Clauses in the New Testament" *Filología Neotestamentari* 6 (1990) pp. 155-7.

ἤ

Mark appears to have used *καί* in the sense of *ἤ* = *vel* but not in the sense of *ἤ* = *aut*. At several places the scribes have corrected this *καὶ* to *ἤ*, probably at iii 33; iv 17; x 38, 40; xiii 21, 32. The confusion does not occur where *ἤ* = *aut*. *ἤ* introduces the second half of a question at ii 9; iii 4(*bis*); iv 21, 30; xi 30; xii 14(*bis*). It introduces an alternative in statements at vi 56; vii 10, 11; x 29; xiii 35.

μέν

μέν occurs rarely in Mark, iv 4; ix 12; xii 5; xiv 21, 38. At xii 5; xiv 21, 38 we have the regular *μέν* ... *δέ* connexion, but at iv 4; ix 12 *δέ* is lacking. At iv 4f its place is taken by *καὶ ἄλλο*, and at ix 12 there is a greater break. The contrasted element may be concealed in *καὶ πῶς γέγραπται ἐπι τὸν υἱὸν τοῦ ἀνθρώπου*.

οὖν

οὖν occurs at xi 31; xiii 35; xv 12. Scribes have added it at iii 31; x 9; xii 6, 9, 23, 27, 37. At xi 31 it is omitted in some manuscripts because of the following *οὐκ*. It has no problems of meaning.

Other Particles

ἄρα occurs at iv 41; xi 13 and *ὥστε* at ii 28; x 8 etc., *εἰ* interrogative at viii 12, and *εἶτα* at iv 17, 28; viii 25. *πλήν* is in a LXX quotation at xii 32.

J.K.Elliott

CHAPTER TEN

AN ECLECTIC TEXTUAL COMMENTARY ON THE GREEK TEXT OF MARK'S GOSPEL

Since it first appeared in 1966, the text of the United Bible Societies' *Greek New Testament* (UBSGNT) has proclaimed itself the standard text of the NT[1]. Originally it was said that UBSGNT would merely be a text for students and translators[2]. Since then UBSGNT has undergone two revisions, the second of which (the third edition of 1975) agrees substantially with the text of Nestle Aland[26] and forms the basis of the *Vollständige Konkordanz*[3], the new computer concordance[4], and the Aland *Synopsis*.

The text of UBSGNT[3], like its predecessors, has only a limited apparatus of 1,400 variation units, all of which have been discussed together with about 600 other variants in a companion volume, *A Textual Commentary on the Greek New Testament*[5]. It fell to Professor B.M. Metzger to write this commentary on behalf of and in co-operation with the editorial committee of the UBSGNT to show how the committee reached its decision on these 2,000 variants. Metzger, with an enviably lucid style, encapsulated the editorial discussions and has thereby enabled us to understand how many of the textual problems encountered by the committee were resolved.

---

1 See K.Aland (ed.), *Synopsis Quattuor Evangeliorum*, 10th ed (Stuttgart, 1978) p. xi.

2 R.P.Markham and E.A.Nida, *An Introduction to the Bible Societies' Greek New Testament* (New York, 1966) p. 1.

3 K.Aland (ed.), *Vollständige Konkordanz zum griechischen Neuen Testament* (Berlin/New York, 1975).

4 H.Bachmann and W.A.Slaby, *Computer-Konkordanz zum Novum Testamentum Graece* (Berlin/New York, 1980).

5 B.M. Metzger, *A Textual Commentary on the Greek New Testament* (London/New York, 1971).

Those of us who criticized features of the *Commentary* when it was first published[6] nevertheless expressed gratitude to the committee in general and to Professor Metzger in particular for allowing us to share in the editorial process through this companion volume. The UBSGNT[3] text, however, must not be thought of as *the* definitive text. Many of its readings have been printed with a high degree of doubt by the editors. This is evident by the increased number of readings accorded the rating letter 'C' (='considerable degree of doubt') and 'D' (='very high degree of doubt') since the second edition. It is also evident from the *Commentary* that the committee responded in different ways to the pull of conflicting arguments and decided on many such occasions to print 'the least unsatisfactory reading'.

Metzger's *Commentary* is a valuable and stimulating starting place for discussing variants. Its failings merely — and inevitably — reflect the failings of the UBSGNT text as a whole. These are primarily its excessive respect for the readings of the so-called great uncials (especially א B) and a cavalier attitude towards principles based on internal evidence. The *Commentary* (like the introductory volume before it)[7] lists the principles on pp. XXVI-XXVIII. Even when these principles are reliable guides — and sometimes they are not[8] — they are often ignored or bypassed in the discussions as reported in the *Commentary*.

Those of us who favour an eclectic Greek NT based primarily on principles of internal evidence inevitably disagree with the text of UBSGNT[3] on many occasions. This article is offered as an example of how eclectic principles thoroughly applied could have produced a different text and is intended not merely to demonstrate how the discussions in the *Commentary* can be expanded or supplemented, but also to show how the *Commentary* is itself a stimulus and a valuable *vade mecum* in initiating such further discussion on variants.

For the sake of space all examples below are taken from Mark's Gospel. I have tried to select variants which demonstrate differing eclectic principles.

---

[6] J.Ross, "The United Bible Societies' *Greek New Testament*", *JBL* 95 (1976) pp.112-121; J.K.Elliott, "The United Bible Societies' *Textual Commentary Evaluated*" *NovT* 17 (1975) pp. 130-150, and "A Second Look at the United Bible Societies' *Greek New Testament*", *BT* 26 (1975) pp. 325-32; G.D.Kilpatrick, *TLZ* 104 (1979) cols. 260-270.

[7] Markham and Nida, *Introduction*.

[8] E.g. II A 4 (c): 'Scribes would sometimes ... add pronouns, conjunctions, and expletives to make a smoother text', and II A 2: 'In general the shorter reading is to be preferred'.

i 4 ὁ βαπτίζων ἐν τῇ ἐρήμῳ

Although the *Commentary* says that "it is easier to account for the addition than the deletion of the definite article before βαπτίζων", the text prints the article, albeit bracketed, presumably because it is found in ℵ. But what the text should print is ὁ *without* brackets. If Marcan usage had been a criterion in determining the text of Mark (as promised in principle II B 1 [a] of the *Commentary*), then it would have been recognized that ὁ βαπτίζων is Mark's normal way of describing John the Baptist.

The *Commentary*, however, refers us to Mark vi 25 and viii 28 where UBSGNT³ prints forms of βαπτιστής — and not to vi 14 or vi 24 where forms of βαπτίζων are printed. In fact there are textual variants at all four of these verses:

vi 14	βαπτίζων ℵ A B C f¹ *Byz*
	βαπτιστής D S W Θ f¹³
vi 24	βαπτίζοντος ℵ B L Δ Θ 565 1596
	βαπτιστοῦ *ceteri*
vi 25	βαπτίζοντος L 700 892
	βαπτιστοῦ *ceteri*
viii 28	βαπτίζοντα 28 565
	βαπτιστήν *ceteri*

In view of the prevailing tendency to call John βαπτιστής in Matthew, Luke, and later Christian writings, it is likely that the direction of change in the text of Mark is away from an original βαπτίζων[9]. Βαπτιστής was introduced into the text by later scribes possibly because of assimilation to parallels at Matt. xiv 2, 8; xvi 14, and Luke ix 19. Mark is likely to have written βαπτίζων throughout as the designation for John. This represents the form of John's name before Christians coined the noun βαπτιστής to describe him. The new noun then became dominant in Christian tradition. In contrast to the argument used by the UBSGNT committee here, at Mark x 47 (Ναζαρηνός/Ναζωραῖος) the *Commentary* says that the editors printed Ναζαρηνός because it is characteristic of Marcan style and that scribes were responsible for introducing the more usual Ναζωραῖος for Mark's less familiar term. This is indeed likely, and the same reasoning should have been applied for the variants βαπτίζων/βαπτιστής.

---

9 See further my article "Ho baptizōn and Mark 1:4", *TZ* 31 (1975) pp. 14-15.

If we accept ὁ βαπτίζων as a title for John at Mark i 4, this helps solve our textual problems in this verse. Some scribes, not recognizing this as a title, have adjusted the verse to make βαπτίζων a verbal participle only. These are the main variants:

(a) βαπτίζων ἐν τῇ ἐρήμῳ καί A K P W Π *pler*. This is the reading accepted in UBSGNT[1,2].

(b) ὁ βαπτίζων ἐν τῇ ἐρήμῳ καί ℵ LΔ cop[bo]. If ὁ is present, καί is difficult to accept as characteristic of Marcan style.

(c) ἐν τῇ ἐρήμῳ βαπτίζων καί D Θ 28 *pc*. Not only has the article been removed, thus preventing βαπτίζων being understood as a substantive, but the two linked participles have been placed closer together to emphasize their dependence on ἐγένετο.

(d) ὁ βαπτίζων ἐν τῇ ἐρήμῳ B 33 892. In accepting this variant as the original, we have a text that conforms to Marcan usage in which John is referred to as ὁ βαπτίζων. Ἐγένετο can be taken as a verb with a force of its own: "John the Baptist appeared in the desert preaching". In view of the significance in the context of John's actual appearing, this is likely, although it would also agree with Mark's style to take ἐγένετο κηρύσσων as periphrastic ("John the Baptist was preaching in the desert ...." ; cf.Mark ix 3).

i 27 Τί ἐστιν τοῦτο; τίς ἡ διδαχὴ ἡ καινὴ αὕτη; ὅτι κατ' ἐξουσίαν· καί

In evaluating the variants in this verse, the UBSGNT editors seem not only to have ignored their principle of taking the authors's style into account but also the fact that the Semitic usage natural to the author could have been responsible for scribal alterations. The editors seem to have been unduly influenced by ℵ B [10].

The *Commentary* does not discuss the variant in C K Δ *et al.*, giving the distinctively Semitic word order ἡ διδαχὴ ἡ καινὴ αὕτη.

---

[10] Other places in Mark where the text in ℵ B seems to have been an important reason for printing its reading are (among others) ii 1; vi 33 (virtually alone), 47; vii 6, 37; viii 13; xiii 2; xiv 10, 52 (ℵ BC only). There are, of course, many other places where the text of ℵ B is printed in preference to variants in other MSS. but where there is neither apparatus in the text nor discussion in the *Commentary*. At iv 8 and 20 (ἕν), 16; vii 4 (βαπτίσωνται), 9, 24, 28; x 26, the *Commentary* shows that the united text of ℵ B has been ignored. Sometimes acknowledgment of a shorter text in ℵ B has resulted in a bracketed text, as in iii 32; vi 23 (πολλά); vi 41 (see below); vii 4 (καὶ κλινῶν),35 (καὶ εὐθέως),37; x 7; xii 23; xv 12 (θέλετε).

G.D.Kilpatrick[11] has drawn our attention to this feature of Semitic style in the NT and to such examples as Mark xii 43 ἡ χήρα ἡ πτωχὴ αὕτη in D Θ 565 f^{13} *pc*. (cf. the same variant in the parallel at Luke xxi 3 in A W Δ *pler*.) and Acts vi 13; xxi 28 where some MSS read τοῦ τόπου τοῦ ἁγίου τούτου. This unGreek word order (article and noun plus article and adjective plus demonstrative) is also to be found in the LXX. We should therefore consider this word order original to Mark. It is the order stylistically-conscious scribes would have avoided.

The MSS which give us this word order in Mark i 27 are for the most part those which also have τίς before ἡ διδαχή, thus creating a second question in the verse. The juxtaposition of two questions is also typical of Mark, e.g. i 24; ii 7, 8-9; iv 13, 21, 40; vi 2; vii 18-19. Scribes also tended to object to this in Mark. This Gospel is characterized by many such redundancies and repetitions. Matthew in using Mark tended to eliminate many such expressions[12]. In this verse D W *et al.* omit the first question τί ἐστιν τοῦτο. Others such as ℵ B Θ etc. omit the second question.

The reading of C K Δ 565^{c} also commends itself as original in another way. As Kilpatrick points out, Mark sometimes follows double questions with a ὅτι clause, e.g. vi 2 (variant 2); vii 18-19. Elsewhere in the NT, ὅτι in the sense of γάρ is found, e.g. at Mark viii 24; John i 16; Rom. ix 7. This also was a feature to which scribes often objected (see variant readings at Mark vi 2; viii 3; xi 18).

That there were so many features characteristic of Marcan style, to which stylistically-aware scribes would have objected, explains the many variants within this verse.

If ὅτι is original to Mark here, the punctuation problems referred to by Metzger disappear. Κατ' ἐξουσίαν has to go with what follows. Verse 22 is more likely to have been a reason for the change by scribes than to have been the pattern for Mark in this respect. As we have seen, stronger and more numerous examples of Marcan style and usage tell in favour of the reading of C K Δ *et al.*

Other places where UBSGNT ignores the reading characteristic of the author's style are frequent. Among those found in Mark are i 39 and ii 1.

---

[11] "Some Problems in New Testament Text and Language" *Neotestamentica et Semitica: Studies in Honour of Matthew Black* (ed. E.E.Ellis and M.Wilcox; (Edinburgh 1969) pp. 198-208. Reproduced in J.K.Elliott (ed.), *The Principles and Practice of New Testament Textual Criticism* (Leuven, 1990) pp. 230-40 (=*BETL* 96).

[12] See W.C. Allen, *A Critical and Exegetical Commentary on the Gospel according to St Matthew* (Edinburgh, 1907) pp. XXIV-XXV (= *ICC*).

At i 39 ἦν should be read, not ἦλθεν [13]. At ii 1 a minority of the committee would have preferred to accept the variant reading, the characteristically Marcan εἰς οἶκον with A C Γ Δ, but the majority overruled them (him?) by insisting on printing the reading of ℵ B. Similarly at ii 4 the majority of the committee ignored the text in accord with Marcan style and printed διὰ τὸν ὄχλον.

Mark viii 13 should read πάλιν ἐμβὰς εἰς τὸ πλοῖον. This is a redundant expression characteristic of Mark (Cf. also xii 23 where the longer text should be printed without brackets for the same reason). At xi 31 τί εἴπωμεν is also likely to be original. (At viii 35 the *Commentary* reports that the committee accepted Marcan style as an argument overruling any possibility that the longer text in Mark was the result of assimilation to the parallels).

i 41 ὀργισθείς

An examination of this famous variant along thoroughgoing eclectic lines would not, I think, have resulted in σπλαγχνισθείς being printed in all three editions of the UBSGNT text with a 'D' rating. That ℵ A B C and the bulk of MSS read it, whereas only D and a few OL MSS and Ephraem read ὀργισθείς, has been the deciding factor, even though many perfectly convincing arguments are capable of being produced — some of them are in the *Commentary* — for accepting the originality ofὀργισθείς. The *Commentary* is not so convincing in suggesting that ὀργισθείς could have come into the text because of a scribe's confusing Aramaic words.

There are several instances where Matthew in particular omits Mark's characteristic references to Jesus' humanity. The Matthaean parallels to Mark i 43; iii 5, 20-21; vi 5-6; viii 12; x 14, 21; xiv 33 provide ample illustration of this. Scribes of Mark were similarly motivated. But we must not expect scribes to have been scrupulous in weeding out every such expression from their exemplars. As Metzger points out, at Mark iii 5 and x 14 Jesus' anger and indignation are recorded by Mark and there are no variants in the MSS. In fact, these comparisons with Mark x 14 and iii 5 should be used to show that ὀργισθείς at i 41 would be entirely characteristic of Mark's picture of Jesus. This, however, should not deflect us from realizing that such changes did occur, and one such example seems to have been here. Admittedly not every human emotion of Jesus has been expunged by scribes, but neither is it likely that human emotions such as anger would have been added by scribes to a text which,

---

[13] See C.H Turner. Notes III and VIII (i).

had it read *σπλαγχνισθείς*, would have seemed to them to be perfectly appropriate and innocuous.

The allegedly slender support for *ὀργισθείς* should not be relevant. At other places in UBSGNT^3 the editors print readings with comparable support, e.g. at John ix 36 *ἀπεκρίθη ἐκεῖνος καὶ εἶπεν, Καὶ τίς ἐστιν, κύριε* against the readings of ℵ B; at Col. ii 2 *τοῦ θεοῦ, χριστοῦ* with P^{46} B Hilary Pelagius and Pseudo-Jerome only; at Acts xvi 12 *πρώτης μερίδος τῆς* with the Provençal and Old German only; or at John iii 27 *οὐδὲ ἕν* with P^{66} P^{75} B 472 only. Despite the fact that the *Commentary* reports that the committee often allowed itself to be overwhelmed by the sheer number of MSS., these and other examples show that it was not always overwhelmed. Mark i 41 is one such place where the minority reading, *ὀργισθείς*, ought to have been printed as the original text.

Matthew is likely to have read *ὀργισθείς* in his copy of Mark. Matthew used *σπλαγχνισθείς* four times of Jesus (Matt. ix 36; xiv 14; xv 32; xx 34) and thus had he found *σπλαγχνισθείς* at Mark i 41 it is likely he would have retained it. In fact, what Matthew seems to have omitted from his copy of Mark was *ὀργισθείς*.

v 22 omit ὀνόματι Ἰάϊρος

Without wishing to open up again the question of "Western non-interpolations", it is perhaps worth reconsidering this text and the reasons for printing it as given in the *Commentary*.

At x 46 Mark names Bartimaeus son of Timaeus, whereas the parallels are silent, and at xv 21 Mark names the sons of Simon of Cyrene. But this is not the normal tendency in the gospels. Assuming Marcan priority, we can see how on so many occasions Mark's impersonal plural verbs have been given subjects by either Matthew or Luke or both. Similarly, names are given to the nameless as the tradition develops[14]. John xi 2 and xii 3 name the woman who anointed Jesus at Bethany. Similarly, John tells us in xviii 10 the name of the high priest's servant and the name of the disciple who cut his ear off.

At x 46 and xv 21 Mark's names stand firm in the MS tradition (though W omits Βαρτιμαῖος at x 46). It is significant here that both Matthew and Luke ignore the names. At v 22, however, Jairus' name does not

[14] See the many examples of this development in an article by B. M. Metzger "Names for the Nameless in the New Testament: A study in the Growth of Christian Tradition" *Kyriakon: Festschrift Johannes Quasten*, ed. P.Granfield and J.A.Jungmann (Münster/Westf. 1970) vol.1 pp. 79-99.

stand firm in the MSS, and even more significantly the Lucan parallel includes the name Jairus without variation.

The words ὀνόματι Ἰάϊρος, therefore, could have entered MSS of Mark from the Lucan parallel, particularly in the wording found in the text of W Θ 565 700 at Mark v 22.

The absence of the name in Matthew is explicable if he did not find the name in his copy of Mark. This is more likely than Glasson's explanation that Matthew's copy of Mark, was equivalent to the Western text of Mark[15], or to say with Metzger in the Quasten *Festschrift* that the shorter text was the result of scribal harmonization to Matthew[16]. Usually harmonizing one account with another resulted in a scribe's adding to his MS from the parallel, not omitting.

The UBSGNT text has again been decided on the basis of external evidence supporting the longer text. The shorter text omitting ὀνόματι Ἰάϊρος deserves to be taken seriously as original.

vi 3 τοῦ τέκτονος υἱὸς καί

This is one of the minority of readings discussed in the *Commentary* where an 'A' rating is given to the reading printed in the text (τέκτων, ὁ υἱός), a reading, that is to say, regarded as "virtually certain". Such confidence does not seem justified.

There are many variants, particularly in the Lucan nativity stories, which avoid describing Jesus as the son of Joseph. For instance, at Luke ii 33, 41, 43 various mss. do not describe Joseph and Mary as "Jesus' parents". Instead they say either "Joseph and Mary" or "Joseph and his mother". Once the virgin birth traditions began to influence and then dominate Christian thinking about Jesus' birth, and once devotion to Mary developed, then passages referring without qualification to Joseph as Jesus' father were frequently altered by scribes.

The variants at Mark vi 3 as a whole seem to fit into this pattern. The UBSGNT text following ℵ AB *pler.* prints the secondary reading. The alternative τοῦ τέκτονος υἱός (καί), far from being due to assimilation to the parallel in Matt. xiii 55, is likely to be original. In fact Matthew does not provide an exact parallel to Mark vi 3.

A man in Jewish literature was more naturally described as the son of his father. This is likely here with Jesus described as son of the car-

---

[15] T.F.Glasson, "Did Matthew and Luke Use a 'Western' Text of Mark?" *ExpTim* 55 (1943-1944) pp. 180-4.

[16] "Names", p. 99, n. 107.

penter[17]. A change in the opposite direction would be less probable, especially in view of the tendency elsewhere to remove references to Jesus' father. Despite the comment of Celsus referred to by Metzger in a footnote to this discussion, it was better for Christian apologists to describe Jesus as a carpenter (just as Paul is described as an artisan) than to have doubts cast on the virgin birth tradition.

vi 22 θυγατρὸς αὐτῆς τῆς Ἡρῳδιάδος

The three main readings here are either "his daughter Herodias" as in UBSGNT, or "her daughter Herodias", or "the daughter of Herodias". The UBSGNT committee, although following ℵ B, were obviously not confident in so doing, as the *Commentary* makes abundantly clear.

We need to decide more positively which reading is the most likely to haven given rise to the alternatives. I would wish to argue for the originality of the reading *θυγατρὸς αὐτῆς τῆς Ἡρῳδιάδος* in A C K Θ *pler*. This could mean "the daughter of Herodias herself", but it is more likely that *τῆς Ἡρῳδιάδος* is in parenthesis. Metzger acknowledges in the *Commentary* that *αὐτῆς* could be a redundant pronoun anticipating a noun and as such is an Aramaism. This seems a likely reason for its removal by scribes. The meaning would be "her (i.e. Herodias') daughter". Such parentheses are characteristic of Mark, e.g. i 2-3; ii 10, 16, 21; vi 14-15; vii 2, 3-4, 19, 26; viii 14; xii 12a; xiii 14; xiv 36. Attempts by scribes to remove the parenthesis in vi 22, and to avoid the redundant pronoun, probably created the alternative readings. These alternatives, particularly the one printed as the text of UBSGNT, have their own problems, particularly in suggesting that the girl herself is called Herodias and is Herod's daughter — a detail which goes against v. 24.

vi 41 μαθηταῖς αὐτοῦ

Metzger's *Commentary* shows that the committee agreed that *μαθηταῖς* defined by *αὐτοῦ* is more likely to have been original. This is surely correct. But the brackets in UBSGNT[3] are unnecessary. They have been added to the text only because the committee wished to acknowledge the reading of the Alexandrian MSS., which by and large have the shorter text, i.e. without the possessive.

---

[17] See R.E.Brown, *The Birth of the Messiah* (Garden City, 1977) pp. 537-541; H.K.McArthur, "Son of Mary" *NovT* 15 (1973) pp. 38-58.

Again, both Marcan and NT usage should have been decisive. Hellenistic Greek made greater use of pronouns than the classical language. Hence, stylistically-conscious scribes tended to remove redundant pronouns (cf. *αὐτῆς* at vi 22). The principle given by Metzger in the Introduction to the *Commentary* (II A 4 [c]) is that scribes would sometimes add pronouns to make a smoother text. But this is not common, particularly in respect of postpositional possessives, which are a feature of Semitic style.

C.H.Turner[18] drew our attention several years ago to the use of the possessive with *μαθητής*, although he did not discuss the variant at Mark vi 41. He stated that originally Jesus' disciples would be known as *his* disciples not *the* disciples. Once *μαθητής* came always to signify Jesus' disciples. scribes felt free to omit the possessive. It is significant that so many of the allegedly great uncials are divided in this matter; hence the UBSGNT apparatus includes many such variants. These can be seen at Matt. viii 21; xv 36; xvi 5; xvii 10; xix 10; xx 17; xxvi 20; Luke xii 22; xx 45; John xx 30, and all are discussed in the *Commentary*. At all these *αὐτοῦ* should be read, and in the case of Matt. viii 21; Luke xii 22; xx 45, and John xx 30 the brackets should be removed as here at Mark vi 41. At Matt. xx 17 not only should *αὐτοῦ* be included in the text but the brackets should be removed from *μαθητάς*. The expression "his twelve disciples" is found at Matt x 1; xi 1; "the twelve", is found only at Matt. x 5; xxvi 14, 47, where the number alone is appropriate in the context.

Variants adding *αὐτοῦ* should also appear in the text at Mark viii 1*; ix 14*; x 10*, 13*, 24; xiv 16*. The verses marked with an asterisk are not discussed by Turner. We can in fact adjust Turner's figures. He says that Mark writes the possessive with *μαθητής* at 32 out of 40 occurrences in the gospel. The true figure is 39 times out of 40. The only real exception is Mark iv 34 (*τοῖς ἰδίοις μαθηταῖς*), where obviously the possessive would not be expected.

All too often the MS. evidence has caused the committee to reject its own arguments concerning the originality of *αὐτοῦ* in the above places.

At other places in Mark — not discussed in the *Commentary* — variants that include the pronoun should be accepted as giving the original text, e.g. Mark i 40 (+ *αὐτόν*); iii 33 (+ *μου*); vii 12 (+ *αὐτοῦ* [*bis*]); viii 25 (+ *αὐτοῦ*). This stylistic feature seems to have been acknowledged in UBSGNT[3], where the brackets around pronouns have been removed at vi 35 and xiv 10.

---

[18] Notes V (iv).

The excessive use of brackets in the UBSGNT text is one of the most disturbing features of the edition. Since the appearance of Metzger's *Commentary*, it has been made clear that all too often this device has been used to indicate division in the committee between printing a text on intrinsic grounds and omitting it because of its ms. support (e.g. Mark v 42; vi 23; x 1).

Here at Mark vi 41 the committee should have been consistent by printing *μαθηταῖς αὐτοῦ* without brackets [19].

ix 38 ὅς οὐκ ἀκολουθεῖ ἡμῖν

The *Commentary* again shows us that the UBSGNT text (*καὶ ἐκωλύομεν αὐτόν, ὅτι οὐκ ἠκολούθει ἡμιν*) has been printed because of its external support. The longer text of A K Π *pler.* is condemned as a conflate reading.

The text printed in UBSGNT seems to be the result of assimilation to the text of the parallel in Luke ix 49. This is especially true of uncial L, which has *μεθ' ἡμῶν* as in Luke. The reading of D W X f^{13} 565 *et al.* (*ὅς οὐκ ἀκολουθεῖ ἡμῖν καὶ ἐκωλύσαμεν αὐτόν* with minor variations) has the effect of transposing the second clause to bring it nearer its subject. This too looks like a secondary text.

The UBSGNT text is secondary. Had it been original to Mark, there is no reason why scribes would have altered it. It makes the two verbs *εἴδομεν* and *ἐκωλύομεν* closely parallel, and, as such, would not demand alteration. If, however, the longer text were original, one can understand that the other major variants are attempts to omit redundant words and to remove the awkwardly placed relative clause. Luke often prunes Mark's redundant expressions. Here is an example of scribes doing the same.

The so-called conflate text is characteristic of Mark and should be the deciding factor in the following places as well. At viii 26 the text of AC *et al.*, reading *μηδὲ εἰς τὴν κώμην εἰσέλθῃς μηδὲ εἴπῃς τινὶ ἐν τῇ κώμῃ*, is likely to be original. And at ix 49 we should accept the text of A K Π *et al.*, *πᾶς γὰρ πυρὶ ἁλισθήσεται καὶ πᾶσα θυσία ἁλὶ ἁλισθήσεται*. The *Commentary* dismisses what appear to them to be conflate readings.

Mark's repetitive style should also be taken into account when discussing the variant *καὶ ἐπιτιμήσας* by W Θ f^1 f^{13} *et al.* at x 14 (cf. ix 34 where the *Commentary* explains that *ἐν τῇ ὁδῷ* is printed precisely because the superfluous text is characteristic of Marcan style).

---

[19] See further my article "Μαθητής with a Possessive in the New Testament" *TZ* 35 (1979) pp. 300-304.

x 2 omit προσελθόντες (οἱ) Φαρισαῖοι

The issue here is whether to include the subject *Φαρισαῖοι* or not. Professor Metzger independently of the majority on the committee in a signed appendix to the discussion in the *Commentary* argues (correctly) for the absence of the subject. The impersonal plural verb is characteristic of Marcan style. Unfortunately his view did not prevail and, as so often, "widespread and impressive support" of certain MSS. encouraged the printing of the longer text.

C.H. Turner[20] lists many examples of the impersonal plural verb in Mark. These include i 21-22, 29-30, 32, 45; ii 2-3, 18; iii 1-2, 31-2; v 14, 35; vi 14, 33, 42-3, 53-4; vii 31-2; viii 22; x 13, 49; xiv 12. The later gospels have often added subjects when following Mark at these places. Similarly scribes often added a subject to the text of Mark. This feature of Marcan style and of scribal activity ought to have been dominant here[21]. "The Pharisees" seems to have been added by scribes from the parallel in Matt. xix 3, even though the wording in the parallel is not exact. The *Commentary* does not explain how or why the words *προσελθόντες οἱ Φαρισαῖοι* were omitted by many scribes if they were original to Mark.

Another instance in Mark of variant readings concerning the impersonal plural of verbs is at xv 10-11. The *Commentary* here explains that *οἱ ἀρχιερεῖς* is likely to be original and that its omission was probably due to stylistically-conscious scribes who objected to the proximity of *οἱ ἀρχιερεῖς* at the beginning of the next verse. But *οἱ ἀρχιερεῖς* at the beginning of v. 11 is secondary, having been added by scribes influenced by the parallel in Matt. xxvii 20 in order to provide the impersonal verb *ἀνέσεισαν* with a subject. The apparatus to Mark xv 10-11 gives the variants for and against the noun in v. 10 but ignores the variants in v. 11. At xv 11, Θ 565 700 read *οἵτινες καί* instead of *οἱ ἀρχιερεῖς*. Ὅστις is not uncharacteristic of Mark when referring to a subject just named (e.g. iv 20; ix 1; xii 18; xv 7), and thus *οἵτινες καί* is likely to be original at v. 11.

---

[20] Note I

[21] That scribes altered Mark's indefinite subjects is recognized in the discussion in the *Commentary* of the variants at Mark xiv 4.

xi 24 λαμβάνετε

The aorist is printed with confidence by UBSGNT because the commitee argued that this tense represents the Semitic prophetic perfect. The variant *λήμψεσθε* is rightly dismissed as coming into Mark from the parallel in Matt. xxi 22, but the reading *λαμβάνετε* deserves consideration as the original text.

Mark, as is well known, is fond of the present tense. In this verse alone four present tenses precede *λαμβάνετε*. Hawkins[22] reckons that there are over 150 historic presents in Mark of which Matthew retains only twenty-one. Some of these twenty-one are doubtless due to assimilation of the text of Matthew to Mark, and a more accurate text of Matthew than Hawkins used would reduce this number. Just as Matthew altered many of Mark's present to aorists[23], so many scribes of Mark did the same. The reverse is less likely to have happened.

Another example of the double standards applying to this text occurs at vi 2 where *ἀκούοντες* is printed with an 'A' rating in the UBSGNT text as typical of Mark's vividness. The aorist *ἀκούσαντες* in D Δ Θ 565 is dismissed as "pedantic". Again, the rules and principles on which this text is built vary depending on the MS. support. What is true at vi 2 should apply at xi 24 also.

---

[22] J.C.Hawkins, *Horae Synopticae: Contributions to the Study of the Synoptic Problem*, 2nd ed. (Oxford, 1909) pp. 143-149.

[23] See Allen, *Matthew* pp. XX-XXI.

CHAPTER ELEVEN

THE TEXT AND LANGUAGE OF THE ENDINGS TO MARK'S GOSPEL

Professor Kurt Aland has indicated that there are several major errors in the citation of the manuscript evidence for the longer and shorter endings to Mark's Gospel in the *apparatus criticus* of currently available printed editions of the Greek New Testament[1].

1.

As the text for these verses is so often the subject for discussion and as textual variants in these verses are to be taken into account below in analysing the distinctiveness of the language and style, the full citation of the evidence for the verses occurring after Mark xvi 8 is presented here. Much of the information in the *apparatus* has been kindly provided for me by the Institut für neutestamentliche Textforschung in Münster. The evidence is as follows.

1) The *longer* ending (Mark xvi 9-20) is included in the following MSS.:

A C D E H K M S U W X Y Γ Δ Θ Π Σ Φ Ω 047 055 0211 f13 28 33 274 (text) 565 700 892 1009 1010 1071 1079 1195 1230 1241 1253 1344 1365 1546 1646 2148 2174 etc.

Lect. 60 69 70 185 547 883.

Lat. (vt. aur c d^{supp}. ff^2 l n o q) (vg). Syr.(c p h pal) Cop.(boh fay) Gothic Arm. ^{MSS} Geo.^{B} Diat. (Arabic, Italian, Codex Fuldensis and Old Dutch).

Justin?, Irenaeus, Tertullian, Aphraates, Apostolic Constitutions, Didymus, Hippolytus, Marinus (as quoted by Eusebius), Epiphanius.

---

[1] K.Aland, "Bemerkungen zum Schluß des Markusevangeliums" *Neotestamentica et Semitica. Studies in honour of Matthew Black* edited by E.E.Ellis and M.Wilcox (Edinburgh, 1969) pp. 157-180. Aland points out particularly errors in the editions of Merk, Bover, Nestle and the United Bible Society. See also K.Aland, "Der Schluß des Markusevangeliums" in M.Sabbe (ed.), *L' Évangile selon Marc* (Leuven, ^{2}1988) pp. 435-70 and 573-5 (=*BETL* 34)

2) The *longer* ending is included in the following MSS. marked with asterisks, or obeli, or with a critical note added:
f1 22 137 138 205 1110 1210 1215 1216 1217 1221 1241 (vid) 1582.

3) The following MSS. add the *shorter* ending *before* the *longer* ending:
L Ψ 083 099 (incomplete up to *συντόμως*) 0112 (omits *πάντα ... μετὰ δὲ*) 274 (mg) 579.
Lect. 1602.
Syr. (h$^{mg.}$) Copt. (sah $^{MSS.}$ boh $^{MSS.}$) Eth.$^{MSS.}$

4) Lat. (vt. *k*) reads *only* the *shorter* ending after Mark xvi 8:
Lat. [vt. *a*] may also have originally contained the shorter ending only.

5) The following MSS. of Mark *end* at xvi 8:
ℵ B (a large space follows xvi 8) 304 (2386 and 1420 have a page missing at this point).
Syr. sin Cop. sa^{ms} Arm.$^{8\ MSS.}$ Eth.$^{3\ MSS.}$ Geo.^{1}, ^{A}.
Eusebius, MSS. according to Eusebius, MSS. according to Jerome[2].

2.

The other main problem concerning these endings which is often the subject of discussion is their language and style.

A discussion is found in an article by Eta Linnemann in which it is claimed that Mark xvi 15-20 is original to Mark and forms part of the actual ending to the gospel[3]. Linnemann maintains a) that the theology of these verses is consistent with the theology of canonical Mark[4], and b) that both Matt. xxviii 18-20 and Luke xxiv 44-53 knew of Mark xvi 15-20. One section of the article devoted to the linguistic and stylistic characteristics of Mark xvi 15-20 concludes: «Aus dem sprachlich-stilistischen Befund läßt sich kein Einwand erheben gegen die These, daß Mk. xvi 15-20 den ursprünglichen Schluß des Evangeliums enthält.»[5]

---

[2] The Coptic evidence has been cited largely from P.Kahle, "The End of St. Mark's Gospel. The Witness of the Coptic Versions" *JTS* N.S. 2 (1951) pp. 49-57.

[3] Eta Linnemann, "Der wiedergefundene Markusschluß" *Zs. Theol. Ki.* 66 (1969) pp. 255-287.

[4] Linnemann (n.3) strongly refutes V.Taylor's arguments for a late date for the ending found in his commentary *The Gospel according to St Mark* (London, 1952) pp. 610-614.

[5] Linnemann (n.3) p. 264.

Linnemann's discussion in this section of the article is however too facile based as it is on a refutation of Morgenthaler's arguments in his *Statistik*[6]. For instance, to disprove Marcan authorship of 9-20 Morgenthaler argues that the number of examples of *καί* (especially *καί* consecutive) in the longer ending is lower than the average for canonical Mark whereas the total number of occurrences of *δέ* is greater than in Mark. Arguments of this type based on averages and percentages can all too easily be questioned as in fact Linnemann does successfully. Similarly, Morgenthaler argues that the longer ending is non-Marcan because of the absence of foreign words. This too is an easy point for Linnemann to destroy. In choosing Morgenthaler's evidence, Linnemann has selected a simple target because the evidence in the *Statistik* for the secondary nature of the longer ending is by no means exhaustive. If Linnemann had tried to argue against the full evidence it would have proved impossible to maintain that part of the longer ending belonged to the original gospel.

Surprisingly though, a thorough discussion of the language and style is not readily accessible.

Commentaries on Mark usually give detailed exegesis of the contents of the longer and shorter endings to the gospel, but the problems connected with the language and style are often dismissed with a statement such as Cranfield's, "In style and vocabulary they (the verses of the longer ending) are obviously non-Markan"[7]. This is typical. Taylor, for instance, also sees it "unnecessary to examine in detail the almost universally held conclusion that xvi 9-20 is not an original part of Mk." because according to him this detail can be found in discussions by Hort, Swete and Lagrange[8]. But these older works do not present a full discussion of the language of the verses. Consequently, there is to my knowledge no thoroughgoing analysis of the language and style of these endings compared with New Testament language in general or with Mark's gospel in particular. Similarly, although there are numerous discussions published on the documentary evidence for the verses after Mark xvi 8, the variants in MSS. containing the longer and shorter endings are not usually taken into account when considering the language and style.

---

[6] R.Morgenthaler, *Statistik des neutestamentlichen Wortschatzes* (Zürich and Frankfurt, 1958) § 10, Wortstatistik und Echtheitsfragen, pp. 58-60, Beispiel 1: Mk. 16, 9-20.

[7] C.E.B.Cranfield, *The Gospel according to St.Mark* (Cambrige, 1963), p. 472.

[8] Taylor p. 610.

3.

The discussion below attempts to remedy these deficiencies.

The Distinctive Features of the Longer Ending, Mark xvi 9-20.

In these notes the name of Mark refers to the author of Mark i 1 - xvi 8 only.

v.9

ἐφάνη. — This is the only occurrence in the New Testament of this verb with reference to the Resurrection appearances although it is used of Elijah re-appearing in Luke ix 8 (cf. Num. xxiii 4 LXX where it is used of God). According to Legg's apparatus[9], the Greek uncial D avoids this verb and reads *ἐφανέρωσεν* but this is clearly a misreading by D due possibly to assimilation to 12 or 14 where *φανερόω* occurs.

παρ' ἧς ἐκβεβλήκει. — This is likely to be the original reading and is a combination not found elsewhere in the Greek New Testament. Several MSS. read *ἀφ' ἧς ἐκβεβλήκει* but this variant is secondary. *ἀπό* has been introduced to the text by assimilation to Luke viii 2 *ἀφ' ἧς δαιμόνια ἑπτὰ ἐξεληλύθει* although it is also possible that some scribes avoided *παρά* because, like the *International Critical Commentary*, they too found this preposition "strange".[10]

v.10

ἐκείνη. — *ἐκεῖνος* as a pronoun is common in the Johannine writings (e.g. John i 8, 18, 33). It is however not characteristic of Marcan style although it is a feature of this ending (see vv. 11, 13, 20). *κἀκεῖνοι* in v.11 for instance is not used of the disciples in Mark.[11]

πορευθεῖσα. — The verb *πορεύομαι* found in Matt., Luke, John and Acts is not a Marcan word. It is however found three times in this longer

---

9 S.C.E.Legg, *Novum Testamentum Graece. Evangelium secundum Marcum* (Oxford, 1935), *ad loc.*

10 E.P.Gould, *The Gospel according to Saint Mark* (Edinburgh, 1896), *ad loc.*

11 This unity of language in Mark xvi 9-20 makes it difficult to uphold Linnemann's (n.3) arguments that 15-20 can be treated separately when refuting Morgenthaler's linguistic points. The textual arguments brought forward by Linnemann are successfully dismissed in another article by K.Aland, "Der wiedergefundene Markusschluß?" *Zs. Theol. Ki.* 67 (1970) pp. 3-13.

ending, vv.10, 12, and 15[11]. Mark does not use the simple form of this verb. At Mark ix 30 the variant reading representing the simple verb is secondary, for scribes tended to remove the prefixed prepositions of compound verbs[12], and *παρεπορεύοντο* should therefore be read at Mark ix 30. Another significant difference from Marcan usage is that Mark tends to reserve the compounds of *πορεύεσθαι* for the present tense, and uses *ἐλθεῖν* for the aorist. Here, however, *πορεύεσθαι* appears in the aorist (cf. also the firm example of the aorist in v.15)[13]. The *v.l.* *ἀπελθοῦσα* here read by K Π 42 131 229 253 481 517 579 892 etc. is to be rejected as secondary. As we have seen, *πορεύομαι* belongs to Pseudo-Mark's vocabulary and it is firmly established in all MSS. at v.15. The *v.l.* has probably been introduced into the text through assimilation to 13 where *ἀπαγγέλλω* follows as here.

τοῖς μετ' αὐτοῦ γενομένοις is also an unusual way of referring to the disciples and is not found elsewhere in the New Testament (cf.*κἀκεῖνοι* above).

πενθοῦσι. — The verb *πενθέω* is non-Marcan.

v.11

ἐθεάθη. — *θεάομαι* is a non-Marcan verb also. It occurs again in 14 in the middle voice.

ἠπίστησαν — *ἀπιστέω* is also non-Marcan. Once more the unity of the language of this ending is demonstrated because the verb also occurs in v.16. At both 16 and here variants are found (D reads *καὶ οὐκ ἐπίστευσαν αὐτῷ* at 11 and 15 reads *μὴ πιστεύσας* at 16) but these are plainly secondary readings intended to avoid the less usual verb *ἀπιστέω*.

v.12

μετὰ ταῦτα is found in Luke and John but not in Mark.

ἐφανερώθη. — *φανερόω* is not used by Mark of Jesus' resurrection appearances although it occurs again in the same context in this section at 14. The *v.l.* *ἐφάνη* read by Θ at v.12 is to be rejected. Θ is notoriously inaccurate when deviating in this section. See the errors of this MS. in reading *πορευθέντες* in 13, *αὐτοῖς* in 11 and *λαλῆσωσι* in 17.

ἑτέρᾳ. — There is no firm example of *ἕτερος* in Mark[14].

---

12 C.H.Turner, Note IX.

13 See further G.D.Kilpatrick, "*πορεύεσθαι* and its Compounds" above.

14 See J.K.Elliott, "The use of *ἕτερος* in the New Testament" *ZNW* 60 (1969) pp. 140f.

μορφῇ. — *μορφή* does not occur elsewhere in the gospels.

v.14

ὕστερον does not occur in Mark. It is not part of his vocabulary as can clearly be demonstrated at Mark xii 6 which contains *ἔσχατον* whereas the parallel in Matt. xxi 37 reads *ὕστερον*.

ἕνδεκα. — This is the only reference to the eleven disciples in Mark i 1 - xvi 20.

ὠνείδισεν. — This is the only example in the New Testament of *ὀνειδίζω* used of Jesus rebuking the disciples.

ἀπιστίαν ... καὶ σκληροκαρδίαν. — This is the only place in the New Testament where these faults are levelled at the disciples.

The so-called Freer logion found after 14 in the Greek uncial W and part of which is found in Greek MSS. known to Jerome has no claim to being original either to Mark's Gospel or to the longer ending. The vocabulary differs sharply from both: *ὅρος* and *προσλέγω* are hapaxes in the Greek New Testament; *ἄφθαρτος*, *δεῖνα*, *ὑποστρέφω*, *ἁμαρτάνω*, *ἀποκαλύπτω* and *ἀπολογέομαι* do not occur in Mark i 1 - xvi 8 or in xvi 9-20; *ὁ Χριστὸς* is not the designation of Jesus by the author of the longer ending.

v.15

ἅπαντα. — There is no firm example of the form *ἅπας* in Mark although it occurs as a variant in Mark i 27; viii 25; xi 32.

κτίσει. — This is the only occurrence in the Gospels of *κτίσις* used in the sense of the sum of what is created rather than the creative act[15]. *κτίσις* in the latter sense is found at Mark x 6; xiii 19.

v.16

κατακριθήσεται. — The passive forms of *κατακρίνω* are not found in Mark.

v.17

σημεῖα. — The plural of *σημεῖον* is not found in Mark in the sense of miracles or wonders regarded as a sign of the divine act although it is fre-

---

[15] This is the interpretation of A.Plummer, *The Gospel according to St.Mark* (Cambridge, 1914), *ad loc.*

quently plural in John with this meaning (e.g. John ii 11, 23; iii 2; vi 2, 14). See also the same usage in v.20.

The separation of *ταῦτα* and *σημεῖα* is not characteristic of normal New Testament word order. Similarly, the use of *ταῦτα* with anarthrous *σημεῖα* differs from the usual usage in the gospels although N.Turner points to examples of the omission of the article after *οὗτος* in Acts i 5; xxiv 21[16]. Of this example he says *ταῦτα* here may be construed as the object of the participle as in fact certain scribes (C^3 *Byz* W 565 etc.) possibly indicate by placing *ταῦτα* next to *τοῖς πιστεύσασιν*.

παρακολουθήσει. — *παρακολουθέω* in the sense "to result" differs from the meaning in the rest of the New Testament (e.g.Luke i 3; 1 Tim. iv 6; 2 Tim. iii 10). This reading is however to be preferred to *ἀκολουθήσει* read by C* L Ψ 892 and others) because *ἀκολουθέω* occurs as a compound verb in 20. The variant reading the simple verb is explicable on stylistic grounds. It can be demonstrated in many other places in the apparatus to the Greek New Testament that scribes tended to avoid compound forms.

v.18

ὄφεις. — *ὄφις* does not occur in Mark.

κἄν in the sense "and if" is not found in canonical Mark. At Mark v 28; vi 56 it is merely an intensification of simple *καί* (in the sense "even", "at least").

θανάσιμον. — *θανάσιμος* occurs only here in the whole of Biblical Greek, although it is found in the apocryphal Acts of John. Biblical Greek prefers the poetic *θανατηφόρος* (which occurs five times in the LXX and in James iii 8).

βλάψῃ. — *βλάπτω* is not found in Mark.

ἐπιθήσουσιν. — This is the only occurrence of *ἐπιτίθημι ἐπί* + Accusative, in Mark. In Mark v 23 the verb is followed by the dative direct, despite the parallel in Matt. ix 18 which reads *ἐπί* + Accusative (but cf. Mark viii 25).

καλῶς ἕξουσιν. — This classical phrase is not found elsewhere in the New Testament.

---

[16] N.Turner, *A Grammar of New Testament Greek* by J.H.Moulton, 3. *Syntax* (Edinburgh, 1963) p. 259.

v.19

μὲν οὖν. — This combination is not found in Mark. *οὖν* itself is rare in Mark there being only two firm examples according to C.H.Turner[17].

ὁ ... *Κύριος* as a Christological title is not found in Mark[18] although it occurs again in 20. The *vv.ll.* adding either 'Ἰησοῦς alone after Κύριος (in C* LKΔ fam.l, 565 etc.) or 'Ἰησοῦς Χριστὸς after Κύριος (in W Lat.[vt.*o*] Copt [boh.^{Mss}]) are secondary. The expansion of divine titles is a characteristic of scribal activity[19].

ἀνελήμφθη. — *ἀναλαμβάνω* is not found in Mark. The verb is used of the ascension only in Acts i 2, 11, 22; 1 Tim. iii 2. Elsewhere in the New Testament this meaning is conveyed by *ἐπαρθῆναι* (Acts i 9), *ἀναβῆναι* (John vi 62; xx 17), *πορευθῆναι εἰς οὐρανόν* (1 Pet. iii 22), or *διεληλυθέναι τοὺς οὐρανούς* (Heb. iv 14).

v.20

ἐκήρυξαν πανταχοῦ. — This expression is not found elsewhere in the gospels.

τού Κυρίου συνεργοῦντος ... σημείων. — The extended genitive absolute found here is a rare New Testament usage. *συνεργέω* is not found elsewhere in the gospels and is found nowhere else in the New Testament with Jesus as subject (if *ὁ Θεός* is read at Rom. viii 28). It is a Pauline word. So too are *βεβαιόω* and *ἐπακολουθέω* neither of which is found elsewhere in the gospels[20].

The Distinctive Features of the Shorter Ending, after Mark xvi 8.

In this section the following words do not occur in canonical Mark: *συντόμως*, *ἐξαγγέλλω*, *σωτηρία*, *ἀνατολή*[21], *ἄρχι* (or *μέχρι*, if the reading of Ψ is accepted as original), and *ἄφθαρτος* (which occurs in the Freer logion).

---

17 C.H.Turner, Note VII (4) ii.

18 *Pace* Linnemann (n.3), p. 281, who wishes to take Mark xi 3 as a parallel to the usage of *ὁ Κύριος* here. Mark xi 3 however is clearly not an example of *Κύριος* as a Christological title. This interpretation is enforced if *χρείαν ἔχω* at xi 3 is used absolutely as at Mark ii 25 and if *αὐτοῦ* is seen as a postpositional possessive, i.e. "its master has need".

19 J.K.Elliott, *The Greek Text of the Epistles to Timothy and Titus*, = *Studies and Documents* 36 (Salt Lake City, 1968), especially pp. 204f.

20 It will be seen from the above that the statement in *The International Critical Commentary* (n.10) p.303, that in the longer ending 19 words and 2 phrases are not found

The following *phrases* are peculiar to this ending:
οἱ περὶ τὸν Πέτρον, ἐξαποστέλλω τὸ κήρυγμα, ἡ αἰώνιος σωτηρία.

δύσις is a New Testament hapax. The perfect participle of *παραγγέλλω* is found nowhere else in the New Testament. The adjective *ἱερός* is found elsewhere only at 2 Tim. iii 15. *μετὰ ταῦτα* is not found in canonical Mark although it occurs at xvi 12 (see above).

Additional Note

Further studies of the endings to Mark include J.Hug, *La Finale de l' Évangile de Marc* (Paris, 1978); W.R.Farmer, *The Last Twelve Verses of Mark* (Cambridge, 1974) and cf. review by J.N.Birdsall *JTS* 26 (1975) pp. 150-60.

---

in canonical Mark represents an undercount. Morgenthaler's figure (n.6), p.59, that 16 of the 92 different words in the longer ending are not found in canonical Mark is also low.

21 Note that *ἀνατολή* occurs in the plural at Matt. xxiv 27; Luke xiii 29 where *δυσμή* is also plural. The v.l. *ἀνατολῶν* here in 274 mg. is plainly secondary as the singular parallels the singular *δύσεως*.

N. Turner

CHAPTER TWELVE

THE STYLE OF MARK

§ *1. Literary Sources In Mark*

Although scholars of various schools have sought to detect literary sources in Mark and to distinguish them by means of linguistic tests, the attempt has never succeeded because the various stylistic features cut right across the boundaries of any literary divisions that have yet been suggested. In consequence it seems that although there may have been literary sources to begin with a final redactor has so obliterated all traces of them that Mark is in the main a literary unity from the beginning to xvi 8, as the foregoing analyistic features will show.

We must except both the Longer and Shorter endings (xvi 9-20) which are full of non-Marcan words and phrases: e.g. *he appeared* (*ephane*) 9, *First day of the week* 9 (i.e. the normal Greek *prote* instead of Semitic *mia* as in xvi 2), *after this* (*meta tauta*) 10 and so on. Cf. V.Taylor, *Mark* 610-615.

§ 2. *Aramaic Influence on the Style of Mark*

On the one hand, it is felt that Mark's style is unpretentious, verging on the vernacular; on the other, that it is rich in Aramaisms. The latter are so much in evidence that early in this century scholars were convinced that Aramaic sources had been translated. Torrey followed them, adducing mistranslations to support the hypothesis (C. C. Torrey, *The Four Gospels*, Oxford 1922; *Our Translated Gospels*, London 1933). To Burney the Aramaic flavour of Mark was not so strong as that of the Fourth Gospel, and he found no mistranslation in Mark (C.F.Burney, *The Aramaic Origin of the Fourth Gospel*, Oxford 1922, 19). Rawlinson thought that the Paralytic narrative might be a translation (ii 1-12), but anything further was "highly improbable." (A.E.J. Rawlinson, *The Gospel according to St. Mark*, London 1925, xxxiii.) Howard concurred with Lagrange that the Greek was translation Greek but he left open the question whether the evangelist translated or whether he was subsequently translated; he inclined to the view that Mark was here and there translating an Aramaic catechetical system of instruction (*Grammar* II 481).

Since Papias indicates that Mark was a catechist, it is conceivable that the Gospel was based on Aramaic catechetical teaching given by the evangelist to Palestinian converts.

Sentence Construction.

Asyndeton.

This is probably where Aramaic influence is strongest in the style of Mark (Taylor, *Mark* 49f, 58; Black 3 55-61). The same is true of the Fourth Gospel. C.H. Turner found 38 examples of asyndeta in Mark, and although many of these may not be abnormal in Greek the number is significant: Note VII (3); Lagrange adds others: M.-J.Lagrange, *Évangile selon Saint Marc,* 5th ed. Paris 1929, lxxf).

Active impersonal plural.

This Marcan mannerism may well evince an Aramaic way of expressing a substitute for the rare passive voice. Thus, *Does the lamp come?* for *Is the lamp brought?* due to misunderstanding the Aphel or Ittaphel of *'t'* (*bring*).

Mark iv 21; B-text; vi 14; vii 19; ix 43; x 13; xiii 26; xv 27. It is not exclusively Marcan: Matthew v 15 (Matthew's Q); ix 2 (from Mark); xvii 27 (M); Luke iv 41 (add. to Mark); viii 2 (L); xii 20 (L). Cf. C.H.Turner, Note I; M.Wilcox, *The Semitisms of Acts*, Oxford 1965, 127ff; *Grammar* II 447f; III 292f; Black[3] 126-128; Taylor, *Mark* 47f, 62; L. Rydbeck, *Fachprosa,* Uppsala 1967, 39-42.

Similar is the impersonal plural with vague subject, e.g. *they were astonished* for *people were astonished* (which is strictly a Semitism, for it reflects a Hebrew idiom in the LXX, as well as Aramaic).

Mark i 22,30,32,45; ii 3,18; iii 2,21,32; v 14,35; vi 33,43,54; vii 32; viii 22; x 2,49; xiii 9,11; xiv 12; xv 14.

Another kind of impersonal plural seems to reflect the eye-witness account of a group of disciples, as C.H.Turner suggested (Note V (i)). Others find difficulty in accepting the suggestion, e.g. V.Taylor, *Mark* 47f; Black[3] 127. To Black, such a plural seems to be "characteristic of simple Semitic narrative."

Mark i 21 (*they went into Capernaum*) 29f; v 1,38; viii 22; ix 14f,30,33; x 32,46; xi 1,11 *v.l.*,12,15,19,21,27; xiv 18,22,26f,32. However, this plural is quite characteristic of Semitic speech.

Use of Participle for a main verb.

Rare in the papyri, it is characteristic of Aramaic and it occurs in the Western text of Mark: i 13; iii 6; vii 25; ix 26; (also Matthew ii 41D). *Grammar* I 224; D.Daube in E.G.Selwyn, *I Peter*[2], (London, 1947) 471ff; Lagrange, *Marc* xc.

Proleptic Pronoun.

Black classes as a genuine Aramaism the proleptic pronoun followed by a resumptive noun (e.g. *he, Herod, had sent*). However, the construction is wider than Mark, and need not indicate the translation of a document unless the non-Marcan instances do too.

It occurs particularly in the D-text: Mark vi 17,18D; v 15D; Matthew iii 4; xii 45D; Luke i 36; iv 43D; x 7; xxiv 10D; Acts iii 2D; vi 7D; vii 52D; xi 27ℵB. (Black[3] 96-100; *Grammar* II 431; Taylor, *Mark* 59f; C.F. Burney, *The Aramaic Origin of the Fourth Gospel* (Oxford, 1922) 85ff). However, in Mark vi 22 where AC read αὐτῆς τῆς Ἡρῳδιάδος, the Old Latin texts understand αὐτῆς (*ipsius*), i.e. *of Herodias herself.*

Conjunctions.

In Aramaic the conjunction *'illâ (but)* has both exceptive and adversative force, which may explain how the Greek *alla* and *ean mē* can appear together in iv 22, and it may account for the textual variants in ix 8. Greek *alla*, in x 40, may have been chosen for its similarity to Aramaic *'illâ* in form and sound, instead of the more appropriate *ean mē*. Thus the sense should clearly be: *To sit ... is not mine to give* (to anyone) *unless it has been prepared for him ....* The Biblical Greek confusion of *ei mē* and *alla* is further seen in xiii 32 = Matthew xxiv 36, as also in Paul.

We must dismiss Burney's suggestion that Aramaic translation or influence accounts for the peculiar use of Greek *hina mē* as meaning *lest* five times in Mark, instead of the more normal *mēpote*. His grounds are that Aramaic has a similar composite term of two words *l*[e]*mâ dī* (Dan ii 18; vi 9, 18) where Hebrew has the single word *pen*. However, the suggestion of direct translation is weak when it is considered that on many occasions Paul wrote *hina mē* when *lest* was meant (e.g. I Cor i 10, 15, 17); he was not translating but his Greek may well have been Semitic in style. The Testament of Abraham is not likely to have an Aramaic original, yet recension A lxxxvii 7 has *hina mē* where recension B cix 23 has *mēpote*. Cf. *Grammar* I 241, and the additional note in J.H.Moulton, *Einleitung in die Sprache des Neuen Testaments*, Heidelberg 1911, 269 n. 1; *Grammar* II 468.

Other Syntax.

Howard has reminded us of *pros* = *with*, reminiscent of Aramaic *lᵉwāth*, though similar to the classical usage (*Grammar* II 467): Mark vi 3; ix 19; xiv 49. One must reject this as evidence for translation, unless one makes the claim also for Paul, where it occurs more than a dozen times. It may well be an Aramaic element in this type of Greek, however.

Black quotes a Targum to illustrate a construction parallel with *katenanti* in Mark vi 41D; cf. also xi 2; xii 41; xiii 3 (*Grammar* II 465; Black^3 116f).
The use of Greek *hen* as multiplicative or distributive in the D-text of Mark iv 8 recalls the same use of Aramaic *ḥadh* (e.g. Dan iii 19); cf. Black^3 124; Taylor, *Mark* 60, and *in loc.* iv 8.
A Marcan and Pauline mannerism is adverbial *polla* (Mark i 45; iii 12; v 10, 23, 38, 43; vi 20; ix 26; xv 3), the frequency of which induced Howard to concede as Aramaic, a parallel to *saggî* (=*many, greatly*); cf. *Grammar* II 446; Lagrange, *Marc* xcviii. However, the adverbial accusative of extent is quite normal in Greek. If this were direct translation from an Aramaic source, why not also Paul and James? (Rom xvi 6,12; I Cor xvi 12,19; James iii 2). Another adverbial expression is *loipon* (esp. xiv 41) with weakened meaning, which Torrey suggested was an over-literal rendering of *mikkeʿ an* (= *from now*), which itself was weakened in Aramaic to little more than *presently, now* (C.C. Torrey, *The Four Gospels*, 303); it is found in Test.Abr., which is probably innocent of Aramaic sources (lxxxiv 27; xcii 19,21; cxi 12; cxiii 16).

Vocabulary.

A.J.Wensinck's unpublished work (Black^3 302) pointed out the unattested Greek use of *poiein* in Mark iv 32, instancing the Onkelos Targum of Gen xlix 15, 21. Further, as Black suggests, Greek *oros* in iii 13 may correspond to Aramaic *ṭura*, with its double meaning of *mountain* and open *country* (Black^3 133, 299). He further suggests that the name *pîstᵉqâ* (Palestinian Talmud) was "simply transliterated, and then taken into the sentence as an adjective" xiv 3 (Black^3 223-225), but it may in fact be a loan-word, naturalized in Greek, and not a translation.

In ii 21 the sense required of *pleroma* is *patch*, and Black's suggestion of a Syriac word which has the double meaning of *patch* and *fill* (*mᵉla*) is interesting; perhaps it may be granted that here, as elsewhere, Semitic usage has enriched the vocabulary of Biblical Greek. This may be said of the next suggestion too. Black notes that the Greek verb *hupagein* in the sense *to die* (Mark xiv 21 and John) has no Greek or LXX parallel, but there was the Aramaic parallel *'zl*; however, the Hebrew *hlk* might also have sufficed. In Mark xiv 41 Black rejects Torrey's theory of mistranslation and substitutes his own, based on the reading of the D-text: confusion of *r* and *d* means that the D-text is a mistranslation of, "the end and the hour are pressing" (Black^3 225f).

Mistranslation of Aramaic *d*ᵉ has frequently been adduced, for *d*ᵉ has a wide variety of usages, and sometimes an obscurity is cleared on the theory of mistranslation of this ubiquitous particle (C.F.Burney, *The Poetry of Our Lord,* Oxford 1925, 145n; *Aramaic Origin* 70; *Grammar* II 434-437; Black^3 71-81; Taylor, *Mark* 58f). T.W.Manson's explanation of the difficult iv 12 (*so that they may see but not perceive* ...) is well known, based on confusion of *who* and *in order that,* both *d*ᵉ (*The Teaching of Jesus,* Cambridge 1936, 76-80).

In Mark iv 22 it has been suggested, not wholly convincingly, that *for there is nothing hid except with the purpose of being revealed* should read, *for there is nothing hid which will not be revealed*; it is claimed that Mark or one of his sources has failed to note that *d*ᵉ might be relative in this context (Burney, *Aramaic Origin* 76). For the same reason the *hos* of the D-text in ix 38 may preserve the true sense of *d*ᵉ, and in iv 41 we ought to understand a relative (Old Lat. *cui*): *whom even the wind and sea obey* (Moulton, *Einleitung* 332; *Grammar* II 436; Black^3 71). Black has accepted Torrey's suggestion that *ti* in Peter's words xiv 68 is a mistranslation of the relative pronoun and we should read: "I am neither a companion of, nor do I know at all, *him of whom* (*d*ᵉ) you speak" (Torrey, *Four Gospels* 303; Manson, *Teaching* 16f; Black^3 79f). Three mistranslations suggested by Wellhausen are of great interest: 1. *Son of Man* for Aramaic *man,* 2. *uncovered the roof* ii 4 for *brought him to the roof,* 3. the improbable *to Bethsaida* vi 45 should be *through Sidon* (W.C.Allen, *The Gospel according to St Mark,* London 1915, *in loc.*).

There is considerable evidence favouring influence of an exclusively Aramaic kind upon the style of Mark, but the case for the translation of documents is somewhat weakened by the fact that here in the same Gospel are instances of both exclusive Aramaisms and exclusive Hebraisms existing side by side. This occurs even within a single verse, e.g. iv 41 where there is the influence of the Hebrew infinitive absolute together with a misunderstanding of Aramaic *d*ᵉ by the use of ὅτι for ᾧ. Therefore unless we can suppose that the sources were composite, parts in Aramaic, parts in Hebrew, the source-hypothesis fails to account for all the Semitic features of style.

§ *3. Hebraic Influence on the Style of Mark*

The style is not free from Hebraism, in spite of Howard (*Grammar* II 446), although the exclusively Hebraic influence is less than that which is common to Hebrew and Aramaic.

Syntax.

When partitive expressions are used as nominal phrases, without either definite or indefinite article, as subject or object of a verb, then the style ceases to be characteristic of normal Greek. It is rare in the non-Biblical language and seems to have originated with the LXX (Gen xxvii 28; II Sam xi 17; 1 Macc vi 48 A, etc.)

As object of a verb: Mark vi 43 (*they took up ... some of the fishes*); ix 37W; xii 2 (*receive some fruit*); xiv 23 (*they all drank some of it*). *Grammar* I 72,102,245; II 433; III 7,208f; *Grammatical Insights* 57f; H.B.Swete, *The Gospel according to St Mark*[3], London 1909, E. Lohmeyer, *Das Evangelium des Markus,* Göttingen 1937, 147n.

The auxiliary use of the verb *add* may reflect Aramaic influence. Cf. G.B.Winer - W.F.Moulton, *A Treatise on the Grammar of New Testament Greek*[8], Edinburgh 1877, 587-590; *Grammar* I 233; II 445; III 227; H.St.J.Thackeray, *A Grammar of the Old Testament in Greek according to the Septuagint,* I, Cambridge 1909, 52f; Allen, *Mark* 169; Taylor, *Mark* 61. However, its common occurrence in the LXX (109 times) argues for its being an idiom of Biblical Greek (Hebrew *ysp*): Mark xiv 25 D (the same construction of the idiom as is found in the LXX).

The addition of a cognate noun or participle to the main verb, which is very rare in Aramaic, is more likely to be Hebraism such as is found in the LXX, through the influence of the infinitive absolute.

Mark iv 12 (*seeing see* and *hearing hear*), 41 (*fear with fear*); v 42 (*amazed with amazement*). Also Matthew Luke John James I Pet Rev LXX e.g. Gen ii 16f; Jonah i 10; 1 Macc x 8 (108 times). Cf. below pp. 47f; Thackeray, *Grammar* 48f; G.Dalman, *The Words of Jesus*, E. T. Edinburgh 1902, 34f; *Grammar* II 443-445; Taylor, *Mark* 61.

Sometimes the aorist indicative is found in a context which is unusual for Greek but which is explained by the influence of Hebrew Stative perfect in the LXX, e.g. *rsh* in Isa xlii 1, *ḥaphēṣ b*ᵉ in Isa lxii 4B.

Mark i 8 *I baptize* (Mt corrects to pres. tense), 11 *I am well pleased,* also in Mt Ac. Cf. W.C.Allen, *A Critical and Exegetical Commentary on the Gospel according to St Matthew,* ICC Edinburgh 1907, 29; *Grammar* I 134f; II 458; III 72; Black[3] 128-130; Taylor, *Mark* 64.

The articular infinitive, very common in the LXX, characteristic of Luke, but rare in the secular papyri, is clearly influenced by the Hebrew *b*ᵉ with infinitive, and is a fairly clear instance of the influence of the LXX upon the Greek of the NT.

It occurs in Mark with four cases: 1. Nom. ix 10; x 40; xii 33. 2. Acc. i 14; iv 5,6; v 4; xiii 22; xiv 28,55B. 3. Gen. iv 3 *v.l.* 4. Dat. iv 4; vi 48B.

As *during* it occurs (but rarely) in Thucydides. *Grammar* I 14, 215, 249; II 448, 450f; III 140-142; L. Radermacher, *Neutestamentliche Grammatik* (Tübingen[2] 1925) 189.

The prolepsis of the subject of a subordinate clause is widespread throughout the NT (Mark, Matthew, Luke-Acts, John, Paul, Revelation), and although it has a few parallels outside Biblical Greek it is clearly a Hebrew idiom, e.g. "God saw *the light*, that *it* was good" Gen i 4.

Mark i 24 (*I know thee who thou art*), vii 2 (*seeing some of the disciples, that they ate*), xi 32 (*all considered John, that he was a prophet*), xii 34 (*seeing him that he had answered*).

Certain Hebrew words are literally rendered. The word *nephesh* has a reflexive function, in Greek replacing the normal pronoun with *psuchē*. It is "a pure Semitism" (Black[3] 102) in Mark viii 36, which Luke alters to more normal Greek. The Hebrew word *liphnê*, literally rendered in the LXX of Amos ix 4 etc., becomes the Biblical Greek *pro prosōpou* Mark i 2. The Hebrew *bayyāmîm hāhēm* (in those days), a very common LXX phrase, is literally rendered in Mark i 9, and the Hebrew *lᵉʻolām* (for ever) becomes logically εἰς τὸν αἰῶνα iii 29, since *ʻôlām* (age) has become identical in meaning with αἰών.

Much has been written on the phrase *believe in the Gospel* i 15, but in view of the massive Semitic complexion of Mark's language it would seem less appropriate to quote classical and vernacular precedents than to suspect the Hebrew phrase *heʼᵉmîn bᵉ* (to trust in) as the real inspiration. Neither verb nor noun with *en* are anything but rare outside Biblical Greek, but the noun with *en* is frequent in Paul. However, it does appear from Pauline usage that to *trust in* involves the prepositions *eis* and *epi*, and so *en* may carry quite a different sense in the primitive Church's terminology, especially as the important formulae, *en Kurio* and *en Christo*, have a theological implication of their own, and so *en* may be taken in sense very closely with Christ and Gospel.

Grammar III 262f; A.Deissmann, *Die NT Formel "in Christo Jesu"*, Marburg 1892; A.Oepke, in *TWNT* II 534-539; M.Zerwick, *Graecitas Biblica* [3], Rome 1955, § 88; N.Turner, "The Preposition *en* in the New Testament," *Bible Translator* 10 (1959) 262ff.

A difficult phrase for translation is τί ἐμοὶ καὶ σοὶ (= Heb. *mah-lī wālāk*): Mark i 24; v 7; Matthew viii 29; Luke viii 28; John ii 4.

The nominative case indicating time is a Hebraism borrowed by Mark and Luke from the LXX (Joshua i 11 A; Eccl ii 16 emended in A ℵ[c.a]) Mark viii 2.

Word-Order.

I. Position of attributive genitive.

Mark's style is conspicuously different from the Ptolemaic Papyri and closer to the LXX, following the order: article — noun — article — genitive (54 times). He never has the position which is common in non-Biblical Greek: article — article — genitive — noun (*Grammar* III 217). Further influence of the Hebrew construct state appears, when the noun in the genitive case follows immediately upon its governing noun, in contrast with the tendency of literary style which is to precede (*Grammar* III 349).

The table will help us to appreciate how the matter stands relatively to Biblical and secular Greek. The number of examples are given for some representative material, and it will be seen that there is a considerable difference between even the more "stylish" parts of the NT and a selection of non-Biblical Greek.

	Genitive before noun	*Genitive after noun*
Mark i-v	none	50
Matthew i-v	i 18	46
Acts (We sections)	xvi 12 xxi 14 xxvii 23,34,42 xxviii 3,17	28
James	3	50
Thucyd. I 89-93	9	7
Philostratus *Vit.Ap.* cc. 1-5	7	7

2. Co-ordinating particles.

The abundance of *kai* and *de* in Mark reflects Hebrew rather than Aramaic use. Moreover, because *waw* must occupy first place in the sentence, Mark prefers *kai* to the second place conjunctions *gar, ge, de, men, oun, te,* and Mark has a *kai: de* proportion of 5:1 (*Grammar* III 332). Mark shares this characteristic with the vernacular too, but this is not to deny that the tendency is Hebraic.

3. Position of the verb in nominal sentences.

Following Hebrew, the copula is almost always in the first-position after the connecting conjunction; the subject immediately follows, and after that the predicate, as in the normal unemphatic and non-interrogative nominal sentence of Hebrew prose.

Exceptions: copula not in first-position v 5; vii 15; xiii 25; xiv 49. Subject not immediately following vii 15; x 32; xiii 25. Where the copula is very closely taken with a ptc, we may be able to distinguish a periphrastic tense from the predicate ptc. e.g. v 5; x 32. Other exceptions are: the placing of a pronoun, etc. first in the sentence for emphasis, where (as in Hebrew) it avoids becoming "a mere appendage to a subject which consists of several words" (e.g. II Kings ii 19 "*good* is the word of Yahweh which you have spoken"); E. Kautzsch, *Gesenius' Hebrew Grammar*, 2nd English ed. by A. E. Cowley, Oxford 1910, § 141n. Also exceptions to the primary position of the verb are iv 38; xiii 25; xv 23, but they are not exceptions to the Hebrew order in nominal sentences without the copula (subject-predicate). Nor is xiv 49 an exception, because *daily* represents the adverbial phrase which may stand at the beginning of a Hebrew nominal sentence (e.g. Genesis iv 7).

4. Position of the verb in verbal sentences.

Contrary to the usual way in non-Biblical Greek, the NT verb tends towards the beginning of the sentence. For instance, the verb in Herodotus has mainly the middle position, according to Kieckers (initial/middle/final: 47/167/71). It is a matter of tendency only. In good prose of the fifth and fourth centuries, the subject tends to precede its verb (K.J.Dover, *Greek Word Order* (Cambridge, 1966) ch. III), but classical authors vary so much that no principle appears to lie behind their choice of word-order; it is rather a matter of emphasis in each particular context. So it is, to some extent, in Biblical Greek; however, here there is definite influence from the normal Hebrew pattern of verbal sentences: verb — subject — object (*Grammar* III 347f). The Biblical Greek verb is followed by personal pronoun, subject, object, supplementary participle — often in that order, which owes everything to Hebrew and nothing to Aramaic, where the verb tends to end the clause, viz. subject — object — verb. Normally in Hebrew the subject immediately follows the verb unless a pronominal object is involved, for that will be inseparable from the verb and will precede the subject.

On our view that Mark's style is largely Hebraic, therefore, a radical change is probably involved in the rendering of Mark ii 15f, which will have to be: "For they were many. There followed him also some scribes of the Pharisees. They noticed him eating ..." The only translation, to our knowledge, which takes this point is the British and Foreign Bible Society's *Mark. A Greek-English Diglot for the Use of Translators*, London 1958, 6.

Also preceding the subject will be a prepositional phrase which includes a pronominal suffix, for that too goes closely with the verb. However, a prepositional phrase which includes a noun will follow the subject, which makes probable the translation of Mark vi 26 as: "he was grieved because of his oaths and guests" (Diglot 15; *Grammar* III 350). A relative phrase immediately with '^{a}*sher*, and a genitive of quality, occur after the noun they qualify; so in Biblical and translation Greek, a prepositional phrase immediately follows the noun which it qualifies, usually with repetition of the definite article; i.e. it does not occur between article and noun as in secular Greek, and even in the free Greek books of the LXX to some extent (M.Johannessohn, *Der Gebrauch der Präpositionen in der LXX*, Berlin 1926, 362ff).

§ *4. Semitic Influence on the Style of Mark*

By "Semitic" we understand those features of syntax which may be either Hebrew or Aramaic; it is not always possible to decide which is the more likely when they are common to both Semitic languages.

Parataxis.

Except in v 4, 25, 27, Mark rather studiously avoids subordinate clauses, in the way of vernacular Greek. The tendency would be Hebraic and Aramaic too; indeed, *kai* is so commonly used in the LXX to render the Hebrew subordinating *waw* that Mark's *kai* may probably be said to have a subordinating function too.

E.g. iv 27 "*while* he rises night and day, the seed sprouts," viii 34 "*if* he will take up his cross, let him follow me," xv 25 "*when* it was the third hour, they crucified him." Perhaps add i 6,11; iv 38; v 21; vii 30; vi 45D. A.B.Davidson, *Hebrew Syntax* 3, Edinburgh 1901, § 141; S.R.Driver, *A Treatise on the Use of the Tenses in Hebrew*[3], London 1892, § 166ff; E. Kautzsch, §§ 116,u, 142,e; *Grammar* ll 423; Black[3] 66f.

Redundancy.

Mark's style tends to be diffuse (cf. Lagrange, *Marc* lxxii-lxxv; *Grammar* II 419f; Taylor, *Mark* 50-52). It tends to repeat apparent synonyms, as also do some other NT authors to a less extent: e.g. *the house's householder* (Luke xxii 11), *straightway immediately* (Acts xiv 10D), *again a second time* (Acts x 15), *return again* (Acts xviii 21; Gal i 17; iv 9), *again the second* (John iv 54), *then after this* (John xi 7 *v.l.*). This, it has been suggested, is an Aramaic mannerism, but it belongs to Hebrew too, corresponding to the parallelism of Semitic speech.

Here are some examples of Mark's redundancy: i 28 *everywhere, in all the district*, 32 *when evening was come, when the sun was set*, 35 *early morning, very early;* ii 25, *he had need, and was hungry;* iv 2 *he taught, and said in his teaching*, 39 *be quiet, be muzzled;* v 15 *the possessed man, the man who had the legion*, 19 *to your home, to your family*, 39 *why ... distressed, why ... weeping?;* vi 4 *family, relatives, home*, 25 *immediately, with haste;* vii 21 *from within, from the heart*, 33 *away from the crowd, on his own;* viii 17 *know, or understand;* ix 2 *privately, alone;* xii 44 *all that she had, all her livelihood;* xiii 19 *the creation, which God created,* 20 *the predestined, whom he predestinated;* xiv 1 *the Passover, and Unleavened Bread,* 18 *at a meal, and eating,* 30 *to-day, to-night,* 61 *he was silent, and answered nothing;* xv 26 *the superscription, which was superscribed.*

The Pleonastic Auxiliary.

Mark is fond of the redundant auxiliary *began to*; it occurs 26 times, and a further three times in D, easily seen in the concordance, and evenly distributed throughout the Gospel. Matthew reduces these instances to six; Luke to two; yet Luke adds 25 others, and it is a Lukan stylistic feature, since 13 are in Proto-Luke. Since Aramaic used *shārî* as an auxiliary verb the idiom has been claimed as a pure Aramaism for the Gospels, and yet the matter cannot be decisive since we have the Hebrew *y'l* hiph. and the late Hebrew *tḥl* hiph. as well as the Latin *incipere*. The verb is relatively frequent in the Testament of Abraham, rec. A (lxxxii 19; lxxxiii 34; cx 25), on each occasion as pleonastic as in the Gospels, without any trace of direct Aramaic influence, but rather of Hebrew.

Black[3] 125f; J.H. Hunkin, *JTS* 25 (1926) 390-402; 28 (1929) 352f; Allen, *Mark* 49f; *Grammar* I 14f; II 455f; Taylor, *Mark* 48, 63f; Lagrange, *Marc* XCIII. C.H.Turner Note VIII (ii).

The Historic Present.

Mark has 151 examples, although there are 151 also in John; and 52 of Mark's concern verbs of speaking. Thackeray suggested that, except with verbs of speaking, Mark indicates thereby a new scene and fresh characters (*The Septuagint and Jewish Worship*, Oxford 1923, 21). The tense is characteristic of vivid narrative in most languages; it may owe something to Aramaic influence in Mark, but it should be noted to the contrary that the historic present occurs some 330 times in the LXX, and thus Hebrew influence is very apparent. As well as Semitic influence, there may have been something theological behind the large use of this tense in Mark. T.A.Burkill reviews with approval Trocmé's view that from Mark's post-resurrection theological viewpoint the past record of Jesus' doings are "construed in terms of the present," and the acts and words of the Crucified One are now being said and done by the living and risen Christ (*New Light on the Earliest Gospel*, Ithaca, N.Y., 1972, 185f).

Periphrastic Tenses. Though these proliferate in Mark, they were not favoured in vernacular Greek (cf. Moulton–Milligan 184f), nor by subsequent copiers and correctors of the NT text, for there are variant readings at Mark i 39; ii 4; iii 1; v 11,40; ix 4; xiii 25; xiv 4; xv 26. They were, however, characteristic of Aramaic and of Hebrew, as witness the LXX. In Biblical Greek they abound more than anywhere else.

Periphrastic imperfect: i 6,13,22,39 ACDW; ii 4,6,18; iii 1; iv 38; v 5,11,40; ix 4; x 22,32(bis); xiv 4,40,49,54; xv 40,43. Present: v 41; vii 15; xv 22,34. Perfect or Plupf.: i 6,33; vi 52; xiv 21D; xv 7,26,46. Future: xiii 13,25. M.-J.Lagrange, *Évangile selon Saint Matthieu* [8], Paris 1948, xci; J. de Zwaan, "The Use of the Septuagint in Acts," *The Beginnings of Christianity*, ed. F.J.Foakes Jackson, K.Lake, London 1922, II 62: P.Chantraine, *Histoire du Parfait Grec*, Paris 1907, ch. IX.

The Article.

1. Aramaic *nāsh* and Hebrew *'îsh* are rendered literally in Mark as indefinite article i 23; vii 11 etc. (cf. concordance under *anthrōpos*). 2. The use of the definite article displays some inconsistency in Mark. Black, following Wensinck, considers that the anomalous practice of all the evangelists may have been influenced by the disappearance of the formal distinction between definite and indefinite nouns in Aramaic, and makes the credible suggestion that Aramaic influence led to some confusion in the normal speech of Greek-speaking Jews. It can further be seen in Paul. Black[3] 93.

Pronouns.

1. The incidence of a resumptive personal pronoun, used after a relative, is too widespread in the Gospels to be explained as vernacular Greek without Semitic influence. It is due either to the *d*[e] construction of Aramaic or, just as likely, to *'*[a]*sher ... lô* in Hebrew.

Mark i 7; vii 25 share the idiom with Biblical Greek in general, e.g. LXX Gen xxviii 13; Matthew iii 12; x 11D; xviii 20D; Luke viii 12D; xii 43D; John i 27,33; ix 36?; xiii 26; xviii 9; Rev iii 8; vii 2,9; xii 6,14; xiii 8,12; xvi 19; xvii 9; xx 8.

2. The construction which allows an expression in casus pendens to be followed by a resumptive personal pronoun is to some extent secular but, alongside all the other evidence for Semitisms, it is more probable that a Semitic idiom lies behind the Greek of Mark and John. While it is possible in Aramaic, it is more likely to have come by way of the LXX, as in Mark's own quotation at xii 10 (cf. also Gen xxxi 16).

Mark i 34D (*and those who had devils he cast them out of them*), vi 16 (*John whom I beheaded, he is risen*), vii 20 (*that which goes out, this defiles*), xiii 11 (*whatever is given you, this speak*).

3. The high incidence of the oblique cases of *autos* is a Semitic tendency due to the pronominal suffix, although the similar tendency in the vernacular doubtless exerted some influence. Arranged in order of Semitic (or vernacular) influence in this respect, Mark, Matthew and John rank the highest in the NT with a figure of one occurrence of superfluous cases of *autos* every two lines, whereas the papyri have one every 13 lines.

Prepositions.

1. The repetition of the preposition before two or more phrases is a prominent feature of Biblical Greek, based on the Semitic practice. It is very pronounced in the style of Mark and Revelation, and least in evidence in that of Luke-Acts and the Pastoral Epistles.

It is particularly marked in the Western text: iii 7 *from Galilee and from Judaea and from Jerusalem and from Idumaea;* v 1; vi 26D *because of his oaths and because of his guests*, 36D *into the fields and into the villages*, 56; viii 31D *of the elders and of the chief priests*; xi 1; xiv 43D *from the chief priests and from the scribes*. *Grammar* III 275; Black[3] 114f.

2. Instrumental *en*.

Although in the vast majority of instances *en* has its fundamental spatial meaning of *in* or *among*, yet there are undoubtedly some important exceptions, not the least of which is the peculiarly Christian usage of this powerful word. Indeed, Mark correctly and more normally has *eis* after *dip* xiv 20 where Matthew has pregnant *en* (Matthew xxvi 23). But in Mark iv 30 *en* must be instrumental (=b^e), as in both Semitic Greek and the Koine (*with what parable shall we set forth the kingdom?*). Sometimes Mark's *en* is temporal: in *rowing* vi 48. The *en dolo* of xiv 1 shows how close we are to the instrumental sense: *by means of guile*. In i 23; v 2 the man is *with* an unclean spirit, but here we may meet the Christian sense of spatial *en* in a spiritual dimension: the man was *in the sphere of* the demon. This is more frequent in the Johannine writings.

En is not likely to express motion in Mark. Except for *epi* c. acc. twice, Mark's rule is invariable for expressing motion after *erchesthai*: i.e. *eis* (22 times) or *pros* (12 times), and so in v 27; viii 38; xiii 26; the preposition will not express *motion* from place to place, but rather the accompanying circumstances or the sphere in which the motion occurs.

Adjectives and Numerals.

In Semitic languages the positive degree does duty for the comparative and superlative. The only analogy to this in the vernacular is the occasional use of comparative for superlative, but the Biblical Greek use of positive for comparitive and superlative has come from the LXX. The use of the cardinal for the ordinal is recognized as Semitic, in Mark xvi 2 (=Matthew xxviii 1 = Luke xxiv 1 = John xx 1,19), coming into Biblical Greek by way of the LXX (Taylor, *Mark* 60).

Mark ix 43 *good (= better) to enter the Kingdom maimed* 45, 47; xiv 21 *good (=better) for him if he had not been born.* LXX instances: Exod. xxv 33 *the first tabernacle* for *the former*, quoted at Heb. ix 2f.; Can i 8 *fair amongst women* for *fairest.* Cardinal for ordinal: Gen. viii 13; Exod xl 2; Ps 23 (24) tit *one* for *first.*

Other Parts of Speech.

1. Wensinck and Black have observed that there is a characteristic way of using the interrogative particle, *What*? to express sarcasm in Semitic languages (Black[3] 121f). Although most of their parallels are Aramaic it is also a Hebrew feature. The fact that almost all instances are in the words of Jesus is not significant for, as Black concedes, ordinary narra tive does not lend itself to questions.

Wensinck had noted its appearance in Luke (especially the D-text): Luke v 22D,41D; vi 2. Black adds the following from Mark: ii 7 *What? Does this man so speak?*, 8 *What? Are you discussing these things ... ?* 24; iv 40; x 18. (LXX Gen xliv 16 *What? Shall we justify ourselves?* etc.).

2. The pleonastic *thus* after verbs of speaking (Mark ii 7, 8, 12) is more likely to be influenced by the Hebrew *kāzôth* (LXX Jg xiii 23; xv 7; xix 30; Isa lxvi 8 etc.) than the Aramaic *kidnâ* (e.g. Dan ii 10), because it occurs in books with a Hebrew background, e.g. Test.Abr. lxxxv 15; lxxxvi 25; lxxxvii 8 cod.; lxxxviii 16; xcvi 8,10; ciii 31.

3. The imperatival *hina*, a Biblical rather than a secular idiom (*Grammar* III 94f), occurs once or twice in Mark. The evangelist uses *hina* in a non-final sense at least as often as a final. It belongs to post-classical Greek but never occurs in so large a variety and concentration as in Biblical books. It may derive from Hebrew or Aramaic. Cf. the informative article by W.G.Morrice, "The Imperatival ἵνα," *Bible Translator*, 23 (1972) 326-330.

Imperatival: Mark v 23 *Come and lay your hands ... !*; x 51 (=Matthew Luke) *Let me see again!*; xiv 49 *Let the Scriptures be fulfilled!* Epexegetical, after a variety of verbs of command and speaking: iii 9, 12; v 10, 18,

43; vi 8, 12, 25; vii 26, 32, 36; viii 22, 30; ix 9, 18, 30; x 35, 37, 48; xi 16, 28; xii 19; xiii 18, 34; xiv 35, 38; xv 21. Ecbatic: vi 2D *so that mighty deeds are wrought by his hands*; xi 28 *who gave you authority so that you do this?*

Word Order.

1. Position of the adjective.

The practice of joining the article and its noun closely together reflects the Semitic necessity to join them as one word. Thus it happens that in a kind of Greek which is influenced by Semitic forms, any matter which qualifies the noun tends to be placed in a separate and subsequent articular phrase, in contrast with secular style which avoids this almost completely.

The table below, arranged in descending order, will illustrate the closeness of Mark's style to that of Rev and the LXX (Gen), and its contrast with that of the vernacular. (The table includes adjectival phrases but not cardinal numerals. Papyri statistics are from Mayser II 2, 54 and involve pap. Tebtunis nos. 5-124).

The close link between def.art. and noun is a feature of the LXX, where separation occurs in only 4% of the incidence of the art. in translated books; in 11% of the incidence in non-translated books, and in 18% of the incidence in the NT epistles (according to the research of J.M.Rife, "The Mechanics of Translation Greek," *JBL* 52 [1933] 247). The NT epistles thus stand halfway between the LXX on the one hand and non-Biblical Greek on the other (Philostratus *Vit.Ap.* 28%; Thucydides I 89-93 39%). On these estimates, Mark, Matthew, Luke's Infancy, document L, and Rev 1-3 stand very much nearer to Semitic Greek than do the epistles (Mark i-iii: 4·7%; Matthew i 8-iv end: 14%; Luke's Infancy: 3·3%; L: 6·5%; Rev i-iii: 9·4%).

	Between art.and noun	*In subsequent articular phrase*	*Proportion*
Papyri of ii-i/BC	140	4 or 5	28:1
Philostratus (sample)	27	1	27:1
Hebrews	15	10	1·5:1
Acts (We)	4	4	1:1
James	7	8	1:1
Rev i-iii	5	16	1:3·2
LXX Gen i-xix	17	56	1:3·3
Mark	7	27	1:3·8
Luke i,ii	2	8	1:4
Rev iv-xxii	21	107	1:5

2. The post-position of demonstrative adjectives.

Again Biblical Greek follows the precedent set by Semitic word-order, and invariably places the adjective after its noun. But this is not as significant as the figures above, because it is only in the translated books of the LXX that there is a spectacular difference between Biblical and non-Biblical Greek in this respect. However, in the frequency of the demonstrative adjective itself there is a marked difference between Biblical and non-Biblical Greek, especially in the attributive use, which is very rare in the Ptolemaic papyri (Mayser II 2, 79-82).

	Pre-positive	*Post-positive*	*Proportion*
Mark	14	31/32	1:2
Matthew	23/24	76/79	1:3
Luke	28	95	1:3
John	32/33	36/38	1:1
Revelation	5	12	1:2·4
LXX: Gen Exod	1	54	1:54
Judith	1	10	1:10
2-4 Mac	4	8	1:2
Philostratus *Vit.Ap.*I	9	22	1:2
Thucyd.II 1-34	9	15	1:1·6

In the following two tables, the figures for the NT agree closely with the LXX, except that Paul, John and Wisdom are less Semitic in this respect. With these exceptions the figures differ markedly from the secular papyri. Even as early as the third century B.C., thirteen examples of independent *ekeinos* were discovered by Mayser for only two attributive (N.Turner, "The Unique Character of Biblical Greek" *VT* 5 (1955) 208-213).

Use of *ekeinos* (NT)

	Independent	Attributive	Proportion
Matthew	4	50	1:12
Luke-Acts	6	50	1:8
Mark	5	18	1:3·6
Revelation	—	2	—
Heb., James, 2 Pet.	6	6	1:1
Pastorals	4	3	1:0·75
Paul	9	4	1:0·5
John and 1 John	59	18	1:0·3

Use of *ekeinos* (LXX)

	Independent	Attributive	Proportion
Minor Prophets	1	59	1:59
Judges	—	36	—
Early Kingdoms	2	69	1:35
Chronicles	—	30	—
Jeremiah	1	30	1:30
Isaiah	2	56	1:28
Daniel LXX	—	28	—
1 Maccabees	2	56	1:28
2 Esdras-Nehemiah	—	26	—
Late Kingdoms	—	25	—
Pentateuch	8	159	1:20
Ezekiel	2	24	1:12
Daniel Th.	2	23	1:11·5
Joshua	2	22	1:11
Judith	2	11	1:5·5
Esther	—	3	—
1 Esdras	3	8	1:3
Job	3	8	1:3
Tobit א	2	5	1:2·5
Psalms	1	2	1:2
Ecclesiastes	—	1	—
Tobit B	1	1	1:1
2-4 Maccabees	14	13	1:1
Proverbs	3	2	1:0·6
Wisdom	12	6	1:0·5
Sirach	1	—	—

§ 5. *Mark's Mannered Style*

Apart from the redundancy which we have already noticed in discussing Semitic features of style, there are other stylistic features of a stereotyped nature which are not necessarily Semitic.

His mannered style is most conspicuous perhaps in his over-use of participles, which incidentally is often reminiscent of Semitic style. The concordance should be consulted for such redundant words as *coming, leaving, rising, answering,* and *saying.*

Accumulation of particles: Mark i 31,41; v 25ff *there being a woman ... having suffered ... having spent ... not having benefited ... coming ... hearing ... coming*; xiv 67; xv 43 (*Grammatical Insights* 66).

Redundant negatives are another contribution to Mark's distinctly heavy style, though several other NT authors share this habit, and it is common in earlier secular authors.

Mark i 44 *see you say nothing to no one*; ii 2 *room for no one not even at the door*; iii 20 *not able not even to* ... , 27 *no one was not able to enter* ... ; v 3 *no one had been able to bind him not yet not even with chains*, 37; vi 5; vii 12; ix 8; xi 14; xii 14,34; xiv 25,60; xv 5; xvi 8.

Mark is particularly fond of clumsy parentheses, often delayed to such an extent that the reader is confused and sometimes entirely misled. Thus, in ii 15, if the parenthesis is restored to its rightful place, the sentence will read: "While Jesus was dining at home many publicans and sinners (there were many such who followed him) came and joined Jesus and his disciples. There followed him also the scribes of the Pharisees." We may do the same for vi 15: "John the Baptist is risen and therefore mighty powers are at work in him, like one of the prophets (some said that he was Elijah and others that he was a prophet)."

Parentheses are very common; we give but a selection: i 2f; ii 10f, 15, 22, 26b; v 42; vi 14f; vii 2f, 11, 19, 25-26a; viii 15, 38-41; xi 32; xii 12a; xiii 10, 14; xiv 36; xvi 3f, 7f. C.H.Turner, Note IV; M.Zerwick, *Untersuchungen zum Markus-stil,* Rome 1937, 130-138; *Grammatical Insights* 64-66.

Another factor contributing to heaviness of style is Mark's inclination to alternate the normal imperfect (220 times) with the sonorous periphrastic imperfect (25 times). C.H.Turner suggested (Note VIII (i)) that the periphrastic imperfect was intended to be the true imperfect, referring to continuous action in the past, and that Mark uses the normal imperfect form as the equivalent of an aorist (doubted by V.Taylor, *Mark* 45). Swete's view was that the normal imperfect-form is used when an eye witness is vividly describing events which took place under his very eyes, especially v 18; vii 17; x 17; xii 41; xiv 55. Just as plausible is the view that the normal imperfect-form represents the conative imperfect, since it is appropriate at ix 38 *we tried to forbid* xv 23 *they tried to give him*.

In addition to the heaviness of style, and germane to it, it is what we choose to call the iconographic nature of Mark's Greek. To some extent all the NT authors share it, but especially Mark and Revelation. They eschew literary virtuosity, conventional rules of syntax, and they succeed in evoking a numinous sense to point the reader upwards by the unclassical barbarism of the style. This is seen particularly in a feature which we must now consider, the over-use of stereotyped expressions and the preference for a set formula. Vincent Taylor assumed that such features were part of the ancient tradition which Mark received (*Mark* 53), but they are characteristic of the evangelist himself and they abound throughout his work. In this respect the language does justice to his somewhat stereotyped theme: viz. to explain the humiliation and passion of Jesus by showing that "the true status of Jesus was a predetermined secret" (T.A.Burkill, *Mysterious Revelation,* Ithaca, N.Y., 1963, 319; cf. also the sequel, *New Light on the Earliest Gospel,* Ithaca 1972, especially 184f, 198f, 214f, 263). This is the theological standpoint which will be found most helpful for the understanding of Mark's mysterious iconographic language. Theologically and linguistically all is predetermined, nothing left to human art or device, all conforming to an iconographic pattern.

Rigidity of style is apparent in some of the repeated expressions: iii 12; viii 30 *he charged them to*; v 43; vii 36; ix 9 *he strictly charged them to*; iii 5,34; x 23 *he looked around ... and said*; i 31; v 41; ix 27 *he took ... by the hand*; vii 17; ix 28,33; x 10 *he entered the house*; viii 27; ix 33; x 32 *on the road.*

This poverty of expression must be deliberate, for it is not due to lack of skill in Greek composition on the part of Mark: he can properly employ his tenses (e.g. v 15ff; vi 14ff; vii 35; ix 15; xv 44), preserving the correct distinction between perfect and aorist, imperfect and aorist, which was quite beyond the powers of some contemporary writers.

The aor. is correctly followed by impf. at vi 41 *he broke* (aor.) *the loaves and kept giving* (impf.). Cf. v 15 *he is in process of being possessed* (pres.), *because he has received the devils* (perf.). In v 18 the aor. ptc. (*the once possessed*) represents the man who in v 15 was constantly possessed (pres. ptc.). The distinction of aor. and perf. is carefully preserved in v 19 (*what the Lord has done for him,* as a finished work, *and did have mercy upon him,* a single act in the past), and xv 44f (*Pilate marvelled that he was already dead* (perf.) ... *and asked if he died* (aor.) *very long ago*). Swete, *Mark* xlix; *Grammar* III 69.

So when Mark economizes, it is deliberately, and not through inadequate knowledge of syntax. Rather than resort to proper names unduly, he will economize with *ho de* and *hoi de,* often to the reader's confusion, and thus marks a change of subject which might have been done more clearly by the use of a proper name. But here he is imitating a classical Greek device, though doubtless the classical writers would have been less ambiguous. The only exception to Mark's rigid use of the *ho de/hoi de* device for change of subject is at x 32, as far as can be discovered, and then it is only apparent, for the witnesses which read *kai* or *kai ho* are probably correct (A, fam 13, etc.), as against *hoi de* in ℵ, B, fam[1], 565, etc. This rigid feature of style is not so much "harsh" (Rawlinson) as "iconographic."

Quite as economical and enigmatic is the phrase *καὶ ἰδὼν αὐτὸν τὸ πνεῦμα συνεσπάραξεν αὐτόν* (ix 20), which seems to defy the laws of language, but Mark may have had some such model as LXX Exod ix 7 in mind: *ἰδὼν δὲ Φαραώ ... ἐβαρύνθη ἡ καρδία Φαραώ*, and perhaps Herm. M. v 14; vii 5.

The vocabulary is economical, too, limited to 1270 words, and specially weak in particles (another feature of Semitic Greek). He has only 80 NT hapax, and only five words entirely peculiar to himself. These are all words compounded with a preposition, of which he is specially fond: *ἐκπερισσῶς* and *ὑπερπερισσῶς*, *ἐπιράπτω*, *ἐπισυντρέχω*, *προμεριμνάω*. Whether Mark invented such words it is impossible to say; they may have belonged to the vocabulary of this circle of iconographic writers, whose habit it was to build up new words from old ones. To us it seems unlikely that he would be much given to invention, for variety is not to his taste: he overworks certain words and expressions, *immediately, which is, why?, again, much, amazed, bring.* In some ways we can detect a tendency towards the vernacular, in that he uses diminutive words which bear no diminutive force: *little daughter, little fish, little girl, small child, little shoe, small morsel, small ear,* but perhaps *little dog* and *little boat* are true diminutives; and he has the vernacular *krabattos.*

One striking example of the economy of vocabulary is the load which *eis* is made to carry, being used 165 times. The overworked preposition appears in some very interesting contexts: viz. with *baptize IN, descend UPON, preach TO, sit ON, beat IN the synagogues, to be AT home or IN the field, speak IN the village, become (into) one flesh, spread ON the road, blaspheme AGAINST.* Nevertheless the idea of motion seems to be included in most of the instances of *eis*, and it is not simply a case of confusion with *en*.

In conclusion, the impression derived from a survey of Mark's style is that he is manipulating none too skilfully but with a curious overall effectiveness, a stereotyped variety of Greek, rather inflexible and schematized, adhering to simple and rigid rules.

Thus, if he uses *pros* with verbs of speaking, it is always before *heautous* and *allēlous*: iv 41; x 26 ADW; xii 7; xvi 3; in the two apparent exceptions, it really goes with the preceding verb xi 31; xii 6 and once it means *against* xii 12. His use of *palin* and *euthus* follows rigid rules: at the beginning of the clause they are mere conjunctions, but adverbial elsewhere (*Grammar* III 229). His use of recitative *hoti* is no less rigid; his rule apparently is not to employ it after a recitative *legōn*, avoiding two recitatives in juxtaposition, for to his mind they both perform the same function, that of quote marks. When in fact they occur together, some 11 times, the *legōn* is not recitative for the main verb is other than one of speaking; where it seems to be recitative (i.e. with *answer, glorify, cry, bear false witness*) then there is always a variant omitting *hoti* and this will probably be correct — unless we are presuming to invent Mark's own rules for him.

§ 6. *Latinisms in the Gospels*

Some features of Marcan style recall Latin constructions and vocabulary. That they are probably more frequent in Mark than in other NT texts, except the Pastoral epistles, may raise the question whether Mark was written in Italy in a kind of Greek that was influenced by Latin. However, supposing that his language is influenced in that way, we presume that it could have happened as well in the Roman provinces.

Syntax.

Whereas Latin influence is possible but improbable in certain simplifications within the Greek language itself, the aoristic perfect, the omission of the definite article, the use of subjunctive to replace optative, the periphrastic tenses, yet the following constructions have some probability, inasmuch as they tend to occur in the particularly Roman parts of the Gospel.

ii 23 *make a way* may be *iter facio,* but it may as well be a Hebraism *'sh derek,* LXX Jg xvii 8, which seems more likely in view of the considerable Hebraic evidence above. iii 6ℵ; xv 1B *making consultation* may be *consilium facere* (*capere*), xiv 65 *received him with blows* may be *verberibus recipere,* xv 15 *make satisfaction* may be *satisfacere* (cf. also Hermas Sim. 6.5.5), xv 19 *place the knees* may be *genua ponere* (= Luke xxii 41; Acts vii 60; ix 40; xx 36; xxi 5; Herm. Vis. 1.1.3; 2.1.2; 3.1.5). But some have found a non-official Latinism in v 43: *he commanded to be given her to eat* may be the construction *duci eum iussit.*

Vocabulary.

Several of Mark's words are obviously transliterations from Latin, and some of them are in other gospels too, but there is nothing very remarkable about transliterations and loan-words, for they occur in all languages.

Aitia = *causa* (papyri). *Census* (papyri). *Crabattus* (papyri). *Denarius* (papyri). *Phragelloō* = *fragellare*. *Praetorius* (papyri). *Kodrantēs* = *quadrans*. The following words are found only in Mark among the gospels: *centurio, xestēs* = *sextarius, speculator.* Luke has avoided some Latin words of Mark but he still has *assarion* (= Matthew), a Greek diminutive of the Roman *as* (one-sixteenth of a denarius), *sudarium* (= John, Ac), *legio* (Matthew Mark Luke), and *modius* (Matthew Mark Luke).

Extent of the Latinism.

In addition to these Matthew has *mille, custodia* and *rationes conferre* xviii 23 (cast up accounts). Luke has *satis accipere* Acts xvii 9, *fora aguntur* xix 38 (cf. also the D-text of Acts, xix 34, 35 marked *ex lat?* in Nestle[25]). Some others are sometimes cited, but their resemblance to Latin would seem to be incidental. The integrity of Hellenistic Greek, outside the NT, was not seriously contaminated by Latinisms, and this is not really surprising, for we would expect subject peoples to avoid aping the conqueror's language. T. A. Burkill very plausibly considers that the use of *legiōn* in connection with the demoniac (Mark v 1-20) betrays anti-Roman feeling (*Mysterious Revelation* 93, n. 12), and we would not consider the extent of the borrowing to be much more significant than this. Rather, external influence on Greek would tend to be other than Latin. Greek language and civilization deeply influenced the Romans; the Romans did not influence the Greek language very much (F.-M. Abel, *Grammaire du Grec Biblique*, Paris 1927, xxxvi).

Codex Bezae.

A question which calls for consideration is whether some of the characteristic Semitisms of the Western text are in reality Latinisms: asyndeta and parataxis may perhaps be in this category. Theoretically, asyndeton is as much a Latinism as an Aramaism, especially perhaps when it occurs in Greek books written in Rome, e.g. the *Acts of Pilate* and *Shepherd* of Hermas. Black at any rate thinks not, because the reading involving parataxis will often occur in non-Western MSS alongside the witness of D; moreover, in several instances, it is the Westcott-Hort text which has parataxis and not D (Black[3] 67).

E.P.Sanders, *The Tendencies of the Synoptic Tradition*, Cambridge 1969, 251; Taylor, *Mark* 45; P.L.Couchoud, "L' Évangile de Marc a-t-il été écrit en Latin?" *Revue de l'Histoire des Religions* 94 (1926) 161-192. The main argument of the latter, which concerns MSS and versions, we do not find wholly convincing.

Abbreviated titles found in this chapter are:

Black[3] = M. Black, *An Aramaic Approach to the Gospel and Acts* (Oxford,[3] 1967)

Grammar = J.H. Moulton, *A Grammar of New Testament Greek* (Edinburgh, I,[3]1908); II with W.F. Howard, 1919-29; III by N. Turner, 1963)

Grammatical Insights = N. Turner, *Grammatical Insights into the New Testament* (Edinburgh, 1965)

Lagrange = M-J. Lagrange, *Évangile selon Saint Marc* (Paris,[5]1929)

MM = J.H. Moulton and G. Milligan, *The Vocabulary of the Greek New Testament* (London, 1930)

Mayser = E. Mayser, *Grammatik der griechischen Papyri aus der Ptolomäerzeit* (Berlin and Leipzig, II, 1 1926; II, 2, II, 3 1934)

END NOTE

C.H. Turner's "Notes on Marcan Usage" do not in any way exhaust the features of Mark's grammar and style that may be found within that Gospel. The distinctiveness of the evangelist's Greek has encouraged others to investigate his language. C.H. Turner himself acknowledged on several occasions his indebtedness to Sir John Hawkins bart., *Horae Synopticae*, the second edition of which had been published by Oxford University Press in 1909. Hawkins listed words and phrases characteristic of each of the Synoptic Gospels and also provided statistics bearing on the origin and composition of each Gospel. Among the latter are details about the historic present in Mark, on his use of particles and instances of anacolouthon and asyndeton.

Since Turner's day many other studies, grammars, lexicons and commentaries on Mark have continued along his path, sometimes with acknowledgements to his "Notes". Among recent works are the following:

M. Zerwick, *Untersuchungen zum Markus-Stil: Ein Beitrag zur stilistischen Durcharbeitung des Neuen Testament* (Rome, 1937)

J.C. Doudna, *The Greek of the Gospel of Mark* (Philadelphia, 1961) (=*JBL Monograph Series* 12)

V. Taylor, *The Gospel according to St. Mark* (London, ^{2}1966)

E. Trocmé, *The Formation of the Gospel according to Mark* (London, 1975)

E.J. Pryke, *Redactional Style in the Marcan Gospel* (Cambridge, 1978) (=*SNTS Monograph* 33)

M. Reiser, *Syntax und Stil des Markusevangeliums im Licht der hellenistischen Volksliteratur* (Tübingen, 1984) (=*Wissenschaftliche Untersuchungen zum Neuen Testament* II, 11)

P. Dschulnigg, *Sprache, Redaktion und Intention des Markusevangeliums* (Stuttgart, 1984) especially pp. 18-27 (=*Stuttgarter Biblische Beiträge* 11)

D.P. Peabody, *Mark as Composer* (Leuven and Macon, Georgia, 1987) (=*New Gospel Studies* 1)

F. Neirynck, *Duality in Mark* (Leuven, revised edition 1988) (=*Bibliotheca Ephemeridum Theologicarum Lovaniensium* 31)

J.K.E.

Indexes

1. Marcan Verses
2. Biblical and Other Texts
3. Themes
4. Greek Words

1. INDEX OF MARCAN VERSES

i 1: 137, 140
i 2: 140, 221
i 3: 140
i 4: 4, 140
i 6: 90
i 7: 177
i 8: 74
i 9: 16, 137, 221
i 10: 110
i 13: 54, 90, 217
i 14: 21, 23, 68, 135, 137
i 15: 68, 135, 175, 221
i 16: 16, 37
i 18: 50, 51
i 20: 51
i 21: 4, 16, 39, 121
i 22: 4, 74, 99
i 23: 226, 227
i 24: 122, 175, 193
i 25: 110, 135, 177
i 26: 110
i 27: 74, 109, 175, 183, 192, 208
i 29: 4, 37, 39, 110
i 30: 4, 39
i 32: 4, 13, 99
i 33: 90
i 34: 183
i 35: 42
i 36: 42
i 37: 68
i 38: 102
i 39: 17, 90, 193
i 40: 68, 97, 175, 198
i 41: 126, 194
i 44: 116, 127, 179, 183
i 45: 93, 95, 151, 153, 166, 183

ii 1: 17, 112, 141
ii 2: 4, 151
ii 3: 4, 13, 55
ii 5: 127
ii 6: 90, 134, 175, 182
ii 7: 63, 193
ii 8-9: 193
ii 8: 74, 103
ii 9: 74, 116, 127, 184
ii 10: 24, 182
ii 11: 24, 116
ii 12: 68, 175
ii 13: 49, 112, 140
ii 15: 25, 42, 51, 83, 232
ii 15f: 145
ii 16: 25, 63, 64, 66
ii 17: 69, 74, 183
ii 18: 5, 90, 181
ii 19: 100, 160
ii 21: 74
ii 22: 25, 183
ii 23: 42, 93, 118, 142
ii 25: 74, 100
ii 26: 26, 74
ii 28: 184

iii 1: 5, 99, 100, 112
iii 2: 5
iii 3: 100
iii 4: 184
iii 5: 180
iii 6: 217
iii 7: 43, 50, 51, 140, 141
iii 8: 50
iii 9: 45, 130
iii 10: 100, 126
iii 11: 69, 127, 175, 179
iii 13: 97, 218
iii 13 ff: 84
iii 14: 55
iii 15: 55
iii 20: 95, 113, 140, 158
iii 21: 10, 69
iii 22: 26, 69, 100
iii 23: 95
iii 24: 95
iii 25: 95
iii 26: 95, 183
iii 27: 75, 183
iii 28: 69
iii 29: 100, 183, 221
iii 30: 26, 100, 183
iii 31: 5, 184
iii 32: 5, 140
iii 33: 175, 184, 198
iii 34: 75, 180
iii 35: 75

iv 1: 45, 49, 93, 112, 113, 140, 141
iv 2: 45
iv 4: 55, 184

iv 5: 55, 100
iv 6: 55, 100
iv 7: 17, 55
iv 8: 17, 18, 55, 56
iv 10: 45, 55
iv 11: 181
iv 12: 179, 219
iv 13: 102, 193
iv 14: 151
iv 15: 151
iv 16: 151
iv 17: 100, 151, 183, 184
iv 18: 17, 151
iv 19: 121, 151
iv 20: 17, 18, 56, 151
iv 21: 69, 184, 193
iv 22: 182, 183, 217
iv 24: 75, 179
iv 26: 160
iv 27: 160
iv 28: 184
iv 29: 183
iv 30: 127, 184, 227
iv 31: 159
iv 32: 96, 218
iv 33: 96, 151
iv 34: 45, 48, 181, 198
iv 35: 45
iv 36: 18, 38, 45, 51
iv 38: 90, 121
iv 40: 100, 193
iv 41: 128, 184, 219

v 1-20: 236
v 1: 39
v 2: 39, 227
v 3: 100
v 4: 128, 224
v 5: 90
v 7: 122
v 8: 110
v 9: 134, 175, 177, 183
v 10: 128
v 11: 56, 90, 182
v 12: 177
v 13: 53, 56
v 14: 6, 18
v 15: 100, 179
v 15ff: 233
v 17: 93
v 18: 130, 142, 232
v 19: 116, 183
v 20: 93
v 21-31: 49
v 21: 49, 112, 113
v 22: 195
v 23: 69, 101, 123, 130, 177, 209
v 24: 49, 50, 141
v 25: 55, 224
v 26: 183
v 27: 127, 224
v 28: 69, 127
v 29: 102
v 30: 103, 127
v 31: 127, 180
v 32: 180
v 33: 102
v 34: 19, 116
v 35: 6, 70, 175
v 36: 151, 166
v 38: 39, 179
v 39: 183
v 40: 121
v 41: 124
v 42: 56, 124, 199
v 43: 130

vi 1: 43, 51, 52
vi 2: 93, 177, 183, 193, 201
vi 3: 196, 218
vi 4: 70
vi 5: 96
vi 7: 55, 56, 93
vi 8: 19, 130
vi 9: 57, 124, 183
vi 12: 130
vi 14: 6, 26, 70, 110, 191
vi 14ff: 233
vi 15: 26, 70, 181, 232
vi 16: 181
vi 17-29: 27
vi 17: 128, 183
vi 18: 70, 183
vi 19: 97
vi 20: 128, 173, 183
vi 22: 124, 197
vi 23: 70, 199
vi 24: 191
vi 25: 98, 130, 143, 176, 191
vi 26: 98
vi 27: 13
vi 28: 13, 124
vi 31: 117
vi 33: 7, 103, 117, 158
vi 34: 49, 93, 101, 183
vi 35: 70, 198
vi 37: 53, 57
vi 38: 55, 101, 116
vi 39: 66
vi 40: 57

vi 41: 48, 55, 180, 197
vi 42: 7
vi 43: 7, 55
vi 44: 55
vi 45: 160
vi 48: 57, 97, 227
vi 52: 91, 183
vi 53: 7, 39
vi 54: 7, 39, 103
vi 55: 93
vi 56: 121, 127, 130, 184
vi 56*b*: 127

vii 2: 23, 27
vii 3: 27, 107
vii 4: 27
vii 5: 183
vii 6: 141, 160, 181
vii 6*a*: 70
vii 6*b*: 70
vii 7: 182
vii 10: 184
vii 11: 181, 184, 226
vii 12: 198
vii 13: 151, 167
vii 14: 112, 113
vii 15: 96, 121, 183
vii 17: 45, 232
vii 18: 27, 121, 128, 193
vii 19: 24, 27, 121, 183, 193
vii 20: 70, 181
vii 24: 97
vii 25: 28, 100, 123, 183, 217
vii 26: 28, 130, 134
vii 27: 124
vii 28: 122, 124
vii 29: 116, 151
vii 31: 8, 113
vii 32: 8, 13, 131
vii 33: 127
vii 34: 180
vii 35: 233
vii 36: 131
vii 37: 177

viii 1: 46, 48, 49, 113, 198
viii 2: 55, 183
viii 3: 193
viii 4: 70, 134
viii 5: 55, 101, 134
viii 6: 55
viii 7: 123
viii 8: 55
viii 9: 46, 55, 182
viii 10: 46
viii 11: 93
viii 12: 63, 184
viii 13: 112, 113, 194
viii 14: 28, 57
viii 15: 28, 75, 177, 179
viii 16: 28, 64, 101, 134, 175
viii 17: 28, 64, 99, 101, 103, 175
viii 18: 179
viii 19: 55
viii 20: 55
viii 22: 8, 13, 40, 127, 131
viii 23: 52, 180
viii 24: 179, 180, 183, 193
viii 25: 113, 180, 184, 198, 208, 209
viii 26: 19, 175, 199
viii 27: 43, 177
viii 28: 71, 191
viii 29: 134, 177, 181
viii 30: 131
viii 31: 54, 86, 93
viii 32: 93, 151, 167
viii 33: 116, 183
viii 34: 46, 50, 51, 98
viii 35: 181, 183
viii 36: 182, 183, 221
viii 37: 182, 183
viii 38: 151, 182, 183

ix 2: 57
ix 4: 91, 179, 221
ix 5: 54, 121, 143
ix 6: 183
ix 7: 175
ix 8: 108, 180, 183, 217
ix 9: 131, 134
ix 9*a*: 110
ix 10: 109, 151
ix 11: 63, 64, 175
ix 12: 131, 184
ix 13: 98, 108, 183
ix 14: 40, 46, 48, 49, 198
ix 15: 40, 49, 140, 233
ix 16: 177
ix 17: 14, 100, 111, 121, 134
ix 18: 131
ix 18*a*: 128
ix 18*b*: 128
ix 19: 14, 128, 218
ix 20: 14
ix 21: 160, 177
ix 22: 183
ix 25: 111, 140, 177
ix 26: 173, 217
ix 28: 63, 64, 134, 177
ix 30: 40, 98, 117, 118, 131, 207

ix 31: 54, 71, 86
ix 32: 128
ix 33: 40, 177
ix 34: 199
ix 35: 55
ix 36-42 (38-41): 29
ix 37: 128, 183
ix 38: 38, 51, 52, 75, 121, 175, 183, 199, 232
ix 39: 96, 183
ix 40: 183
ix 41: 71, 183
ix 43: 57
ix 45: 57
ix 49: 199
ix 50: 101, 182

x 1: 8, 49, 112, 113, 118, 140, 158, 199
x 2: 8, 44, 128, 135, 200
x 6: 181, 182, 208
x 8: 183, 184
x 9: 75, 79, 184
x 10: 20, 48, 114, 198
x 13: 8, 43, 48, 127, 198
x 14: 75, 182, 199
x 17: 118, 121, 135, 232
x 19: 104
x 20: 122
x 21: 50, 101, 116, 180
x 22: 91, 151
x 23: 87, 121, 180
x 24: 48, 75, 87, 112, 114, 151, 198
x 25: 75
x 26: 109, 177
x 27: 75, 180, 183
x 28: 50, 75, 93, 142
x 29: 76, 184
x 30: 58
x 32: 40, 50, 55, 71, 94, 114, 128, 142, 182, 233
x 32*a*: 91
x 32*b*: 91
x 33: 51, 71, 86
x 34: 54
x 35: 58, 98, 118, 122, 131, 143, 175
x 35 ff: 87
x 36: 98, 143
x 37: 131
x 38: 184
x 40: 181, 183, 184, 217
x 41: 58, 94
x 43: 183
x 45: 182, 183
x 46: 41, 46, 49, 88, 118, 195
x 47: 94, 122, 137, 142
x 48: 131
x 49: 8, 175
x 51: 121, 131, 143, 180
x 52: 51, 116, 180

xi 1: 41, 58
xi 2: 14, 116, 121
xi 3: 112, 114
xi 7: 14
xi 8: 20, 111, 181
xi 9: 50, 135, 175
xi 11: 41, 55, 180
xi 12: 41
xi 13: 101, 184
xi 15: 41, 94
xi 16: 131
xi 17: 71, 129, 181
xi 18: 49, 140, 193
xi 19: 41
xi 20: 41
xi 21: 41, 121
xi 22: 100
xi 23: 183
xi 24: 201
xi 27: 41, 114
xi 28: 128, 131
xi 29: 151
xi 30: 184
xi 31: 80, 109, 175, 184, 194
xi 32: 108, 141, 183, 208

xii 1: 94, 142
xii 4: 105, 114
xii 5: 181, 184
xii 6: 101, 175, 184, 208
xii 7: 71, 109
xii 8: 80
xii 9: 76, 80, 184
xii 10: 226
xii 12: 102
xii 12*a*: 31, 128
xii 12*b*: 128
xii 13: 128, 151
xii 14: 122
xii 15: 14, 103
xii 16: 14
xii 17: 76
xii 18: 177
xii 19: 71, 122, 131
xii 20: 58, 76
xii 21: 58
xii 23: 76, 80, 182, 184, 194
xii 24: 76
xii 25: 182, 183

xii 26: 176, 182
xii 27: 183, 184
xii 28: 71, 135
xii 29: 71
xii 32: 71, 122, 184
xii 34: 128
xii 36: 76
xii 37: 49, 76, 80, 184
xii 38: 98, 179
xii 41: 46, 179, 232
xii 42: 46, 58, 59
xii 43: 46, 71, 155, 193
xii 44: 181

xiii 1: 111, 118, 122
xiii 2: 59, 180
xiii 3: 20, 135
xiii 5: 76, 94, 142, 179
xiii 6: 72, 76, 175
xiii 7: 76, 183
xiii 8*a*: 76
xiii 8*b*: 76
xiii 9: 8, 20, 31, 179, 182
xiii 10: 8, 21, 31
xiii 11: 8, 31, 183
xiii 14: 32, 182
xiii 15: 21
xiii 16: 21
xiii 17: 182
xiii 18: 182
xiii 19: 208
xiii 20: 108, 183
xiii 21: 184
xiii 22: 182
xiii 23: 77, 179, 181
xiii 24: 108, 183
xiii 26: 179
xiii 27: 59
xiii 28: 102, 182
xiii 29: 102
xiii 30: 72
xiii 31: 151, 181
xiii 32: 182, 184, 217
xiii 33: 102, 179
xiii 34: 77, 131
xiii 35: 59, 80, 102, 184
xiii 36: 52

xiv 1: 10, 59, 128, 182, 227
xiv 2: 141
xiv 3: 77, 218
xiv 4: 109, 133, 182
xiv 5: 53, 60, 96, 155, 182
xiv 6: 77
xiv 7: 96, 97
xiv 8: 77, 101
xiv 10: 55, 89, 105, 128, 198
xiv 11: 128
xiv 12-17: 88
xiv 12: 9, 43, 129, 131, 143
xiv 13: 43, 60, 116
xiv 14: 72, 129
xiv 16: 48, 198
xiv 17: 43, 55
xiv 18: 42, 72
xiv 19: 77, 94
xiv 20: 21, 55, 60, 89, 227
xiv 21: 117, 181, 183, 184
xiv 22: 42
xiv 25: 72, 111, 220
xiv 26: 42, 52
xiv 27: 42, 72, 183
xiv 28: 108, 183
xiv 29: 108, 183
xiv 30: 60, 72, 129
xiv 31: 136
xiv 32: 42, 89
xiv 33: 94
xiv 35: 131
xiv 36: 33, 108, 183
xiv 38: 181, 184
xiv 39: 114, 151
xiv 40: 91, 112, 114
xiv 41: 61, 77
xiv 42: 129
xiv 43: 55, 89
xiv 44: 177, 182
xiv 45: 121
xiv 47: 125, 129
xiv 48: 159
xiv 49: 91, 108, 183, 218
xiv 50: 52
xiv 53: 158
xiv 54: 50, 91
xiv 55: 232
xiv 57: 72
xiv 57f: 176
xiv 58: 61, 72
xiv 60: 64, 177
xiv 61: 115
xiv 62: 179
xiv 63: 77, 129
xiv 64: 77, 135
xiv 65: 94, 129
xiv 67: 137, 180
xiv 68: 60, 176
xiv 69: 72, 94, 112, 115, 142
xiv 70: 115, 182
xiv 71: 73, 94
xiv 72: 73, 129, 142, 160

xiv 72*a*: 60
xiv 72*b*: 60

xv 1: 50, 61
xv 2: 135
xv 4: 115, 177
xv 6: 182
xv 7: 91, 182
xv 8: 11, 94
xv 9: 11, 143, 175
xv 10: 11, 200
xv 11: 11, 132, 200
xv 12: 80, 115, 143, 184
xv 13: 115, 136
xv 14: 136, 182
xv 15: 132
xv 18: 94
xv 20: 132
xv 21: 132, 195
xv 22: 14
xv 23: 232
xv 25: 61, 182
xv 26: 91
xv 29: 176
xv 31: 129
xv 33: 61
xv 34: 33, 61, 134, 175
xv 36: 176
xv 39: 182
xv 40: 92, 179, 182
xv 41: 52
xv 43: 92
xv 44: 233
xv 46: 92
xv 47: 179

xvi 2: 228
xvi 3: 34, 109, 111
xvi 4: 34, 179, 180
xvi 6: 23, 77, 137
xvi 6*b*: 78
xvi 7: 34, 73, 89, 108, 117, 129, 179, 183
xvi 9-20: 203

2. INDEX OF BIBLICAL AND OTHER TEXTS

Gen. i 4: 221
xxvii 28: 220
xxxi 16: 226
xlix 15, 21: 218

Num. xxiii 4: 206

2 Sam. xi 17: 220

3 Reg. xviii 4, 13: 57

1 Chron. xvii 6: 65

Isa. xlii 1; lxii 4: 220

Dan. ii 18; vi 9, 18: 217

1 Macc. vi 48: 220

Matt. ii 41: 217
iv 25: 51
viii 1: 51
ix 18: 209
ix 36: 195
x 1: 84
x 2: 56
xii 15: 51
xiii 2: 49
xiv 1: 137, 138
xiv 2: 191
xiv 8: 191
xiv 13: 51
xiv 14: 195
xv 17: 157
xv 32: 195
xvi 14: 191
xviii 23: 236
xx 17: 138
xx 30: 137, 138
xx 34: 195
xxi 1: 138
xxi 8: 49
xxi 12: 138
xxi 37: 208
xxvi 8: 138
xxvi 51: 138
xxviii 9: 138
xxviii 15: 152

Luke i 3: 209
ii 33, 41, 43: 196
ii 52: 137, 138
iii 21: 137, 138
iii 23: 138
iv 1: 137, 138
iv 8: 138
v 8: 138
v 10: 138
v 15: 151
vi 19: 49
vii 9: 51
vii 12: 49
vii 17: 152
viii 2: 206
ix 1: 55
ix 8: 206
ix 11: 51
ix 19: 191
ix 36: 138
ix 49: 52, 199
ix 50: 138
x 1: 56
xiii 17: 49
xviii 40: 139
xxii 11: 224
xxii 39: 52
xxii 48: 139
xxii 52: 139
xxiii 28: 139
xxiii 29: 51
xxiv 15: 139

John i 8: 206
i 16: 193
i 18, 33: 206
ii 9: 160
ii 11, 23: 209
iii 2: 209
iii 27: 195
iv 54: 224
vi 2: 209
vi 12: 7
vi 14: 209
ix 36: 195
xi 2: 195
xi 7: 224
xii 3: 195

Acts i 2: 210
i 5: 209
i 9, 11: 210
i 13: 56
i 22: 210
vi 13: 193
x 15: 224
xi 24: 49
xi 26: 47, 49
xiv 10: 224
xvi 12: 195
xvii 9: 236
xviii 21: 224
xix 26: 49
xix 38: 236
xxi 28: 193
xxiv 21: 209

Rom. iv 3: 67
ix 7: 193
viii 15: 33

1 Cor. i 10, 15, 17: 217
xv 3-5: 89
xv 5, 6-8: 44

2 Cor. viii 23: 44

Gal. i 17: 224
iv 6: 33
iv 9: 224

Phil. ii 25: 44

Col. ii 2: 195

2 Thess. ii 6, 7: 32

1 Tim. iii 2: 210
iv 6: 209

2 Tim. iii 10: 209
iii 15: 211

Heb. iv 14: 210

1 Pet. iii 22: 210

Rev. i 13: 159
xiii 18: 32
xiv 14: 159
xxi 14: 44

Testament of Abraham lxxxii 19: 225
lxxxiii 34: 225
lxxxvii 7: 217
cix 23: 217
cx 25: 225

Barnabas Epistle: 66

Cyprian *de eccl. unit.* **22:** 106
ep. **lii 1:** 105
lix 2: 106
Ps.-Cypr. *ad Nouatianum* **14:** 106

Hermas *Mand.* **iii 2:** 104
Mand. **viii 5:** 104
Similitudes: 65
II 10: 65
V 6.4: 65
VI 5. 5: 105
VIII 1.4: 65
VIII 2.8: 66
VIII 6. 2: 65

Irenaeus *adv.hereses.***:** 67
II xxxii 1 (xlviii 4): 120
III xxxi [xxii] 2: 67
IV x 1 [v 3]: 67

Jerome *Tractatus in Marc.* **xiii 32-33 et xiiii 3-6:** 156

Martyrium Polycarpi **vi 1, 2:** 106

Pliny *ep. ad Traianum* **96:** 104

Tertullian *ad Scapulam* **4:** 120
de fuga **12:** 120

3. INDEX OF THEMES

Absence of λέγων (λέγοντες) after verbs introducing a statement or a question: 133
Active impersonal plural: 216
Adjective:
  Position of the adjective: 229
  Adjectives and Numerals comparative and superlative: 228
  Post-position of demonstrative adjectives: 230
Adverbial *polla*: 218
Aramaic Influence: 215
Article:
  The Article: 226
  Articular infinitive: 220
Asyndeton:
  Asyndeta or absence of particles in Mark: 74
  Asyndeton: 216
Attributive: Position of attribute genitive: 222
Auxiliary:
  Auxiliary and quasi-auxiliary verbs: 90
  Pleonastic Auxiliary: 225

Causal ὅτι: 183
Clauses: Parenthetical clauses: 23
Comparative: Adjectives and Numerals comparative and superlative: 228
Conjunctions: 217
Co-ordinating particles: 222
Crowd:
  Movements of Jesus and his disciples and the crowd: 36
  'The crowd', or 'the multitudes': 49

Demonstrative: Post-position of demonstrative adjectives: 230
Diminutives in Mark: 123
Disciples:
  'His disciples' 'the disciples' (*οἱ μαθηταὶ αὐτοῦ, οἱ μαθηταί*): 47
  Movements of Jesus and his disciples and the crowd: 36
  Singular followed by mention of the disciples (or the Twelve): 42
  'The disciples' and 'the Twelve': 82
  The Lord, the disciples, and the multitude: 45

Ekeinos:
  Use of *ekeinos* (LXX): 231
  Use of *ekeinos* (NT): 230
Einai: Periphrastic εἶναι and Participle: 173
En: Instrumental *en*: 227

Genitive: Position of attribute genitive: 222

Hebraic Influence: 219
Hina: Imperatival *hina*: 228
'His disciples' 'the disciples' (*οἱ μαθηταὶ αὐτοῦ, οἱ μαθηταί*): 47
Historic Present: 225
Hoti:
  Causal ὅτι: 183
  Interrogative ὅτι: 63
  Recitative *hoti*: 234
  Recitative ὅτι (after λέγειν or similar verbs): 68

Idou: ἰδού in narrative: 81
Imperatival *hina*: 228
Imperfect: Periphrastic imperfect: 232
Impersonal:
  Active impersonal plural: 216
  Impersonal plural followed by the singular: 39
Infinitive: Articular infinitive: 220
Influence:
  Aramaic Influence: 215
  Hebraic Influence: 219
  Semitic Influence: 224
Instrumental *en*: 227
Interrogative:
  Interrogative εἰ: 184
  Interrogative ὅτι: 63

Jesus:
  ὁ Ἰησοῦς and Ἰησοῦς: 137
  Ἰησοῦς in Luke: 138
  Ἰησοῦς in Matthew: 138

(Jesus): Movements of Jesus and his disciples and the crowd: 36

Latinisms in the Gospels: 235
Legon:
Absence of λέγων (λέγοντες) after verbs introducing a statement or a question: 133
List of verbs followed by λέγων: 176
Recitative λέγων: 175
Lord: The Lord, the disciples, and the multitude: 45

Mathetai: 'His disciples' 'the disciples' (οἱ μαθηταὶ αὐτοῦ, οἱ μαθηταί): 47
Movements of Jesus and his disciples and the crowd: 36
Multitude:
'The crowd', or 'the multitudes': 49
The Lord, the disciples, and the multitude: 45

Narrative: ἰδού in narrative: 81
Negatives: Redundant negatives: 231
Numerals:
Adjectives and Numerals comparative and superlative: 228
Use of numbers in St Mark's Gospel: 53

Over-use of participles: 231

Parataxis: 224
Parentheses: 232
Parenthetical clauses: 23
Participle:
Periphrastic εἶναι and Participle: 173
Over-use of participles: 231
Particles: 63, 181
Co-ordinating particles: 222
Particles absent from Mark: 78
Perfect: 160
Stative perfect: 220
Periphrastic:
Periphrastic εἶναι and Participle: 173
Periphrastic imperfect: 232
Periphrastic Tenses: 225
Pleonastic Auxiliary: 225
Plural:
Active impersonal plural: 216
Impersonal plural followed by the singular: 39
Polla: Adverbial *polla*: 218
Position:
Position of attribute genitive: 222
Position of the adjective: 229
Position of the verb in nominal sentences: 222
Position of the verb in verbal sentences: 223
Post-position of demonstrative adjectives: 230
Prepositions: 227
Present: Historic Present: 225
Prolepsis of the subject: 221
Proleptic Pronoun: 217
Pronouns: 226
Proleptic Pronoun: 217

Recitative:
Recitative *hoti*: 234
Recitative ὅτι (after λέγειν or similar verbs): 68
Recitative λέγων: 175
Redundancy: 224
Redundant negatives: 231

Semitic Influence: 224
Sentences: Position of the verb in verbal sentences: 223
Singular:
Impersonal plural followed by the singular: 39
Singular followed by mention of the disciples (or the Twelve): 42
Stative perfect: 220
Subject: Prolepsis of the subject: 221
Superlative: Adjectives and Numerals comparative and superlative: 228
Syntax: 235

Tenses: Periphrastic Tenses: 225
The Article: 226
'The crowd', or 'the multitudes': 49
'The disciples' and 'the Twelve': 82
'The disciples': 'His disciples' 'the disciples' (οἱ μαθηταὶ αὐτοῦ, οἱ μαθηταί): 47
The Lord, the disciples, and the multitude: 45
The Twelve: 'The disciples' and 'the Twelve': 82
Titles used in addressing Christ: 121

Twelve:
- Singular followed by mention of the disciples (or the Twelve): 42
- 'The disciples' and 'the Twelve': 82

Use of *ekeinos* (LXX): 231
Use of *ekeinos* (NT): 230
Use of numbers in St Mark's Gospel: 53
Use of Participle for a main verb: 217

Verbal: Position of the verb in verbal sentences: 223

Verb:
- Verb at the end of the sentence, after noun or personal pronoun: 126
- Position of the verb in verbal sentences: 223
- Auxiliary and quasi-auxiliary verbs: 90
- List of verbs followed by λέγων: 176
- Use of Participle for a main verb: 217
- Verbs of seeing: 179

Vocabulary: 234

4. INDEX OF GREEK WORDS

ἀγανακτεῖν: 133
ἀκολουθεῖν: 50, 171
ἀλλά: 107, 183
ἀναβλέψαι: 180
ἀποκρίνεσθαι: 134
ἀποστερεῖν: 104, 120, 179
ἄρα: 184
ἄρχομαι: 93

βλέπειν: 179
βοᾶν: 134

γάρ: 182

δέ: 181
διαβλέψαι: 180
διαλογίζεσθαι: 134
διαστέλλεσθαι: 134
διδάσκαλε: 121
δύναμαι: 95
δώδεκα: 43, 82

ἑαυτοὺς: (πρὸς) ἑαυτοὺς: 108
εἰ: 184
εἶναι: 173
ἐκ, ἀπό: 110
ἐκεινος: 230, 231
ἐκπορεύεσθαι: 157
ἐμβλέψαι: 180
ἐν: 16, 227
ἐπάνω: 155
ἐπερωτάω (ἐρωτάω): 134
ἐπιτιμάω: 135
ἐπιτιμᾶν: 170
ἔρχεσθαι: 157
εὐθύς: 168, *euthus* 234
ἔχω: 99

ἤ: 184

θέλω: 97
θεωρεῖν: 179
θυγάτριον: 123

Ἰησοῦ: 122
ἰδού in narrative: 81
ἵνα: Imperatival *hina*: 228
ἰχθύδιον: 123, 124

κεφαλιόω: 105
κηρύσσειν: 135

κοράσιον: 124
κράζω: 135
κυνάριον: 124
κύριε: 122

λαλεῖν: 136
λέγων:
  Absence of λέγων: 133
  Verbs followed by λέγων: 176
  Recitative λέγων: 175
λόγος: 151, 166

μαθηταί: 47, 82
μέν: 181, 184

ναί: 78, 130

ὁ Ἰησοῦς and Ἰησοῦς: 137
οἰκία: 169
οἶκος: 169
ὁρᾶν: 179
ὅτι:
  Interrogative: 63
  Recitative: 68, *hoti* 234
  Causal ὅτι: 183
οὖν: 79, 184
ὀφθῆναι: 179
ὄχλος: 49
ὄψεσθαι: 179

παιδίον: 125
παλίν: 111, 168, *palin* 234
περιβλέπεσθαι: 180
πλήν: 184
πολλά: 172
  adverbial *polla*: 218
πορεύεσθαι: 117, 121, 126, 157
προδοῦναι: 105
πυγμῇ: 107

ῥαββεί (ῥαββουνεί): 121

σανδάλιον: 124

ὑπάγω: 116

φέρειν: 13

ὡς: 159
ὥστε: 184
ὠτάριον: 125

SUPPLEMENTS TO NOVUM TESTAMENTUM

ISSN 0167-9732

2. STROBEL, A. *Untersuchungen zum eschatologischen Verzögerungsproblem auf Grund der spätjüdische-urchristlichen Geschichte von Habakuk 2,2 ff.* 1961. ISBN 90 04 01582 5
6. *Neotestamentica et Patristica.* Eine Freundesgabe Herrn Professor Dr. Oscar Cullmann zu seinem 60. Geburtstag überreicht. 1962. ISBN 90 04 01586 8
8. DE MARCO, A.A. *The Tomb of Saint Peter.* A Representative and Annotated Bibliography of the Excavations. 1964. ISBN 90 04 01588 4
10. BORGEN, P. *Bread from Heaven.* An Exegetical Study of the Concept of Manna in the Gospel of John and the Writings of Philo. Photomech. Reprint of the first (1965) edition. 1981. ISBN 90 04 06419 2
13. MOORE, A.L. *The Parousia in the New Testament.* 1966. ISBN 90 04 01593 0
15. QUISPEL, G. *Makarius, das Thomasevangelium und das Lied von der Perle.* 1967. ISBN 90 04 01595 7
16. PFITZNER, V.C. *Paul and the Agon Motif.* 1967. ISBN 90 04 01596 5
17. BELLINZONI, A. *The Sayings of Jesus in the Writings of Justin Martyr.* 1967. ISBN 90 04 01597 3
18. GUNDRY, R.H. *The Use of the Old Testament in St. Matthew's Gospel.* With Special Reference to the Messianistic Hope. Reprint of the first (1967) edition. 1975. ISBN 90 04 04278 4
19. SEVENSTER, J.N. *Do You Know Greek?* How Much Greek Could the first Jewish Christians Have Known? 1968. ISBN 90 04 03090 5
20. BUCHANAN, G.W. *The Consequences of the Covenant.* 1970. ISBN 90 04 01600 7
21. KLIJN, A.F.J. *A Survey of the Researches into the Western Text of the Gospels and Acts.* Part 2: 1949-1969. 1969. ISBN 90 04 01601 5
22. GABOURY, A. *La Stucture des Évangiles synoptiques.* La structure-type à l'origine des synoptiques. 1970. ISBN 90 04 01602 3
23. GASTON, L. *No Stone on Another.* Studies in the Significance of the Fall of Jerusalem in the Synoptic Gospels. 1970. ISBN 90 04 01603 1
24. *Studies in John.* Presented to Professor Dr. J.N. Sevenster on the Occasion of His Seventieth Birthday. 1970. ISBN 90 04 03091 3
25. STORY, C.I.K. *The Nature of Truth in the 'Gospel of Truth', and in the Writings of Justin Martyr.* A Study of the Pattern of Orthodoxy in the Middle of the Second Christian Century. 1970. ISBN 90 04 01605 8
26. GIBBS, J.G. *Creation and Redemption.* A Study in Pauline Theology. 1971. ISBN 90 04 01606 6
27. MUSSIES, G. *The Morphology of Koine Greek As Used in the Apocalypse of St. John.* A Study in Bilingualism. 1971. ISBN 90 04 02656 8
28. AUNE, D.E. *The Cultic Setting of Realized Eschatology in Early Christianity.* 1972. ISBN 90 04 03341 6
29. UNNIK, W.C. VAN. *Sparsa Collecta.* The Collected Essays of W.C. van Unnik Part 1. Evangelia, Paulina, Acta. 1973. ISBN 90 04 03660 1
30. UNNIK, W.C. VAN. *Sparsa Collecta.* The Collected Essays of W.C. van Unnik Part 2. I Peter, Canon, Corpus Hellenisticum, Generalia. 1980. ISBN 90 04 06261 0
31. UNNIK, W.C. VAN. *Sparsa Collecta.* The Collected Essays of W.C. van Unnik

Part 3. Patristica, Gnostica, Liturgica. 1983. ISBN 90 04 06262 9
33. AUNE D.E. (ed.) *Studies in New Testament and Early Christian Literature.* Essays in Honor of Allen P. Wikgren. 1972. ISBN 90 04 03504 4
34. HAGNER, D.A. *The Use of the Old and New Testaments in Clement of Rome.* 1973. ISBN 90 04 03636 9
35. GUNTHER, J.J. *St. Paul's Opponents and Their Background.* A Study of Apocalyptic and Jewish Sectarian Teachings. 1973. ISBN 90 04 03738 1
36. KLIJN, A.F.J. & G.J. REININK (eds.) *Patristic Evidence for Jewish-Christian Sects.* 1973. ISBN 90 04 03763 2
37. REILING, J. *Hermas and Christian Prophecy.* A Study of The Eleventh Mandate. 1973. ISBN 90 04 03771 3
38. DONFRIED, K.P. *The Setting of Second Clement in Early Christianity.* 1974. ISBN 90 04 03895 7
39. ROON, A. VAN. *The Authenticity of Ephesians.* 1974. ISBN 90 04 03971 6
40. KEMMLER, D.W. *Faith and Human Reason.* A Study of Paul's Method of Preaching as Illustrated by 1-2 Thessalonians and Acts 17, 2-4. 1975. ISBN 90 04 04209 1
42. PANCARO, S. *The Law in the Fourth Gospel.* The Torah and the Gospel, Moses and Jesus, Judaism and Christianity According to John. 1975. ISBN 90 04 04309 8
43. CLAVIER, H. *Les variétés de la pensée biblique et le problème de son unité.* Esquisse d'une théologie de la Bible sur les textes originaux et dans leur contexte historique. 1976. ISBN 90 04 04465 5
44. ELLIOTT, J.K.E. (ed.) *Studies in New Testament Language and Text.* Essays in Honour of George D. Kilpatrick on the Occasion of His Sixty-fifth Birthday. 1976. ISBN 90 04 04386 1
45. PANAGOPOULOS, J. (ed.) *Prophetic Vocation in the New Testament and Today.* 1977. ISBN 90 04 04923 1
46. KLIJN, A.F.J. *Seth in Jewish, Christian and Gnostic Literature.* 1977. ISBN 90 04 05245 3
47. BAARDA, T., A.F.J. KLIJN & W.C. VAN UNNIK (eds.) *Miscellanea Neotestamentica.* I. Studia ad Novum Testamentum Praesertim Pertinentia a Sociis Sodalicii Batavi c.n. Studiosorum Novi Testamenti Conventus Anno MCMLXXVI Quintum Lustrum Feliciter Complentis Suscepta. 1978. ISBN 90 04 05685 8
48. BAARDA, T., A.F.J. KLIJN & W.C. VAN UNNIK (eds.) *Miscellanea Neotestamentica.* II. 1978. ISBN 90 04 05686 6
49. O'BRIEN, P.T. *Introductory Thanksgivings in the Letters of Paul.* 1977. ISBN 90 04 05265 8
50. BOUSSET, D.W. *Religionsgeschichtliche Studien.* Aufsätze zur Religionsgeschichte des hellenistischen Zeitalters. Hrsg. von A.F. Verheule. 1979. ISBN 90 04 05845 1
51. COOK, M.J. *Mark's Treatment of the Jewish Leaders.* 1978. ISBN 90 04 05785 4
52. GARLAND, D.E. *The Intention of Matthew 23.* 1979. ISBN 90 04 05912 1
53. MOXNES, H. *Theology in Conflict.* Studies in Paul's Understanding of God in Romans. 1980. ISBN 90 04 06140 1
55. MENKEN, M.J.J. *Numerical Literary Techniques in John.* The Fourth Evangelist's Use of Numbers of Words and Syllables. 1985. ISBN 90 04 07427 9
56. SKARSAUNE, O. *The Proof From Prophecy.* A Study in Justin Martyr's Proof-Text Tradition: Text-type, Provenance, Theological Profile. 1987. ISBN 90 04 07468 6
59. WILKINS, M.J. *The Concept of Disciple in Matthew's Gospel, as Reflected in the Use of the Term 'Mathetes'.* 1988. ISBN 90 04 08689 7
60. MILLER, E.L. *Salvation-History in the Prologue of John.* The Significance of John 1:

3-4. 1989. ISBN 90 04 08692 7

61. THIELMAN, F. *From Plight to Solution.* A Jewish Framework for Understanding Paul's View of the Law in Galatians and Romans. 1989. ISBN 90 04 09176 9
64. STERLING, G.E. *Historiography and Self-Definition.* Josephos, Luke-Acts and Apologetic Historiography. 1992. ISBN 90 04 09501 2
65. BOTHA, J.E. *Jesus and the Samaritan Woman.* A Speech Act Reading of John 4:1-42. 1991. ISBN 90 04 09505 5
66. KUCK, D.W. *Judgment and Community Conflict.* Paul's Use of Apologetic Judgment Language in 1 Corinthians 3:5-4:5. 1992. ISBN 90 04 09510 1
67. SCHNEIDER, G. *Jesusüberlieferung und Christologie.* Neutestamentliche Aufsätze 1970-1990. 1992. ISBN 90 04 09555 1
68. SEIFRID, M.A. *Justification by Faith.* The Origin and Development of a Central Pauline Theme. 1992. ISBN 90 04 09521 7
69. NEWMAN, C.C. *Paul's Glory-Christology.* Tradition and Rhetoric. 1992. ISBN 90 04 09463 6
70. IRELAND, D.J. *Stewardship and the Kingdom of God.* An Historical, Exegetical, and Contextual Study of the Parable of the Unjust Steward in Luke 16: 1-13. 1992. ISBN 90 04 09600 0
71. ELLIOTT, J.K. *The Language and Style of the Gospel of Mark.* An Edition of C.H. Turner's "Notes on Marcan Usage" together with other comparable studies. 1993. ISBN 90 04 09767 8

C. H. Turner pioneered the study of the language and style of Mark's Gospel in a series of articles in the 1920s entitled 'Notes on Marcan Usage'. All but one appeared in the *Journal of Theological Studies* – one further 'Note' is published now for the first time. It is Turner's articles, reprinted with editorial additions, that form the backbone of the present book. Comparable articles by those who have followed in C. H. Turner's footsteps (G. D. Kilpatrick, J. K. Elliott, N. Turner) are also included. Some of these are published for the first time.

These studies into language, style and usage are relevant for work not only on exegesis, but also on the textual criticism of the Gospel and on the synoptic problem.

This volume makes Turner's essays accessible in one place and these together with the other studies form a convenient reference tool for Marcan scholars.

J. K. Elliott is Reader in New Testament Textual Criticism in the Department of Theology at the University of Leeds.